Public
Management
Reform
and
Innovation

Public Management Reform and Innovation

Research, Theory, and Application

Edited by
H. George Frederickson and
Jocelyn M. Johnston

THE UNIVERSITY OF ALABAMA PRESS

Tuscaloosa and London

Copyright © 1999
The University of Alabama Press
Tuscaloosa, Alabama 35487-0380
All rights reserved
Manufactured in the United States of America

1 2 3 4 5 6 7 8 9 / 07 06 05 04 03 02 01 00 99

Cover design by Shari DeGraw

∞

The paper on which this book is printed meets the minimum requirements
of American National Standard for Information Science—Permanence of
Paper for Printed Library Materials, ANSI Z39.48-1984.

Library of Congress Cataloging-in-Publication Data

Public management reform and innovation : research, theory, and
application / H. George Frederickson and Jocelyn M. Johnston,
editors.
     p.   cm.
   Includes bibliographical references and index.
   ISBN 0-8173-0964-0 (cloth : alk. paper)
   ISBN 0-8173-0971-3 (pbk. : alk. paper)
   1. Public administration—United States.   2. Administrative
agencies—United States—Management.   3. Administrative
agencies—United States—Reorganization.   4. Civil service
reform—United States.   I. Frederickson, H. George.   II. Johnston,
Jocelyn M., 1955–
   JK421 .P814   1999
   351.73—ddc21   98-58024
                                                                  CIP

British Library Cataloguing-in-Publication Data available

Contents

Introduction

H. George Frederickson

IF THERE IS A single word that would characterize public management at the closing of the twentieth century and the opening of the twenty-first century, it is *change*. Today, the practice and study of public management is most commonly described by the use of such words as reform, reorganization, reinvention, reengineering, innovation, the learning organization, creativity, taking risks, and being entrepreneurial. In many ways this makes sense. The end of a century and a millennium is a period of stocktaking as well as a time for striving to improve, to make things better. Part of the instincts toward change as the critical variable in modern public management is rhetoric and fluff. Some of it, however, reflects a commitment to serious institutional and managerial improvement, and some of it is quality social science that describes, catalogues, and analyzes public management change. And that is the exact purpose of this book.

Starting in 1990, a group of about sixty specialists and scholars from the academic fields of public management, public policy studies, political science, and public administration began a series of conferences, meetings, exchanges of papers and scholarship, and general scholarly interaction. The initial purpose was to bring together theoretical and research specialists from the fields of public administration and public policy, it being generally agreed that the two fields were unnecessarily distant and estranged. After a series of meetings and planning sessions, the National Conference on Public Management Research was held at the Maxwell School of Citizenship and Public Affairs at Syracuse University in October 1991. The Second National Conference on Public Management Research was held at the Robert La Follette School of Public Affairs at the University of Wisconsin in October 1993, and the Third National Conference on Public Management Research was held at the Department of Public Administration at the University of Kansas in October 1995.

These sessions brought together a community of scholars with a shared interest in empirical social science research on public organizations, broadly defined, and on the development of testable theories of public policy and management. These conferences have had the particularly desirable effect of creating a shared body of knowledge and a generally agreed-upon vocabulary to describe that body of knowledge. These years of scholarly interaction have established a foundation on which contemporary theories of public policy and management can be built. These meetings have also directly produced significant collections of research and theory (Bozeman 1993; Kettl and Milward 1996), although they are by no means all of the scholarship of the persons associated with this ongoing enterprise.

This book is a product of the Third National Public Management Research Conference held at the University of Kansas in October 1995. The editors decided to select several papers (not all) that present significant field research or theoretical arguments having to do with the dominant conference themes—change, reform, and innovation. Taken together, they constitute the most complete, as well as the most advanced, treatment of public management reform and innovation available.

The Purposes of the Book

The main purpose of the book, then, is to set out the metes and bounds of research and theory on public management reform and innovation. It is written to describe and define the subject matter; to present data and information on field research on many aspects of the subject; to formulate theory that explains or accounts for how public organizations change, adapt, reform, and innovate; and to present empirical research and theory dealing with how public managers and policy makers presume to bring about public organizational change. The purposes of the book are met by dividing the subject into several parts—theories and concepts of reform and innovation in public administration; the effects of political and institutional context on public management reform and innovation; the organizational and bureaucratic factors that influence the management of innovation and reform; and the special importance for reform and innovation of democratic politics on modern governance.

Audiences for the Book

Given these purposes, there are several audiences for the book. First, these days those who study and practice public administration are especially attuned to issues of change, reform, and innovation. Much of the available modern literature on the subject is anecdotal and based on so-called best practices. Some of it is primarily hortatory and presented as a handy guide to better public management, often without an empirical warrant. And much of it is prescientific and pretheoretical.

This book provides an alternative perspective on change in public management and public organizations, a perspective based on solid empirical research and careful theoretical development. So, the first audience for the book is that group of students, scholars, and theorists who have a serious interest in public management reform and change. Second, many who practice public administration are careful students of theoretical development in the field. These "reflective practitioners" will find this book useful. Third, there is a wider body of persons interested in organizational change and innovation, persons associated with such fields as education administration, business administration, health care administration, social services administration, and so on. They will also find this book of interest.

The Perspective of the Book

For the first three quarters of the twentieth century, most public sector reforms, particularly in democratic polities and especially in the United States, were aimed in the direction of professionalizing government, strengthening the executive in the separation of powers, and stamping out graft and corruption. The features of these reforms are well known—a merit-appointed professional civil service with extensive protections; elaborate bidding, purchasing, auditing, and budgeting rules and procedures; stronger mayors, school superintendents, governors, and presidents; the council-manager form of government at the city level; and the erosion of the power of political parties. By any measure, these reforms were extraordinarily successful. Virtually all of the important initial theories of public administration and public policy were developed during this period—the principles of public administration, rational-decision theory, measurement of program performance, goal-oriented management, and concepts of democratic administration. Most of these theories were associated with the values of efficiency and economy or their combined value, effectiveness. Theories of fairness or social equity were also influential, however.

In the last quarter of this century there has been a movement away from these theories in the direction of market theories, which now guide most contemporary reform. Beginning with Niskanen (1971), Ostrom (1973), Downs (1967), and others, the logic of economics colonized the field. By the late 1990s the public management reform agenda included concepts of competition; privatization; contracting out (or in); reduction of transaction costs; management and policy entrepreneurs; citizen as customers; fees for service;

vouchers; reductions in purchasing and other corruption-control rules and regulations; reductions in civil service requirements and rules; decentralization; and unit autonomy.

These new theories of administration were combined with the logic and sentiments associated with antitax and antigovernment movements to create the best-known form of modern government reform—reinventing government. Osborne and Gaebler (1992) introduced this phrase and with it a virtual snowstorm of catchy symbols and metaphors taken not from academic theory but from journalism and modern business management jargon. First, they named the problem—it is bureaucracy. They then described the ten things to do to solve the problem (steering rather than rowing, empowering employees and customers, building a better government that costs less, and so on). These authors based this modern theory of reform on the logic of "best practices," stories of management successes, often told by the managers who carried them out, which could be copied by other managers to stamp out bureaucracy. By the late 1980s virtually every candidate for executive office (mayors, governors, presidents) was campaigning on a reinventing government platform, and it proved to be very good politics indeed. Cities and states across the country were and are busy reinventing government. Bill Clinton practiced these concepts while governor of Arkansas and, after being elected president, assigned Vice-President Al Gore to the task of developing the National Performance Review, the federal government version of reinventing government. The federal civilian work force has been reduced by more than 10 percent in only four years. There are now hundreds of "reinventing laboratories" in the national government, regular "hammer awards" to those who are breaking bureaucracy, several innovation alliances designed to help reinvent government, and an army of reinvention consultants. It could fairly be said reinvention is everywhere and is based essentially on a combination of shrinking the size of the government work force, using the logic of the market model, and following the steps of reinventing government. These developments are probably as near to a public sector reform hegemony as has been experienced.

Because most contemporary public sector reforms are a part of this hegemony, many chapters in this book are empirical studies of these reforms, theoretical arguments about these reforms, or critiques of these reforms. The most direct are chapter 9, "The Pain of Organizational Change: Managing Reinvention" by Patricia W. Ingraham and Vernon Dale Jones, an evaluation of the Clinton administration's administrative reforms, and chapter 14, "Reinventing Government: Lessons from a State Capital" by Francis S. Berry, Richard Chackerian, and Barton Wechsler, an evaluation of Governor Lawton Chiles's reform program in Florida. Both chapter 8, "Implementing

Mission-Driven, Results-Oriented Budgeting" by Fred Thompson and Carol K. Johansen, and chapter 7, "Good Budgetary Decision Processes" by Patrick D. Larkey and Erik A. Devereux, evaluate the modern reform agenda in terms of its effects on the processes and substance of the allocation of public funds—budgeting. Lois R. Wise and Per Stengård, in chapter 6, "Assessing Public Management Reform with Internal Labor Market Theory: A Comparative Assessment of Change Implementation," examine applications of the modern reform agenda using theories of labor markets in the United States and Sweden as their empirical referents. Using one of the central features of the reinventing approach to reform, contracting out and contracting in, Eric Welch and Stuart Bretschneider in chapter 11, "Contracting In: Can Government Be a Business?" have serious reservations. Finally, in chapter 5, "Where's the Institution? Neoinstitutionalism and Public Management," Karen G. Evans and Gary L. Wamsley critique the logical assumptions and theoretical soundness of the reinventing government approach to public sector reform.

Fully half of the book, then, deals directly with contemporary applications of market model reform, coupled with downsizing government, mostly packaged together under the rubric "reinventing government." This emphasis is fitting, given the fact that most modern public sector innovations and arguments for change are based on the premises and assumptions on which the reinvention approach is built. In addition to being fitting, this emphasis on the reinvention agenda is also timely. President Clinton has been reelected, and Vice-President Gore continues to lead the National Performance Review, and their approach continues to be very successful politics. Good politics, however, is not necessarily the same thing as good government. All of the chapters of this book referred to above evaluate this reform agenda asking these questions: Is this good politics? Is this good government? Is this good administration?

The opening four chapters of the book take up the more general issues associated with theories and concepts of public sector organizational and managerial change. In chapter 1, "One Hundred Theories of Organizational Change: The Good, the Bad and the Ugly," Lawrence B. Mohr sketches the logic, assumptions, successes, and failures of theories of public sector organizational change and the evidence of their actual effectiveness. Mohr capably sets the tone of the book and clearly distinguishes the book's message from the hype and hustle often associated with considerations of public sector reform. In chapter 2, "Theoretical Foundations of Policy Intervention," Janet A. Weiss applies the logic associated with modern approaches to public sector administrative reform to interventions in public policy, assessing the appropriateness and effectiveness of such interventions. In chapter 3, "Do Goals Help Create Innovative Organizations?" Robert D. Behn takes up a common feature of the modern reform agenda—the need for goal clarification and agreement—and evaluates the likelihood of greater or less administrative, organizational, or policy innovation in the face of goal clarification and agreement. He asks, "Is it simply easier, and therefore more likely, to be innovative and creative when there is greater understanding of organizational goals and greater commitment to them?" One of the favorite arguments in the contemporary approach to reform is that effective leaders should be entrepreneurial (approximately meaning institution building and promotional). In chapter 4, "Innovation by Legislative, Judicial, and Management Design: Three Arenas of Public Entrepreneurship," Nancy C. Roberts examines the effects of different public sector settings on the capacity for and probability of innovation.

An important feature of modern public sector reform has to do with the role of interest groups, policy-advocating organizations, and so-called policy entrepreneurs (such entrepreneurs can be found anywhere—among legislators, in interest or advocacy groups, in appointed executive office, and in the civil service) in change and reform. In chapter 12, "Interest Groups in the Rule-Making Process: Who Participates? Whose Voices Get Heard?" Marissa Martino Golden examines empirically how change and resistance to change really occur and why. Then, in chapter 13, "Dialogue between Advocates and Executive Agencies: New Roles for Public Management," Linda Kaboolian describes the critical role played by public administrators in balancing the need to be politically responsive, to be innovative, and to protect the public interest. These two chapters consider especially the role of politics in public sector reform and how both politically appointed and merit-based public administrators relate to the politics of reform.

Each chapter of the book is a careful, clear-eyed analysis of public sector reform and innovation. The authors purposely took this approach to distinguish this work from the reform advocacy literature most commonly associated with government reform. It should not be assumed, however, that the authors of the chapters in this book are not advocates, that they have no agenda or point of view. We do. First, our perspective is rooted in constitutional democratic government, in the rule of law, and in the legitimate and critically important role of public administrators to implement law and public policy. We share a strong commitment to democratic responsiveness. Nevertheless, we have an equally strong commitment to the importance of expertise, professionalism, and high standards of managerial competence in public administration. We tend to see the logic and assumptions of the application of the market model to public affairs, as well as the politics of downsizing, from the perspectives of constitutional democratic government and the role of public managers in the day-to-day operations of that government. We tend to favor innovation and change, but we insist that such innovation and change be not only good politics but also good government both in the short run and in the long run. We are dedicated to an understanding that the effectiveness of innovations might not be universally good, which is to say that innovation can be better for some citizens and their interests than for others. We tend, therefore, to take fairness and equity seriously. Finally, we insist on evidence and verification as standards of empirical observation and analysis. Public sector reforms and changes, like other social phenomena, are observable, describable, and, with sufficient evidence, can form the basis of generalizations and theory. Careful theory, thus developed, can and should guide future reform and change. (Lawrence Mohr in chapter 1 has some reservations about these last two points.)

Themes in the Book

The primary themes running through the chapters in this book are the following. First, context matters. This is a book about reform, innovation, and change in the public sector. Nonetheless, the dominant model for this reform is taken from the private sector. Many of the chapters herein deal in one form or another with the issue of the suitability and effectiveness of features of the market model applied to public and governmental organizations. Karen G. Evans and Gary L. Wamsley in chapter 5 state boldly that the market model has very limited usefulness in the public sector because it robs us of our ability to find a public interest or to establish and sustain collective institutions. Patrick D. Larkey and Erik A. Devereux in chapter 7 trace the history of reform, particularly as applied to public budgeting, and determine that the application of business logic to public funding decisions has had a mostly negative effect on the quality of those decisions. Eric Welch and Stuart Bretschneider in chapter 11 find the application of concepts of competition and efficiency through the logic of "contracting in" to have limited efficacy in government. In chapter 4 Nancy C. Roberts describes different patterns of innovation in public sector organizations depending on whether they are legislative, judicial, or administrative. These and other chapters demonstrate the long-standing contention in public administration that the public sector is not just somewhat different from business and industry but is greatly different. It is nevertheless the case that most contemporary public management reforms are imported to government from business, primarily by elected political leaders. Still, there is widespread support for the "new public management" approach to reform both on the part of scholars in public management, particularly those associated with economics, and on the part of practitioners looking for ways to improve organizational performance.

Second, the combination of downsizing and reinventing tends to elicit bureaucratic resistance. Standing alone, many of the features of contemporary reform, such as contracting out, privatization, deregulation, unit autonomy, encouragement of risk taking, and the like, have long been in the public management innovation tool bag. But when managers are faced with implementing these innovations at the same time that they are experiencing staff cuts, resistance is natural. Public managers tend also to be policy advocates. When they see or think they see reduced policy effectiveness coming with reform, they will resist. Reformers may choose to view this resistance as merely bureaucratic comfort with the status quo and tendencies to resist change. As Fred Thompson and Carol K. Johansen in chapter 8, Patricia W. Ingraham and Vernon Dale Jones in chapter 9, Eric Welch and Stuart Bretschneider in chapter 11, and Frances S. Berry, Richard Chackerian, and Barton Wechsler in chapter 14 all demonstrate, resistance to reforms is more often a correlate of perceived threats of reduced policy effectiveness than it is simply bureaucratic obstinacy.

Third, one of the serious challenges in public sector reform can be traced to the unique features of the separation of powers and the juxtaposition of public management between elected legislators, the lawmaking process, the law, and legislatively appropriated funds on the one hand and elected executives and their policy leadership on the other hand. Public managers are charged with implementing the law and spending public funds on the tasks for which they were appropriated. When elected executives set a reform agenda that runs counter to the law or is understood to circumvent by executive fiat either the law or the intent of lawmakers, public managers face a serious dilemma. One of the more sophisticated features of the National Performance Review was the conscious emphasis on reforms that could be fully implemented by the executive branch by executive order or the regulation-making process. The reforms, then, have tended to be rather rapidly implemented as policy discretion fully within the power of the president. Such an approach, however, limited reforms to less fundamental changes because fundamental reforms called for in the reinventing agenda, such as multiyear budgeting, require legislative approval.

Fourth is the assumption that public sector reform and change is or should be managerial. This theory assumes that the problems with governance are mostly managerial and that clever people can devise management solutions even to flawed policy. Several of the chapters in this book illustrate that the fundamental problems with government can be traced to flawed policy and that it is difficult, if not impossible, to fix bad policy by improved management. Indeed, improvement management of poor policy can make things worse. For example, Kenneth Meier determined in *The Politics of Sin* (1994) that American drug policy is so flawed that better management of that policy has only made our drug situation worse. One important reason for the emphasis on management as against policy reform is political. It is simply easier politically, particularly for elected executives, to tinker with management than to try to get elected legislators to change laws and macropolicies. The management approach to reform is the flip side of bureaucrat bashing. In bureaucrat bashing it is said that the problems with government have to do with the management of public policy. In the management approach to reform it is assumed that the solutions to government problems are mostly managerial. So, bad bureaucracy is the problem, and good bureaucracy is the solution.

The authors and editors intend that readers come away from this book with an ample understanding of the prospects and problems associated with contemporary reform in American public administration.

References

Bozeman, Barry, ed. 1993. *Public Management: The State of the Art.* San Francisco: Jossey-Bass.

Downs, Anthony. 1967. *Inside Bureaucracy.* Boston: Little, Brown.

Kettl, Donald F., and H. Brinton Milward, eds. 1996. *The State of Public Management.* Baltimore: Johns Hopkins University Press.

Meier, Kenneth. 1994. *The Politics of Sin.* Armonk, N.Y.: M.E. Sharpe.

Niskanen, William A. 1971. *Bureaucracy and Representative Government.* Hawthorn, N.Y.: Aldine de Gruyter.

Osborne, David, and Ted Gaebler. 1992. *Reinventing Government: How the Entrepreneurial Spirit Is Transforming the Public Sector.* Reading, Mass.: Addison-Wesley.

Ostrom, Vincent. 1973. *The Intellectual Crisis in American Public Administration.* University, Ala.: University of Alabama Press.

I | Theories and Concepts of Reform, Innovation, and Intervention in Public Management

In his discussions of the current state of theory in the field of public management, Lynn (1994, 1996) has argued that analytic approaches to theory building and theory testing are crucial to providing coherence in this maturing field. While he acknowledges the importance of advising the practice of public management, Lynn stresses the need for a firm theoretical foundation to support that advice. The chapters in this section represent progress in this area. Each of these chapters addresses—directly or indirectly—theoretical issues in public management. The first two chapters (Mohr, Weiss) include direct treatments of "theory" itself, with emphases on social science theory in general and theories of innovation in particular. The third and fourth chapters (Behn, Roberts) address theory more indirectly, providing conceptualizations of innovation that can be viewed as important refinements of existing public management theories.

Lawrence B. Mohr's chapter assesses the validity of prevailing theories in social science and organization study. Under his careful eye, the current state of understanding from which we study innovation and reform is subjected to strict scrutiny. Using the framework provided by historical research, Mohr reminds us that the generalizability and explanatory power of current social science theories are still weak. The discipline of history suffers from a similar problem, he writes, yet historians do not abandon research because their theories fail to predict with precision. Mohr suggests that public management scholars should learn from historians and should acknowledge that despite the limitations of social science theoretical models, theories nonetheless foster deeper understanding of the relevant issues, refine our view of organizational change and innovation, and provide "useful" frameworks for study.

Before delving into "the good, the bad, and the ugly" theoretical approaches that prevail in contemporary social science and innovation theory, Mohr warns us that in these areas of inquiry "there can be no [universal] laws" or explanatory principles with consistent, complete external validity. Those of us conducting social science research are well acquainted with the problem that excludes perfect validity (or what Mohr refers to as "stable generalizations"): we are unable to specify precisely all conditions under which certain events can be expected to occur, nor can we predict that an event will occur even if all necessary conditions are present. Because we study human behavior, we are limited to probabilistic explanations and "creative-selective generalizations." Social science research is not purely "trade," Mohr argues, nor is it purely "art." Rather, it combines elements of both (usefulness and beauty) in the form of "craft." [1]

Mohr provides elegant descriptions of the predominant theoretical approaches in innovation theory and social science, which include variance theories, process descriptions, and encounter theory. His strongest endorsement is reserved for encounter theories, such as the garbage can model introduced by Cohen, March, and Olsen (1972), which explain organizational change and innovation within the framework of probabilistic encounters.

Janet A. Weiss characterizes innovation theories as theories of "intervention." She refines the notion of policy theory by identifying three major theoretical components (or "interrelated theories"): a theory of the problem, a theory of desired outcomes, and a theory of intervention. According to Weiss, the theory of intervention explains how action (intervention) will evoke the desired outcomes and alleviate the problem. To demonstrate her propositions, Weiss uses the example provided by the final report of the National Performance Review (NPR). The report, viewed as a policy theory, includes a theory of the problem (government needs fixing; government does not work) and a theory of desired outcome (a government that puts people first and that serves its customers more efficiently). Like many policy theories, however, the NPR's attempt to articulate a theory of intervention fails to link adequately the problem and the desired outcomes, in part because of insufficient attention to political factors—factors that may compromise the suggested administrative interventions. In this respect, the policy theory embodied in the final NPR report is similar to many other policy theories: experts agree on the theory of the problem and may agree on the theory of desired outcomes, but they may repudiate the theory of intervention prescribed in the larger theory.

Weiss identifies and describes the core elements of successful intervention theory: agents, targets, time/place, and mechanisms. The agent is charged with the responsibility of executing the intervention. Selection of the agent matters because of the crucial role the agent plays and because of the "symbolic message" associated with the agent. The target consists of people, groups, communities, or organizations at which the desired outcome is directed. Symbolism can also affect the selection of the target, Weiss suggests. For example, the target of antismoking efforts may be identified as individual smokers rather than tobacco companies in order to accomplish the political objective of avoiding

confrontation with powerful, organized interests. The desired outcome is reduced tobacco consumption, but the selection of the target can influence the
intervention and the final outcome of the policy initiative. The time/place
element refers to the fact that intervention must be concrete rather than abstract.

The element of mechanism contained in the theory of intervention is of
paramount importance. Weiss devotes significant attention to this element and
proposes a taxonomy of mechanisms consisting of incentives, authority, and
ideas. She suggests that her taxonomy is similar in nature to the mechanisms of
control—exchange, authority, and persuasion—described by Lindblom (1976).
She draws distinctions between her work and that of Lindblom, however, if
only because of her explicit focus on U.S. domestic policy. Weiss points out
that most policies and interventions do not rely on one "pure" mechanism, but
rather incorporate combinations of the three mechanisms, thereby enhancing
the effectiveness of the intervention. She concludes that the most effective
interventions are those that rest on sound theories of the problem and of desired outcomes, which use combinations of the three intervention mechanisms
and which clearly recognize that the designation of multiple targets may be
necessary.

Robert D. Behn's chapter emphasizes the importance of goals in fostering
organizational innovation. He notes that the presence of goals does not guarantee innovation but that they enhance the probability of successful innovation. Behn identifies five intermediate steps, or linkages, that he has observed
in his research. Of equal importance, he specifies two barriers that may overwhelm the contribution of goals to innovation: the difficulty of obtaining
consensus on goals and the resistance of organizations—especially government
organizations—to change.

Goals, Behn contends, can displace "process" as the primary focus of organizations. Thus, goals can "redefine success" for the organization and its leaders. If this happens, then the first of Behn's linkages is established. Second,
goals, properly structured and communicated, can simulate "crisis," which in
turn can "get everyone thinking and behaving innovatively." Crisis facilitates
a redirection away from organizational process toward the objectives contained
in the goals. Third, as key agents in the organization respond to the goals, leadership develops at all levels of the organization, which further enhances the
probability of innovation and goal success. Fourth, new goals may provide incentives for the organization to communicate with other organizations and to
take advantage of the experiences and knowledge they may offer. Finally, goals
can lead to shifts in public values and perceptions of the organization.

Behn notes that the barriers that may interfere with the contributions of goals to innovation will vary across different organizational types and different goals. For example, obtaining consensus on the goals of reducing welfare dependency will be difficult relative to goals related to more straightforward activities such as providing adequate fleet maintenance for government agencies. Similar variations will apply to resistance to organizational change—resistance will be higher in certain types of public organizations.

In her chapter, Nancy C. Roberts explores related themes and provides a model that articulates the relationship between organizational innovation and entrepreneurship. Her theoretical conceptualization identifies two important limits on innovation: the institutional context and the level of change required by the innovation. In the Roberts model, innovation is represented as process with time dimensions. The process consists of various phases, but idea initiation, idea design, and idea implementation are key to a successful innovation process. The success of the innovation, however, also requires a "driver," or an actor who will steer and push the process along. That actor is the entrepreneur. Entrepreneurship can be individual or collective, according to Roberts.

One of Roberts's objectives is to clarify two different recommendations that public management theory commonly offers to entrepreneurs. Should entrepreneurs "grope along" as they guide the innovation process, experimenting, responding to feedback as they steer, building "craft knowledge" about the issue? Or, alternatively, should they engage in systematic analysis and planning? Roberts uses three examples (or institutional contexts) to refine her theoretical concept of innovation. She examines the innovation process and key entrepreneurs in a legislative context, in a judicial context, and in a management context (which is the most relevant context for our purposes). Her analysis leads her to conclude that "groping along" is most characteristic of innovation by management design (i.e., organizational innovation): it is "iterative, incremental, and disorderly." Management is more conducive to an incremental innovation style in part because of the types of innovative ideas that managers "drive." In legislative and judicial contexts, Roberts argues, ideas tend to be more "radical." In a management setting, incremental policy changes pose less challenge to the policy decision power of legislatures and courts. Of more importance, they generate less resistance to change, which is crucial in bureaucratic organizations.

These four chapters offer substantial contributions to our understanding of the state of theory in the fields of innovation and public management and to actual existing sets of theories. Mohr and Weiss provide elegant, well-reasoned assessments of the current condition of theoretical development. Behn and Roberts offer specific, precise theoretical descriptions of innovation and innovation management. The four authors have set the stage for the theoretical refinements that follow.

Note

1. See Lynn (1996) for additional discussion of the "craft" of public management scholarship.

References

Cohen, Michael D., James G. March, and Johan P. Olsen. 1972. "A Garbage Can Model of Organizational Choice." *Administrative Science Quarterly* 17: 1–25.

Lindblom, Charles. 1976. *Politics and Markets: The World's Political-Economic Systems.* New York: Basic Books.

Lynn, Laurence Jr. 1994. "Public Management Research: The Triumph of Art over Science." *Journal of Policy Analysis and Management* 13, no. 2 (spring): 231–59.

———. 1996. *Public Management as Art, Science, and Profession.* Chatham, N.J.: Chatham House.

1 | One Hundred Theories of Organizational Change
The Good, the Bad, and the Ugly

Lawrence B. Mohr

My purpose in this chapter is to present and defend some recently derived views on the subject of theory in the social sciences and to illustrate them with reference to the field of innovation in organizations. In a recent publication (Mohr 1996), I claimed to demonstrate that neither universal nor probabilistic laws governing human behavior are possible. The analyses were based on an investigation of certain concepts and processes that seem to me basic to social research, including the definition of causality and the nature of the physiological mechanism that generates intentional behavior. With the treatment of laws added to these investigations, the whole suggests the need for a second look at the goals and methods of explanatory social science research. In this chapter, I concentrate on goals rather than methods, first sketching out the background arguments in this connection and then applying the results to innovation theory.

Expectations for Theory in Social Science

Encounters and Laws

The case against universal laws of human behavior hinges on the notion of "encounters," coupled with the conclusion that "operative reasons" in a certain physiological form are the physical causes of all intentional behavior. By universal law in this context I mean an explanation for human behavior that holds universally (given a very small allowance for measurement error and irreducible random perturbation) for a specified subclass of people under a specified set of conditions. In other words, universal does not mean all people, but any subset as long as it is not left partially vague. Also, the proposed applicability of the law might be narrowed substantially by stipulating that it holds only under certain conditions and not under all conditions, but those conditions must also be specified in order for the proposition to be a valid law. In the end, I argue that it is impossible to specify such conditions for any explanation of any intentional behavior, which is tantamount to saying that there can be no laws.

17

Encounters

I have also suggested elsewhere that a good deal of prominent scientific work, including both Mendelian and Darwinian theory, is pointed toward the theoretical explanation of *encounters* rather than of simpler events (see "process theory" in Mohr 1982, 44–70). An encounter, or probabilistic encounter, is a *compound* event conceptualized as the status relative to each other of two or more free, component objects or events. By "free" I mean the opposite of a fixed frame of reference or a given. For example, when we speak of a motion upward or downward, we mean relative to the earth so that the earth is taken as a fixed frame of reference, and the motion is simply the motion of one object and not an encounter. The earth in this sense does not count because it is considered fixed rather than free. Similarly, whereas the collision of two billiard balls on a table is an encounter, the motion of one of them afterward may be considered the motion of a single object. It does not have to be considered, for example, as an encounter involving the ball and the table because the table may be considered as not free; it may be taken rather as a fixed frame of reference.

An automobile accident—a collision between two cars—is an example of a probabilistic encounter. If we conceptualized an event as two ships passing in the night, that would be an encounter in just the same way. The accident and the passing as such are not motions of one or more objects but rather a juxtaposition of things—a status of things relative to one another. I argue at length (Mohr 1996) that encounters cannot be covered by laws. No law can be specified, for example, that correctly predicts or determines that an accident will take place or that the ships will pass in the night. The compound event is inherently probabilistic. One car might be caught by a red light, or have a flat tire, or swerve at the last moment so that no accident takes place. One might try to specify a lot of initial conditions, including a statement such as "provided there is no red light, flat tire, or swerving," but in order to predict with certainty one would have to account for everything in the universe. Otherwise, in principle, something one did not think of could always come up.

If the accident does indeed take place, one can easily see how each car followed known physical laws under the totality of circumstances that actually prevailed. Moreover, one does not have to *name* all of the circumstances, such as "sound tires" and so forth, but rather can consider most of them as unidentified background or context. One can have a complete, lawlike explanation of the accident given those circumstances together with the fact that the accident happened. Before the accident does take place, however, the laws cannot tell you that it will.

Events are commonly conceptualized as encounters. "Winning" at roulette, for example, is an encounter between a certain bet and the stopping place of a little ball. Because it is not something that receives a force and that thereby moves, the winning is not covered by the laws of physics. The following are some additional examples: a tie for first place; sole possession of first place; bumping into an old friend; stumbling over a root; getting caught in the rain; agreement; job satisfaction; and so forth.

Reasons

A reason is defined roughly as the combination of a desire and a certain kind of belief: for example, the desire to overcome people's resistance to a change and the belief that getting them to participate in decision making will overcome their resistance. This desire and belief together become a reason for getting them to participate. As used here, a reason is a physiological phenomenon and does not have to be conscious, although it may at times be that, too. We all know that we sometimes do things without being conscious of why beforehand, or even afterward, and indeed it might take a psychoanalysis to figure it out. Nevertheless, the reason was there in unaware, physiological form and operated. An *operative* reason is the reason that at a given time is the strongest. I have argued (Mohr 1996, chapter 3) that operative physiological reasons are the causes of intentional behavior.

Laws

I hope one can begin to see from this brief characterization of a longer argument why it is that there can be no universal laws governing human behavior. Behavior results from an encounter, namely, the encounter of a reason with other reasons, such that the strongest one wins and the behavior pertinent to it is selected. It might be true, therefore, that a person or an organization adopted an innovation in order to acquire enhanced status, but there can be no law that the desire to acquire enhanced status will lead to innovation. That particular reason for innovating might sometimes be weaker than some other reason for doing something else, and the innovation might not only fail to take place then and there, but it might well never take place in spite of the continued existence of the reason.

We commonly consider that although there are no universal laws governing human behavior, there may be probabilistic ones. There are indeed probabilistic laws in physics, such as the laws of the rate of radioactive decay of the various elements, and in biology, such as the Mendelian laws of segregation and independent assortment. Each of these always depends on a strictly random process that, paradoxically enough, will produce an utterly stable and reliable distribution of outcomes. Intentional human behavior is assuredly probabilistic, as the above paragraphs indicate, because what is done always depends on the probabilistic encounter of reasons of various strengths with other reasons. Furthermore, many social scientists offer explanations for behavior that are probabilistic in the sense that they incorporate a stochastic component. In a regression model, for example, for each combination of values on the independent variables, each possible value of the dependent variable has a stipulated probability of occurrence. This probability is defined by the parameters of the regression surface together with the parameters of the distribution of the random disturbance term.

Nevertheless, such a probabilistic *model* cannot be a probabilistic *law.* The reason is that the *parameters* are not stable across populations and time periods, meaning that outcomes conditioned on any particular values of the independent variables have two sources of variation rather than one—the local parameters as well as the disturbance. The local parameters do not vary randomly, which would imply the absurd result of strictly random human behavior, but neither do they vary in response to specifiable causes, which (by simply including the causes in the model) would imply human behavior with stable conditioned means across populations and time periods. Instead, the parameters vary in response to encounters, which in turn depend on heredity, context, and experience. The parameters, in short, are variable but unpredictable, which negates any claim to lawlike status.

Implications for Theory

The point I want to emphasize is that the categorical disavowal of laws leaves explanatory social science in a challenging position. If we cannot aspire to stable generalizations, to what then can we aspire? Anytime we explain innovation, good leadership, and so forth, whether it be by a quantitative analysis or a case study, it must be with the thought that this explanation cannot be generalized in any systematic way beyond the population and time period studied or sampled. No amount of accumulation of research will change this fundamental fact in any way, and indeed, in areas such as innovation and human relations theory, which represent some of the most relentlessly studied areas in our field, we are as far from stable generalizations as ever. Each study we carry out for the purpose of explaining the behavior of individuals or groups is in this sense "historical," or history bound (Gergen 1973).

The above is not meant to imply that it is pointless to carry out explanatory research, but only that the disavowal of laws calls on us to pause and give some thought to discovering and articulating just what might be the point of such research. Otherwise, we are likely to either continue to operate as though some universal or probabilistic laws were likely eventually to result or be vulnerable to the criticism that we have not been reflective enough about why we do what we do and how, therefore, we can tell the good research from the bad. I wish here to offer one kind of answer to these questions, but the general issue seems to me important enough that one would hope for further proposals and discussion.

Because all explanatory social research must be "historical," I take my cue from the position of the discipline of history—not, I might add, from the raisons d'etre explicitly offered by historians, for these have been few (Carr 1963; Turner 1981), but rather from the apparently prevailing attitudes toward the study of history in society.

Why study history? Why care about the past? The best answer probably involves the observation that human beings are addicted to stories, i.e., to accounts of the causes and consequences of human action, and it seems that these accounts and stories help us, as individuals, to regulate our own affairs. The question might well be raised, of course, whether that vague purpose is enough to justify the activity of large segments of several major academic disciplines—history, anthropology, area studies, and so forth. With some elaboration and specification, I propose that it is indeed enough. Admittedly, it is difficult to say precisely why we are so committed to learning about the way in which certain things happened in the past. Nevertheless, and this is the important point, one cannot foresee the slightest diminution in the inclination to remain so committed. Somehow, we do believe—and I simply accept this as a valid orientation—that an understanding of important past events is valuable enough to receive skilled attention, even when we recognize that such understanding cannot be extended in any systematic way to the prediction, explanation, or control of future events (Scriven 1966, 250).

This orientation provides us with a clue in our quest for a perspective on the role of explanatory social science: good research and ideas are apparently those that impart this sort of understanding of the past, with the proviso that such understanding must be useful. The idea is to impart through the research a *consummate causal understanding* of the past behavior investigated such that all pertinent challenges and questions regarding that behavior and our explanation of it are answerable from the data and their logical extensions. How nearly this is accomplished will in turn be affected primarily by the set of events or variables we choose to investigate and the creativity and quality of the way in which we conceptualize them, as well as the quality of measurements, analyses, and presentation. Understanding as a goal of research is a venerable idea; the well-known *verstehen* school has an institutionalized position in the philosophy of social science, often seen as a rebuttal and alternative to positivism (a brief summary pertinent to the present discussion may be found in Warnke 1984; see also Scriven 1966, 250–54). What is different in the present treatment, without attempting a philosophical exposition, is that understanding here *embraces* at its very core the notion of causation, rather than setting itself up in opposition to it. This is accomplished primarily through the role of operative reasons, which are at the basis of the understanding of human behavior and which at the same time are causally related to it.

As noted, moreover, we commonly think that understanding the background of a certain behavior in depth teaches something valuable in terms of future conduct; therefore at best something is to be learned from such research products in terms of behavioral expectations in similar circumstances. When we know enough of just the right facts about a situation to be able to understand thoroughly the behavior of the actors, we believe that the information we tuck away has a good chance of being reused with profit at some future time. This form of memory suggests a process of *creative-selective generalization*. Generalizability of this sort is indefinite, but it is also common, and this creative-selective sort is, I suggest, the best kind of theoretical generalization we can aspire to in social science (recognizing that probability sampling permits no generalization beyond the population sampled and the past time period studied).

Let us now view the two notions of consummate causal understanding and creative-selective generalization together as complementary criteria of quality in explanatory research and introduce one more concept that forms a bridge between them. Simply establishing a causal connection between organizational size and innovation in a piece of research, for example, might be a reasonable start toward understanding that relation, but if it were left at that, the nature of the connection would be hidden away in a black box, and creative-selective generalization would therefore be difficult. The idea is that particular research on size and innovation should be instructive in thinking about the same or a similar issue in new contexts. Perhaps in the next few time periods, the same relation might reasonably be expected to hold in the same population of organizations, but as we change populations, or leave the time period far behind, then whether we can apply these findings at all, and whether fully or partially, will depend on relevant similarities between the two contexts, and just which dimensions are relevant is in turn likely to be revealed only through a thorough understanding of the modus operandi of size on innovation in the context studied. Thus, in social science, the particular program of research does not induce or even test a strict regularity, nor does it present a partial law or contribute to the eventual development of a law. What it does at best, instead, is present us with a *significant possibility* (Scriven 1966, 246–51)—a way in which behavior frequently does indeed unfold, even if not always (possibility), and a finding that is both aesthetically appealing and important for the world to know about (significant).

In the use of the term "significant possibility," the word "significant" may readily be seen to connote importance. That is, private individuals may be drawn to stories and accounts that are of interest mainly to themselves, but academic disciplines, as large social investments, should devote their explanatory side to behaviors that have broad importance. I mean the idea of significance to have a further connotation as well, however, namely, to suggest the aesthetic side of the academic enterprise. Social science is a kind of craft. It is not strictly a trade, such as carpentry, or an art form, such as sculpture, but is rather a mixture of the two, analogous to cabinet making. It takes its value in being both useful and beautiful. The aesthetic side has always suggested characteristics such as parsimony, the intriguing juxtaposition of ideas, and the unusual and skillful use of methodological tools. I will use terms such as "the aesthetic dimension" and "intriguing" to denote this meaning of "significant."

Getting the craft combination right has, I think, been troublesome for social science, especially the aesthetic side. One influential scholar views the situation as follows: "The aesthetic norm . . . has little bearing on behavioral science in its present state, which may be characterized—without undue offense to anyone, I trust—as one of almost unrelieved ugliness" (Kaplan 1964, 310). There is undoubtedly a good deal of truth in this observation, yet I find that some theoretical sallies have fared at least somewhat better than others on this criterion.

The best explanatory research generates strong, causal insight into human affairs. By this inclusive term I mean to include in brief the three concepts just referred to: research that imparts a consummate causal understanding of a relation such that we are presented with a significant possibility that we can use, by means of creative-selective generalization, to illuminate and inform potential iterations of this relation in other contexts. In this sense, it is wrong to denigrate a strong, causal insight—the observation that exceptionally high morale had a profound effect on productivity in the Hawthorne studies, for example (Roethlisberger and Dickson 1939)—on the ground that it does not hold in all cases. The danger may lie more in our ever thinking that it might. If a theory does indeed present a significant possibility based on a thorough understanding, it stands at a high level of accomplishment within social science and indeed at the highest level possible within the domain of explanatory theory.

Kuhn (1962) referred to what he called "normal science." This is research on a certain topic that follows in the wake of the seminal scholarship on that topic. The phenomenon is important because most science is normal science. It is often considered that the function of normal science is to amplify, specify, or otherwise elaborate or modify the basic laws originally propounded in the seminal research. Perhaps it works that way in those sciences that do deal in the discovery of universal or nearly universal laws, but it follows from the foregoing that normal science cannot have the same meaning and function in the social disciplines. Because there are no laws (beyond the physical ones), laws in our disciplines cannot be elaborated. Moreover, although normal science must still relate to seminal insights, this cannot be in the sense of bringing the original insight closer to being a law by explaining away a piece of the original error variance. The latter orientation has, I think, been a distraction. Thinking about what normal science can properly hope to do in our areas, I suggest that it should function in large measure to provide additional and more modest insights that supplement and fill out the original, strong insights—elaborating and modifying them, perhaps, or discovering some of the significant conditions under which they have been valid or have failed to be valid. The result would be to contribute understanding of related situations and to broaden or sharpen the possibilities for valuable selective generalization.

Application: Theories of Innovation and Change

It may be an exaggeration to say that there have been one hundred theories of organizational change, yet change seems so frequently to be extremely difficult for individuals and groups, while at the same time being crucial for getting important things done, that we have been motivated to give it a great deal of attention across all of the disciplines contributing to organization theory. The result has been many theoretical approaches to what is nominally, at least, the same behavior. Thus, we can use innovation theory to illustrate extent of adherence to the norms suggested above with some basis for comparison across the examples. I will not strive here for one hundred, but will rather review six or eight general approaches, many of which contain a large number of individual theories or models with different specific content. Still, much is omitted. In each case, I will evaluate the quality of the theory on each of the criteria elaborated above. To summarize the performance of each example across the various criteria, I will offer an overall subjective rating of the theory on a quantitative scale of 1 to 5, with 5 being highest or best.

Variance Theories

Variance theories is a term drawn from a former publication (Mohr 1982), by which I mean theories oriented toward explaining variance in one variable by means of variance in others. It is a dangerous approach in that it lends itself naturally to expression as an equation (e.g., a regression equation). First, equations are the prototypical form for laws so that one is drawn toward an orientation to regularities. Second, the investigator and his or her audience are likely to become focused on R-squares and significance levels—attached to any variables at all—at the expense of a search for the variables or factors that would most enhance understanding.

Determinants Theory

One variant, which had a heyday in the sixties and seventies, is to use number of innovations adopted, or earliness of adoption, as a dependent variable in a correlation or regression format while stringing together any number of possible determinants or predictors as independent variables. These have included bureaucratic characteristics such as specialization, formalization, and centralization; fugitives from two-step flow theory (to be reviewed below) such as centrality in a social network; demographic descriptors such as the age of the organization or its chief executive; and economic considerations such as organizational size and wealth. One might think of the form as "determinants theory." A large number of studies of this sort have been conducted, perhaps more than any other type, and many early examples were reviewed in Zaltman, Duncan, and Holbek (1973) and Rogers and Shoemaker (1971). The studies had the merit of benefitting from a certain amount of objectivity, but they fell afoul of the problem of encounters and the impossibility of laws: the individual determinants tended to work well in some studies but poorly in others, with the signs of some associations even veering from positive to negative across studies (Rogers and Shoemaker 1971). Determinants theories in the innovation area therefore get low marks from the standpoint of usefulness, or serving as a basis of creative-selective generalization. This is especially true in that the simple listing of a string of determinants will rarely provide and communicate an understanding of the innovative behavior studied. Determinants theories also fare poorly on the aesthetic dimension. They might be taken as aspiring to be intriguing by employing statistical techniques, which were still relatively novel and interesting in the sixties (although diffusing rapidly in the seventies), but scholars have tended to apply the statistical procedures mechanically. In addition, a laundry list of variables on the right-hand side exemplifies the opposite of parsimony and the antithesis of elegance; it is just the kind of theorizing, I would guess, that helped to give Kaplan the impression of unremitting ugliness.

Determinants theories fare well in importance because innovation itself and most of the individual areas of innovation studied are indeed of great importance, but this will be true of all of the theoretical approaches to be reviewed here, so that importance is a constant in the present analysis (it should not be forgotten, however, in the analysis of other areas).

I would score determinants theory a 1.

Adoptability

Many studies in the variance theory mode have looked at the innovation rather than the adopter as the unit of analysis (e.g., Fliegel and Kivlin 1966; see also Downs and Mohr 1976, 711–12). The question asked is, "What determines the variation in the speed or extent of adoption of innovations of various sorts?" The determinants, then, are descriptors of innovations, such as their understandability, their ability to reduce costs, and so on. The above comments on determinants theory would be applicable essentially without change to this group as well.

Motivation-Resources Theory

A variant that does at least feature a persuasive functional organization of the determinants (as opposed to a laundry list) is motivation-resources theory, suggested by Mohr (1969, 123–25) and elaborated in Downs and Mohr (1976; see also Atkinson 1957; Palmore and Hammond 1964). The approach has general applicability because almost any behavior can be seen, and usually constructively so, as being determined multiplicatively by the motivations involved in undertaking it and the resources available to do it successfully (or the barriers, which are negative resources). The apparent universality or near universality of the model comes from employing an exhaustive *classification* of causes—the classes being motivation and resources—rather than the causes themselves. Creative-selective generalization, on the other hand, would have to be based on an understanding of an act of innovation in terms of the particular causes—individual, concrete motivations and resources—that were pertinent to it in the instances studied. Unfortunately, in moving to the particular we lose the smack of generality that was so appealing in the abstract classes. If there is to be true theoretical generalization, the loss must be recaptured by a consummate causal understanding involving the particulars, and even then it can be recaptured only in part, that is, we must settle for a more modest scope of generality than the near universal scope of "motivation and resources." For example, in one research project of this genre that I carried out myself, I used the public health ideology of the local health officer and the size (expenditures) of the health department to predict innovations in local public health agencies (Mohr 1969). The ability to generalize these results creatively is meager, however, because I did not develop an understanding of just how ideology and size led to innovation in the organizations studied. I did not recognize the need to do so at the time and was instead oriented toward statistical performance. Had I been able to develop a sound understanding of the modus operandi of ideology and size, a good basis for limited but perhaps important generalization might have been produced.

Causal understanding at the abstract level is satisfactory in this variant because what the theory says is that people add up the costs and benefits (i.e., the negative and positive motivations), and, if the balance is favorable, they adopt, provided that the appropriate resources are in adequate supply. Seen in this way, motivation-resources theory is a subtype of rational-choice theory. The rational-choice approach can be intriguing if particular motivations and resources are imputed that are themselves intriguing given the kind of behavior considered, but to offer only "motivation" and "resources" in the abstract is not intriguing in the same way. On the contrary, it is hard to imagine anything more boring theoretically than rational choice—a theory of human behavior that says only that, all in all, people do what they want and are able to do. As noted, a really productive causal understanding would have to come at the level of the individual innovation or innovation type and its concrete causes, but to my knowledge there have been no studies in the motivation-resources mode that have attempted to accomplish this.

The theory is parsimonious at the abstract level; credit is due there. There would also seem to be a potential for parsimony at the concrete level. Value, however, would depend on understanding and generalizability based on such concrete cases, and that remains to be demonstrated.

I would score motivation-resources theory a 2.

Theoretical Process Descriptions

The theoretical process descriptions model is another approach to explanation entirely. It tries to capture the process by which the adoption of an innovation comes about.

The Two-Step Flow Theory

An early variant was the two-step flow theory, coming out of rural sociology and education and then, later, medical sociology (again, reviewed extensively in Rogers and Shoemaker 1971). Here, the unit of analysis is the community of adopters, that is, the theory describes the process by which a community of farmers or doctors or state highway departments or school districts adopts a new technology or practice. It says that the earliest adopters are individuals or organizations who are attuned to and take their cues from the mass media or other external sources. These then become opinion leaders. Others in the community take heart from their example and follow suit, some needing just a few role models and others not taking the plunge until almost all of the community has gone before them. The theory is extremely powerful in giving a basic understanding of how a community of adopters takes on something new (but only sometimes—this is a possibility, not a regularity). It does not impart a thorough understanding because, as the research was done, it did not go very far toward revealing *why* a community does things in this manner. There would be many ways of conceptualizing and approaching that aspect. In normal science, the two-step flow researchers tended to get stuck on identifying roles, such as pioneer, early adopter, laggard, and so on, and straying into determinants research, with little success, to learn what kinds of people were likely to fill the various roles. In the end, we understood little about why communities might operate in this fashion and so cannot be very creative in our selective generalization. What was needed and never supplied was a certain amount of intensive analysis of community dynamics in this regard, complete with narratives of the kinds of lives various individuals led as background to the ways in which they fit into the larger picture and contributed more or less to the generation of community motion. The two-step flow theory is a parsimonious and powerful idea that can be (and was) used extensively in the applied world even though the mechanism it proposed was sketchy and superficial. It went essentially nowhere theoretically after the initial, seminal scholarship.

I would score it a 3.

Lewinian Field Theory

A theoretical process description that is similar in its simplicity, cast at the individual rather than the community level, is due to Lewin (1951). Capturing the brunt of his "field theory" in its least complicated form, Lewin proposed that innovation proceeds by a process of unfreezing, moving, and refreezing. Of the three stages, the first, unfreezing, is by far the most important. The idea is that in order for people to change in a certain way, they first must become unstuck from a preferred pattern of outlook or behavior that holds them back. Positive and negative forces with respect to change are both active. In that circumstance, unfreezing will be unlikely to result by increasing forces that push in the new direction because that sort of pushing will simply arouse and strengthen the forces of resistance. The most efficacious route is through the undermining of those initial forces of resistance.

Unfreezing-moving-refreezing achieves parsimony nicely at the abstract level, although the fuller field theory is not quite so simple. As we will see in a moment, there is also an attraction of parsimony in the ideas of group discussion and participation in decision making that are suggested as being key vehicles to achieve unfreezing in some concrete instances. The job of imparting a thorough understanding in this case was better achieved than in the two-step flow theory, although apparently not well enough. In Lewin's elaboration of "field theory" (1951) and his descriptions of reducing the resistance of wartime housewives to changes in dietary preferences through group discussion (1947), we do get some amount of feeling for why it was that unfreezing took place in particular illustrations. The quest for understanding, however, relied almost entirely on explanations in technical language rather than, for example, on some amount of description of the actual lives and reactions of people. In a highly influential piece, Coch and French (1948) applied the theory with noteworthy success to reducing resistance to change through participation in decision making in a formal organization. What followed, however, was something of a disgrace (Leavitt 1965). Social scientists began to use their skills in small-group leadership to manipulate workers in discussion sessions into arriving at decisions that were preordained by management. Not only did guilt ultimately and appropriately set in, but the manipulators were by no means always successful, perhaps because of insufficient skill but perhaps also because this emphasis in Lewin's theory is only a significant possibility, whereas it seemed to be taken more as a strict regularity. The *desired* and presumed scope of generalization tended to be universal rather than creative and selective. In sum, causal understanding seems not to have been strong enough to permit good creative-selective generalization, and the apparent orientation toward universal generalization would have been too ambitious even if causal understanding had been much stronger.

I would score the theory a 3.

Field Theory and Determinants Theory Conflated

There is another example of normal science in connection with this theory, namely, the attempt to reformulate the abstract version as a statistical model (Zand and Sorensen 1975). The cited treatment does not try to augment the original strong insight concerning the process of change with additional significant possibilities that would elaborate or modify it. Instead, the attempt is to convert the theoretical process description into a variance theory by making variables out of the basic concepts (unfreezing, for example) and viewing them as determinants of another variable, the successful completion of the change. The original theory, however, does not suggest that each stage is an independent determinant of success, but shows rather how innovation unfolds if and when it does take place. It would not be contradicted, for example, if there were unfreezing and moving but no successful adoption of a new practice. In part, the theory is being made to suffer here by bringing to center stage the aspect of *control,* or the successful introduction of change. At the same time, it must be admitted that Lewin and his early followers were themselves strongly oriented toward control, as in the tradition of overcoming the resistance to change. In any case, the statistical format changes the original sense of the theory in a basic way while doing little or nothing to increase understanding. Striving to bring a strong insight such as Lewin's closer to the functional form of an explanatory law does not seem to have been at all successful. This variant cannot be scored any higher than other determinants theories of innovation.

Innovation-Process Theory

Theoretical process descriptions at a much more concrete level were attempted by Eveland, Rogers, and Klepper (1977) and Pelz (1985). The thrust of these theories is to identify the successive stages in the process of organizational innovation in terms of what people actually do. Eveland, Rogers, and Klepper (1977) find agenda setting, matching, redefining, structuring, and interconnecting. Pelz finds concern, search, appraisal, design, commitment, implementation, incorporation, and diffusion. The enlightening aspect of these theories, it seems to me, is simple: to bring to our attention that these particular hurdles must be jumped if an organization is going to take on something new. In terms of applied creative generalization, for example, one might think about whether a given organization will adopt a certain innovation by taking the adoption process mentally through the proposed stages and judging whether certain ones are likely to prove to be sticking points in that organization. There is, therefore, some potential utility. None of the cases described by these authors, however, seems to increase our understanding of an innovation process. I doubt that any could because I do not think that we get a grasp on a process by memorizing a list of concrete tasks. The contrast in elegance and insight between this direct sort of process theory and the more analogical or metaphorical sort exemplified by Lewin's theory or the two-step flow model is pronounced. There is indeed something ugly about a would-be theory comprised of a list of nitty-gritty tasks of this sort. On the other hand, it is superior to a list of unorganized determinants, as in variance theory, in that it is unified by comprising an account that unfolds in the flow of time—or at least it would be superior if we did not learn from Pelz (1985) that two or more stages can occur simultaneously and that the given order of stages is not necessarily constant. In this light, creative-selective generalization for the process as a whole would be extremely limited.

I would score the direct, list-of-activities sort of theoretical process description a 1+.

Diffusion Theory

Last in our review of theoretical process descriptions is a consideration of diffusion theory at the population level, that is, the theory that an innovation diffuses over time through a population of potential adopters according to the equation of a mathematical curve, such as an S-curve (Griliches 1957; Hagerstrand 1968). What is intriguing aesthetically about this theory is that innovation is shown to behave like a communicable disease; it follows the typical pattern of cumulative proportion of victims over time (or space, as in Hagerstrand 1968). Yet, there is no bug—no infectious organism that passes from person to person. What does pass from person to person, and how is it communicated? Therein lies both the great potential and the great challenge of diffusion theory, but the challenge has not been met, and the potential has not been realized. What is at issue is understanding. In epidemiology, we understand the parameters of particular S-curves by coming to understand the process of person-to-person transmission of a type of organism, whether by mosquitos, water, sexual contact, air, animal bites, or what have you. In the field of innovation, we have a stunted theory if we know only the shape of the curve but have not conceptualized just what is transmitted and how. The entire theory remains at the symbolic (mathematical) level; there is little operationalization of the underlying transmission process (Pahre 1996). In the case of this theory of innovation, it is unavoidable that generalization be creative and selective; there is truly little basis for universalizing. That is so because diffusion curves are apparently quite different for different innovations (although only S-curves tend to be publicized). Pause to consider the standard hybrid corn and penicillin examples on one hand, which underwent S-curve diffusion, and contact lenses, participative management, hot pants, strong-mayor government, democratic republics, and toll roads on the other. The differences can be well understood only by the creative conceptualization of what is actually going on that we would call "transmission" in each of these cases. Thus, there is a good start in diffusion theory, particularly in the aesthetics, but critical progress is needed.

Score it a 2+.

Encounter Theory

An encounter theory reveals that the event to be explained is a probabilistic encounter and specifies the elements of the conjunction that make up the encounter. In the theory of natural selection, for example, a species gets its start as the result of an encounter—that between a new, hereditary genome resulting from a mutation, and the elements of an environment. This has proven to be a theory of incredible interest, richness, and challenge, with results concerning one characteristic, species, or grouping constantly being used creatively and selectively to develop and test hypotheses about others. In organization theory, the approach is exemplified most prominently by the garbage can model of organizational choice (Cohen, March, and Olsen 1972), where a choice is conceptualized as a probabilistic encounter between a quantity of energy embodied in a stream of participants and a smaller load of required energy embodied in a stream of problems. There is a great deal of variety in the reasons for the interest in and value of an encounter theory. It is not just a matter of explaining something important that recurs. For example, whereas the theory of natural selection is most interesting for the many implications of "successful" encounters that occur, the garbage can model is more interesting in terms of lack of success—i.e., choices *not* made because choice opportunities became overburdened by problems.

Routine Change

It should immediately be expected that the routine change theory will score high on the aesthetic or "intriguing" component of "significant possibility" because the very idea of routine change is surprising, even counterintuitive. Almost all other theorizing about innovation and change sees it as something explicitly planned and as a possibility that stimulates conspicuous resistance—anything but routine. March (1981) suggests, however, that a large proportion of significant change in organizations results, often almost imperceptibly, from encounters between the execution of a few routine processes, on one hand, and details of the context in which the execution of the processes occurs, on the other. In this way, for example, "an organization of evangelists becomes a gym with services attached" (570), or a regulatory agency may become more hostile to the organizations it regulates, who hire many of its departing officials, because this practice may produce "a pattern of turnover in the regulatory agency in which friends leave the agency, and only those unfriendly to the organization[s] remain" (567). Much of the spirit of the important hypothesis of path dependence (e.g., David 1985) is subsumed under this encounter theory.

The basic idea is lovely. As with motivation-resources theory, it is simple at the level of the abstract. Parsimony is lost somewhat when descending from the general statement of the theory because there are several possible stable processes of change (March specifies six, but that is just one conceptualization). Similarly, there is a ready though sketchy understanding of the occurrence of change in this way at the general level, but the basic need for understanding must be fulfilled, as always, by more localized studies. There have, however, been few (see Mohr 1985 for an application of the theory to the sweeping adoption of computers by organizations). Thus, there is little if any generalization of actual research results to instances or types of routine change. In my view, the similarities to the theory of evolution by natural selection are strong. There could be a whole field or subfield here addressed to the understanding of a wide range of organizational change, in which hundreds of instances of routine change might be studied, with insights that serve to elaborate the theory itself and that are applied in the progressively more rich and powerful analysis of further instances of routing change and, therefore, of general organizational behavior. Yet, in more than fifteen years since the appearance of March's article little has happened in the way of normal science. It is of course impossible to say why for certain, but I suggest that the *motivation* for further development has not been great. Unlike natural selection, where scientists have been spontaneously driven to develop a large and multifaceted descriptive science, interest in organizational innovation and change has been mainly normative. That is, we have wished to understand this phenomenon mainly in order to be able to influence it. Given March's admonition, which is undoubtedly correct, that knowledge of routine change will have only small payoff in terms of the ability to control it or to introduce intentionally planned change, there seems to be little interest. There has in fact been only slight pursuit of encounter theories altogether, perhaps because, by their very nature, they fail to point in the direction of specific prediction and control.

Here, then, is an excellent theory that seems to suffer much because it does not comport very well with the goals of researchers in the area of innovation. I score it a 4–.

Conclusion

Viewing the many theories of innovation in terms of the criteria derived from methodological inquiry, certain patterns emerge. In particular, there is a fairly consistent failure to pursue the requirement of understanding except at the most abstract level. Instead, inputs are related to outputs only by a black box so that generalization can only be universal rather than creative and selective—a usage that must always fail and perhaps make the theory seem less successful than might otherwise be the case. Second, the analysis reveals that, as much as we might claim *not* to be interested in general laws, that kind of orientation is seen to have dominated innovation research in practice. Among the approaches reviewed, only routine change theory has been satisfied with the more modest but potentially more efficacious claim to the discovery of a significant possibility. Third, theories that emphasize the process of innovation have fared relatively well. Some of these have failed by being too concrete. There has seemed to be more potential in achieving a basic understanding of the process through a fairly simple, metaphorical sort of model instead of a concrete one, which then might be specified and elaborated through the understanding of individual, real processes of innovation that follow the metaphorical pattern. But fourth, whereas there have been many excellent models and ideas at the abstract level—two-step flow theory, Lewinian field theory, diffusion theory, and routine change theory, there has been a failure to upgrade the utility of these in the normal science following the seminal scholarship. The primary reason seems to be a predilection for broad applicability over the understanding of individual processes of innovation in the respective theoretical terms. In addition, we have perhaps been too quick to want to show how to act on the world instead of tending to the business of elaborating a descriptive science. Last, encounters have figured both positively and negatively in the study of innovation. Routine change theory conceptualizes innovation as an encounter and thereby adds creatively to theoretical possibilities. Other approaches, however, have not recognized that all intentional human behavior results from encounters, so we have tended to expect more stability and predictability than there can ever be. Consequently, social science tends to seem disappointing. Its substantial successes are undervalued, and its even greater potential remains largely unexploited.

Note

A prior version of this chapter was delivered at the Third National Public Management Research Conference, University of Kansas, October 5–7, 1995.

References

Atkinson, John W. 1957. "Motivational Determinants of Risk-Taking Behavior." *Psychological Review* 64: 359–72.

Carr, Edward H. 1963. *What Is History?* New York: Knopf.

Coch, Lester, and J. R. P. French. 1948. "Overcoming Resistance to Change." *Human Relations* 1, no. 4: 512–32.

Cohen, Michael D., James G. March, and Johan P. Olsen. 1972. "A Garbage Can Model of Organizational Choice." *Administrative Science Quarterly* 17, no. 1: 1–25.

David, Paul A. 1985. "Clio and the Economics of QWERTY." *Economic History* 75, no. 2: 332–37.

Downs, George W., Jr., and Lawrence B. Mohr. 1976. "Conceptual Issues in the Study of Innovation." *Administrative Science Quarterly* 21, no. 4: 700–714.

Eveland, J. D., Everett M. Rogers, and Constance M. Klepper. 1977. "The Innovation Process in Public Organizations: Some Elements of a Preliminary Model." Grant No. RDA 75–17952. Ann Arbor: Report to the National Science Foundation, University of Michigan.

Fliegel, Frederick C., and Joseph E. Kivlin. 1966. "Attributes of Innovations as Factors in Diffusion." *American Journal of Sociology* 72: 235–48.

Gergen, Kenneth J. 1973. "Social Psychology as History." *Journal of Personality and Social Psychology* 26: 309–20.

Griliches, Zvi. 1957. "Hybrid Corn: An Exploration in the Economics of Technological Change." *Econometrica* 25: 501–22.

Hagerstrand, T. 1968. *Innovation Diffusion As a Spatial Process.* Chicago: University of Chicago Press.

Kaplan, Abraham. 1964. *The Conduct of Inquiry.* San Francisco: Chandler.

Kuhn, Thomas S. 1962. *The Structure of Scientific Revolutions.* Chicago: University of Chicago Press.

Leavitt, Harold J. 1965. "Applied Organizational Change in Industry: Structural, Technological, and Humanistic Approaches." In *Handbook of Organizations,* edited by James G. March. Chicago: Rand McNally.

Lewin, Kurt. 1947. "Frontiers in Group Dynamics." *Human Relations,* 1, no. 1: 5–42.

———. 1951. *Field Theory in Social Science.* New York: Harper.

March, James G. 1981. "Footnotes to Organizational Change." *Administrative Science Quarterly* 26, no. 4: 563–77.

Mohr, Lawrence B. 1969. "Determinants of Innovation in Organizations." *American Political Science Review,* 63, no. 1: 111–26.

———. 1982. *Explaining Organizational Behavior: The Limits and Possibilities of Theory and Research.* San Francisco: Jossey-Bass.

———. 1985. "Forces Influencing Decision and Change Behaviors." In *Organizational Strategy and Change,* edited by J. M. Pennings et al. San Francisco: Jossey-Bass.

———. 1996. *The Causes of Human Behavior: Implications for Theory and Method in the Social Sciences.* Ann Arbor: University of Michigan Press.

Pahre, Robert. 1996. "Mathematical Discourse and Crossdisciplinary Communities: The Case of Political Economy." *Social Epistemology* 10, no. 1: 55–73.

Palmore, Erdman B., and Phillip E. Hammond. 1964. "Interacting Factors in Juvenile Delinquency." *American Sociological Review* 29, no. 6: 848–54.

Pelz, Don C. 1985. "Innovation Complexity and the Sequence of Innovating Stages." *Knowledge: Creation, Diffusion, Utilization* 6, no. 3: 60–67.

Roethlisberger, F. J., and W. J. Dickson. 1939. *Management and the Worker.* Cambridge: Harvard University Press.

Rogers, Everett M., and F. Floyd Shoemaker. 1971. *Communication of Innovations.* New York: Free Press.

Scriven, Michael. 1966. "Causes, Connections and Conditions in History." In *Philosophical Analysis and History,* edited by William Dray. New York: Harper and Row.

Turner, James. 1981. "Recovering the Uses of History." *Yale Review* 70, no. 2: 221–33.

Warnke, Georgia. 1984. "Translator's Introduction." In *Understanding and Explanation: A Transcendental-Pragmatic Perspective,* edited by Karl-Otto Apel. Cambridge: MIT Press.

Zaltman, Gerald, Robert Duncan, and Jonny Holbek. 1973. *Innovations and Organizations.* New York: Wiley.

Zand, Dale E., and Richard E. Sorensen. 1975. "Theory of Change and the Effective Use of Management Science." *Administrative Science Quarterly* 20, no. 4: 532–45.

2 | Theoretical Foundations of Policy Intervention

Janet A. Weiss

In Graham Allison's influential account of the Cuban missile crisis, the president's discovery of Soviet missiles in Cuba became the point of departure for three kinds of policy arguments that Allison called the rational policy, organizational process, and bureaucratic politics models (Allison 1971). The value of these models was that each offered a way to understand what was happening in Cuba and to make sensible proposals about what United States officials might do next. Allison's point was that the three models offered distinctive accounts with different implications for action. I will focus on Allison's recognition that policy deliberation, decision making, and argument are grounded in policy makers' models of the world that offer them guidance about how, when, and why to act. These models of the world frame what is happening and point toward alternative courses of action that may make sense. Participants in policy debates may or may not make their models explicit to themselves or to others. Nevertheless, for the observer, and especially the academic researcher, recognizing the logic that guides the arguments and actions of policy participants helps to render intelligible the resulting policy decisions and their aftermath. Whether or not participants share common models, articulating the models in play helps to clarify the domains of agreement and disagreement and reveals possibilities for acceptable action.

In scientific explanation, such models of the world are usually called theories. Theories organize information and data into patterns that can be interpreted. These interpretations form the basis for a conclusion about the situation at hand. A theory sets boundaries around the problem or event, identifies critical variables, sorts evidence and argument into categories that are and are not pertinent to the question at hand, and usually draws attention to cause and effect relationships. I use the word "theories" in this discussion to describe conceptual models of the world held by nonscientists, indeed held by all participants in which policy making takes place, no matter how primitive the theories may be. Such theories used in policy making and implementation would often fail tests of rationality, internal consistency, or grounding in systematic evidence. Whether they have these "scientific" qualities or not, theories offer those who use them a way to organize and focus thinking about the problem at hand. Other words have often been used to describe these theories, such as paradigms, conceptual frameworks, ideologies, or cognitive maps. I use "theories" to emphasize the explanatory and filtering role these theories serve for participants in policy making. Like scientific theories, policy theories may turn out to be compatible or incompatible with data and make accurate or inaccurate predictions about future events. Like scientific theories, alternative theories may be invoked by one's critics to explain the same set of circumstances. The critical role of policy theories in the policy design process is that they help people to develop positions and to take action on complex, uncertain, and difficult matters.

As I have looked at policy theories in use in actual policy deliberations, I find that public policies must be grounded, explicitly or implicitly, in not one but three interrelated theories: a theory of the problem, a theory of desired outcomes, and a theory of intervention. These distinct but interdependent theories offer an account of the phenomenon that policy makers are attempting to address, the outcomes they seek to produce, and the means of intervention they intend to employ. The three theories are often packaged as a single argument. The distinctions among them are typically not explicit; they are certainly not put forward by policy advocates labeled as such. Nevertheless, it is helpful to think of the arguments, assumptions, and rationales supporting particular policy initiatives as theories of these three kinds.

All three theories make causal claims; they argue that a given pattern of behavior has been (or will be) caused by a configuration of forces in the world. All three are essentially behavioral: they explain or predict changes in human behavior—the actions of citizens, firms, governments, communities, or other groups. All make both normative and positive claims about the problem at hand. Typically, all three theories are contested. The embrace of a particular theory of the problem (or outcome or intervention) by one group does not mean that other policy makers or other groups affected by the problem share the same theory. Frequently these differences in theoretical assumptions remain implicit and lead to arguing past one another rather than squarely confronting different predictions or priorities. The theories used by policy makers may be internally coherent, realistic, and carefully targeted; or they may be incoherent, simplistic, or hopelessly out of whack with real people and their real lives. Policy proposals are incomplete without attention to all three theories, although any given proposal may not give equal emphasis or be equally clever about its three components.

The three theories rely on one another to form a coherent policy package. They remain conceptually distinct and independently subject to scrutiny, however. The theory of the problem sets the boundaries of the problem, offering at least a rough account of its causes and consequences; why does it occur here and now? This theory speaks to the past (where did the problem come from) and the present (how we experience the problem now). The theory of desired outcome asks what outcomes would be preferred to the current problem, offering at least a rough account of the potential causal forces that might bring this better outcome to pass: which actors and which behavior will make these outcomes more likely to occur? This theory speaks to the present (what we prefer now) and the future (which determinants might bring about the future desired state). The theory of intervention asks how government action (or inaction) is likely to elicit behavior that will lead to desired outcomes. Like the theory of desired outcomes, it speaks to both present (what are the possibilities for government action currently available to us) and future (how can these be used to elicit future change in the actors who are capable of bringing about desired outcomes). The trio of theories bridges the diagnosis of the past with predictions about the future.

In many cases these theories are not articulated or examined critically in the light of available evidence. Thus they remain half-articulated and half-understood. The relations among the theories may also be ill specified, even contradictory. Nonetheless, all three contribute to the fit between the policy and the world in which the policy will take shape. To understand the consequences or to offer guidance for the effective pursuit of particular policies, researchers can begin by making explicit the trio of theories implicated in policy proposals and examining them critically.

Note that I treat policy design in this discussion as the search for action patterns that can bring about desired outcomes. This is not because policy making is an objective, systematic, deliberative search for means to agreed-upon ends. Particular policies represent action plans for improving given social outcomes, but they also serve as vehicles for public officials to express commitments and values, to accumulate reputational credit with voters, to embarrass the political opposition, to maneuver for support for future policy initiatives, to attract press attention, to repay favors, to please potential campaign donors, or to save money. Although policies have value in these (and other) particularistic ways for public officials, the instrumental objective of accomplishing intended outcomes for some espoused public purpose remains a nontrivial concern. Finding ways to address problems and take advantage of opportunities facing society is not the only thing that public officials do. Probably it is a small fraction of what they do. Nevertheless, it is a consequential part of what they do and thus worth taking seriously as the starting point of my analysis.

Examples of such theories are shot through all policy deliberations. Sometimes they must be excavated from below the surface of positions and arguments. Sometimes they are an explicit focus of attention and debate. Sometimes they are some of both. Take, for example, "From Red Tape to Results: Creating a Government That Works Better and Costs Less," the final report of the National Performance Review (NPR), chaired by Vice-President Al Gore in 1993. The National Performance Review was commissioned by President Clinton to reinvent the federal government, to "radically change the way the government operates" (National Performance Review 1993, i). Its report offers hundreds of policy proposals for accomplishing this, each bundled with its trio of policy theories. The report spells out the logic justifying its general approach, making many of its theories accessible, if not always entirely coherent.

The proposals are organized into broad rubrics that share critical elements of their policy theories. Thus the problem motivating policy intervention is described as follows: "Public confidence in the federal government has never been lower. . . . People simply feel that government doesn't work. . . . We have spent too much money on programs that don't work. . . . Red tape and regulation [are] so suffocating that they stifle every ounce of creativity. . . . In the name of controlling waste, we have created paralyzing inefficiency. . . . Many federal organizations are monopolies, with few incentives to innovate or improve. . . . Success offers few rewards; failure, few penalties. . . . Politics intensifies the problem. In Washington's highly politicized world, the greatest risk is not that a program will perform poorly, but that a scandal will erupt. Hence control system after control system is piled up to minimize the risk of scandal" (National Performance Review 1993, 1–3). The theory of the problem may be sketched as follows. Government is expensive but does not perform effectively in the eyes of the public. This problem has been caused by (1) the lack of positive incentives for good performance and (2) political risk aversion that leads to excessive procedural controls. The report also puts forward a theory of desired outcome. The desired outcome is "a government that puts people first, by cutting unnecessary spending, serving its customers, empowering its employees, helping communities solve their own problems, and fostering excellence" (7). The theory identifies causal forces that can bring about this outcome: federal employees. "The people who work closest to the problem know the most about how to solve the problem" (9).[1] With the right administrative systems to work in, according to the NPR, federal employees will be free to bring about dramatically improved performance in line with the desired outcome.

But how to get from where we are to where we want to be? The report is less explicit about its theories of intervention, but it offers policy proposals grounded in several theories of intervention to bring about these outcomes. A number of proposals rest on a theory in which the causal mechanism is decentralization of authority, such as permitting agencies to design their own performance appraisal systems or to conduct their own recruiting and hiring. This decentralization is predicted to lead to personnel decisions in the agencies that are superior to the decisions currently made by the central Office of Personnel Management (OPM). These better personnel decisions are predicted to lead to better performance, made possible by selection and retention of better staff.

In the NPR report, as in other policy discussions, particular proposals can be understood in light of their three component theories. The justifications for particular proposals make these three kinds of arguments. The theories are not always satisfactory or coherent. The theories are often disputed. Still, they offer a logic for action, which guides policy makers toward some policies and away from others. Making the theoretical logic more explicit offers policy researchers the opportunity to comment on the logic and offer evidence about the linkages.

With regard to the NPR report, several preliminary observations emerge from making the theories explicit. The report's theory of the problem identifies two major sources of constraints on performance: administrative and political. The theory of the desired outcome concentrates on the administrative sources of better outcomes and devotes less attention to the contributing role of political risk aversion. Thus there is some logical overlap in the theory of the problem and of the desired outcome, but the theory of the desired outcome is less complex than the theory of the problem.

The theory of intervention is even more streamlined than the theory of the desired outcome. If we want administrative systems that empower employees, how can we bring that about? One answer preferred by the authors of the report is to give federal employees more authority and discretion. Decentralization of authority over, say, the procurement or personnel function is theorized to lead to better decisions at the agency level, and these decisions are expected to translate into better agency performance. People at the agency level know their own needs; once they have the authority to make their own decisions, they will make decisions that will lead to better satisfaction of those needs. This theory does not grapple with either of the factors highlighted in the theory of the problem: the absence of positive incentives for good performance (whose needs will be satisfied, and how are these needs connected to performance?) or the political risk aversion that leads to excessive procedural controls (how will legislators respond to failures or errors of judgment by agency officials?). Still, the theory offers a logic for intervention based on the predictions about the consequences of reallocating authority over important administrative decisions.[2]

A few of the report's recommendations, however, are guided by a logic of intervention remote from the theory of desired outcomes. For example, some proposals advocate centralizing authority over federal agencies (such as the proposed National Science and Technology Council, Trade Promotion Coordinating Committee, or Federal Coordinating Council for Economic Development) (National Performance Review 1993, 51–53). The logic of intervention here is that agencies engaged with the same problems need a centralized structure to overcome fragmentation and help them work together on common priorities. This is not crazy, but it is based on a much different logic from the claim that decentralizing authority will improve agency performance. Moreover, it seems little connected to the dominant theory of the desired outcome, which holds that empowered federal employees are able and willing to improve government performance.

Particular interventions advocated in the report might have been offered in the context of different problems or desired outcomes. For example, changing federal personnel policies to give hiring responsibility to agencies might have been an intervention offered in tandem with a theory of desired outcome focused on reducing the number of federal employees or agencies (by making OPM and/or its employees dispensable) or might have been offered in the context of a theory of the problem alleging intractable incompetence or corruption within OPM. Specific interventions acquire meaning in policy debates only within a theoretical context defined by all three theories.

Note also that you may agree with the report about the theory of the problem and even about the theory of desired outcome without endorsing the same theory of intervention. Some critics of the report seem to take just this posture.[3] They agree with the diagnosis of the problem and with the desired outcome. Nevertheless, they suggest that different modes of intervention, such as changes in law or public expectations of government rather than changes in administrative practice, are the best way to move toward more effective government performance.

Explicating the three theories, exploring their linkages, and distinguishing among them can be valuable in two important ways for policy researchers. First, the distinctions help to organize policy arguments and debates in a way that facilitates the accumulation of knowledge about public policy design and consequences. For example, it may be easier to pull together research on the theory of the problem when it is held apart from issues of desired outcome or potential intervention. Also, research on the consequences of alternative interventions can be compared across different problem contexts with varying outcomes in mind. Second, the distinctions among the three kinds of policy theory help to focus research attention on gaps in the chain of logic leading to policy consequences.[4] In the following sections I suggest how the three policy theories may draw on social science theories and results, exploring the potential contributions of these perspectives to policy design. I am especially interested in enriching our theoretical vocabulary about intervention. As I noted in the discussion of the National Performance Review report, theories of intervention are often simpler and less behaviorally sophisticated than theories of the problem. Although social science is short on crisp advice about theories of intervention, the framework I propose gives policy researchers a way to bring social science perspectives to bear on the discussion of intervention to see what value can be added.

Theories of the Problem

The importance of the theory of the problem (often characterized as problem definition) has been emphasized repeatedly in the policy literature. Of the many undesirable states of affairs that may merit government attention, only some secure a place on the crowded public agenda. For problems to receive sustained scrutiny with an eye to ameliorative action, they must be defined in a way that packages a characterization of the problem with a causal story about its origins and consequences. In these theories, some aspects of the problem (and some people, groups, or institutions connected with the problem) are prominently featured while others are treated as insignificant. Analysts have often recognized that such definitions have clear implications for subsequent action (Weiss 1989; Rocheford and Cobb 1994; Nelson 1984; Gusfield 1981).

Theories of the problem often invite research attention. The tools and theories of social science lend themselves rather well to characterizing social circumstances and exploring their causes. The multiplicity of perspectives among policy researchers permits characterization of problems along multiple dimensions. Thus sociologists, economists, and anthropologists may all contribute to analyzing and defining the problems of poverty. They even may acknowledge the value of each others' contributions to describing the problem without necessarily sharing a common theory of a desired outcome or preferred intervention.

Because they are consequential for future action, theories of the problem also invite political struggle. Much policy debate is about whether and how to define problems, where to locate responsibility for problems, and how to understand the role of government in those problems. Policy struggles are triggered by conflicting characterizations of problems, with their differing allocations of blame and responsibility for causes and consequences. These political struggles also signal that values are necessarily invoked in defining problems. Social conditions are not described neutrally in policy debates. They are labeled as good or bad, opportunities or threats, constructive or destructive for the public or some significant social group. The incidence of children living in poverty is not simply a statistic. It acquires policy meaning when it is portrayed by some actors as a negative social condition that calls for corrective action (a portrayal that is disputed by others).

Some significant political debates rest on general consensus about problems and focus instead on theories of desired outcome or theories of intervention. Nearly everyone agrees that violent crime is undesirable and that we want less of it. We disagree, however, often quite violently, about the desirable outcomes of anticrime policies and about the kinds of intervention that might lead to less violent crime. We want more jobs and businesses in poor communities but disagree about how to effect that. We agree that we want children to learn more in school but disagree about exactly what they should learn or how to make the learning happen. Theories of the problem describe what we do not want. Yet, only when policy analysts begin specifying what we do want and (even more strongly) specific proposals for intervention do the trade-offs and interdependencies implicated in particular social conditions become clear. Thus disagreements about desirable future states and about means of intervention arise even after general agreement on the problem.

Theories of Desired Outcome

The theory of the problem analyzes how the problem developed. The theory of the desired outcome analyzes a future preferred state. Thus the latter is always more speculative and relies on subtly different kinds of argument. The theory of the problem is often a story about blame and credit; the theory of desired outcome is about responsibility and opportunity. It is not a mere statement of preferences or goals. Like the other two kinds of theory, the theory of desired outcome tells a causal story. It explicates the desired state and identifies potential causes of the desired state, typically by designating actors who may help to bring the desired outcome to pass. A theory of desired outcome seeks potential sources of improvement in the outcomes that policy makers designate as important.[5] Much policy talk is in abstract language: reducing dependency or increasing economic development in large cities, for example. The theory of desired outcomes presses beyond characterizations of wishes or values to an analysis of what the outcome would look like in practice. Theories of desired outcomes, just like theories of problems, always incorporate moral, value, and political judgments as well as empirical claims about patterns of social outcomes.

The theory has two critical elements. One is the description of the social reality that is preferred to the current unsatisfactory condition. Second is the identification of social actors who are responsible for the preferred social state. Policy must be based on a theory that locates at least partial control over the desired outcome in the hands of some actors and identifies patterns of behavior on their part that are connected to the desired outcome. These actors may be individuals, government agencies, households, firms, or other institutional entities.

Of course the theory of desired outcome used by policy makers may be wrong, at least in part. It may identify desired social realities that are worse than the status quo in the eyes of critical actors. It may attribute control over outcomes to actors who have no control. It may focus attention on behavior that has little connection to the intended outcome. Right or wrong, the theory of desired outcome makes causal attributions that direct policy toward actors and behaviors that are predicted to make desired outcomes more likely.

The desired outcome may be tightly linked to the problem, but it may also be only loosely coupled. A theory of the problem that bemoans welfare dependency may be linked to a theory of desired outcome that aims to reduce out-of-wedlock births, a related but far from identical empirical phenomenon. Both the problem and the desired outcome are subject to redefinition, based on understanding of one another, and the two theories inform one another. Without knowing an advocate's theory of the problem, it is often difficult to understand why the advocate embraces a particular theory of desired outcome. What is the problem that the desired outcome is intended to replace?

The theory of the desired outcome may draw heavily on the theory of the problem. Sometimes a policy problem is caused by actors who need to change their behavior in order to stop causing that problem. For example, the problem may be defined as mass hunger caused by severe food shortages, which were created by hoarding and black markets in scarce commodities. The theory of desired outcomes might set as a goal easing the food shortage and identifies two groups of actors who can contribute to that goal: households that have been hoarding food and participants in black marketeering. In this case the two theories overlap substantially in content and attention (see figure 1 [A]). Sometimes, however, the two theories may be distinct; the causes of the problem and the causes of the desired outcome may be very different. The theory of the problem may attribute hunger and food shortages to natural disaster and destruction of crops. To get more food into the region, policy makers need to

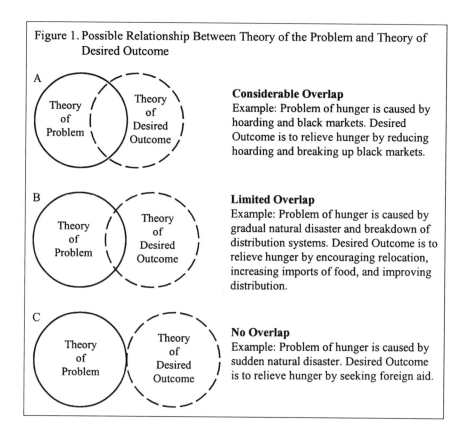

Figure 1. Possible Relationship Between Theory of the Problem and Theory of Desired Outcome

Considerable Overlap
Example: Problem of hunger is caused by hoarding and black markets. Desired Outcome is to relieve hunger by reducing hoarding and breaking up black markets.

Limited Overlap
Example: Problem of hunger is caused by gradual natural disaster and breakdown of distribution systems. Desired Outcome is to relieve hunger by encouraging relocation, increasing imports of food, and improving distribution.

No Overlap
Example: Problem of hunger is caused by sudden natural disaster. Desired Outcome is to relieve hunger by seeking foreign aid.

focus on theories of the *desired* outcome, that is, more food, and not on the monsoon or drought that led to the shortage in the first place. They must develop theories that locate actors who can generate more food, regardless of the reasons that shortages developed. They might, for example, focus on increasing imports of food by distributors or relief organizations (see figure 1 [B] and [C]). The theory of desired outcome identifies the actors whose behavior can produce outcomes that policy makers seek, whether or not these actors were responsible for creating the outcome in the first place. The designated actors need not have full control over the outcome; they seldom do. It is important, however, not to limit attention to those actors who have contributed to the problem in the first place.

Theories of desired outcome vary in ways that are important for the ability of policy makers to design effective interventions. Three dimensions of variation are especially critical: the type of outcome desired, the actors identified as possible contributors to the desired outcome, and the nature of the behavior associated with the outcome.

The outcome defined as desirable may range from concrete and specific to expressive and symbolic. It may involve drastic change in the status quo or modest adjustment. It may be a long-established arena of government action or be entirely new territory for policy making. It may enjoy considerable social support or be the focus of significant social conflict. These differences shape the possibilities for intervention. Intervention is easier when desired outcomes are concrete, enjoy broad social support, require modest changes from the status quo, or continue an on-going stream of government activity; it is more difficult when desired outcomes are expressive, trigger social conflict, break new ground for government action, or require major social change. The resources and skill required for intervention are likely to be higher in the latter cases. Often theories of desired outcome incorporate multiple goals or objectives, just as the NPR report was not content to reinvent government that worked better but added the goal of making government cost less at the same time. As more outcomes (or more criteria for evaluating outcomes) are incorporated into the theory, it also becomes more difficult to design an intervention to achieve all the desired goals.

The second important source of variation emerges from the designation of actors whose behavior is pertinent to the outcome. Actors may be individuals, household, firms, other levels of government, other countries, or the component parts of government itself. Such actors may have considerable independence from the government or may be highly dependent on the government (even direct government employees). They may be politically powerful or have little influence. They may or may not have large material stakes in the status quo or in the proposed outcome. There may be large numbers of actors whose behavior is pertinent to the outcome, or only a few. They may be a very heterogeneous collection, with widely varying interests in the proposed policy, or they may be very similar. Such variation in the theory of desired outcome has consequences for the capacity of policy makers to design an intervention that elicits the desired behavior from the actors. When the actors are powerful, numerous, and very different from one another, it is more difficult to find a scheme that elicits the intended response from them all. The difficulty of effective intervention is likely to be lower when policy makers direct their attention to a smaller, weaker, or more homogeneous group of target actors.

A third important source of variation in theories of desired outcome is the level of uncertainty about how designated actors produce the desired results. Can government officials specify which behavior is required, as for example when the desired outcome is a dam or the distribution of funds? Or must the policy allow for a variety of actions, depending on context and circumstance, as for example when the desired outcome is provision of mental health care or crime prevention? How much control do the actors have over their own behavior that is important to the outcome? How much discretion do actors have? This depends on the institutional context of behavior and the type of behavior involved. How tightly linked is the behavior to other behavior? When the target behavior is social interaction, as for example in the case of negotiation or child rearing, the actor who is the focus of the theory of desired outcome necessarily has partial control over the outcome. When the theory of desired outcome cannot specify the behavior that the actors should engage in, perhaps because the technology of production is highly uncertain or because of enormous variability in the circumstances surrounding production, it becomes more difficult to elicit the desired behavior from the actors. When the actors themselves have limited control over the behavior, perhaps because the behavior is interdependent with other actors, such as the product of market dynamics, or embedded in institutional, religious, professional, or social practices that are difficult to influence, intervention again becomes more challenging to design.

Theories of Intervention

Having developed a theory of the desired outcome, policy makers must figure out what government can do to produce that outcome. The plan for exercising policy influence is the theory of intervention. This theory works within the context of the problem and desired outcome as defined in the other two theories. The intervention needs to be appropriate to the policy makers and the actors and to the behavior of interest. The elements of intervention that must be specified in a theory of intervention are: agent (who should intervene), target (whose actions are to be changed in some way), mechanism (how to intervene), and time and place (when and where a concrete social intervention takes place).

The agent of intervention may be the agency or office with responsibility for carrying out the policy at hand. Policy makers have limited choices of agents when they contemplate various forms of intervention. Some agents are units of government that work directly with targets; some government agents work only indirectly with targets, relying on market dynamics or social forces that occur outside of government. Variations in the policy makers' level of government or branch of government limit the agents to whom policy makers can assign responsibility. Thus the Congress or the president can assign intervention to a federal executive agency to carry out policy directives, but the federal courts typically cannot do the same. Local city councils have different options at their disposal than their federal counterparts, sometimes making them more likely to succeed in intervention, sometimes making them less likely to succeed. Within these choices limited by the structure of the governmental system, the policy makers may select agents that are most likely to carry out the intervention successfully. This assignment of responsibility is consequential because different agents have vastly different capabilities to carry out policies with respect to targets. The power of the agent with respect to the target is a major consideration. Along with power of the agent is the willingness of the agent to use its power on the influence tasks specified by the policy. The assignment of responsibility for intervention is also politically consequential. The designation of an agent sends a clear symbolic message to targets (and other citizens) about the policy makers' intent. The electoral cycle or political viability of a regime may also influence policy makers' choice of agents, making some agents, such as the military or police, too risky to use (or, in other cases, too risky not to use).[6]

The target of intervention is the people, groups, organizations, or communities who are connected to the policy outcome. The selection of the target is often (but not necessarily) guided by the theory of desired outcome. When promising targets are identified in the theory of desired outcome, the intervention may be designed to influence them (see figure 2 [A]). Intervention, however, might be directed at actors who were prominent in the creation of the policy problem but have little control over the desired outcome (as in figure 2 [B]). Worse yet, intervention may be directed at actors who cannot affect the desired outcome, but who were chosen as scapegoats for policy attention (figure 2 [C]). For example, policies designed to reduce federal paperwork may tie the hands of such federal bureaucrats as the Census Bureau or the Bureau of Labor Statistics, who generate paperwork in the course of carrying out congressional mandates for information collection. These bureaucrats did not cause the problem of excess paperwork; their information activities originated in legal mandates.[7] Nor can they readily reduce their information collection if the mandate to collect the information remains in force. The policy ends up constraining their activities without addressing any of the actors who are more closely connected to the desired outcome. When policy intervention is targeted at actors or behaviors that are not plausibly connected to desired outcomes (as in figure 2 [B] and [C]), desired results are unlikely to ensue.

Like the selection of agents, the selection of targets has large political significance (Schneider and Ingram 1993). It assigns blame, credit, stigma, and power to various individuals and social groups. These political considerations may lead policy makers to avoid confrontations with targets whose behavior is

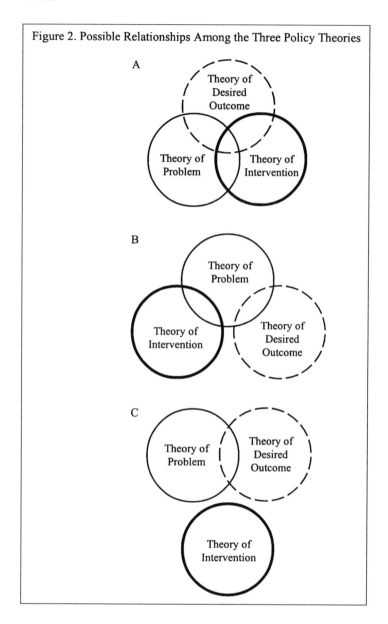

Figure 2. Possible Relationships Among the Three Policy Theories

A

Theory of Desired Outcome

Theory of Problem

Theory of Intervention

B

Theory of Problem

Theory of Intervention

Theory of Desired Outcome

C

Theory of Problem

Theory of Desired Outcome

Theory of Intervention

most closely connected to the desired outcome. Thus, for example, antismoking policy is more often directed at individual smokers than at powerful companies that grow, sell, and market tobacco products.

Time and place of intervention may seem unnecessary to specify. Yet, policy intervention does not succeed in changing behavior because it is intended or espoused in the abstract. It changes behavior if it reaches real people in actual times and places (Giddens 1984). Arranging for policy to be translated into concrete acts by individuals with implications for targets is a significant challenge for any theory of intervention.

Specifying a time and place for intervention also makes it clear that all intervention occurs at particular historical moments. In each time and place, other events have happened over the years with influence over the actors and their behavior. These past events give the actors a context in which to interpret their own behavior and the intervention of any agent. The past also creates a context in which the agents understand the behavior of the target actors. Any intervention is embedded in the context of these past or concurrent relationships and experiences. Moreover, all the parties understand that time continues. The expectation of future interaction between agents and actors influences interaction in the present. Today's intervention happens today, but tomorrow may bring opportunities for reciprocity, retaliation, or some new domain of interdependence. Each policy intervention is one in a stream of influences, from the government and elsewhere, on the outcome of interest.

Mechanisms of Intervention

In many cases, policy makers find that their theories of desired outcome lead them to identify large numbers of actors whose behavior bears on the outcomes of interest. Often these actors are heterogeneous, geographically dispersed, and engaged in behavior that is difficult to observe and measure. Under these circumstances, interventions are required that are capable of working under a broad range of circumstances with different kinds of actors.

A long history of analysis in social science points to three mechanisms or instruments that are powerful over very broad ranges of social behavior and social circumstances: incentives, authority, and ideas. These instruments are powerful over individuals, institutions, and larger social and economic units. Indeed, these are three nearly ubiquitous currents of social and political life.

Various scholars have suggested that a handful of generic mechanisms or instruments constitute the fundamental repertoire of government intervention.[8] The proposed taxonomies have two purposes: (1) to bring to policy makers' attention the range of options available to them to achieve their preferred outcomes so that the full range can be systematically considered, and (2) to identify common strengths and weaknesses within families of instruments by examining how they work under differing circumstances. By looking at the theory of intervention that justifies government activity, we can see common advantages and disadvantages to policy designs that rely on a common instrument. We can examine the patterns of implementation of each instrument, looking for systematic variation. We can search for circumstances in which a given instrument works well or poorly. Each instrument is a tool in the sense that it is valuable to public officials under some circumstances for achieving desired ends. Unlike hammers and chisels, however, policy instruments take shape only in social interaction and vary considerably depending on the circumstances in which they are used by one or more parties to the interaction.

Each effort to construct a taxonomy reflects the authors' implicit theories of intervention. For example, Weimer and Vining (1989) propose five categories of instruments: freeing, facilitating, and simulating markets; using subsidies and taxes to alter incentives; establishing rules; supplying goods through non market mechanisms; and providing insurance and cushions. This typology comes from a view of public policy as a corrective to market failure and to some extent as a second generation corrective to government failure. The market thus serves as the organizing framework for understanding the causes of policy problems and outcomes. Government intervention becomes a substitute for market forces when market outcomes are unacceptable or when previous government efforts to compensate for market outcomes do not yield the desired outcomes. The typology of instruments thus points to the ways in which market failure can be addressed through government intervention (Weimer and Vining 1989; Hood 1983; McDonnell and Elmore 1987; Salamon 1989; Stone 1988).

The taxonomy I propose has three basic mechanisms: authority, incentives, and ideas. Authority is defined as a grant of permission from the target individuals to the authority figure to make decisions for them for some category of acts. These decisions may be resource allocation decisions or behavioral control. Examples of public policies that rely on authority include direct government intervention, rules, mandates, and prohibitions. Incentives are defined as the direct or indirect use of sanctions or inducements to alter the calculus of costs and benefits associated with given behavior for the target individuals. Examples of public policies that rely on incentives are subsidies, social insurance, grants, and taxes. Ideas are defined as the generation and use of information, communication, or symbols communicated to target individuals that change what they think or think about with respect to the target behavior. Examples of public policies that rely on ideas include training, education, research, statistics, and technical assistance.

The reason for plunging into the vexing problems associated with any such taxonomy is to create a taxonomy in which each instrument relies on a distinct, powerful mechanism of social influence. It maps most closely to the elemental mechanisms of control described in Charles E. Lindblom's 1976 *Politics and Markets: The World's Political-Economic Systems.* These three, he suggests, are crucial to the construction of political and economic systems in modern times. Lindblom characterizes exchange as a relationship in which each party offers a benefit in order to induce a response. The exchange relationship is the central mechanism in markets and permits control over a wide range of social behavior by offering the appropriate incentive. Authority in Lindblom's account exists whenever people permit someone else to make decisions for them for some category of acts. People accept a rule of obedience to others for a variety of reasons, whether voluntary or coerced: for tradition or employment, for efficiency or reverence. Whatever the reason, authority is "the core phenomenon that makes government possible" (22). Governmental authority often operates through law and other rules specifying who can exercise what kind of control over whom in what circumstances. Persuasion is less clearly linked to macrolevel systems of social organization, but is an ubiquitous and powerful form of social control that, like exchange and authority, influences a wide range of consequential social behavior.

Politics and Markets argues that the exchange relationship is the foundation of market-oriented economies and that the authority relationship is the foundation of government. Persuasion can form the basis of a system of massive unilateral indoctrination of citizens and/or consumers, although this seems not to happen in real societies in any lasting way. Indeed, none of these systems exists in pure form. All existing societies combine the three; what is interesting is how much and when they rely on each. Lindblom takes as a central puzzle that modern societies must grapple with how much to rely on markets as compared to government, that is, how to combine exchange and authority. As a result, persuasion becomes less prominent in his analysis than the other two. Indeed, it does not even make it into the book's title.

Being less interested than Lindblom in the awesomely ambitious questions of sociopolitical structure and organization, I focus on the design of effective public policy within modern democratic societies and within the United States in particular. My taxonomy adopts the perspective of policy makers seeking actions to take. Authority, incentives, and ideas are the essential mechanisms that can be used and combined to create specific policy interventions. By comparing ideas to authority and incentives, the distinctive roles of ideas in policy design will become clearer.

Authority

Governmental authority is the power to make decisions that are accepted as legitimate and binding. Lindblom says authority "exists whenever one, sev-

eral, or many people explicitly or tacitly permit someone else to make decisions for them for some category of acts" (Lindblom 1976, 17). People grant
such permission to government for various reasons, such as respect for expertise, fear of physical coercion, tradition, or reverence, that make authority legitimate. The authority relationship grants government officials routinized
permission to control other people directly. It also may become routinized
permission to control resources by virtue of the grant of permission to act
on behalf of others in allocating collective resources. Governmental authority
is not synonymous with either hierarchy or force, although it often takes the
form of hierarchy and is backed by the government's claim to a monopoly on
the legitimate use of physical force.

Any organization can be seen as a network of authority relationships in
which some members are granted authority by others to control designated
sectors of activity and resources. Governments, too, can be seen as systems
of authority over citizens and over other organizations. A central feature of
governmental authority is that a government claims (without challenge from
a rival claimant) authority for its orders over those of every organization
(Lindblom 1976, 21). A government may seldom choose to exercise its priority,
but the claim to priority is distinctive. This is true even when, as in the United
States, multiple levels of government exert simultaneous authority over the
same group of citizens. Federal, state, county, and local government, for example, may all claim jurisdiction over social activities, such as environmental pollution or drug abuse, at a given site. Each level of government has permission
from its citizens to exert control over these activities. In addition, all exercise
this permission but do so in a way that acknowledges that other governments
have overlapping grants of authority.

Authority is necessarily implicated in all instruments of public policy. All
acts of government rely in some way on the generalized authority granted to
government by citizens to exercise control over activities or resources in some
domains. Public policy could not happen at all without the authority of a legitimate government to act. Nevertheless, not all public policies make primary
use of this authority as their central mechanism for achieving change. Within
the context of the general grant of authority to act, some policies rely not on
the specific exercise of authority but on incentives and/or ideas as their core
mechanisms of social control. Even if authority is the essential backdrop to all
policy interventions, it is not necessarily the mechanism that gets the job done.

When authority is the core mechanism for achieving social outcomes,
policies fall into roughly two categories (many finer distinctions being glossed
over for the time being). The first category is when government uses authority
in order to take direct action on individuals, groups, organizations, or natural

phenomena to achieve its desired objective. Leman (1989) calls this direct government. Weimer and Vining (1989) call it supplying goods through nonmarket means. Hood (1983) calls it organization. The common causal story is that government uses permission to organize people and collective resources in order to operate directly on some target actors who are capable of contributing to improvement in some problem or social dilemma. In granting that permission, citizens (or at least most citizens) agree to treat the actions of government as acceptable and legitimate. Examples include delivering mail by the U.S. Postal Service, printing currency by the Bureau of Engraving and Printing, building a dam by the Army Corps of Engineers, paving the streets, or sending monthly checks to Social Security recipients.

The second general type of authority instrument is when government officials create rules, laws, or mandates that tell individuals, groups, or entities what to do or not do. These rules may be supplemented with elaborate schemes of monitoring and enforcement.[9] They may be rules about who may write further rules. They may represent an agreement among officials with authority, with no formal capacity for enforcement or sanctions at all. These instruments are used by government officials to extend authority into a vast range of human behavior. By creating rules to control how people and institutions behave (which may be other units of government or entities outside of government such as households or firms), policy makers can extend the exercise of authority over many kinds of behavior in a way that is efficient and powerful. It is efficient because once the rule of obedience has been accepted, it need not be invoked anew each time. It is powerful because it can control behavior in the designated domain even when government officials cannot or have not prescribed the details of behavior they desire. Of course the power is always contingent upon the acceptance of authority by citizens or entities, the permission they grant to government to make certain decisions on their behalf. If the citizens or entities such as business firms revoke their permission, as they sometimes do because they question the legitimacy of the government as a whole or because they believe the government should not control specific domains of activity, then the authority relationship loses control over those domains.

Examples include schemes of regulation in which activity is required or forbidden. This differs from assuming public ownership or control of economic activity; in the case of regulation, authority is lodged in a government agency not to conduct the activity itself but to set standards or constrain behavior by a variety of other public and private entities who carry out the activity for their own reasons. Other examples include laws that apply to everyone (such as international treaties, legal prohibitions, or laws granting authority to designated agencies to carry out certain activities), to specific groups or activities (such as licensure or certification requirements), or to individual cases (such as civil or criminal litigation). Other kinds of rules give people formal rights. Government may adopt rules that create expectations or standards of behavior (such as rights to a free public education, to work, or to privacy) and enforce those rights on behalf of individuals or groups. These are all examples of authority-based strategies for government officials to effect changes in social outcomes.

The exercise of authority is fraught with difficulties. When used as a policy instrument it may fail for a number of reasons. The authority invoked in a policy intervention may be too weak, leading to little change in the target actors. Conversely, it may be too strong, leading to counter-mobilization and resistance. Authority may be granted to an agent who cannot exercise it effectively or conscientiously. A grant of authority for one intervention is counteracted by another grant of authority for another purpose. The use of authority may generate side effects that undercut the value of the intervention. These examples illustrate potential failures of the theory of intervention. Additional sources of possible failure reside in the theory of desired outcome—failures in which authority is directed at targets who are not capable of bringing about the desired outcome or at behavior that is not connected to the desired outcome. Clearly, the selection of authority as a primary mechanism of intervention is no guarantee of results. Policy makers benefit from an appreciation of the limits of authority in particular instances.

Government uses authority in unique ways. Note, however, that many other institutions and groups in society also possess authority and use it to accomplish their objectives. Private firms, religious organizations, community organizations, professions, universities, families, and others claim authority over some of the same behavior that the government seeks to influence with its policy interventions. The exercise of authority in any given policy intervention occurs in the context of other sources of authority, whether these reinforce or compete with the policy intent. Understanding these multiple sources of authority can help policy designers gauge the likely effect of a new or additional intervention.

Just as government authority competes with other sources of authority, so too authority operates in a world suffused with incentives and ideas. Each new policy intervention must work in the context of many pressures and forces bearing on the target actors. For example, intervention with authority to change the behavior of target actors may run into obstacles created by patterns of incentives that reinforce the status quo. In crafting a theory of intervention, policy designers must grapple with the multiple pressures on the target actors, knowing that they are trying to influence behavior that is embedded in many layers of social interaction.

Incentives

Policy interventions that use incentives rely on manipulation of sanctions or inducements to alter the calculus of costs and benefits associated with given behavior for the target individuals. The basic premise is that the target individuals, in rational pursuit of their own interests, will be influenced by a change in the payoffs to alternative courses of action and will be more likely to pursue an alternative if the net benefits of that alternative have increased. Thus the intervention harnesses the pursuit of self-interest by target actors to the desired outcome.[10]

Governments typically have at their disposal a wide range of sanctions or inducements to encourage responses from a broad range of target actors. The simplest is money in exchange for goods or services. Government officials may purchase designs for new submarines, services to mentally ill homeless persons, management of nuclear weapons plants, or advice about tax collection software from private firms or nonprofit suppliers. This huge and increasingly important domain of government activity relies on contracts as the mechanism to elicit the target behavior.[11] Transfers of resources to individuals to provide them with retirement or subsistence income is another use of money, although not the same kind of quid pro quo seen in a contract. Such transfers do not require an explicit commitment from the target actor to behave in accord with policy objectives. Still, the purpose of the transfer is to change the target actors' behavior, perhaps to keep the recipient from starving, begging, going homeless, or otherwise manifesting the consequences of dire poverty. Transfer policies rely on the self-interest of the recipients to use the government funds to bring about the desired outcome.[12]

Somewhat more complicated are interventions in which the policy attempts to make some alternative actions more or less attractive to the target actors by using benefits or costs. Grants or subsidies may be used to encourage target actors to engage in more economic development of inner cities, home ownership, or provision of preventive health care to indigent children. Charges, taxes, or penalties may be used to encourage target actors to engage in less alcohol consumption, generation of solid waste, development of wetlands, or securities manipulation. When target actors are government agencies, benefits and costs may include increases in the amount or flexibility of use of budget or staff. These interventions rely on actors making their own judgments about the net value of alternative actions and responding to objective changes in anticipated consequences.

Another category of incentive-based instruments involves government interventions directed at behavior embedded in private markets to elicit different outcomes. Here the government policy changes incentives, but policy makers do not know which actors will change as a result. Unlike the case of grants or charges, where policy makers decide precisely whom to pay or penalize, government officials may have little idea of which households, firms, or other entities they will influence with a market intervention. Indeed, the response sought by government officials is not the behavior of any actor in particular, but a different pattern of aggregate behavior. In this category fall such examples as loan guarantees, freeing, facilitating, and simulating markets.[13] For example, deregulating a previously regulated sector such as airlines or telecommunications is an intervention based on assumptions about manipulating incentives for target actors (whether existing private firms or new entrants) to be more efficient and innovative. Auctions, tradable permits, and the privatization of formerly public sector activities are further ways of achieving change in unspecified groups of target actors by rearranging incentives operating on those actors.

What these instruments have in common is their reliance on incentives. They share a causal theory that rational, self-interested actors will respond to changes in incentives. To achieve changes in any particular behavior, government officials may intervene in the system of incentives that govern the behavior. If policy makers have used the mechanism of incentives wisely, the people whose behavior is of interest will find it in their interest to behave in accord with the preferences of the policy makers. This common causal theory may be shared by a number of instruments that rely on the theory in different ways. As we have seen in the case of both authority and incentives, a common elementary mechanism may result in a wide variety of manifestations. As each instrument is used with targets by agents in particular institutional contexts, it must be adapted to the coloration of that context. Hence, it appears in many guises. I suggest, however, that the family resemblances are strong enough to justify for my purposes the broad and inclusive categories used here.[14]

Just as authority has many weaknesses as a policy mechanism, so too do incentives. Incentives may not work because ineffective incentives were applied. Perhaps the incentives were too weak to counteract other incentives bearing on the same behavior. Perhaps the theory of intervention may have been fine, but a misguided theory of desired outcome led policy makers to structure incentives for the wrong set of actors, i.e., actors who did not have the capacity to affect the desired outcomes. Perhaps the capacity of the agent of intervention to manipulate the incentives was inadequate. In short, incentives do not always work. Instrument design is guided by a theory of intervention, but that theory may be wrong, incomplete, or misplaced. This is the case for all three families of instruments.

Ideas

Ideas are the third major instrument for eliciting desired policy outcomes. Policy makers persuade the target actors to change their behavior by trying to change what they think or think about with respect to the target behavior. The means of persuasion are ideas, which I define broadly to include what people think and think about. Ideas include what other researchers have called information, persuasive messages, facts, cognitive frames, social or professional norms, rhetoric, symbols, ideology, arguments, deliberation, learning, and passions. In the pure case of influence with ideas, people change what they do because a policy intervention has led them to change what they think, without necessarily changing anything else about authority or incentives operative in the situation.

As with authority and incentives, a wide variety of interventions may rely on ideas as the basic instrument. One kind of intervention occurs when government officials possess information that they distribute to actors who need or want it, or who are believed by policy makers to need it, so that they may produce the desired outcome. Examples of this top-down variety include technical assistance, dissemination of research findings, statistical systems, public information campaigns (including the Smokey Bear campaign of the U.S. Forest Service), counseling, and, more ominously, propaganda and indoctrination. These words describing the first few examples are technocratic; the last two ring of political fear. Tocqueville (1969) warned of the immense tutelary power of majoritarian government in the United States.[15] The phrase "tutelary power," like Lindblom's "preceptoral system," has a decidedly negative tone. Tutelary power has always had the potential to undermine the possibilities of freedom and democracy by preventing citizens from even knowing what they want from government. The phrase can be read in ways that are more positive, however. Tutelary power teaches and informs, and there has always been a strain of American political thought that endorses informed citizens and education as bulwarks of democracy.[16] In her account of "solutions" commonly offered to policy problems, Stone (1988) suggests that changing people's behavior by operating on their minds and their perceptions of the world arouses deep ambivalence in American political analysis: "Of all the means of coordinating and controlling human behavior, none is more widespread, more complicated, or less well understood [than ideas]" (249).

A second kind of idea-based intervention occurs when policy sets in motion a process of information collection or learning. Government officials may not themselves have the information required to produce the outcome, but they ask or enable other actors to generate or share such information. In this second category, common examples include training, research, reporting and record keeping (Weiss and Gruber 1984), auditing, demonstration projects, labeling and disclosure, and public hearings (including the conservation planning done in Coachella Valley to protect endangered species; see Innes et al. 1994). These interventions rely on learning as a means to achieve the desired outcomes. They are typically less top-down in orientation than the first category, however, and invite more active participation by the target actors. Education is an example of a mechanism of intervention that cuts across the two types. Sometimes education is conducted as though it were a process of knowledge transfer from the teacher who knows the curriculum to passive students who are supposed to receive it. This tends to fall in the top-down mode. Education, however, can be a process in which teachers and students participate in a mutually influential, interactive experience from which learning emerges. In such cases, it resembles the more interactive category in which the target actors are active participants.

The family of ideas-based policies is quite heterogeneous. This diversity of approaches is directly linked to the number of ways in which people can be influenced by ideas. In other works, I explore a number of psychological processes that policy interventions can tap to elicit change in target actors, ranging from information processing to evolving values. For now, it is important to note that nearly all policy-related ideas have both cognitive and normative content. In communicating what is and what may be, they also send strong signals about what should be. In some uses, ideas may be tilted toward more cognitive content, as for example in labeling of chemicals used at work sites. The intervention predicts that workers who learn more about their own exposure to chemicals will take constructive steps to avoid the most damaging health consequences in whatever way is appropriate to the situation (whether this means using personal protective equipment, pressuring employers for safety measures, or seeking other employment). In other uses, ideas may be tilted heavily toward normative messages, as in child abuse prevention campaigns that emphasize that good parents discipline their children without violence. Still, ideas are never merely objective or technical interventions. Intervening with ideas carries values, at least implicitly, into the relationships between policy maker and targets.

Some analyses of incentives include information as a resource that is scarce and valuable and hence can be properly understood within an incentive framework. Thus one way to improve market outcomes may be to correct asymmetries of information in markets, for example by requiring disclosure to consumers about product ingredients. Some informational limitations, however, can be resolved by means completely different from idea-based instruments. Thus hierarchy can be a solution to informational limitations in market transactions (such as information impactedness), showing that some informational problems may be efficiently addressed with an authority instrument. Although informational limitations may create the policy problem, it does not follow that the intervention should necessarily rely on ideas as the mechanism of intervention. In a similar vein, problems that originate in perversities of authority and incentives need not be addressed with authority or incentive instruments. Idea instruments are often useful under circumstances where the origins of the problem have little to do with information.

Ideas are also featured as an instrument in some treatments of authority. These focus on expertise (control over information) as one important basis of authority—the reason why people grant authority to government over certain domains of activity. It is certainly possible to categorize policy instruments, including those that I have labeled ideas, in other ways. These other ways obscure what they have in common and highlight some of their differences. My claim is that something useful can be learned by examining their common reliance on changing minds as the elementary mechanism of intervention. That, at least, is the point of this exercise.

Ideas used as policy instruments are not necessarily true, correct, or accurate. To be effective components of policy intervention, they need not be true. They are effective when they influence the behavior of the actors who contribute to policy outcomes. To speak of ideas as instruments is neither to advocate nor to assume rationality, nor to imagine a society of philosopher kings and queens who deliberate wisely over all of their choices. All of us are persuaded, educated, informed, distracted, and otherwise influenced by ideas in daily life. Commercial advertising, political campaigns, and religious teaching all rely on that aspect of human nature (Lindblom 1990).

Any attempt to influence how people think or behave must compete with other sources of influence and arguments supporting alternate courses of action. Some of this competing debate has the character of deliberation, the considered airing of multiple views to find the wisdom in each. Some of the debate seems to be cacophony. Some seems to be systematic manipulation of communication channels to emphasize some arguments and to exclude others. Some of the information flow is from government to citizens. Some is from citizens to government. Much is lateral, citizen to citizen or government to government. Much is mediated by the press, which imposes its own stamp and priorities on the flow. No idea, and indeed no instrument of any sort, has the luxury of operating in isolation from other influences. The question for each family of policy instruments, then, is, how can this instrument make a differ-ence in the mix of competing constraints and influences that already shape the behavior that policy makers seek to influence?

Combinations

Confronting real cases of real problems, policy makers design interven-tions that rely on combinations of instruments and almost never use only one. Several reasons explain the scarcity of "pure" cases of single instruments. First, all three mechanisms—authority, incentives, and ideas—are present in some form in essentially all relationships between government and target ac-tors, whoever the target actors may be. Authority is omnipresent because the government's authority to act legally and with some acceptance of its legiti-macy is a precondition for public policy to happen at all. Incentives are omni-present because any act of government (like those of any other actor in an interdependent system) leads to the allocation of resources; any resource allo-cation decision has the effect, intentional or willy-nilly, of influencing the in-centives facing other actors who stand in some interdependent relationship with the policy maker. Ideas are omnipresent because policy interventions never speak for themselves; they need to be communicated, explained, and jus-tified as citizens and target actors learn what the policy means and implies for the target actor's behavior.

If all three mechanisms are present in all policy interventions, why go to the trouble of distinguishing among them—because interventions assign dif-fering balance and emphasis to the three mechanisms in ways that are conse-quential for how they work. Recognizing that no instrument stands entirely alone, some policy interventions are dominated by one of the three instru-ments, others by two, and still others giving significant roles to all three.

The second reason that actual policy interventions are not pure cases is that new policy interventions are typically tried in circumstances in which previous policy interventions have been carried out. Thus today's new crime prevention policy follows in the wake of many previous efforts at crime pre-vention. These earlier interventions have left a legacy of institutional arrange-ments that tend to persist. The earlier interventions have themselves drawn from the same basic set of policy mechanisms—authority, incentives, and ideas—and have created patterns of government action (and inaction) that are part of the problem that today's policy makers confront. Even when a new intervention explicitly undoes some earlier policy, the new intervention oper-ates in a context defined in part by those prior government activities.

Another reason that policy interventions frequently rely on combinations of mechanisms is that combinations have the potential to be more effective.

The policy design problem is not which instrument to choose, but rather how to design interventions likely to succeed in influencing the target actors. Under many circumstances, multiple instruments will be valuable to that effort. This poses further design challenges. The three basic mechanisms do not necessarily combine in simple, additive ways. Instead, some combinations seem to achieve significant synergy; others seem to work at cross-purposes.

Why are multiple instruments useful? Partly because target actors are themselves using multiple instruments. Government in a democracy does not have exclusive control of any instrument of social influence.[17] The versatility of authority, incentives, and ideas means that many actors are using them simultaneously with government. Corporations, unions, families, religious groups, social movements, professional groups, and political activists are attempting to achieve their own goals through these same instruments. When policy makers design an intervention, they cannot imagine a world in which all else is held equal. They must anticipate the consequences of using an intervention in a world in which other actors are using the same instruments to achieve a mix of complementary and conflicting outcomes. The awareness of interdependencies combined with the possibility of active counter-mobilization tends to point toward multiple channels of influence to increase the likelihood of successful intervention.

This recognition points to two ways to explore the use of any particular mechanism of intervention, such as ideas. The first focuses on policies in which ideas are the primary or dominant mechanism of intervention. The second focuses on how ideas combine with authority or incentives or both.

Reflections on Theories of Intervention

Theories of intervention provide a logic for government action within a context defined by the theory of the problem and the theory of desired outcome. Better understanding of the logic of intervention is thus one step toward understanding when and why particular policies work the way they do. Nevertheless, better understanding of intervention without appreciation of the importance of the other two theories in motivating and focusing intervention will do little good. The overall success or failure of a policy cannot be assigned to the logic of intervention that the policy uses. As each policy is justified by all three theories, all three contribute to its potential for positive (or negative) consequences. Disagreements about policy may be located in any one of the three theories. With that said, understanding the logic of intervention is one way in which social science research can inform the complex and uncertain work of policy design.

A comparative analysis of alternate modes of intervention is potentially useful because the theories of the problem and the desired outcome seldom fully constrain the possibilities for intervention. They do define the substantive context for intervention. Yet, having defined an outcome and identified target actors and target behavior, most theories of desired outcome leave open multiple pathways by which government may bring about the desired changes.

Returning to the example of the National Performance Review, the desired outcome of a federal government that works better and costs less can be approached in a number of ways suggested in the various reports of the NPR and in the follow-up actions of federal agencies. These interventions make use of various agents, various targets, all three mechanisms, and an array of times and places.

For example, a number of recommendations focus on making federal agencies more helpful in their relationships with states and localities. Recommendations to achieve this more helpful stance include cabinet secretaries and agency heads (the agents) delegating authority (the dominant mechanism) to states and localities (the target actors) by granting selective waivers from federal regulations or mandates on request for limited periods of time. The same outcome is behind the proposal that the federal government consolidate federal grants (incentive mechanism) to state and local governments in six broad areas (job training, education, water quality, defense conversion, environmental management, and motor carrier safety). Here the theory of intervention predicts that state and local governments will use their allocation of federal funds more efficiently than they used funds with more strings attached. The agent in this intervention must be the Congress, however, not the agencies alone. Yet a third pathway to achieve a similar benefit for state and local governments can be found in the recommendation to create a federal coordinating council for economic development. This council (the agent) would serve as a central source of information for states and localities about federal programs and would provide a unifying framework for planning regional development efforts. The dominant mechanism is the shared information and coordination based in ideas, with some implication that the council might also bring federal funding (incentives) and administrative decisions (authority) in line with the new strategic framework. In all of these examples, the goal of flexibility and support for state and local governments is accomplished through changing differing aspects of the relationship with federal agencies (National Performance Review 1993, 38–39, 53).

The NPR report also describes alternate policies that share the desired outcome of empowering federal employees to improve the quality of their work. The proposed policies include cutting out management layers and eliminating supervisory positions (using authority), having bonuses or penalties for meeting agreed-upon performance objectives (incentives), and upgrading the training offered to employees at all levels of the hierarchy to enhance their productivity (ideas) (65–91). The eclectic set of recommendations recognizes that many interventions may lead to the desired result.

Nevertheless, they lead there in quite different ways and are grounded in quite different assumptions about behavior and change. The active causal ingredient in each family of instruments differs from the others. To understand the likely consequences of the NPR proposals or other possible interventions, researchers need to come to grips with the ways in which these instruments may achieve their intended result. The conceptual framework suggested here offers a way to partition the conceptual, political, and administrative dilemmas implicit in particular policy proposals. The three theories may help analysts to be clearer about their claims and predictions and about the sources of their disagreements with others. The framework also urges analysis to open up the black box that is at the center of any given policy proposals: how will it get the job done?

Answering this question proceeds through several stages. The first stage is to desegregate the policy proposal into its three parts: problem, desired outcome, and intervention. The claims and the arguments implicit in the policy may then become clearer, along with any obvious logical inconsistencies in those claims.

The second stage is to assess the coherence and plausibility of the three theories in light of previous evidence, including social science research. Note that many kinds of evidence are potentially valuable: evidence about the boundaries and nature of the problem, the desired outcomes and those actors positioned to influence those outcomes, the actors who are the agents of intervention, the actors who are the targets of intervention, the mechanisms of intervention, and the time and place in which the intervention will occur.

The third step is to consider the policy intervention from the perspective of the target actors. Instead of assuming that agents know how their interventions will influence the behavior of target actors, policy researchers enrich their understanding of the likely effects of policy intervention by asking about the implications of intervention for the target actors themselves. This forces policy designers into simultaneously thinking top-down and bottom-up: seeing the intervention from the perspective of the policy makers trying to achieve a desired outcome, and seeing the intervention from the perspective of the target actors whose behavior is the focus of the change effort (but who may or may not know about—much less share—the desired outcome). This dual perspective tends to complicate matters. Simplified models of impact tend to break down as policy makers or researchers look at how target actors understand and respond to efforts to change their behavior.[18] The stylized versions of the three instruments presented in this chapter seem far from adequate in dealing with the complex, fluid, and uncertain realities of policy relevant behavior.[19]

To develop more effective theories of intervention, researchers need to probe into the possible influences that policy can exert on the behavior of individuals, groups, households, firms, nonprofit agencies, government agencies, and those other entities I have grouped under the label of target actors. Long thought about the conditions of effective intervention leads me to a generally modest stance about the relationship between intervention—any kind of intervention—and desired outcomes. Yet, it also leads me to consider more actively interventions that work along multiple paths, using combinations of mechanisms and more than one set of target actors. Such combinations are valuable in their own right, affording more than one shot at effective influence. Under some circumstances, they may also have political and symbolic value in recognizing that more than one actor and more than one social process are implicated in most important policy problems. Most of all, the framework offered here leads me to the conclusion that policy researchers can, and should, continue to participate alongside the policy-making communities in the ongoing conversations about policy problems, outcomes, and, especially, interventions. Although we social scientists often do not know how and when our knowledge and theories can add value, every now and then we may find ways to enrich and enlarge the stock of intelligence from which policy designers may draw.

Notes

This chapter was prepared for presentation at the National Public Management Research Conference, October 1995. I am grateful to the Center for Advanced Study in the Behavioral Sciences, the University of Michigan Business School, and the National Science Foundation for support of this work.

1. Specific policy proposals, however, often implicate other actors, most often Congress and the president but also state and local governments, nonprofit agencies, federal contractors, and private firms.

2. Some of the critics of the NPR report have identified the neglect of political factors in the problem and in potential interventions as the major flaw in the report (e.g. Moe 1994). Others celebrate the focus on reconfiguring administrative systems as a potentially powerful influence on government performance.

3. Of course some disagree with all three theories supporting the report's recommendations.

4. For a similar argument about theory-driven evaluation research, see Weiss (1995) and Chen and Rossi (1983).

5. This is Elmore's basic insight in his discussion of backward mapping. Elmore (1979) explains how the behavior one wants to produce is different from understanding the problem one wants to change and requires a different analytical approach.

6. Allison's discussion (1971) of bureaucratic politics is useful in understanding the implications of the choice of agent.

7. In the case of the Census Bureau, a constitutional mandate. Of course, not all bureaucrats are innocent of causing excessive paperwork burdens. Some federal managers have contributed to the problem and are appropriately selected as targets of interventions to reduce paperwork. Many are not, however.

8. I will use mechanism and instrument interchangeably in this discussion.

9. When penalties or sanctions are applied to those who do not comply, this introduces an incentive mechanism into the intervention.

10. As Schultze (1977) puts it, the public use of private interest.

11. See, for example, Kelman (1990). Of course, contracting is more difficult with some kinds of target behavior than others.

12. As I said at the beginning of the chapter, policy intervention may be motivated by political or particularistic benefits as well as for the purpose of bringing about change in target actors. Transfers are often interpreted as bids for political advantage by elected officials rather than policies to bring about public purposes. Nevertheless, the stated purpose of the policy may be carried out, even if the policy was partially or largely motivated by the search for political advantage.

13. Salamon (1989) discusses loan guarantees. Weimer and Vining (1989) give substantial attention to what they call freeing, facilitating, and simulating markets.

14. For other purposes a more desegregated taxonomy will be more useful.

15. Tocqueville (1969) has a chapter titled "The Power Exercised by the Majority in America Over Thought."

16. Dryzek (1990). Also think of the fundamental importance of communicative rationality emphasized by Habermas (1984) and other critical theorists.

17. Although government has a monopoly on the *legitimate* use of physical force, it has no monopoly on force or coercion. No other actors can invoke force on the scale of the government (at least not in the United States), but many invoke it to achieve limited purposes in particular times and places.

18. This is one of the big differences between policy analysis (top-down) and program evaluation (which tends to be bottom-up in the sense that it examines outcomes, often by looking at outcomes for the targets of policy). Policy analysis generally

paints a simpler and more optimistic picture of intervention than program evaluation researchers do.

19. This chapter is drawn from a book manuscript (Weiss, in preparation) in which I go on to discuss how theories of intervention can become more sophisticated in their behavioral assumptions.

References

Allison, Graham. 1971. *Essence of Decision: Explaining the Cuban Missile Crisis.* Boston, Mass.: Little, Brown.

Chen, Huey-Tsyh, and Peter Rossi. 1983. "Evaluating with Sense: The Theory-Driven Approach." *Evaluation Review* 7: 283–302.

Dryzek, John. 1990. *Discursive Democracy: Politics, Policy, and Political Science.* New York: Cambridge University Press.

Elmore, Richard. 1979. "Backward Mapping: Implementation Research and Policy Decisions." *Political Science Quarterly* 94: 601–16.

Giddens, Anthony. 1984. *The Constitution of Society.* Berkeley, Calif.: University of California Press.

Gusfield, Joseph. 1981. *The Culture of Public Problems: Drinking-Driving and the Public Order.* Chicago: University of Chicago Press.

Habermas, Jürgen. 1984. *The Theory of Communicative Action: Lifeworld and System.* Translated by T. McCarthy. Boston: Beacon Press.

Hood, Christopher. 1983. *The Tools of Government.* Chatham, N.J.: Chatham House.

Innes, Judith, Judith Gruber, Michael Neuman, and Robert Thompson. 1994. *Coordinating Growth and Environmental Management through Consensus Building.* Berkeley, Calif.: California Policy Seminar.

Kelman, Steven. 1990. *Procurement and Public Management.* Washington, D.C.: American Enterprise Institute Press.

Leman, Christopher. 1989. "The Forgotten Fundamental: Successes and Excesses of Direct Government." In *Beyond Privatization: The Tools of Government Action,* edited by L. Salamon. Washington, D.C.: Urban Institute.

Lindblom, Charles E. 1976. *Politics and Markets: The World's Political-Economic Systems.* New York: Basic Books.

———. 1990. *Inquiry and Change: The Troubled Attempt to Understand and Shape Society.* New Haven, Conn.: Yale University Press.

McDonnell, Lorraine, and R. Elmore. 1987. "Getting the Job Done: Alternative Policy Instruments." *Education Evaluation and Policy Analysis* 9: 133–52.

Moe, Ronald. 1994. "The 'Reinventing Government' Exercise: Misinterpreting the Problem, Misjudging the Consequences." *Public Administration Review* 54: 111–22.

National Performance Review. 1993. *From Red Tape to Results: Creating a Government That Works Better and Costs Less.* Washington, D.C.: U.S. Government Printing Office.

Nelson, Barbara. 1984. *Making an Issue of Child Abuse: Political Agenda Setting for Social Problems.* Chicago: University of Chicago Press.

Rochefort, David A., and Roger Cobb, eds. 1994. *The Politics of Problem Definition: Shaping the Policy Agenda.* Lawrence, Kan.: University Press of Kansas.

Salamon, Lester, ed. 1989. *Beyond Privatization: The Tools of Government Action.* Washington, D.C.: Urban Institute.

Schneider, Anne, and Helen Ingram. 1993. "Social Construction of Target Populations: Implications for Politics and Policy." *American Political Science Review* 87: 334–47.

Schultze, Charles. 1977. *The Public Use of Private Interest.* Washington, D.C.: Brookings.

Stone, Deborah. 1988. *Policy Paradox and Political Reason.* Glenview, Ill.: Scott, Foresman.

Tocqueville, Alexis de. 1969. *Democracy in America.* Edited by J. P. Mayer. New York: Harper Perennial.

Weimer, David, and Aidan Vining. 1989. *Policy Analysis: Concepts and Practice.* Englewood Cliffs, N.J.: Prentice-Hall.

Weiss, Carol. 1995. "Nothing as Practical as Good Theory: Exploring Theory-Based Evaluation for Comprehensive Community Initiatives for Children and Families." In *New Approaches to Evaluating Community Initiatives,* edited by J. P. Connell et al. Washington, D.C.: Aspen Institute.

Weiss, Janet A. 1989. "The Powers of Problem Definition: The Case of Government Paperwork." *Policy Sciences* 22: 97–121.

Weiss, J. A., and Judith Gruber. 1984. "Using Knowledge for Control in Fragmented Policy Arenas." *Journal of Policy Analysis and Management* 2: 225–47.

3 | Do Goals Help Create Innovative Organizations?

Robert D. Behn

Like organizations in the private sector, those in the public sector need to be innovative to accomplish their missions. Even while the public is demanding lower taxes from government, it is also demanding that public agencies improve their performance.[1] Moreover, improving performance requires more than the faithful implementation of well-established routines. Improved performance requires innovation (Behn 1987).

Innovation, in turn, requires innovative leadership. Such leaders conceive, foster, develop, and implement innovative ways to improve performance and achieve their organization's mission. Nevertheless, top-level leadership is no longer enough. If innovation—and thus improved performance—depends on the few people at the top of an agency, progress will be slow and marginal. Real innovation—innovation that significantly improves performance of an entire organization—depends on the behavior of the entire organization. It requires that everyone—from the agency's leadership team, to its middle managers, to its front-line supervisors, to its front-line workers—be engaged in the task of developing new and better mechanisms for achieving the agency's mission. Real innovation—innovation that has a significant impact on overall performance—requires an innovative organization.

The Five Linkages

How can such an innovative public agency come into being? Can the right environmental circumstances automatically beget one, or does it require a conscious act to create one? And if it does, who must do what?

Innovative organizations are not self-generating. Somewhere, sometime, some group of people may have spontaneously spawned their own thoroughly innovative organization. Nevertheless, such events are as rare as the Red Sox winning the World Series. Innovative organizations—just like innovations themselves—require the initiative of leaders. Yet what should those leaders do?

One answer is: create goals. Give the organization something very specific to accomplish. The leadership team of a public agency can convert it into an

70

innovative organization by giving the entire agency some explicit objectives to pursue. In her study of seventeen human-services innovations, three of which were accomplished in large public agencies,[2] Olivia Golden (1990) found that in "all three of the large organizations . . . the managers developed new types of outcome and performance measures (adoptive placements, job placements, measures of children's health and education status) and new channels for collecting and reporting the information" (244). These managers engaged people in the task of pursuing innovative ways to achieve their mission by explicitly measuring and publicly reporting performance.

This is not necessarily the only way to create an innovative organization. Other organizational leaders may find other strategies equally as effective. Nor is this approach guaranteed to produce results in all situations. Circumstances may conspire to thwart any effort at innovation. Nevertheless, establishing goals has worked in the past. Public leaders have found that goals can get people throughout their organization to think and behave innovatively. Thus, other leaders should be able to do the same in the future.[3]

Establishing specific goals for an agency to achieve can contribute in five different ways to the conversion of a routine-bound organization into an innovative one:

1. Goals redefine the meaning of success.
2. Goals can get everyone thinking and behaving innovatively.
3. Goals can foster leaders at all levels in the organization.
4. Goals can encourage organizations to reach out to other institutions whose work is helpful (or even necessary) to achieving these goals.
5. Accomplishing goals can change public values.

These five linkages provide an explanation of how establishing specific goals can help create innovative organizations.

I have noticed these five linkages in action in three innovative organizations about which I have written:

• The Massachusetts Department of Public Welfare (Behn 1991);
• Homestead Air Force Base (Behn 1992); and
• The Bureau of Motor Equipment (BME) in the New York City Department of Sanitation.

Thus the five linkages reflect an attempt to synthesize some important lessons from these three examples of innovative organizations.

Nevertheless, these five linkages between specific goals and innovative organizations are not always connected.[4] Establishing goals does not automatically produce an individual innovation, let alone create an entire innovative organization. Merely articulating goals in not enough. After all, if it was that easy—if simply creating a goal or two converted unimaginative people into innovators—many public administrators would be inventing goals. If this one readily available and easily movable organizational lever is linked to so many other desirable actions through a public agency, many managers would be grabbing it. It all sounds just a little too wonderful.

And it is. Unfortunately, there are two big reasons why goals may not work. The first reflects the nature of politics; the second, the nature of organizations:

1. It is politically difficult to get agreement on goals.
2. All organizations are resistant to change, and government organizations are explicitly designed to resist change.

Goals sound nice, but political conflict and organizational rigidity can easily neutralize their effectiveness.

Not all of these five linkages were present in all three of these innovative organizations. Consequently, to provide a coherent illustration of these linkages, I have chosen to include a hypothetical example of an elementary school that has established the goal of raising its students' average math and reading scores by fifty points.

Next year the school might have a much different goal. It might choose to focus on the arts or on athletics. It might have been successful in achieving this year's fifty-point increase in math but not in reading and thus decide that next year's goal should emphasize reading. The goal is not fixed; it can be changed next year—or even this year if circumstances warrant. For now, however, this year's goal for the school is to raise student math and reading scores by an average of fifty points.

Creating an Innovative School

The leadership of an elementary school—the principal, teachers' union, and parents' association—decide to improve the students' learning. After numerous discussions (i.e., debates), they decide to establish the goal of raising the students' average math and reading scores by fifty points. But will this make a difference in the behavior of the school's teachers, or of its principal, union leaders, and parents?

The overall issue is: Can such a goal help turn the school into an innovative organization? The specific question here is: Can the goal of raising math and reading scores by fifty points activate the five linkages?

Linkage 1: Goals redefine the meaning of success. Specific goals are often essential to accomplishing something specific. Without specific goals to focus attention on specific results to be achieved, people in government agencies will continue to focus solely on process: Have all the rules and regulations been properly followed? If so, we are—by definition—doing a "good job." After all, public employees can easily get into trouble by violating the most mundane of rules. In contrast, producing significant results will rarely generate much attention. Little wonder that public employees scrupulously follow the rules rather than focus on results; they are merely responding to the incentives that we, as citizens, have created for them. They are doing precisely what we told them to do. We have told public employees that the definition of a "good job" is complying with the rules, and they have adhered to our commandments (Behn 1994, 2–3).

By giving a public agency a specific goal to achieve, its leaders can change the definition of a good job.[5] Indeed, unless such a clear target for everyone to achieve is actually created, nothing specific will be achieved. Everyone is left to determine his or her own definition of a "good job."

Throughout the 1970s, the number of sorties flown by the U.S. Tactical Air Command (TAC) dropped annually—from twenty-three sorties per plane per month in 1969 to just twelve in 1977. To General Wilbur L. Creech, who took command of TAC in April 1978, this was a sign of declining readiness. With fewer sorties, TAC's pilots were receiving less training and, thus, were less prepared for combat. To revive TAC, Creech established a contract with the commander of each of his wings. For example, for fiscal year 1979, Colonel William A. Gorton, commander of the 31st Fighter Wing at Homestead Air Force Base, had the goal of flying seventeen thousand sorties. And the trend in sorties flown did reverse itself, increasing annually to more than twenty per plane per month by 1984 (Behn 1992).

In the early 1980s, the Massachusetts Department of Public Welfare had no goals. The people who worked there just filled out the forms and issued the checks, though actually they were not doing a very good job at that. When Charles Atkins and his leadership team took over in 1983, the top goal was to reduce the error rate to the federally established level. Atkins did not become commissioner to conquer the error rate, however. He took the job with the expressed purpose of placing fifty thousand welfare recipients in jobs over a five-year period. Nevertheless, for fiscal year 1984, the top goal was reducing the error rate; the second goal was placing five thousand welfare recipients in jobs. By fiscal year 1986, job placements had displaced the error rate as the top goal; by fiscal year 1987, the error rate was below the federal maximum; and by the end of fiscal year 1988, the department had indeed placed more than fifty thousand welfare recipients in jobs (Behn 1991).

In 1978, the New York City Department of Sanitation did not have enough operating sanitation trucks to collect the city's trash and garbage. On any day, the Bureau of Motor Equipment, which maintained and repaired the city's sanitation trucks, could provide only three-quarters of the vehicles needed. In this case, the goal was rather obvious: provide all the vehicles that the collections division needed to pick up the city's trash during normal hours (i.e., without overtime). Moreover, the new leadership team—Norman Steisel, commissioner; Ronald Contino, deputy commissioner for support services; and Roger Liwer, director of materials management—made some quick progress. By focusing the maintenance effort on this obvious goal, they provided, during their first full fiscal year on the job, 97 percent of the trucks needed.

All three public organizations—a city support agency, a state social service agency, and a federal military unit—improved performance significantly. All three defined the performance to be achieved by establishing specific goals for the organization to accomplish (as well as specific goals for various subunits) and then focused the attention of everyone within the organization on those goals. In all three organizations, the leadership used specific goals to redefine the meaning of success.

Linkage 1 in Creating an Innovative School:
Redefining the Meaning of Success

Unless an elementary school is charged with raising its students' math and reading scores by fifty points, it will believe it has satisfied its obligation by hiring only teachers with the proper credentials, putting them and the students in certified rooms, and following meticulously the approved curriculum. By creating the fifty-point goal, the school's leaders define clearly, for everyone to see, the meaning of a "good job" for the school as a whole, for each individual classroom, and perhaps even for each parent.

Linkage 2: Creating goals can get everyone thinking and behaving innovatively. The underlying theory linking specific goals and innovation is simple: If people feel a responsibility for helping the organization to achieve a specific goal, they will worry less about process and more about outcomes. They will apply themselves and their intelligence less to following the plethora of rules and more to producing the desired results. They will think about what they can do individually and collectively to help achieve the goal.

In a crisis, people think and act quite innovatively. That is because in a crisis everyone understands the purpose to be achieved. Everyone knows what needs to be accomplished and feels a personal responsibility to help solve the crisis. (Moreover, during a crisis, the rules about process become less important.) In the absence of a crisis, goals can become the purpose that can focus people's attention and energy. Indeed, goals can be a way of creating a (artificial?) crisis. Goals are the moral equivalent of a crisis.

At the Bureau of Motor Equipment, the crisis already existed. Trash and garbage were not being collected, and BME's mechanics were in danger of losing their jobs through privatization. Still, what should people do about the crisis? What were BME's various shops (i.e., the paint shop or the body shop), let alone individual mechanics, supposed to do to alleviate the crisis?

BME's leadership provided the operational definition of the crisis: the gap between the number of sanitation vehicles needed daily and the number that BME provided. Moreover, BME's leadership created a clear goal: put on the road every day the number of vehicles that the collection division needs.

As a result, BME's mechanics started working harder. Of more importance, they also started working smarter. After all, the task was not simply to repair trucks more speedily; there were limits to what that could accomplish. Therefore, they had to repair trucks smarter. They had to make repairs so that they lasted longer. When they conducted routine maintenance on a truck, they had to make adjustments to prevent obvious needs to make future repairs. Indeed, BME's mechanics began identifying the causes of frequent repair problems and designing measures to prevent these problems from ever occurring. For example, to prevent the signal lights that were mounted on top of the bumpers from being repetitively smashed, they cut a hole in the bumper and mounted the lights inside for protection. Indeed, to reduce maintenance and repair problems further, BME mechanics began to influence the specifications for the new trucks that the department purchased and then even the design of these trucks by manufacturers.

By establishing a clear goal, BME's leadership was able to get its front-line workers to think innovatively about how to achieve this goal—and to implement their innovations as well.

> ## Linkage 2 in Creating an Innovative School:
> ### Getting Everyone to Think and Act Innovatively
>
> If all the teachers in an elementary school have the goal of raising their students' average math and reading scores by fifty points—if that goal is dramatized and repeated so that no one doubts its importance or the commitment to achieving it—they will become creative about what they might actually do to help raise the scores of their students by fifty points. For example, the fifty-point increase may be easier to achieve for poorly performing students than for excellent ones. Consequently, this goal may shift the teachers' focus away from the students with whom they find it easiest to work and onto the students who need the most help.

Linkage 3: Goals can foster leaders at all levels in the organization. Leaders are important. They can foster and implement innovations. They can support the innovations of others. They can create innovative organizations. Yet, when these leaders leave, the innovativeness of the organization atrophies and eventually disappears. Thus, among other things, these leaders need to leave behind other leaders.

In addition, goals can help foster the development of such leaders. If different subunits within the organization also have subgoals, someone—or some group—will have to assume formal (or informal) responsibility for achieving these subgoals. In the process, these people will not only develop their own leadership skills; they will also establish a reputation for leadership. Regardless of whether the subunit creates its own goals or has its goals imposed from the outside, the existence of these goals encourages leadership.

In fact, it may not be that the goals themselves *directly* get everyone in the organization thinking and acting innovatively (as suggested by Linkage 2). Rather, it may be that the goals encourage some people in the organization (regardless of their informal roles) to take personal responsibility for some aspect of achieving a goal and thus to exercise leadership to get others to understand how they can contribute too. (That is, Linkage 3 may activate Linkage 2.) Alternatively, the goal might get everyone thinking innovatively and create leaders who now help coordinate all the innovative activity. And, of course, rather than actually create leaders, the goals could bring out latent leadership capabilities—or the goals could both create and bring out leadership. It hardly matters.

At TAC, Colonel Gorton had tried things, been beaten down, and had given up: "One time, with another Wing that I was involved in, we tried to do a number of things on occasion. And we just kind of quit because our higher headquarters wouldn't even tolerate that" (Behn 1992, 4). But in General Creech, Gorton found a leader who remotivated his own lost innovativeness. By giving Gorton a specific goal to achieve and the flexibility to use his resources to achieve that goal, Creech rekindled in Gorton his propensity to be an innovative leader.

Then, by dividing his seventeen-thousand sortie goal among the base's four squadrons, and by establishing a sortie goal for each squadron for each month, Gorton brought out leadership there. He linked the rewards for the flight crews and the maintenance crews to their squadron's goal—and further linked the rewards of those working in supply and support to the achievement of those goals. As a result, he encouraged leadership within the traditionally detached support units; even there, people began to think innovatively about how they could contribute to the effort to fly more sorties.

At the Massachusetts Department of Public Welfare, the responsibility for leadership was not owned and retained by headquarters. Every local welfare office had an annual job placement goal, which was also subdivided into monthly goals. Consequently, the director of every local welfare office had to become a leader. Obviously, a director could borrow innovative ideas employed in other offices. (Indeed, headquarters made sure that all fifty local offices knew about the innovative ideas successfully implemented elsewhere.) Nonetheless, these ideas always had to be adapted to the peculiarities of the local situation. Consequently, each local office had to develop its own strategy to achieve its monthly placement goal. This effort to invent innovative ways to achieve the monthly goal encouraged not just the local office director but also front-line supervisors within that office to exercise leadership in creating their own innovations.

Linkage 3 in Creating an Innovative School:
Fostering Leaders at All Levels

If not only the school but also each classroom has the goal of raising student math and reading scores by fifty points, each teacher might begin to think innovatively about how he or she could engage other teachers at the school to work innovatively to improve math and reading scores. Perhaps an assistant principal might do this. Perhaps someone in the math department might try getting others to focus attention on those students whose math scores were easiest to raise. Perhaps someone in the art department might try to get others to teach *more* arts by finding or developing art modules that directly improved reading skills.

Linkage 4: Goals can encourage organizations to reach out to other institutions whose work is helpful (or even necessary) for achieving these goals. Why build complicated working partnerships or coalitions? They are difficult to manage. Everyone has a different idea about what the coalition should do. In addition, maybe someone will even violate some rules; then everyone will be blamed. The human tendency is to work solely within one's own boundaries.

If an organization is charged with achieving a very specific goal, however, it may be forced to go outside. In thinking about the multiple barriers to achieving its goal, the organization may discover problems that it cannot solve directly. What to do? The obvious solution is to engage others who have the knowledge, authority, contacts, tools, influence, or capabilities to solve these problems. Goals encourage people to move out from behind the boundaries of their organization in an attempt to mobilize others who might have a more direct ability to overcome these problems.

The Massachusetts Department of Public Welfare lacked the in-house capability to achieve its placement goal. It had few people with job placement, job counseling, or employment-training skills. It could, of course, have chosen to create those competencies, to build the internal capacity to perform all the functions necessary to get jobs for welfare recipients. Instead, however, it chose to build alliances with other institutions—with the state's Division of Employment Security to place welfare recipients directly into jobs and with the nonprofit agencies established under the Job Training and Partnership Act to provide basic education, training for specific jobs, and then job placement. As a result, local welfare offices did not control the resources for achieving their own goals; they too had to build alliances (though the central office provided the overall structure and funding).

New York's Bureau of Motor Equipment could itself make only after-the-breakdown repairs plus some minor changes in equipment to prevent some of the more blatantly repetitive repairs. The real key to more efficient maintenance was the original design of the vehicle. And, in its search for continuous improvement, BME found a way to influence the design of sanitation vehicles by private firms with the expressed purpose of reducing maintenance costs.

Linkage 5: Accomplishing goals can change public values. Why does the public believe that government is incompetent? Is it because those who make this argument publicly and aggressively are cleverly (but wrongly) persuasive? Is it because the public knows (correctly) that government actually accomplishes very little? Or is it because the public is rarely told what the government is attempting to accomplish, let alone when it has been successful?

This final linkage is based on the assumption that the public does not inherently hate government. Citizens do, however, want to get something for

---

Linkage 4 in Creating an Innovative School:
Reaching Out to Others Who Can Be Helpful

If the goal is raising the math and reading scores of elementary school children, and if teachers conclude that parental support is essential to getting the students to apply themselves diligently to their math and reading assignments, then these teachers will begin to think innovatively about how to involve parents.

Linkage 5 in Creating an Innovative School:
Changing Public Values

Cutting taxes earmarked for education makes perfect sense if the school system is doing no better this year than it was doing five years ago when it had 10 percent less money. Why not cut education expenditures back by 10 percent? Nevertheless, if the school system is accomplishing something—if (in the jargon of total quality management) it is demonstrating continuous improvement—maybe the public will change not only its attitude toward funding the schools but also its attitude toward the work of other government agencies.

---

their taxes. Furthermore, people see (or hear about) a lot of waste and silliness and rarely learn of any specific accomplishments.

In Massachusetts, the welfare department's Employment and Training Program (ET) did change public attitudes about at least that agency's ability to produce results—the agency not only set and achieved annual goals; it also announced those successes at a public ceremony, citing each local office that achieved its own annual goal, and then published those achievements through each district's local media. "The polls say that 85 percent of the people are in favor of ET, our welfare program," reported the governor's chief of staff. "Can you name another state where 85 percent of the people are in favor of welfare?" (Behn 1991, 88).

Conventional political theory would suggest that the offices of the driver's license bureau would be significantly nicer than those of the welfare department. After all, middle-class voters visit the driver's licenses offices, whereas only the poor frequent welfare offices. Nevertheless, the leadership of the Massachusetts Department of Public Welfare was able to use the achievement of its goals to obtain the resources from the legislature necessary to improve significantly its fifty local offices—to make them much nicer than the drab facilities of that state's Registry of Motor Vehicles.

The logic connecting goals and innovativeness is straightforward. There are five linkages—five different ways in which goals work to improve the innovativeness of public agencies. The critique of the effectiveness of these five linkages is, however, equally straightforward: Traditional political and organizational behavior will overwhelm any effort to use goals to create an innovative public agency.

Problem 1: It is politically difficult to get agreement on goals. Politics is about the choice of society's goals. That is what makes politics so controversial. We do not agree about which goals society—or its government institutions—ought to pursue. Consequently, the mere decision to have a public agency focus its energies on one specific goal (or even two or three such goals) can alienate a variety of stakeholders. Some may not disagree with the chosen goal but, nevertheless, have very different priorities. Others may think the agency should pursue precisely the opposite goal. The more explicit the goal is, the more there is to disagree with, and thus the more controversial it is likely to be. Little wonder that public agencies concentrate on process.

By choosing to pursue a specific goal, an agency's leaders invite trouble: public protests, critical journalistic commentary, internal dissension, legislative hearings, budgetary constraints, even personal abuse. The purpose of choosing a specific goal is to concentrate people's attention on innovative ways to achieve that goal. Yet it may produce precisely the opposite result. By publicly emphasizing one goal over others, the agency's leaders may create so much disagreement that no one has time to do anything but cope with the political controversy.

At the Bureau of Motor Equipment, this was not a problem. Providing the number of trucks that the collection division needed was not controversial. Indeed, that seemed to be BME's entire job. No one complained about BME's goal.

At the Tactical Air Command, General Creech's real purpose was to improve readiness. Flying sorties was not the end in itself. Rather, it was the means by which that TAC's flight and maintenance crews maintained and enhanced their readiness. Consequently, it is easy to assert that Creech chose the wrong goal. After all, sorties are really an input to the training process. They are hardly an output, let alone the outcome. So some could argue that Creech should have selected a goal that more directly measured TAC's readiness.

This, however, is an analytical argument, not a political one. Only the unilateral-disarmament types will quarrel that TAC ought not to be flying sorties.

For TAC, flying sorties was quite politically acceptable. TAC was supposed to fly sorties. No one complained about TAC's goal.

Finding jobs for welfare recipients does, however, raise some political issues. Few would disagree with the idea that both society and the individual families would be better off if the family could, through productive employment, escape welfare. Nevertheless, people do not agree on how to achieve that widely held purpose. Today, the political imperative seems to be that you do not help welfare recipients find jobs so much as to tell them—or force them—to do so. In the 1980s, however, there were various political currents that the leadership behind the Massachusetts Employment and Training program needed to navigate. Theirs was a voluntary program, though some (including Governor Michael Dukakis) thought it should be mandatory. On the other hand, even though the program was formally voluntary, advocates for the state's welfare recipients were concerned that the monthly goals would encourage local welfare offices to make it de facto mandatory. Nevertheless, by working with the welfare advocates to mitigate their concerns while producing results with which the supporters of mandatory programs had difficulty finding fault, the department's leadership neutralized both political challenges.

Agencies benefit from choosing less politically controversial goals. Thus, output goals (job placements or trucks on the road) or even input goals (sorties flown) have an advantage over outcome goals because often it is the outcomes that are the most controversial.

Of course, we really care not about outputs or inputs but about outcomes—but the output of job placements is obviously connected to the outcome of family independence. Similarly, BME's output of working sanitation trucks is an input to the collection division's output of picking up the trash and thus to the Department of Sanitation's outcome of a clean city. And the input of flying sorties is a prerequisite for the outcome of TAC readiness. These correlations are not perfect. Those in the agency can achieve their goals without achieving their real mission. Consequently, while using a single input or output goal to motivate behavior, the agency's leadership needs to measure a lot of other variables to be sure that in the process of realizing their input or output goal they are also achieving their true mission (Behn 1991, 74–76).

The challenge is to identify not so much an outcome goal but a "productive goal"—one that helps the organization *produce* against many of its key purposes. A productive goal is one that motivates people and units throughout the organization to accomplish not only that specific goal but also others that contribute to the organization's overall mission. Although sorties flown is an input goal, it is also a productive goal because it directly helps a squadron or wing produce trained pilots and thus, also directly, helps TAC achieve its readiness purpose. Collection trucks in service is a productive goal because trucks are necessary (given the strategy adopted by the New York Department of Sanitation) to achieving the department's purpose of collecting trash. Finding jobs for welfare recipients is a productive goal because it helped the agency improve the welfare of individual families.

Sometimes the most productive goal may be obvious or noncontroversial. In other situations, however, obtaining agreement on a goal will require leadership. Those seeking to establish goals will have to consult stakeholders. They will have to build a working consensus, compromising with some while convincing others, because if the leadership is unable to focus the agency's work on achieving some clear goals, it will be unable to use goals to create an innovative organization.

Problem 1 in Creating an Innovative School:
The Difficulty of Getting Agreement over Goals

Not everyone will want the school to concentrate on math and reading scores. Some will want to emphasize history or science. Others will prefer a curriculum that focuses on the "whole child" or makes enhanced self-esteem a coequal purpose. Nevertheless, math and reading do have certain advantages. They are essential. Moreover, a curriculum that focuses on improving math and reading can—simultaneously—teach history and science and, by raising individual test scores, improve individual self-esteem. Having improved reading and math skills is not just an important outcome goal; it can also be a productive goal.

Problem 2: All organizations are resistant to change, and government organizations are explicitly designed to resist change. As the length of the preamble to any authorizing legislation demonstrates, we ask public agencies to accomplish multiple objectives. Rarely do we tell a public agency to concentrate on one specific goal (or even on three). As a result, a public agency will have different units pursuing different parts of its authorizing legislation. We do not want these different units to change direction every time the agency gets a new boss. That is the old Wilsonian separation between politics (the choice of policy) and administration (the implementation of that policy).

Moreover, for any public agency, we fix the key dimensions from the outside. We place multiple line items in the budget; we define narrow personnel categories, job descriptions, tight salary ranges; we create seniority and bumping rights; and we firmly control hiring and promotion. Unelected public administrators are supposed to have the freedom to administer professionally the policies established by the elected officials—but not too much freedom. We have designed our public agencies to be predictable—to be even more resistant to change than other large institutions.

Thus, when a new agency head—or even an established leadership team—announces that the agency has a new specific goal for the year, the response may be nothing more than a polite yawn. It's the "We-Be" syndrome again: "We be here before you're here; we be here after you're here."

In the face of organizational apathy, cynicism, resistance, or sabotage, leaders have to be persistent. At Homestead Air Force Base, the wing met its first month's goals but did it in a sloppy and unsafe manner. So Colonel Gorton decided to stop flying, telling his base: "Shut 'em down until you guys get healthy and we start operating like a professional outfit." As he recalled, "That got everybody's attention" (Behn 1992, sequel, 12–14). At the Massachusetts Department of Public Welfare, Atkins kept talking about his job placement goals. He would go to the monthly meetings of the local office directors and distribute a page with two columns. In one column, he listed each local office that had made its job placement last month; in the other column, he listed those offices that had not made their goals. Slowly, the managers of the various local offices began to sign onto the new goal (Behn 1991, chapter 4).

Moving public agencies is, indeed, difficult. With persistence, however, leaders can overcome that inevitable resistance.

Problem 2 in Creating an Innovative School:
Organizational Rigidity and Resistance

Some teachers will disagree with the principal's goal for raising reading and math scores. Some will agree but figure: Why bother? This principal will be gone soon too. Still, some teachers will sign on. Some will even make progress. Then, slowly, others—wanting to prove that they too are good teachers—will start working on improving their own students' math and reading scores.

Analyzing an Alternative Approach: The Strategy of Unobtrusive Leadership

Using specific goals to motivate organizational behavior is a very explicit, very aggressive, very conspicuous strategy of leadership. The leader is very precise about ends (though much less clear about means) and publicly stimulates individuals and units to produce (somehow) these desired ends. It is not very subtle. And it may not always work.

For example, Michael Cohen and James March (1986) offer a much less obtrusive strategy for the leaders of "organized anarchies." Specifically, they focus on situations in which the goals are "either vague or in dispute,"[6] the production technology is not well understood, and participation in the organization is fluid (2–3). Cohen and March developed their recommendations for leadership by studying the organized anarchies of American colleges and universities, but their three characteristics can describe government agencies as well.

Among other things, Cohen and March suggest that the leaders of organized anarchies should manage unobtrusively while overloading the system with a variety of proposals, some of which will be accepted, if only by default. Do not get too attached to any one idea, they warn the leader, but if you can put forward enough ideas, some will make it through. Cohen and March also suggest that leaders should facilitate opposition participation so as to teach their antagonists how little power and control exists within the organized anarchy, to dramatize to them how difficult it is to accomplish anything, and thus to convince opponents to lower their expectations—particularly as to what they demand the leader accomplish.

Cohen and March also advocate persistence. Theirs is a much more subtle persistence, however, not aimed necessarily at accomplishing one specific goal but rather simply at accomplishing something, almost anything.

To Cohen and March, the university is a can of worms. Consequently, they advocate a deliberate but subtle garbage can[7] strategy: Give people lots of meaningless forums in which to debate all their concerns. For example, a committee to study the future of the university is a great "garbage can." It will attract all sorts of people who have nothing to do but argue and debate (indeed, who may be able to do nothing but argue and debate). Be sure to feed these committees regularly, giving them big questions to examine in endless detail, but do not worry that they will produce anything useful or harmful. They will not. Indeed, they cannot.

Furthermore, do not try to mobilize these people or anyone else, argue Cohen and March. Neutralize them. Meanwhile, you, the unobtrusive leader, move a few real things along slowly in the direction you desire.

Cohen and March's strategy would not create an innovative organization. In fact, they essentially give up.[8] They accept their organized anarchy's lack of goals as an inherent condition, immutable. And, indeed, it may be extremely difficult to organize a university to rally around one or a few explicit goals. Nevertheless, that may reflect the ways in which we have chosen to construct universities. By consciously recruiting people with diverse views—indeed, by placing a premium on such intellectual diversity—universities make it almost impossible to achieve consensus on goals. Thus, because a university can never have a specific goal to pursue, it cannot become an "innovative organization" in the sense that people throughout the university are thinking up and implementing innovative ways to achieve these goals.[9]

Public agencies, however, may be much less anarchic than universities. They benefit from advantageous selection.[10] The people who have chosen a career in the United States Air Force may be diverse in a number of dimensions, but most of them would agree that the United States needs a strong defense, and few would object to flying sorties as a way to train pilots. Moreover, those who fly planes and those who fix them like their work. Motivating a pilot to fly or a mechanic to get inside an engine is not particularly difficult. Some members of Congress may think that TAC should be flying fewer sorties, but inside the House and Senate Armed Services Committees and their appropriations subcommittees on defense, there will be few dissenters.

The same applies to those mechanics who work in New York City's Bureau of Motor Equipment. They like fixing trucks. Indeed, they are proud of their work. Furthermore, neither citizens of New York nor the members of its city council will disagree significantly about BME's real purposes.

A social service agency, however, may look more like an organized anarchy. When those who now work at the agency first chose to enter the social service field, they may have been young and idealistic. The years of working with an endless stream of welfare recipients, however, may have converted them into cynics. In addition, there are the citizens, legislators, and journalists, whose participation in the affairs of the welfare department is certainly episodic and unpredictable. Furthermore, we know little about the technology of converting a family from dependence on welfare to economic and psychological self-sufficiency. Maybe the managers of social service agencies ought to accept that they head "organized anarchies"—that they have "impossible jobs" (Hargrove and Glidewell 1990)—and thus give up on the ambitious goal of creating an innovative organization.

Then, however, that pesky existence theorem reappears. It has been done. It is not impossible. A public agency may look like an organized anarchy—something that is completely incapable of focusing its creative energies on the innovative pursuit of an explicit mission. Yet persistent but very real people have converted the potential anarchy of a social service agency into an innovative organization. Furthermore, when they have done so—whenever public leaders have created innovative organizations—they appear to have done it by focusing the organization on the pursuit of an explicit goal, thus activating the five linkages between specific goals and innovative organizations.

Notes

The author thanks the Ford Foundation for its support in the preparation of this chapter.

1. And how to motivate large public agencies to improve performance is certainly one of the big questions of public management (Behn 1995).

2. All seventeen were either winners or finalists in the first year (1986) of the Ford Foundation Awards Program for Innovations in State and Local Government (Golden 1990).

3. This is the existence theorem argument: The three examples here provide the "existence theorem." They "prove" that goals *can* help create innovative organizations (provided that my analysis of these organizations does, indeed, establish a causal link between the goals and the organization's innovativeness). Consequently, if other public leaders in other similar circumstances establish similar goals, they may be able to foster similar innovativeness throughout their organization.

4. Indeed, it may be that these are not the correct linkages. Interpreting history is not a flawless undertaking. It may be that other features of these organizations and their leadership produced the innovativeness that I saw—or it may have just been dumb luck (Behn 1991, 209–12). Then again, as Branch Rickey often said: "Luck is the residue of design."

5. For a discussion of the importance of defining what a "good job" is, see Vaill (1991, chapter 3: "Winning Is Only the Thing You Think Winning Is").

6. I use the word "goal" in a slightly different way than Cohen and March do. Their "goal" is a basic, overarching purpose of the organization—such as preventing the spread of communism. My "goal" is a specific operational task that a specific unit can complete in a specific period of time—such as flying seventeen thousand sorties in a year. Furthermore, Cohen and March are interested in the role that their overarching purposes (or goals) play in making decisions. In contrast, I emphasize the use of specific operational goals to motivate organizations and people. Nevertheless, there is enough similarity to make this discussion worthwhile.

7. For the original discussion of the concept of the "garbage can" in organizational behavior, see Cohen, March, and Olsen (1972).

8. This may be a little unfair. It may be not so much that Cohen and March have given up as that the university presidents whom they studied and whom they concluded were most "effective" had given up. Cohen and March apparently found no university president who was able to articulate goals and then get the university to pursue them in any systematic way.

Employing the unobtrusive strategy in the organized anarchy of a university may be the only sane alternative. Nevertheless, this approach does have consequences. Without organizational goals, the guardians of process inevitably win. The overhead units within most universities exercise so much power over daily operations precisely because there exist no competing values on which to base a decision—or even an argument. Cohen and March's unobtrusive strategy may help the university president deflect a variety of attacks; indeed, it may prevent individuals from organizing any coherent assault against the president. Yet this unobtrusive strategy also ensures that the overhead units can use the rules about process to prevent line personnel from undertaking innovative initiatives that the president might actually find valuable.

Several years ago, an academic colleague, someone who had worked at a large state university, in state government, and in the private sector, visited Duke. As we walked around the campus, I explained to him some of the vagaries of our operations. At one point, he blurted out: "Why do you do it that way? You don't have a legislature."

An emphasis on process over outcomes is not exclusively a product of legislatures, however. Process can easily win over outcomes in any organization that fails to establish specific outcome goals to pursue. Whenever there are no goals, process wins. Legislative bodies have a difficult time establishing clear outcome goals, but they can come to a quick agreement about process values—e.g. equity, fairness, or (superficial) efficiency—particularly if some obvious process value has been recently violated and it is necessary to ensure that this particular value is never violated again.

In that sense, universities are like legislatures. There is no agreement about what outcomes to pursue, but there is a major concern for such process values as equity and fairness. Whenever the leaders of universities—like leaders of legislatures—refrain from any effort to establish goals, process wins. Organizations that have no common purposes to provide coherence to daily work can find a convenient substitute in rules.

9. Actually, universities do have one explicit goal for their individual faculty members—research publications—and that goal does encourage much individual innovativeness. Because universities typically evaluate faculty by the strength of their individual publication records, and because universities usually establish a clearly understood (if unwritten) publication goal as the requirement for tenure, faculty can be quite innovative in their efforts to achieve their own personal goals. This, of course, contributes to the university's overall research reputation but does not help it achieve anything more coherent.

10. "Advantageous selection" is the opposite of the economist's "adverse selection."

References

Behn, Robert D. 1987. "A Curmudgeon's View of Public Administration: Routine Tasks, Performance, and Innovation." *State and Local Government Review* 19 (spring): 54–61.

———. 1991. *Leadership Counts: Lessons for Public Managers from the Massachusetts Welfare, Training, and Employment Program.* Cambridge, Mass.: Harvard University Press.

———. 1992. "Homestead Air Force Base." Case, sequel, and teaching note. Durham, N.C.: Governors Center at Duke University.

———. 1994. Bottom-Line Government. Unpublished essay. Durham, N.C.: Governors Center at Duke University.

———. 1995. "The Big Questions of Public Management." *Public Administration Review* 55, no. 4 (July/August): 313–24.

Cohen, Michael D., and James G. March. 1986. *Leadership and Ambiguity.* 2d ed. Boston: Harvard Business School Press.

Cohen, Michael D., James G. March, and Johan P. Olsen. 1972. "A Garbage Can Model of Organizational Choice." *Administrative Science Quarterly* 17, no. 1: 1–25.

Golden, Olivia. 1990. "Innovation in Public Sector Human Services Programs: The Implications of Innovation by 'Groping Along.'" *Journal of Policy Analysis and Management* 9, no. 2: 219–48.

Hargrove, Erwin C., and John C. Glidewell. 1990. *Impossible Jobs in Public Management.* Lawrence, Kan.: University Press of Kansas.

Vaill, Peter B. 1991. *Managing as a Performing Art: New Ideas for a World of Chaotic Change.* San Francisco: Jossey-Bass.

4 Innovation by Legislative, Judicial, and Management Design
Three Arenas of Public Entrepreneurship
Nancy C. Roberts

T HE BASIC QUESTION of this research is how to reconcile two different recommendations given to public entrepreneurs. The literature advises them to both grope along and, alternatively, systematically analyze and plan their way through the innovation process. Practitioners receive what seems to be contradictory advice on how to innovate in the public sector. Public entrepreneurs are to grope along in pursuit of a general direction of change, experimenting with various initiatives as they proceed. Exploration and learning from experience rather than pursuit of well-defined and analyzed plans characterize this approach (Behn 1988; Golden 1990). Through trial and error, they tinker with existing practices and assemble familiar stuff in new ways, prompting evolutionary rather than revolutionary change (Sanger and Levin 1992). Alternatively, public entrepreneurs are to move an innovative idea systematically and strategically through the various stages of the innovation process—initiation, design, and implementation. Analytical in the development and assessment of the idea, and political in its defense, they prompt incremental as well as radical change (Roberts 1992; Roberts and King 1996).

How can we account for these diverse descriptions and prescriptions of public entrepreneurship and innovation? This is the basic question addressed in this chapter. We begin with the assumption that descriptions of public entrepreneurship and innovation, as well as advice to practitioners, are basically sound. There are occasions when experimentation and groping along occur and make sense. There are other occasions when analysis and planning are fundamental to entrepreneurship and innovation. What is needed is a theory of entrepreneurship and innovation that specifies the scope conditions under which public entrepreneurs either grope along or strategically analyze and plan. Without such a theory, we have no way to qualify our recommendations or reconcile what seem to be competing perspectives on entrepreneurial behavior.

The chapter is divided into three sections to accomplish this task. The first section presents a conceptual framework on which to build a theory of public entrepreneurship and innovation. Attention to definitions and units of analysis

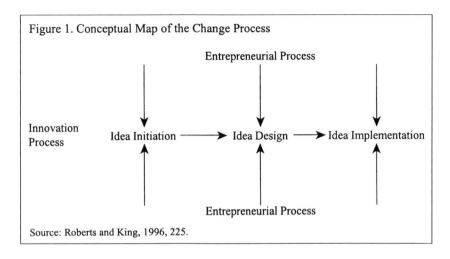

Figure 1. Conceptual Map of the Change Process

Source: Roberts and King, 1996, 225.

minimize the confusion that often accompanies discussion of these concepts. The next section presents well-known examples of public entrepreneurship and innovation—innovation by legislative design, innovation by judicial design, and innovation by management design. Section three analyzes these cases in terms of the conceptual framework and notes the range of entrepreneurial behavior exhibited. The chapter concludes by identifying two scope conditions—institutional context and the level of change inherent in the innovative idea—that delimit the theory. Taking both of these conditions into consideration, it is possible to account for the competing advice given to practitioners and aspiring public entrepreneurs.

Conceptual Framework

Often confused as one process, two interrelated processes are involved in getting a new idea accepted into practice (Roberts and King 1996). The first is innovation—the translation of a new idea from its initial state to its actualization in practice as a full-blown innovation. The second process is entrepreneurship—the energy force driving the innovative idea forward on its path to innovation. Figure 1 illustrates the relationship between these two processes. The horizontal dimension represents the innovation process and the vertical dimension represents the entrepreneurial process.

Representing two vectors in time and space, the two processes work in tandem to produce an innovation. The entrepreneurial vector tracks the entrepreneur who galvanizes energy for and counters resistance to the new idea. The innovation vector tracks the different manifestations of the new idea as it moves through time. The unit of analysis of the innovation process is the idea. The unit of analysis of the entrepreneurial process is the entrepreneur.

Innovation Process

Innovation is defined as the culmination of a series of transformations on a new idea in order to move it from its initial state through its eventual implementation into practice (Roberts 1992; Roberts and King 1996). A new idea can be anything from a new technology, service, or product to a new administrative process or procedure (Daft and Becker 1978). The central element in any new idea is its departure from existing conditions. It is considered innovative if it deviates from current activity and is viewed as new by the relevant unit of adoption (Zaltman, Duncan, and Holbek 1973).

Numerous schemes exist to characterize a new idea. Rogers and Kim (1985) characterize a new idea in terms of its compatibility, relative advantage, complexity, trialability, and observability, among others. Compatibility is the degree to which an idea is perceived as consistent with the existing values, past experiences, and needs of the social system. Relative advantage is the degree to which an idea is perceived as better than the one it supersedes. Complexity is the degree to which an idea is perceived to be relatively difficult to understand and use. Trialability is the degree to which an idea may be experimented with on a trial basis. Observability is the degree to which the results of an idea implemented into practice are visible to others.

Pelz and Munson (1982) also characterize new ideas in terms of their levels of innovation. Entrepreneurs can invent brand new ideas themselves (level: origination). They can modify the ideas that originate with others for use in their situation (level: adaptation). Or they can take ideas directly from other settings without modification (level: borrowing).

Noting that new ideas imply a certain degree of change, Roberts and King (1996) suggest locating a new idea on a continuum depending on the nature of change it represents. Incremental change would anchor one end and radical change the other. Radical change is defined as the reconfiguration of existing system parts to form a new whole. It differs from first-order, incremental change, which makes minor modifications to parts of a system without changing the parts' underlying relationship to one another. Radical change represents a discontinuity from the previous order, which fundamentally alters the relationship of parts to the whole. It is irreversible, transformative change based on a new set of ordering principles. In reality, there are probably degrees of radicalness moving into degrees of incrementalism. Somewhere on the continuum we would locate the innovative idea based on the type of change it represents, either modifications to existing practice or a radical departure from it.

However an idea is characterized, there is widespread agreement that discernible phases can mark the idea's translation into practice (Roberts 1992; Roberts and King 1996). Initiation or creation highlights the emergence and development of an innovative idea and the association of the idea with some need, problem, or concern. Design translates the innovative idea into a concrete form for review. Perhaps it is manifested as a prototype, or a proposal that specifies the details of the innovative idea—whom it would benefit, what it would cost, its advantages over other alternatives. Implementation brings the innovative idea into actual practice where its merits are assessed. If it survives this process, we know it as an innovation. Consequently, for each innovation phase there is a different by-product. The innovative idea, as solution to some problem, emerges from initiation. The prototype evolves from the design phase, and innovation itself emerges from implementation.

The trajectory of new ideas through the phases of the innovation process can vary widely. Some ideas can incubate for years in the initiation phase, whereas others require little time in each phase before they become a full-blown innovation. Pelz and Munson (1982), for example, found that the duration of each phase varies, depending on the originality of the innovation. The more original the new idea, the more time it requires in all phases. We also know that trajectories of innovative ideas can take an orderly, sequential path from initiation, design, and implementation. Others can follow more complex, disorderly, divergent trajectories that proliferate and feed back on themselves, creating patterns that looks like fireworks displays (Schroeder et al. 1989). The lines demarcating the phases are also not hard and fast. Innovative ideas of low originality, borrowed from other locales, tend to follow an orderly sequence with identifiable markers from phase to phase. On the other hand, the more novel the innovative idea, the more overlap there tends to be among the phases (Pelz and Munson 1982). In practice what this means is that entrepreneurs can be working on initiation and design, or design and implementation, at the same time. Thus, a clear distinction among the phases is not always expected, and sometimes we only can say in retrospect when a phase begins and ends.

Entrepreneurial Process

Entrepreneurs are the drivers of innovation. They supply the energy to move the innovative idea through the various phases of the innovation process. Two expressions of entrepreneurship are possible: individual and collective. An individual entrepreneur initiates a new idea, links it to some problem or need, designs it into a prototype or proposal, and implements it into practice where it survives evaluation. We categorize individual entrepreneurs depending on their location in the policy system. A political entrepreneur holds elective public office. An executive entrepreneur holds an appointive leadership position in a government bureau. A bureaucratic entrepreneur works in government in a nonleadership position. A policy entrepreneur pushes an innovative idea from outside government (Roberts 1992; Roberts and King 1996).

Entrepreneurship has its collective form as well, although little evidence exists to suggest which form predominates. Individual entrepreneurs can join forces and work as a team with other entrepreneurs to push an idea through all phases of the innovation process. Alternatively, individuals whose responsibilities direct their attention to certain functional aspects of the innovation process (e.g., policy intellectuals, policy champions, policy administrators and implementors, and policy evaluators) can coordinate their resources and energy to push an idea into practice (Roberts 1992; Roberts and King 1996).

Although interrelated, the processes of entrepreneurship and innovation are conceptually distinct. The innovation phases represent functional requisites, the hurdles the idea must overcome to become a full-fledged innovation (Pelz and Munson 1982). If a new idea is not initiated, designed, and implemented, it will not be able to attain the developed status we attribute to innovation.

The functional requisites of innovation do not imply that the actions of individual entrepreneurs follow the same sequential logic. To assume that an entrepreneur would be expected to go through a predefined set of activities, such as initiation, design, and implementation, and in that order, confuses the general phases of the innovation process with the entrepreneur's behavior and decision making at the individual level of analysis. These are two very different issues. The phases or requisites describe innovation in global terms, stating the necessary conditions for an idea to develop as an innovation. On the other hand, entrepreneurs can go through a much messier process that follows no predetermined set of activities (Lambright and Teich 1979; Van de Ven and Angle 1989). As Kingdon reminds us, "Events do not proceed neatly in stages, steps, or phases. Participants do not first identify problems and then seek solutions for them; indeed, advocacy of solutions often precedes the highlighting of problems to which they become attached" (Kingdon 1984, 215). Characterizing the innovation process as either planning or groping along (Golden 1990; Sanger and Levin 1992; Levin and Sanger 1994) thus confounds the trajectory of the innovative idea over time with the activities and behaviors of the entrepreneur. These are two very different processes with two very different units of analysis. Ideas do not plan or grope along; entrepreneurs do.

Groping along versus analysis and planning describe two general modes of behavior entrepreneurs employ when searching for ideas and pushing them forward on the path to innovation. When planning, entrepreneurs pay careful attention to identifying and developing and the 'right' innovative idea, relying on analysis to aid in its selection. They take care to refine their idea into statute and policy, planning as much as they can in advance to avoid implementation problems. Ideally, they establish controls and incentives as part of the supporting structure to ensure that implementation actions will be congruent with the original policy idea (Golden 1990).

When groping along, entrepreneurs develop a conception of a problem and some consensus around it. Starting with a general direction (not a well-defined policy), they pay little attention to framing the initial idea. Their intent is to act quickly and experiment with alternative ideas. Through this exploration they build "craft knowledge" about the problem and their capacity to deal with it. They test new ideas through experience, and the role of analysis is limited. Minimal plans are needed to get a specific idea implemented in some form. Attention is directed to results of actions, and actions are modified based on trial-and-error experience. Analysis naturally follows action rather than preceding it. Entrepreneurs learn and adapt through error correction, regarding divergent actions of implementors as reason to adjust policy, not to sanction the implementors for modifications (Behn 1988; Golden 1990).

Viewed in this light, entrepreneurship, whether the mode is groping along or analyzing and planning, becomes the engine of change, and entrepreneurs are its catalysts. Entrepreneurs attract resources, garner support, manage meaning, focus direction and attention, and overcome resistance, all in an effort to gather momentum and push their new ideas forward on the path to innovation.

Examples of Public Entrepreneurship and Innovation

Three examples of public entrepreneurship and innovation will be illustrative. They represent different arenas of innovation, each with its own constraints to mold and shape entrepreneurial behavior.

Auto Safety Legislation of 1966

Abraham Ribicoff of Connecticut, a former state governor, House member, and secretary of the Department of Health, Education, and Welfare, was elected to the Senate in 1962 and assigned to the Government Operations Committee (Drew 1966; Walker 1977). Within two years, he acquired a subcommittee chairmanship and used this platform to launch an investigation of the federal government's efforts in the area of traffic safety, a subject that had captured his interest and attention while he was governor of Connecticut. In fact, he had earned the nickname "Mr. Safety" for his crackdown on speeders. He announced hearings to address the "fantastic carnage" on the highways and introduced a bill to expand federal research into traffic safety and to authorize grants for vehicle inspection and driver-education programs. Joining Ribicoff on the subcommittee was Senator Robert Kennedy.

Ribicoff also brought in a young, thirty-two-year-old lawyer from Winsted, Connecticut, to advise the committee. A graduate of Princeton and the Harvard Law School, this attorney had practiced law in Connecticut where he also had been a part-time advocate of a new approach to traffic safety. Giving up his law practice, he moved to Washington in 1964 to devote himself full-time to the cause of safety and consumer protection. The young attorney was Ralph Nader.

On arrival in Washington, Nader served as a consultant to a group in the Department of Labor that was studying traffic safety, and beginning in early 1965, he was advising Ribicoff's staff on the auto safety bill—what areas to study, which witnesses to call, what questions to ask. By the summer of 1965 he was pressing the staff to publicize that many new cars were sold with defects and some with serious safety hazards. By November, his *Unsafe At Any Speed* (1965) had been published, receiving front-page coverage in the *New York Times* and largely favorable reviews. Subtitled *The Designed-in Dangers of the American Automobile,* the book was a well-documented criticism of the automobile industry's concern for style over safety.

In the meantime other congressmen had been showing their interest in the problems of traffic safety. Lawrence A. Ernest of Whitefish Bay, Wisconsin, had written in March of 1964 to his senator, Gaylord Nelson (D), complaining about the lack of safety standards for automobile tires. Although there was earlier legislation, thanks in large measure to the efforts of Congressman Kenneth Roberts (D, Alabama) (legislation that required standards for brake fluid, seat belts, and safety standards for passenger cars the General Services Administration [GSA] bought for the government each year), these efforts had attracted little attention. So in mid-1964, Representative Nelson introduced a bill to require federal safety standards for tires, and by early 1965, becoming interested in all aspects of automobile safety, Nelson introduced a second bill to require that the GSA safety standards be applied to all cars.

Sensing a growing interest in traffic safety, President Johnson instructed Joe Califano, his special assistant in charge of the 1966 legislative program, to work up a transportation program that would include a traffic safety bill. The news was especially gratifying to "Young Turks" within the Commerce Department who had been attempting to push the department into a meaningful role in traffic safety. (The Commerce Department's charter to promote American business was viewed as incompatible with regulating American business.) The president's bill proposing a highway safety act was the strongest car-safety proposal before the Congress, but it was denounced as a "no-law law" by Ralph Nader and criticized by Ribicoff for permitting too much time before safer cars reached the American public. Instead, Ribicoff urged interim standards for all cars based on the GSA standards and a requirement that the secretary of the Commerce Department set safety standards.

Annoyed at Senator Ribicoff for moving in on his committee's jurisdiction, Senator Warren Magnuson, the powerful chairman of the Senate Commerce Committee, began to assert his influence over issues of traffic safety. Displacing the original sponsors, Senators Ribicoff and Gaylord Nelson, Magnuson took up Nelson's tire bill in 1965 and told his staff to prepare for final action on a revised bill in 1966. The bill was to pass in March of 1966 at the same time Magnuson opened his Commerce Committee hearings on President Johnson's bill. He also announced that he would sponsor amendments that would require the GSA standard to be applied to all cars by January 1967 and the secretary of the Commerce Department to set additional standards one year later.

Ribicoff reopened his own subcommittee hearings shortly after the president's state of the union address and called Ralph Nader as a congressional witness. In early March, reports that Ralph Nader was being followed circulated in the press. Detectives were asking relatives and friends about his sex life, his politics, and his attitudes toward Jews. Issuing a press release just before midnight on March 9, General Motors admitted it had initiated a routine investigation of Ralph Nader. Ribicoff then opened a hearing to assess whether a witness (Nader) before his subcommittee had been harassed. These hearings provided high drama and focused national attention on the issues of safety standards. James M. Roche, the president of General Motors, personally appeared and publicly apologized to Ralph Nader in front of a packed hearing room and TV cameras. Judging by the lengths that an auto company would go to discredit Nader, many came to believe that Nader was right in his criticisms of the auto companies.

As a consequence of all this controversy and heightened interest and Nader's technical advice to the committee's staff, a major coalition in the Senate emerged to support expansion of the federal government's efforts to regulate the automobile industry and to ensure public safety. After some negotiations, the Commerce Department and the White House also got in line for mandatory standards. Staff members (Gerald Grinstein and Mike Pertschuk) then drew together the administration's bill, amendments proposed by several senators, nine Nader changes incorporated into amendments submitted by

Senator Vance Hartke (D, Indiana), and six major and some minor changes sought by Cutler (the lobbyist for the automobile industry) and fashioned them into a bill with which all could live. The Senate then went on to pass the bill by a vote of 76 to 0.

In a unanimous vote, the House passed its own version of a combined tire and auto safety bill. House and Senate committees were able to iron out the remaining differences, and the final bill was cleared for the president's signature. By January 31, 1967, the secretary of Commerce would require all new cars to meet the safety standards similar to those already issued by the GSA for government-purchased cars, and by January 31, 1968, the secretary would issue additional safety standards to appear in the 1969 models.

Advancement of Minority Rights

The NAACP, the National Association of Colored People, and its independent Legal Defense Fund, founded in 1939, had struggled for years to advance minority rights. Coming to the conclusion that they would be unable to attain their goals in the legislative and administrative arenas, they chose the judicial forum as the most expedient avenue to advance their cause.

Their strategy involved the recruitment of well-trained and experienced attorneys in civil rights law and the development of a network of cooperating attorneys who were sympathetic to their efforts. This network kept attorneys abreast of potentially good test cases to sponsor in pursuit of their policy goals. In addition, they sought direct sponsorship of cases at the trial court level to give their attorneys more control over the course of litigation and put them in a better position to establish a good record for later appeal. The ultimate purpose was to obtain "judicial invalidation of restrictive covenants through liberal interpretation of the state requirement of the Fourteenth Amendment" (O'Connor and Epstein 1984, 67).

Another factor in their strategy was the cultivation of support from other litigators. Filing amicus curiae briefs, especially ones from the U.S. government, lent legitimacy to their claims and increased their chances of garnering major policy changes from the Court. Ultimately their strategy was successful. In *Shelley v. Kraemer* 334 U.S. 1 (1948), the Court was forced to deal with state judicial policies that allowed the enforcement of restrictive covenants. By continuing a similar strategy and expanding their base of precedents, the NAACP achieved an even greater success in the *Brown v. Board of Education* case 347 U.S. 483 (1954), which outlawed segregation in the schools.

While crediting disadvantaged groups in the initiation of new policy ideas, legal scholars also acknowledge that the justices themselves were active participants in this process of judicial entrepreneurship (Pacelle 1990). Their attitudes and values formed the backdrop of their decision making regarding whether to accept some case and reject others. Furthermore, justices signaled litigants about their interests and preferences by extending or reducing the time for case selection, by the consistency of their decisions in related cases, and by the language of their decisions (Pacelle 1990).

If justices did not have the necessary cases before them to pursue their interests, they were able to manipulate the cases that were before them. Using a method known as "issue fluidity," the justices were able to expand or contract an issue raised in a litigant's brief to suit their own designs (Pacelle 1990, 3–4). Instances of issue fluidity can be found in other landmark cases that established or fundamentally altered the law. *New York Times v. Sullivan* changed the nature of libel law. *Roth v. United States* took issues involving alleged obscenity and placed them under the First Amendment. *Monroe v. Pape,* a search-and-seizure case, opened a new area of civil rights litigation. *Griswold v. Connecticut* created the right of privacy and was the basis of *Roe v. Wade* (Pacelle 1990). In these instances, justices and litigants formed a union that fundamentally altered the laws of the land and public practice. This path to change has extended well into the court system, especially the Supreme Court, and has been a strategy emulated by organized interest groups attempting to follow their pattern of success (Caldeira and Wright 1988; Cortner 1968; Cowan 1976; Greenberg 1977; Kellogg 1967; Kluger 1976; O'Connor 1980; Vose 1959, 1972).

Tax Collection in Massachusetts

Ira Jackson was appointed commissioner of the Massachusetts Department of Revenue in 1983 (Behn 1988). The department had been rocked by scandal and was under attack. Brought in to clean things up, Jackson wanted to enhance his agency's reputation as being tough on enforcement, generate more revenues to help solve the state's budgetary problems, and improve agency morale. His job would be challenging. He was not a tax attorney, and he did not know anything about managing tax collection. When he arrived on the job, he found no agency annual report, no transition document, and no mission statement. No book on tax administration existed to teach him how to run the business, nor was there much guidance on how to manage the agency.

On being sworn in, he decided not to sign the traditional papers delegating authority to various deputy commissioners and bureau chiefs. (The law assigns all department authority to the commissioner.) Instead, during the first month in office, he held extensive interviews. He used these interviews as opportunities to learn about every manager in his department and about the authority each would be delegated. Only when he reached a measure of confidence that a manager could do a job did he delegate authority to the person.

The process was exhausting, but it disciplined him to learn about the agency and what everybody did. Of more importance, the interviews became a vehicle for controlling his department.

Having selected his executives, Jackson did not set out to develop a comprehensive strategy for the department. Rather, department strategy emerged from trial and error. It evolved as people tried things and learned from their successes and failures. Indeed, he encouraged their experimentation and interest in testing out various ideas and hunches on how to improve department performance. As a consequence, within the first six months, he and his staff had taken a series of very tough enforcement actions. Designed to prepare the public for the upcoming tax amnesty period and to increase voluntary compliance, they closed restaurants delinquent in turning over their meal-tax revenues to the state. They seized yachts and airplanes registered in Delaware by owners who wanted to avoid Massachusetts excise tax. Through this process, Jackson was able to increase revenue collection significantly without increasing taxes. Aggressive enforcement, including commercial property seizures, recouped over $200 million in unpaid taxes. He went on to propose other new ideas—giving his agency additional enforcement power and creating a tax amnesty program that eventually yielded $60 million in back taxes.

Case Analysis

Each of these cases represents a different institutional arena or location for public entrepreneurship and innovation. As alternative venues for change—legislatures, courts, and public bureaus—they illustrate innovation by legislative design, innovation by judicial design, and innovation by management design, respectively. Each consists of unique cognitive, normative, and regulative structures and activities that provide stability and meaning to social behavior. Each is also governed by its own habits and rules of conduct, including formal structures and cultural norms that are expected to set up different constraints and options for behavior (March and Olsen, 1989; Scott, 1995).

Innovation by Legislative Design

Innovation by legislative design is innovation by statute or law. It is achieved by completing a series of institutional requisites specified in federal or state constitutions. It begins with an innovative idea that is thought to solve some problem or meet some need. The idea, fashioned into a proposal, is introduced into the legislature. If convinced of its potential, legislators champion the idea, fashion it into a bill, and place it on the formal decision agenda. If it picks up enough support, the bill is given a hearing, and ultimately a vote on its merits is taken. If enacted, the bill becomes law. Once passed into law, it is translated into programs by bureaus charged with its implementation and evaluation in practice.

The automobile safety legislation of 1966 is an good example of innovation by legislative design. The idea of regulating automobile manufacturers was initiated by concerned citizens and legislators. It was refined and designed by congressional representatives, staff, and committees and turned over to the Department of Commerce for implementation on its enactment. Its evolution through time left markers or artifacts (e.g. idea, proposal, bill, law, program) to document its movement through the hurdles of the innovation process. Once the details of the case were known, it was possible to identify the idea's trajectory and describe its translation into accepted practice.

We note that public entrepreneurship in this instance was collective in form. Citizens and specialists, each attending to his or her area of interest and expertise, pooled their resources and coordinated their efforts to push the idea forward. Through various avenues, policy intellectuals and advocates (e.g. Nader, citizens, Young Turks in Commerce, legislators, staffers, President Johnson) convinced influential members of Congress to champion the idea and give it a hearing. Their mode of action was deliberate and strategic, and they relied on analysis and planning to make their case.

Innovation by Judicial Design

Innovation by judicial design is innovation through the courts and judicial interpretation of the law. Ordinarily, we do not think of jurists as innovators or the judicial process as opportunity for innovation. A case is brought before the court, and the prosecuting and defense attorneys argue its merits based on the evidence. The jury weighs the information and renders its verdict. Taking the jury's verdict and legal precedent into account, the judge makes the final determination. Lower court decisions can be challenged on appeals to higher state and federal courts, with final authority resting with the Supreme Court. Although judges can be appointed or elected, whatever their avenue to office, lay people usually see their roles as interpreting the laws, not making them.

As we have seen, there is latitude in the judicial process. In fact, some scholars describe the interaction between Supreme Court justices and the litigants who bring them the cases as being a "shared enterprise" of entrepreneurship (Pacelle 1990, 2). Initiated by the NAACP and supported by receptive jurists, radical changes in policy emerged from "judicial lobbying" and collective entrepreneurship, a strategy that has since been employed by other groups pursuing litigation to achieve their policy goals (see O'Connor and Epstein [1984] for a review). On the basis of these and numerous studies,

Richard Cortner (1968) formulated a theory of interest group use of the courts. "Disadvantaged groups," such as the NAACP, are highly dependent on the judicial process as a means of pursuing their policy interests, usually because they are temporarily, or even permanently, disadvantaged in terms of their abilities to attain successfully their goals in the electoral process, within the elected political institutions, or in the bureaucracy. If they are to succeed at all in the pursuit of their goals they are almost compelled to resort to litigation (287; see also O'Connor and Epstein 1984, 68).

The markers and artifacts of innovation by judicial design were easy to discern. There were test cases, litigants' and amicus curiae briefs, jury verdicts, judicial rulings, appeals, and eventually Supreme Court decisions that advanced the idea of minority rights in housing and education. Finding a test case ended the phase of initiation and began the design phase when jurists, litigants, and their lawyers formed and shaped the idea as a way to address the problem of discrimination. Implementation and evaluation followed the Supreme Court's ruling as the idea was molded into programs. The trajectory was lengthy—spanning decades—and iterative as the idea cycled and recycled through initiation and design before a test case was able to activate a ruling from the Supreme Court and prepare the idea's implementation in practice. Entrepreneurial behavior was collective in form. Litigants, lawyers, and judges formed a shared enterprise to push the idea of minority rights. Their mode of action was deliberate, strategic, and analytical.

Innovation by Management Design

Innovation by management design is organizational innovation—innovation initiated and developed within a public bureau. The organization is the setting because the innovation is designed and implemented in order to provide a new technology, process, or procedure to improve bureau performance. Although perhaps not initiated and designed by upper management within the organization (in fact it may have come from employees from the "bottom up"), ultimately, in its evolved state, the new idea requires the blessing and resources from management if it is to be sustained as an innovation over time. Hence, it is titled innovation by management design.

Descriptions of innovation by management design do vary, but for the most part scholars agree that the innovation process begins with a new idea, however vaguely formulated. The idea is shaped and formed as it passes through organizational hurdles set up to win management interest and support. If the idea is found acceptable, organizational experimentation begins. If, after testing, management finds the innovative idea produces results considered to be desirable, they officially adopt it as part of organizational practice. Numerous examples of entrepreneurship in public organizations can be found in the literature (Behn 1988; Doig and Hargrove 1987; Golden 1990; Levin and Sanger 1994; Osborne and Gaebler 1992; Sanger and Levin 1992).

The case of tax collection in Massachusetts is a good example of innovation by management design. The ideas—new policies in tax collection initiated by organization members to deal with delinquent payments and violation of the law—began the innovation process. Initiation and design phases to mold and shape the ideas were of relatively short duration as managers moved quickly into the implementation phase. On successful evaluation and testing, the ideas established new organizational policies for dealing with tax evaders. The markers or artifacts were identifiable as ideas, proposals, and programs. The trajectory, as best as can be determined from the details, was iterative as the idea cycled and recycled through initiation, design, and implementation. Entrepreneurship seemed to be both individual and collective. The commissioner was involved in driving the new ideas through all phases of the innovation process, yet the process was collective as organizational members joined forces, proposed new ideas, and began to experiment with them. Finally, the mode of entrepreneurial behavior has been described as groping along (Behn 1988). The commissioner initially had no comprehensive strategy or plan, but as people tried some things and failed with others, one design emerged through interactions and experimentation.

Comparison of Institutional Settings

Table 1 identifies some of the major differences between the cases of innovation by legislative and management design. Innovation by legislative design follows one clearly specified idea from initiation through design and implementation. Regulation of automobile manufacturers positioned the idea toward the radical side of the change continuum, although it was not an extreme example because the law could be considered an adaptation of other laws regulating business. The innovation process took more than four years, and the idea's trajectory was sequential through initiation, design, and implementation. The outcome measures of the idea were specified in advance, and the alignment between the initial idea and the innovation was high. Little change to the idea occurred during implementation because there were controls built in to ensure compliance with the law. Entrepreneurship was collective in form, and entrepreneurial behavior for the most part was strategic, analytical, and planned.

In contrast, innovation by management design followed a multitude of programmatic ideas vaguely specified during initiation and design to fit a broad agency direction. Specification awaited experimentation and trial-and-error learning during implementation. Administration of the law to penalize

Table 1. Comparison between Innovation by Legislative and Organization
Design in Two Processes

Dimension	Legislative Design	Organization Design
Innovation Process		
Artifacts, markers	Ideas, proposals, bills, law, program	Ideas, proposals, program
Change implied in idea	Radical	Incremental tinkering
Nature of idea	Adapted	Borrowed
Specification of idea	One idea clearly specified	Multitude of programmatic ideas vaguely specified to fit broad agency direction
When idea specified	Initiation, design, before implementation	Culmination of implementation; evolved in practice
Duration of phases	Four years	Within year
Trajectory of idea	Sequential	Iterative
Outcome measures of idea	Specified in advance	Evolved in practice
Alignment between initial idea and innovation	High	Low
Change to idea during implementation	Less fundamental, less frequent	Greater change, more frequent
Toleration for idea deviation during implementation	Low	High
Constraints/controls on ideas	Use of controls and incentives for alignment	Few controls, learn from experience
Entrepreneurial Process		
Form	Collective	Individual, collective
Mode	Strategic, analytical, contingency planning	Groping along
Role of analysis	Extensive, comprehensive	Limited
Planning period	Extensive	Minimal (months to a year)

tax evaders, ideas borrowed from other state agencies with more efficient and
effective tax collection, was on the incremental side of the change continuum.
The duration of the innovation process for the initial idea was less than a year,
and the idea's trajectory was iterative as ideas were modified and revamped
through initiation, design, and implementation. Outcomes evolved through

practice, so alignment between the idea and the innovation was low. Because the goal was to learn from practice, few controls or constraints were needed to check behavior. Entrepreneurship was both individual and collective in form and characterized as groping along.

Although it may be argued that this description of innovation by management design is an artifact of the selected case, that argument holds less weight when considered against other research. Examining innovation by management design in seventeen human services programs, Golden (1990) also found that groping along best described the way innovation came about. Similarly, Sanger and Levin (1992), in their analysis of more than twenty-five successful innovations in public bureaus, found that entrepreneurs had an opportunistic bias toward action. Their process was not neat; it was iterative, incremental, and disorderly. Using bits and pieces of what was available in new ways to meet changing circumstances, entrepreneurs tinkered and depended on analysis after a policy direction was chosen, using it to shape policy rather than to choose between competing policies ahead of time. Innovation did not occur from revolutionary breakthroughs, but from trial-and-error learning and experimentation in the field during implementation. Altering their course of action based on operational results, entrepreneurs promoted evolutionary change; they combined old and familiar things in new ways, usually borrowing and adapting ideas from others. Thus, there is growing evidence that groping along fits the organizational context and innovation by management design.

The evidence on entrepreneurial behavior through legislative design is less clear. Studies of policy innovation through the legislative process do follow the phases from initiation to design (agenda setting and enactment) and implementation. In addition, phases are broken down into separate units for analysis: initiation (Polsby 1984); agenda setting (Cobb and Elder 1983; Nelson 1984; Downs 1972; Peters and Hogwood 1985); enactment (Redman 1973; Reid 1980); and implementation (Pressman and Wildavsky 1973; Bardach 1977). Nonetheless, there is a greater range of entrepreneurial behavior reported. Under certain circumstances, entrepreneurs have been found to devote little time or energy to research on alternatives, and, in fact, alternatives to problems they experience are discovered during the search process. In a manner similar to groping along, they rely on satisficing and choose the first good alternative that comes their way (Polsby 1984). Alternatively, under other circumstances, entrepreneurs follow the pattern of strategic analysis and planning as outlined above. They canvas alternatives, weigh long-term consequences, and develop elaborate justifications to support their solutions during initiation and design in order to prepare for implementation (Polsby 1984). Clearly there must be other factors at play besides the institutional setting. The issue is how to account for the greater range of entrepreneurial behavior in legislative arenas compared to organizational ones.

The answer may lie in the nature of the innovative idea. Ideas vary on a number of dimensions, as noted earlier. If innovation means doing something different from current practice, the issue is how much change is implied in the innovative idea—incremental modifications to the status quo or radical change that reconfigures a policy?

Legislative and judicial arenas offer greater opportunities to initiate a range of new ideas. The Constitution specifically accords Congress the right and the responsibility to make new laws—whether they be incremental or radical. Although jurists are supposed to settle conflicts between the branches of government, they can and do engage in issue expansion to alter the laws fundamentally, prompting a range of incremental and radical changes. Bureaucrats, on the other hand, function to implement the laws and work within the intent and parameters established by legislatures and courts. Notwithstanding the creativity and flexibility required in bureaucratic implementation, fundamental change is therefore more likely to come from innovation by legislative design or judicial design rather than from innovation by management design.

Although suggestive and not definitive, evidence does seem to point in this direction. Zegans (1992), for example, found in his interviews that public sector executives viewed politicians as having the responsibility to make new policy. From these executives' perspective, an effective legislature sets broad policy direction and makes choices about fundamental policy changes, especially those that require new expenditures or a major change in policy direction. He quotes one executive as saying: "For what it's worth, I think major new policy initiatives have to come from elected officials. I mean, staff can have ideas, maybe bounce and buzz off of [sic] them. But, ultimately, if you're going to affect segments of your public, either in offering a new service or taking something away that's been there before . . . that's their (the legislature's) call (149).

This conservative role definition, self-imposed or system imposed, permits executives fewer degrees of freedom and makes the pursuit of radical ideas within bureaus less attractive. Given these constraints, it is reasonable for bureaucratic entrepreneurs to resort to evolutionary tinkering rather than to push for more radical shifts in policy. Unwilling to risk going beyond their charge, managers use what is at hand to combine old and familiar things in new ways.

The advantage of this incrementalism is less resistance to change, and less resistance means fewer resources have to be allocated to justify new ideas. Why spend scarce budget dollars for analysis and planning when resistance is minimal and competing ideas are few? In a resource-constrained bureau, it makes sense to minimize the investments for new ideas and let things evolve as they will.

In contrast, when entrepreneurs push more radical ideas, whether in legislative or judicial arenas, they tend to prompt greater resistance. Greater resistance requires more time and energy. Dealing with resistance means building a case with data and analysis to support one's position. It means orchestrating experts to attest to the idea's viability. It means strategically coordinating larger numbers of people to champion the idea through the more complex innovation process in legislative and judicial arenas. The more radical the idea, the greater the resistance. The greater the resistance, the greater the investment in time and resources needed to defend the idea and overcome the resistance to it. If there is evidence of new ideas that range from incremental to radical emerging through legislative and judicial processes, then it is reasonable to assume that one would find variation in entrepreneurial behavior to serve in the defense of innovation.

Conclusion

Drawing on a conceptual framework to distinguish entrepreneurship from innovation, this chapter has argued that the apparent contradictions in entrepreneurial behavior reported in the literature can be explained if two scope conditions are taken into account—the institutional context and the nature of the innovative idea.

Institutional context is important because research reveals a different mode of entrepreneurial behavior in organizational settings. As illustrated in the case of tax reform in Massachusetts, entrepreneurs in public bureaus tend to grope along and tinker around the edges of existing practice. Yet institutional context does not tell the whole story. Groping along has been reported in legislative contexts, although entrepreneurs in these settings also exhibit a mode of behavior characterized by strategic analysis and planning, as seen in the case concerning automobile safety and the case involving minority rights.

Here is where the nature of the innovative idea becomes important. Entrepreneurs in public bureaus are incrementalists. Their comfort zone and ideas do not take them far from modest adjustments to the status quo. Pushing ideas that represent incremental change has the advantage of provoking minimal resistance from organizational members and stakeholders, which in turn requires comparatively few resources to sustain the entrepreneurial effort. Seen in this light, groping along is energy efficient and compatible with the resource-limited world of public bureaus.

In contrast, when pursuing more radical ideas, usually in legislative and judicial arenas, entrepreneurs prompt greater scrutiny and questioning. Their ideas tend to be resisted from those defending current practice. They are challenged to demonstrate the validity of their new ideas and to justify them with data and analysis before moving ideas into the design stage and beyond. Entrepreneurial action in this situation has to be more strategic and analytical to offset the large amount of resistance generated.

No doubt other factors also account for entrepreneurial behavior. New ideas can be analyzed on various dimensions, as suggested above. Nevertheless, what is important to remember is that by specifying the scope conditions, we can ultimately reconcile the different descriptions and prescriptions in the literature. If these observations hold for larger samples, public entrepreneurs would be advised to analyze and plan strategically when pursuing radical change in legislative and judicial arenas and to grope along when promoting incremental change by management design.

References

Bardach, Eugene. 1977. *The Implementation Game: What Happens after a Bill Becomes a Law.* Cambridge, Mass.: MIT Press.

Behn, Robert D. 1988. "Management by Groping Along." *Journal of Policy Analysis and Management* 7 (fall): 643–63.

Caldeira, G. A., and J. R. Wright. 1988. "Organized Interests and Agenda Setting in the U.S. Supreme Court." *American Political Science Review* 82, no. 4: 1109–27.

Cobb, Roger W., and Charles D. Elder. 1983. *Participation in American Politics: The Dynamics of Agenda Building.* 2d ed. Baltimore: Johns Hopkins University Press.

Cortner, R. C. 1968. "Strategies and Tactics of Litigants in Constitutional Cases." *Journal of Public Law* 17: 287–307.

Cowan, R. B. 1976. "Women's Rights through Litigation: An Examination of the American Civil Liberties Union Women's Rights Project, 1971–1976." *Columbia Human Rights Law Review* 8: 373–412.

Daft, R., and S. Becker. 1978. *Innovations in Organizations.* New York: Elsevier.

Doig, Jameson W., and Erwin C. Hargrove, eds. 1987. *Leadership and Innovation.* Baltimore: Johns Hopkins University Press.

Downs, Anthony. 1972. "Up and Down with Ecology: The Issue Attention Cycle." *Public Interest* 28: 38–50.

Drew, E. B. 1966. "The Politics of Auto Safety." *Atlantic Monthly* 95–102.

Golden, Olivia. 1990. "Innovation in Public Sector Human Services Programs: The Implications of Innovation by 'Groping Along.'" *Journal of Policy Analysis and Management* 9, no. 2: 219–48.

Greenberg, J. 1977. *Judicial Process and Social Change: Constitutional Litigation.* St. Paul, Minn.: West.

Kellogg, C. 1967. *NAACP: A History of the National Association for the Advancement of Colored People.* Baltimore: Johns Hopkins University Press.

Kingdon, James W. 1984. *Agendas, Alternatives, and Public Policies.* Boston: Little, Brown.

Kluger, Richard. 1976. *Simple Justice: The History of* Brown vs. Board of Education *and Black American Struggle for Equality.* New York: Alfred A. Knopf.

Lambright, W. Henry, and Alfred H. Teich. 1979. "Policy Innovation in Federal R & D: The Case of Energy." *Public Administration Review* 39: 140–47.

Levin, Martin A., and Mary Bryna Sanger. 1994. *Making Government Work.* San Francisco: Jossey-Bass.

March, James G., and Johan P. Olsen. 1989. *Rediscovering Institutions: The Organizational Basis of Politics.* New York: Free Press.

Nelson, Barbara J. 1984. *Making an Issue of Child Abuse: Political Agenda Setting for Social Problems.* Chicago: University of Chicago Press.

O'Connor, K. 1980. *Women's Organizations' Use of the Courts.* Lexington, Mass.: Lexington Books.

O'Connor, K., and L. Epstein. 1984. "The Role of Interest Groups in Supreme Court Policy Formation." In *Public Policy Formation,* edited by R. Eyestone. Greenwich, Conn.: JAI Press.

Osborne, David, and Ted Gaebler. 1992. *Reinventing Government: How the Entrepreneurial Spirit Is Transforming the Public Sector.* Reading, Mass.: Addison-Wesley.

Pacelle, R. L. 1990. "The Supreme Court's Agenda and the Dynamics of Policy Evolution." Paper presented at the American Political Science Association Meeting, San Francisco.

Pelz, D. C., and F. C. Munson. 1982. "Originality Level and the Innovating Process in Organizations." *Human Systems Management* 3: 173–87.

Peters, B. Guy, and Brian W. Hogwood. 1985. "In Search of the Issue Attention Cycle." *Journal of Politics* 47: 238–53.

Polsby, Nelson W. 1984. *Political Innovation in America: The Politics of Policy Initiation.* New Haven, Conn.: Yale University Press.

Pressman, Jeffrey L., and Aaron Wildavsky. 1973. *Implementation.* Berkeley, Calif.: University of California Press.

Redman, Eric. 1973. *The Dance of Legislation.* New York: Simon and Schuster.

Reid, T. R. 1980. *Congressional Odyssey: The Saga of a Senate Bill.* San Francisco: W. H. Freeman.

Roberts, Nancy C. 1992. "Public Entrepreneurship and Innovation." *Policy Studies Review* 11, no. 1: 55–71.

Roberts, Nancy C., and Paula J. King. 1996. *Transforming Public Policy: Dynamics of Policy Entrepreneurship and Innovation.* San Francisco: Jossey-Bass.

Rogers, E., and Joung-Im Kim. 1985. "Diffusion of Innovations in Public Organizations."

In *Innovation in the Public Sector,* edited by R. L. Merritt and A. J. Merritt. Beverly Hills, Calif.: Sage.

Sanger, J. B., and M. A. Levin. 1992. "Using Old Stuff in New Ways: Innovation as a Case of Evolutionary Tinkering." *Journal of Policy Analysis and Management* 11, no. 1: 88–115.

Schroeder, R. G., A. H. Van de Ven, G. D. Scudder, and D. Polley. 1989. "The Development of Innovative Ideas." In *Research on the Management of Innovation,* edited by Andrew H. Van de Ven, Harold L. Angle, and Marshall Scott Poole. New York: Harper & Row.

Scott, W. Richard. 1995. *Institutions and Organization.* Thousand Oaks, Calif.: Sage.

Van de Ven, Andrew H., and Harold L. Angle. 1989. "An Introduction to the Minnesota Innovation Research Program." In *Research on the Management of Innovation,* edited by Andrew H. Van de Ven, Harold L. Angle, and Marshall Scott Poole. New York: Harper & Row.

Vose, Clement E. 1959. *Caucasians Only.* Berkeley, Calif.: University of California Press.

———. 1972. *Constitutional Change.* Lexington, Mass.: Lexington Books.

Walker, J. L. 1977. "Setting the Agenda in the U.S. Senate: A Theory of Problem Selection." *British Journal of Political Science* (October): 423–45.

Zaltman, Gerald, Robert Duncan, and Jonny Holbek. 1973. *Innovations and Organizations.* New York: Wiley.

Zegans, M. D. 1992. "Innovation in the Well-Functioning Public Agency." *Public Productivity and Management Review* 16, no. 2: 141–56.

II | Reengineering, Reform, and Innovation as Design Science
The Roles of Institutions and Political Contexts

Public management scholars increasingly recognize the importance of the institutional contexts in which individuals function and the role of those institutions' structures on management reform: "institutions do matter" (Ferris and Tang 1993). At the very least, the incentives that shape individual behavior are often determined by the institutions within which individuals act (Ostrom, Schroeder, and Wynne 1993; Knott 1993). Each of the chapters in this section addresses the importance of specific institutional contexts to public management reform. The first chapter provides an explicit, general discussion of the dangers of conducting public management scholarship in an institutional vacuum and of assuming that reform emphases on market mechanisms are necessarily desirable or practical (Evans and Wamsley). The second chapter examines human resource management reform within a framework that contrasts institutional incentives in the United States and Sweden (Wise and Stengård), and the third and fourth chapters focus on budgetary reform and the need to alter existing institutional incentives (Larkey and Devereux; Thompson and Johansen). Taken together, they provide ample evidence that institutional contexts are crucial to valid public management research.

Karen G. Evans and Gary L. Wamsley focus on public management in the context of institutions of governance. Using a narrative framework based on *The Wizard of Oz,* they suggest that "much like Dorothy and company, public administration and public management scholars both seem to be on a journey of self-discovery." Yet the authors are concerned with the implications of a public management identity that extricates itself from the institutional framework provided by public administration—that is, a framework concerned with "the evocation of citizenship and the evolution of institutions of governance." The authors emphasize that effective management is a crucial component of governance, but they question the emphasis on the "means" of governance rather than its ultimate objective—the establishment of government institutions that "support the practices of democracy and . . . enhance the life opportunities of citizens."

Evans and Wamsley argue that because public management research and

111

government *reinvention* often focus on the orthodox values of public administration—efficiency, economy, and effectiveness—they may overlook vitally important values required of democratic institutions and may reduce the citizen's role to that of a customer, thereby eroding the "citizen-administrator nexus" on which true governance depends. By neglecting the institutional context, public management risks the possibility of contributing no more than the administrative science offered by early public administration scholarship—the value-neutral, "pure" management that we associate with nongovernment organizations and with the politics-administration dichotomy. Evans and Wamsley remind us that "management, whether effective or not, does not take place for its own sake."

Lois R. Wise and Per Stengård provide an empirical assessment of the management of reform, comparing the experiences of Sweden and the United States between 1983 and 1993. The political institutions in which these two cases were embedded, the authors argue, were important determinants of the process *and* the success of fundamental government reform. They begin by emphasizing that public management research must look beyond the rhetoric of reform and must critically evaluate the extent to which reform has actually occurred. Their study uses internal labor market theory to provide such an evaluation, and they justify their approach by pointing out that personnel and human resource management often dominates reform rhetoric. In essence, Wise and Stengård conclude that Sweden was successful in reorienting its labor market system to external market forces, whereas the United States was not.

The authors define internal labor market systems as those that provide a set of formal and informal rules for its employees. Such systems typify large national civil service systems, and they feature many of the conditions which we identify as "bureaucratic." Bona fide reform, the authors argue, would involve the transition of a government personnel system to one that incorporates market incentives. Thus, human resource management becomes more businesslike. Wise and Stengård offer a theoretical framework that identifies factors affecting the ability of government to make this transition. They hypothesize that reform should be enhanced by smaller government agencies (Sweden's are smaller), by a more external economic orientation (i.e., reliance on export activity, which is greater in Sweden), by weaker labor unions (found in the United States), and by an administrative style that is oriented toward consensus (characteristic of Sweden). The central focus of their model, however, is the extent to which reform responsibility is decentralized. Sweden, which used a relatively decentralized approach, was much more dependent on discretionary action by line managers in the design and implementation of reform, whereas the United States relied on centralized direction from the Office of Personnel

Management (OPM). In order to evaluate the success of reform, the authors examine efforts to reform national government employee compensation, job security, and deployment and staffing patterns. In general, they find that OPM retained significant control over these issues in the United States, whereas in Sweden responsibility for decisions in these areas was successfully shifted to agency managers. They conclude that the decentralized model exemplified by Swedish reform efforts has led to more effective changes in human resource management.

Patrick D. Larkey and Erik A. Devereux analyze the impact of the numerous reform efforts in the federal budget process. In the authors' view, the reforms have been disappointing. They argue that budgetary reforms are inadequate because they fail to alter the incentives imbedded in the institutions in which budgeting occurs. Consequently, political and bureaucratic actors involved in the budgetary process have no reason to change their behavior. In addition, budgetary reform is stymied by our inability to predict adequately the consequences of adopting any particular reform; we know too little about the causal mechanisms associated with changing the process, and the research required to design better reforms is "infeasible intellectually and/or politically."

Larkey and Devereux identify five classes of attempted budgetary reforms. *Rationalizing* reforms include the famous Planning, Programming, Budgeting Systems (PPBS) approach. Also included in this class is the more recent National Performance Review (NPR) emphasis on "mission-driven, results-oriented" budgeting. A review of similar past "rational" reforms leaves Larkey and Devereux pessimistic about the potential for successful NPR reform. The other classes of reforms include *ad hoc norms* or standards that the process should meet (i.e., comprehensiveness); *power shifting* from the executive to legislative branch; *control* style reforms in which "we have auditors auditing the auditors"; and *democratizing* reforms, which attempt to enhance responsiveness to citizens. Larkey and Devereux argue that none of these classes of reforms have offered noticeable improvement in the budgetary process, due in part to the "inherent complexities and dynamics" of the process. They reserve most of their criticism for the democratizing reforms, noting that "the logic of democratic accountability and responsiveness often has little to do with the outcomes of the policy process" and that "democratizing reforms failed because they are founded on models of how people *should* behave rather than how they *do* behave." The authors offer various suggestions for "modest" improvements in the federal budgeting. These include the establishment of a new nonpartisan body to establish economic figures and assumptions; an acknowledgment that the process must be more closed in order to facilitate the tough decisions necessary to good; the elimination of existing geographic imbalances in congressional budgetary decisions; and, perhaps most interesting, a "pay for performance" scheme for members of Congress in which pay would be based on the extent of balance in the budget. The common denominator in the authors' proposals is an explicit attempt to alter the behavior of individuals through incentives designed to improve the budgetary process.

The NPR recommendations for "mission-driven, results-oriented" budgeting is formally addressed in the Fred Thompson and Carol K. Johansen chapter. They point out that this objective requires "a wholesale transfer" of private sector budgeting practices to the public sector. In fact, they argue, restoration of the budget process that existed before the implementation of the 1921 Budget Act would result in a process that incorporates many positive aspects of private budgeting. Thompson and Johansen review New Zealand's efforts to reform its budget process and conclude that the New Zealand reforms offer a model for the United States to study and perhaps emulate.

One key feature of the New Zealand reform is a closer relationship between an agency's performance and future agency appropriations. Agency managers are given some responsibility for capital investments, but because the financial performance of the agency is key to its evaluation and appropriation, incentives exist for careful capital spending decisions at the agency level. This model bears some resemblance to the use of "responsibility centers" in private sector budgetary management. These centers represent one strategy used by private firms to delegate authority to lower organizational levels. The manager of a responsibility center, or organizational unit, is given significant flexibility and responsibility, and the manager's reward is related to the performance of his or her center.

Thompson and Johansen suggest that in the United States, governmental budgeting frequently incorporates the *form* of private sector budgeting, but not its content. They offer various suggestions for improving the transfer of private practices. The annual, comprehensive executive budget should be abandoned; instead, executive agencies should be free to propose changes in their operations at any time. Of course Congress must and should approve new initiatives, but once approved, these initiatives should be reviewed only if they fail or if circumstances change significantly; in other words, congressional budgeting should be more selective. Agencies should receive permanent authority, seeking congressional permission only for changes that entail significant substantive or financial consequences. In short, congressional budgeting should, whenever possible, adopt the *permissive, continuous,* and *selective* features of private sector budgeting. In addition, incorporation of private sector attention to temporal considerations—i.e., paying closer attention to the net *present* value of alternatives—would enhance budgetary results.

Each of these chapters clearly recognizes that effective public management research must pay closer attention to the contexts of individual action—contexts imbedded in our political institutions. For example, budget officials frequently operate in a context in which incentives operate against reform. Thus, if the Thompson/Johansen budgeting model is to be successfully implemented, it must overcome many of the institutional barriers cited by Larkey and Devereux. In short, if public management scholarship minimizes—or ignores—the influence of institutional constraints and incentive systems, our view of public management will be incomplete at best. The greater danger is that in the absence of institutional considerations, public management scholars will draw invalid conclusions.

References

Ferris, James M., and Shui-Yan Tang. 1993. "The New Institutionalism and Public Administration: An Overview." *Journal of Public Administration and Theory* 3, no. 1 (January): 4–10.

Knott, Jack H. 1993. "Comparing Public and Private Management: Cooperative Effort and Principal-Agent Relationships." *Journal of Public Administration and Theory* 3, no. 1 (January): 93–119.

Ostrom, Elinor, Larry Schroeder, and Susan Wynne. 1993. "Analyzing the Performance of Alternative Institutional Arrangements for Sustaining Rural Infrastructure in Developing Countries." *Journal of Public Administration and Theory* 3, no. 1 (January): 11–45.

5 | Where's the Institution?
Neoinstitutionalism and
Public Management

Karen G. Evans and Gary L. Wamsley

In 1900, L. Frank Baum wrote what he called "a modernized fairy tale"—a story that has been so immortalized in film that some elements have become a part of our ordinary vocabulary. Baum decried the "horrible and blood–curdling incidents" included in the tales of Anderson and Grimm that were intended to teach moral truths to young readers. Baum believed that values and morality had indeed become an integral part of modern education[1] and that therefore children's literature should simply be entertaining. It no longer needed to use fear and violence to teach values or to drive home moral points. He claimed, in the introduction to the work, that his was a simple story of wonderment and adventure—one that nearly a century later still enchants all who read it (Baum 1985, introduction).

Despite Baum's disclaimers of any intent but enchantment, interpretations of his work are as interesting as the story he wrote. For example, Henry M. Littlefield (1964) described *The Wizard of Oz* as a metaphor for the Populist movement of the late nineteenth century. He saw the protagonists in the following way: Dorothy was "Miss Innocent Everybody," the Scarecrow was the beleaguered farmer, the Tin Woodsman was the abused wage laborer, and the Cowardly Lion was the Populist spokesman William Jennings Bryan. The Wicked Witch of the East, of course, represented the power-hungry finance capitalists of New York, and the humbug Wizard was their agent cum confidence man who dealt in illusions that led the Populist agenda to self-destruct.

Our understanding of self and the world, indeed human existence itself, is grounded in metaphors. Metaphors are the basis for our language and our ability to form abstractions (Lakeoff and Johnson 1980). Thus, the metaphor is a powerful tool for understanding and explaining complex ideas. By definition, however, a metaphor cannot exactly fit the phenomenon it seeks to illuminate. One danger in using metaphors is that, if the analogies are not relatively simple, the message can be easily lost in the metaphor. The metaphor one uses must also be readily recognizable and familiar to the audience. Another danger is our being "captured" by a powerful metaphor and, thereby, losing sight of the differences between it and the phenomenon to which it is applied. Although we acknowledge these potential dangers, we nonetheless believe that *The Wizard of Oz* has metaphorical power that can explain much that is troubling about public management today and can suggest some possible remedies.

We see *The Wizard of Oz* as an allegorical tale of a mythic journey in which the protagonists must overcome seemingly insurmountable obstacles to obtain what they *perceive* as missing in themselves. It is, in other words, the archetypal arduous journey of self-discovery that humankind has used to entertain and instruct going back as far as Homer's *Odyssey*. For Dorothy and Toto, stranded by a tornado in an alien land, "home" is the missing element. For the Scarecrow, it is the "brains" that will give him respect as a man among men. For the Tin Woodsman, having lost his human heart along with his human form, the missing element is the ability to be a part of a feeling and loving community. For the Cowardly Lion, the goal is the courage to stand for what is right and the confidence in that stand that can make him truly the king of beasts. Each of these travelers represents one problem of interest to public administration and public management—finding compelling purpose (home); gaining credibility (brain); erasing the barriers between government and citizen (heart); and a legitimate role in governance (courage). The Wicked Witch of the East in our Oz represents powerful negative forces that must be overcome on the journey, and the Wizard represents the hope of help that turns out to be illusion.[2]

The Yellow Brick Road: A Shared Ontological Quest

For a variety of reasons, some of which are less than edifying and which we will not discuss here, a number of scholars and academic programs use the term "public management" (PM) rather than "public administration" (PA) to describe their work.[3] Indeed, the term "PM" grows in popularity in practicing venues as well as in academia, though many cannot even articulate a reason for their choice of usage. We see scholars who choose either label (PA or PM) enmeshed in a complex and evolving relationship with one another, with the phenomena they seek to describe and explain, and with the practices they inform. Nevertheless, whatever their differences, all, in our estimation, are involved in searching for an answer to the existential questions put so eloquently by Ross Perot's 1992 running mate, Admiral Stockdale: "Who am I? And why am I here?"

We see both PA and PM as engaged in an ontological quest, though with varying degrees of consciousness. Neither have been able to attain any broad consensus as to whether they are nascent disciplines, disciplines, interdisciplinary fields, or applied fields. Furthermore, they cannot agree as to the paradigmatic state of their subject. Some hold that their field of inquiry is in a pre-paradigmatic stage, others believe that it has had a succession of paradigms, and some will claim it has a dominant paradigm now. In addition, more than a few would not be able to agree on a definition of a paradigm. Regardless of their chosen designation, PA and PM scholars also vary widely in their awareness of and concern for the related field (or fields?) of practice and the practitioners who struggle there daily. Do these practitioners constitute an occupation, a nascent profession, or a profession? Like you, the reader, we have our opinions on all these matters, but our point is that any group (or groups) of people who have run about asking questions as fundamental as these surely is engaged in an ontological quest of the first order, whether they know it or not.

Much like Dorothy and company, PA and PM scholars both seem to be on a journey of self-discovery. While projecting critical stereotypes onto one another, they make assumptions about what is missing in their and the others' research and practice, and both hope to find an all-powerful Wizard (a theory, a methodology, a concept) that can answer their ontological queries. To the extent that they are conscious of their ontological angst or do not simply ignore or suppress it, they share it with one another in their respective conference papers and journal articles. In this way, they seek affirmation from peers that *their* quest is on the right track, that *their* lines of inquiry will finally achieve something like the status accorded disciplines, and that *their* respective practitioners will receive the rewards, both material and nonmaterial, accorded to professionals.

Like Dorothy and company, they may not find these things until they have reached some equivalent of the Emerald City and completed the tasks assigned them by the Wizard. Perhaps then they will come to see that the elements they think they are lacking are already lying within them awaiting discovery and that this self-discovery can lead to an appreciation of what they share and an understanding of how they might cooperate rather than compete.

As we use the "Oz" metaphor, who or what might constitute the Wicked Witch of the East? For PA and PM, the Witch could be seen as an amalgam of: (1) the tenets of the conventional wisdom about how government ought to be structured and conducted and the role PA and PM have played in that process (as manifested in the writings of Luther Gulick and a succession of reorganization studies); (2) the demands of functionalist social science (behaviorism's persistent desire to mimic the hard sciences and the enthusiastic compliance by PA and PM scholars and practitioners in that desire); and (3) the particularistic needs of a succession of partisan political elites both to marginalize the role of PA/PM in governance and to use them for partisan purposes (e.g., the Roosevelt administration's need to preserve New Deal programs or the Clinton administration's use of the National Performance Review as a prophylactic against Republican charges that Clintonites love "big government").

What about the Wizard? In the original story he is a trickster, an illusionist who ballooned into Oz and created the Emerald City by requiring that all citizens wear green-colored glasses—to maintain better the illusion that the walls were encrusted with precious gems. Our Wizard may be seen as those reformers who are always quick to rush forward from the groves of academe or the ranks of practitioners with glittering promises to "fix" our "broken" government once and for all by means of administrative reform of one sort or another.

The Emerald City can be seen as the state of false consciousness that PA and PM sustain by wearing metaphorical green glasses, thereby maintaining certain comfortable illusions. Of course, we have borrowed the term "false consciousness" from Karl Marx, who used it in reference to the inability of a social class to perceive its "real" interests or its role in society due to mental blinders concealing its exploitation by other classes. When we use the term, we refer to an ontological stance based on an economic rationality that does not allow us to recognize the extent to which we are used by partisan actors for their advantage. We believe that both PA and PM suffer from such a false consciousness—they fail to see that by defining their roles as "just management," they enable partisan elites to use them as scapegoats. In this, they and the nation-state are ill-served.

If it is useful to conceive of the Witch and the Wizard in these ways, can PA and PM hope to gain anything more than an illusion of transformation from this journey? Or will they, like the travelers in Baum's tale, be forced to find the answers for and in themselves and in a more cooperative relationship across the artificial management/administration divide they have created? Will they be able to see beyond the illusions they have accepted and, in part, created, and break the constraining patterns to re-envision government and their appropriate roles in it?

Both public management and administration have primarily addressed the instrumental side of public organizational life, which, if words have any shared meaning, can fairly be called "management."[4] When they have concentrated on the lower level of public organizational life, means-ends calculations and instrumental rationality can fairly be said to be more prevalent and appropriate. It makes sense to speak of "management" in such a context, but for many scholars, public management has become the label of choice, regardless of context. Because they have sought to address different audiences (public administration primarily to career administrators and public management to top-level careerists and political appointees), the result has been to confound sensible definition of "management," and thus we find the terms "management," "administration," and "governance" used almost synonymously in both literatures.

Both public administration and public management have known that the phenomena they treat are not to be confined to the lower sector of organizational life. Public management, after all, has been forced to deal with the issue of power as a result of its focus on the top executive layer, where the political calculus assumes primacy. Moreover, public administration, whatever its many shortcomings, has always contained a significant, albeit a minority, faction that has insisted that the phenomena it addresses are part of something larger than management.[5] Neither public administration nor public management, however, have come to a clear understanding of what those phenomena really are or what their implications might be for theory and practice. By disassociating itself from public administration, public management runs the risk of making the same mistake as have many in public administration: ignoring the institutional context in which it inevitably operates—a web of instrumental *and political* rationality, where management, the subordinate part, serves to camouflage the primacy of political rationality, not just at the top but throughout the institution.

Setting aside the conceptual confusion that is currently prevalent in public management and has long been a feature of public administration (Noordegraaf 1995, 2), this chapter will distinguish between management and governance while at the same time showing their interrelatedness. We will go on to address what we think are two key responsibilities of governance that both public management and public administration have given too little attention—the evocation of citizenship and the evolution of institutions of governance.

We want to state clearly what lies beneath our metaphoric placement of public management and public administration in the land of Oz. We believe that both have been caught up in shortsighted, short-term "fixes"—that neither has been able to step outside the political and economic aspects of academia and the politics of running the government long enough to ask what purposes government should serve (Stokes 1994; Bozeman 1993; Newland 1994). We would argue that this reductionism—based on the premise that means can be separated from the ends they serve—is a poor foundation for the search for meaning in the action contexts of the public sector. Means and ends are always inextricably tangled—management, whether effective or not, does not take place for its own sake. Overlooking this is a critical flaw, in our view, for anyone who truly seeks answers to ontological questions. Government, at all levels including the managerial level, is constitutive (Cook 1992).[6] It requires a translation of thought into action undertaken in the name of all of us (the public) and thereby defines what or who we are.

We believe that government should exist for purposes that go beyond serving the needs of a power elite, distributing largesse as the vector sum of interest group pressures, or even as a corrective to market inadequacies. Government should exist as well, and perhaps primarily, to facilitate our efforts to develop ourselves as citizens both individually and as part of a collective life—in other words, to help make us capable of governing ourselves and being, as the U.S. Army's commercials say, all that we can be. At a minimum that would entail steering a course toward ends that benefit both the individual and the collective whole. Yet this implies that goals are of paramount importance in governance when in fact it is the course and the act of steering and rowing the course—the journey and, most important, the quality of the relationships involved in the journey—that matter the most.

There is nothing new in this view of government and governance. Indeed, it stretches back to Aristotle, who believed that humans reached the zenith of their potentialities in self-governance. It is in this spirit that we believe the terms "govern" and "governance" should come into play in a republic such as ours. Management, tied as it is to short-term, teleological instrumentality, is an essential but insufficient condition for such a human endeavor as governance. In contrast, governance demands the long-term view, focusing on relations that enable us to discover and define ourselves and the meaning of our lives. Governance requires us to envision what we might become, as citizens and as a nation, in order that our visions be realized (Evans 1997b).

Politics is a realm of obfuscation, illusion, and perceptual manipulation. PA and PM pay a dear price for being an organic part of that realm. In our metaphor, Oz is a land where scholars and practitioners involved in government reform get caught up in an illusion that good generic management practices constitute the sum total of the role civil servants can play in governing. We are led to believe, blinded by apparent "successes" of the past, that no other role is possible or legitimate. With alternate visions denied credibility, we are doomed to retrace the steps taken by our counterparts through history and to repeat their mistakes. Taking this metaphorical journey through Oz may reveal ways in which we can cast off the blinders and begin to see ourselves and our potentialities in a clear and unobstructed light. Re-envisioning government in terms of what may be possible is the first step toward making the vision real.

We invite you now to join us as we travel the Yellow Brick Road, retracing the journey through Oz once taken by Dorothy and her companions. Each of the original travelers has a tale to tell—one of significance for public administration and public management today. Who knows? We may develop some clearer ideas as to what "home" for PA and PM ought to be. We might even click the heels of the ruby slippers[7] and find ourselves restored to a more serendipitous conceptual setting for both PA and PM—one in which we can resolve our ontological quest by defining a legitimate role in the governance process, one that is equal to both the challenges our nation faces and the potential we in PA and PM bring to those challenges.

The Scarecrow's Quest: Theorizing, Not a Theory

The Scarecrow, Dorothy's first companion, decides to accompany her to the Emerald City to ask the Wizard for a brain. He has decided that as long as his head is stuffed with straw, he cannot count in the world. Dorothy neither agrees nor disagrees with the Scarecrow's self-assessment; she is simply glad not to be alone on the road. However, as the journey proceeds, as difficulties begin to crop up, it is clearly the Scarecrow who comes up with solutions to the problems at hand—no simple feat for one without a brain.

Like the Scarecrow, PA and PM scholars in their search for a comprehensive theory or conceptual breakthrough often look outward to other disciplines. Although there is nothing wrong with drawing on other disciplines and fields, there are serious problems with the assumption that we can and must create or find *a* theory for such a multifaceted phenomenon as public administration/management—not a discipline but an interdisciplinary field with ties to a practice with aspects of a nascent profession. *Theorizing* about aspects of PA and PM—from a general ontological stance that rests on constitutional values and draws on philosophical pragmatism and democratic theory—will take us further. In searching for *a* theory, PA and PM scholars are pursuing something that we think is both unattainable and inappropriate. Furthermore, we impede theoretical development when we drastically discount or totally disregard the practical wisdom and ordinary working knowledge bases that arise from the practice.

Much has been made of the research diversity or lack of a solid theoretical orthodoxy in the studies of public administration and public management (Behn 1995; Rainey 1991, 1993). Rather than considering the lack of *a* theory to be problematic, we would suggest that such a lack may, in fact, prove beneficial if the goal of our research is arriving at a better understanding of the practice of governance and its relationship to the practice of citizenship in the United States. Bozeman (1993), in his attempt to define PM better, differentiates among three types of public management knowledge: theory-seeking knowledge built from empirical or conceptual work; wisdom knowledge, which he characterizes as "theoretical, craftlike, descriptive, or personalistic"; and "ordinary knowledge," which is informal, intuitive, uncredentialed, and direct (29). He identifies the pervasiveness of what he describes as ordinary knowledge as a significant barrier to a creditably integrated and certified knowledge standard for the field. As he sees it, the problem with the inclusive nature and diversity of public management research is that it resists the establishment of an agreed-upon truth test—and that validity, associated with ordinary knowledge and wisdom knowledge and with applied or practice-related research, is often incompatible with the credibility achieved by the results of more rigorous, empirical work.

Bozeman's concern is that theorizing about PM, if it does not establish a credo of its own with regard to standards for theory-building knowledge, may well end up a collection of new "proverbs of public management" (Bozeman 1993, 37). He is concerned that premature prescription may reduce otherwise likely elements of theory to the level of mere "wisdom." The community of researchers and scholars, he believes, must retain social control of the research agenda and of its knowledge output, lest practitioners limit the public management project to the production of ordinary knowledge (39). This concern has merit if one's goal is the building and protection of disciplinary walls (with the inevitable outcome that practitioners are excluded except as objects of study).

Because we see ours as a field of scholarly inquiry in support of a professional practice, not as an academic discipline, we take exception to the intensity and direction of some of Bozeman's concerns, specifically about the usefulness of wisdom and ordinary knowledge. Yet he has acknowledged that "employing a fuzzy definition of the term *theory*" may be the best way to maintain a healthy and creative relationship between theory and practice (39). Although it has both respectability and stature, empirical and conceptual knowledge traditionally associated with the scientific method has been difficult to achieve in any of the social sciences. The quest for the level of certainty rightly or wrongly attributed to such knowledge not only has exhausted our resources but also has too often come up empty, as might be expected when the subject is individual or collective human behavior. Although it is not generalizable to the same extent as the tenets of such "science," anecdotal and particularistic practitioner lore has general value in giving direction to our theorizing and in the sense that it reflects back to those working in the field that the reality they perceive in their daily activities is not an aberration but rather a shared and therefore meaningful experience (Schmidt 1993; Hummel 1991). In addition, this knowledge derived from intimate contact with the processes and people one "manages" may be the only available information on which to base judgments. Intuition and feeling may be impossible to describe or teach, but they form the basis for much organizational and political decision making.[8]

Rather than deplore this state of affairs, we want to point out its advantages for public administration and for public management. Ordinary knowledge arises from the context of the work itself. Much like Giddens's (1987) "ordinary talk," the conversation that takes place in—and the narratives arising from—the workplace shape and define the meaning of events. Unlike their more "scientific" counterparts, these narratives change and evolve in the act of telling and listening—they are not frozen like texts or other cultural artifacts to which one cannot immediately respond. As Giddens describes it, "Meaning and reference are ordinarily closely combined in talk. . . . Because it is carried on and organized within practical contexts of action . . . meaning is sustained through the constant connecting of talk with the modalities of day-to-day experience" (219). Ordinary knowledge, therefore, is the product of interaction within the totality of its occasioning situations—a conversation that includes all relevant information, not merely "the facts" as derived by standard methods of science and one that not only allows but also requires reflexivity.

John Dewey's philosophical pragmatism provides us with a context for accepting the validity of ordinary knowledge to underpin theorizing about public management. Although never denying the importance of empirical methods, Dewey (1958) encouraged us to see knowing as an activity that enables action, not as an end state. Dewey believed that philosophy should not remain in intellectual isolation from the common activities of humankind but rather that it could have value only in service of such activities. Dewey denied the privilege of absolute foundations and the value of knowledge as an end state. Knowing, in temporary and partial stages, rather than frozen and absolute knowledge, permits the evolution of human thought and the development of coherent human activity.

The human or social sciences have consistently sought the certainty perceived to exist in the natural or physical sciences. They have sought a theory that would help us explain or understand the "Truth," so it is understandable that we sometimes feel uncomfortable with ordinary knowledge, accumulated wisdom, or theorizing as a basis for or result from our work. The world of human endeavor, however, is an uncertain and contingent world, and even the physical sciences have a hard time these days in pinning down what constitutes foundational reality. For example, no matter how solid and fixed the physical world appears to be, quantum theorists tell us that at the elemental level of the atom matter and energy are merely two aspects of the same entity, showing one aspect over the other as a function of probability and of the type of measurement. At the most fundamental level, then, all that we see and touch, what we ourselves are, is "a pregnant void—stable patterns of probability striving to connect with other patterns of probability" (Kofman and Senge 1993, 14). Although this vision of physical reality flies in the face of our commonsense observations, we must acknowledge along with today's hard sciences that uncertainty is the condition within which we must operate. Moreover, theorizing, without searching for *a* theory, may be the best guide we can have for our actions within that matrix of uncertainty.

The Scarecrow's new brains, as provided by the Wizard, were a mixture of wheat bran and sharp pins—not real brains at all. Nothing had really changed except the Scarecrow's perception of himself. Appreciation of the practical wisdom of our practitioners—accepting theorizing rather than insisting on finding *a* theory—may help us as we face social and economic uncertainty, once we acknowledge that we cannot establish, for all time, the "one right way" to think about the phenomena that are the purview of public administration and public management. We have to face up to our inability to "get it right" for once and for all times (Stivers 1996).

If I Only Had a Heart: Individualism and Community

The second companion, the Tin Woodsman, is found by Dorothy and the Scarecrow rusted into immobility. When properly cleaned and oiled, he tells his new friends how he came to be transformed from a human forester to his present state. Although he joins the travelers to request a heart, stating that he misses being able to feel emotion, it is the Tin Woodsman who becomes teary-eyed at the thought of accidentally killing an ant on the road. Although denying the feelings that he has, he asserts that once he has a heart he can rejoin human society as a participant in all of its aspects.

From the outset, American public administration saw itself as working closely with citizens to reform government. The PA program at Syracuse University was founded as the Maxwell School of *Citizenship* and Public Affairs and has inscribed on its walls the uplifting rhetoric of the oath of the Athenian citizen. These early efforts, however, came to emphasize efficiency and economy—the development of "scientific" expertise—and moved away from evoking the potential of citizens. The lack our Tin Woodsman feels is the lack of connection that has resulted from the separation of public administrators and managers from the rest of our society—our abandonment of commitment to associational and institutional life.

We conceive of institutions in two ways—as more or less intentional social constructs or organizations and as broadly based constitutive elements of the social order such as the family. In both of these conceptions of "institution," we can find promise and pathology. The promise lies in the government institution as a carrier of tradition, in adopting an "agential perspective"—a public space where primacy is given to discovering the ever-changing public interest (Wamsley 1990) and a locus for the construction of meaningful interaction between the public servant and the citizen (Stivers 1990). The pathology can be identified with the unfortunate adoption of instrumental means as ends in themselves, making citizens objects of manipulation and allowing the practices of governance and citizenship to wither away from an integral position in daily living to an almost quaint, but nonetheless passé, occupation for the few.[9]

However tightly we would perhaps like to hold to the notion that we can separate facts—or administrative actions—from the values—political and moral judgments—that they purport to serve, we must acknowledge that such separation is impossible. In light of this difficulty, we can see that management, as a set of skills and competencies, is easier to understand and explicate than is the complex world of governance, where politics clouds the view. The linkage between ends and means is, however, irreducible, as can be demonstrated by Harmon's (1995) treatment of this issue in the context of administrative responsibility. Building on MacIntyre's (1984) discussion of practices, he argues two connections between the two: "First, . . . a means, including the factual knowledge relevant to its exercise, has an inescapably moral component because it would not exist except for the presence of ends or values in whose service it is employed. Second, and conversely, ends served by practices are transformed by the practices themselves. And because practice is necessarily a social activity, the ends in whose service a particular practice is engaged are in themselves social products, which therefore can be judged only in terms of the social context within which they are produced" (195). And, imperfect though they may be, our institutions of government provide the sociopolitical context within which both the ends and means of government are generated and wherein they are constantly being iteratively renegotiated.

The study of the institutional influences on the development of our culture are many and varied. Selznick (1957) delineated the substantive difference between the organization—as an instrumental entity—and an institution—where value and meaning are distilled and preserved—largely through the auspices of vital executive leadership. He also recognized the interdependence of the institution and the larger environment of which it is a part. It is largely from this early work of Selznick that the organic metaphor of organization arises and to which the understanding of the institution as constitutive can be traced.

Douglas (1986) points out that institutions confer identity; they classify and bound the world; and they act as repositories for selected memory and choose to forget those elements that no longer resonate with the dominant themes of society. They are capable, in other words, of mediating the emergence of collective meaning in daily situations for their members or participants within the context of tradition.

Giddens (1984) sheds considerable light on the interrelatedness of individual human actors and the institutional contexts in which they act. He argues that, instead of viewing structure as a rigid, external limit on human agency, one should see it both as a product of the recursive activities of situated actors and as the medium within which and from which those actors make meaningful action. "Structure is not to be equated with constraint but is always both constraining and enabling" (25).

Sullivan (1995) underscores the message first delivered by Tocqueville—that associational life in America, which is vital to the maintenance of democracy—is supported by an institutional order that acts as a school of civic virtue. As Sullivan puts it, it was "the institutional order, the patterns of normative, sanctioned interaction themselves, which worked through daily life to shape the imagination and character of the citizens" (173). It is the mutually creative, enabling relationship between the individual and the institution that, in the case of government, serves to shape and refine the practices of both governance and citizenship.

Even from our avowedly institutionalist stance, we recognize the importance in American political culture of the ethos of individualism. What we decry is the exaggerated notion that sees that person as an atomistic and isolated individual whose relationship with others is confined to competition for and exchange of scarce resources. The calculus of the market and the erosion of citizen practices and associational life have brought us to this extreme—the naked self unconnected with community except through a contract delineating rights. Radical individualism, "with its myths of solitary beatitude (godliness), has persistently underrated the human need for association, community, and species identification" (Barber 1984, 112). We are inescapably social beings—we are defined by, as well as defining agents of, our society.

We generally must accept that the individual in both the modern and the postmodern world cannot survive alone; like the Tin Woodsman, the individual rusts into immobility in isolation. Since the closing of the frontier at the end of the last century, the opportunity to live the largely mythological American life of splendidly isolated individualism began to disappear. By holding onto that myth too long we have foregone a coherent sense of self in relation to new frontiers of opportunity. Today's interconnected life—where specialization in labor has made it impossible for us to supply all of our own needs—precludes the actuality of the individual in the classic sense and, worse, connects the notion of individualism to corporate and personal profit and wealth. Our exaggerated sense of privacy and our geographical mobility have left us little by way of community life in the social or political sense. Our life has become corporate life, and this corporate life works in ways that deny our full intellectual and creative capacity. We find ourselves, therefore, both incapable of sustaining a healthy individualism and bereft of the comfort of interconnected community (Evans 1997a).

John Dewey (1954, 1988, 1991) argued that the individual self arises out of his or her community. The community, associations, and "publics" within which people live make possible the individual's realization of his or her capacities and capabilities. As more and more of Americans' associational life is lived inside corporate organizations, as work has ceased to be a self-directed, creative endeavor, the individual increasingly has lost touch with the human context that makes one whole. Dewey recognized as early as the 1920s that Americans are "lost individuals"—that we individually have become both economically and politically disempowered.[10] Our rootlessness, although identified by many as the problem, is really the presenting symptom of the problem—an artificial opposition of the individual and society (Campbell 1995, 160–61). Individuals will always be, Dewey (1988) recognized, at the center of American life, "but what an individual actually *is* in his life-experience depends upon the nature and movement of associational life" (275).

What we call society is nothing but the system of relationships of individuals to each other. Dewey (1988) saw these relations as "interactions not fixed molds. The particular interactions that compose a human society include the give and take of participation, of a sharing that increases, that expands and deepens, the capacity and significance of the interacting factors" (82). If what we call an institution is not composed of such dynamic interactions, it is a "fossil of some past society" (83). Throughout his scholarly life, in many contexts ranging from education to technology to politics, Dewey understood that the social group, and only the social group, provided people a chance to develop individuality. As Campbell (1995) summarizes, "Once we can recognize the importance of developing a social place and overcome the attempt to divorce the individual from society, we can come to see the individual as *being in process,* as developing in the course of social interaction and by means of society's facilities" (164).

In this age of technological sophistication and specialized expertise, the gap between democratic government and its citizens has grown exponentially. This has created both an inarticulate yearning for union and the kind of distrust and disdain for government that has undercut government's ability to serve any ends effectively. This yearning, like the Tin Woodsman's, "is real and must be answered responsibly by nourishing, nontoxic forms of democratic community if it is not to be answered by deformation of the human spirit" (Barber 1984, 112).

Some such sense of community becomes necessary when situations arise affecting all of us and we disagree about the means by which to confront them. Our individual preferences will not suffice to answer the question such a situation poses. This area where a collective *"we"* rather than an individual *"I"* must prevail is the realm of politics. As Barber (1984) defines it, "The need for politics arises when some action of public consequence becomes necessary and when men must thus make a public choice that is reasonable in the face of conflict despite the absence of an independent ground of judgment" (122). Without a community of deliberative democracy (Gutmann and Thompson, 1996), such collective decisions become problematic; without institutions, the maintenance of any sense of community becomes impossible.

We have addressed the need to attend to the political and thus the institutional side of public management. We must, however, acknowledge the problematic character of politics as it is presently played out in the American system and perhaps in other democracies as well (Greider 1992). Increasingly, policy is formulated, implemented, and adjudicated at the nexus between citizens (individuals and groups) and administrative institutions rather than being worked out through the channels of voters, parties, and elected officials. In the American system, the partisan struggle for power has become increasingly ideological and increasingly distant from the citizen-administration nexus and from the networks and policy subsystems where so much public policy evolves. It may be that, as our party system declines in its ability to involve citizens and articulate real choices, we need to conceive of a politics that is appropriate for the citizen-administrator nexus.

Charles Taylor (1995) offers a possible visualization of such a politics, one that situates dialogue about the common good outside of our formal politics—which have become so pathological—in a public sphere where "debate breaks out, and continues, involving in principle everybody, and this is perfectly legitimate" (192). In the best sense of institutional tradition, such conflict is appropriate because a living tradition, according to MacIntyre (1984), "is an historically extended, socially embodied argument, and an argument precisely in part about the goods which constitute that tradition" (222). This meaningful argument is what we have lost. Taylor's (1995) public sphere contrasts with formal politics in that it is "constituted by nothing outside of the common action we carry out in it: coming to a common mind, where possible, through the exchange of ideas" (194). We could create a space for deliberation—while preserving constitutional tradition—which occurs "without the mediation of the political sphere (the struggle for office), in a discourse of reason outside power, which nevertheless is normative for power" (192–93). In such a space, illuminated by openness, we may respect each other as moral actors and grant each other legitimacy even when we disagree on the substance of each other's positions (Gutmann and Thompson 1996).

What Baum's Tin Woodsman sought was an ability to feel that was already firmly embedded within him. The Wizard's implantation of a silk heart filled with sawdust did nothing to increase his sensitivity and tolerance—his love for his fellow creatures. Those were inherent qualities that he already possessed but did not recognize. Similarly, we in PA and PM have the concepts, the skills, and the feelings necessary to evoke civic virtue and public happiness[11]—to improve the relationships among people and between the people and their government. We can—and sometimes even manage to—use those skills in the course of our professional practices. What we think we need from the Wizard is permission to act on our feelings. Then those skills can blossom, and we can evoke those relationships.

The Courage to Resist: Public Administration's Complicity in Reform

The Cowardly Lion, although he had a terrifying roar, confessed to a lack of courage when confronted with the dangers of our uncertain world. He joined the travelers in order to ask the Wizard for the courage commensurate with his traditional role—as king of the beasts. Although he confessed his fear, when the companions were confronted with danger, it was the Lion who stood between that danger and his weaker friends.

Like the Cowardly Lion, we in public management and public administration have all too often taken the path of least resistance when faced with political challenges to the legitimacy of our involvement in policy making. We have readily and meekly fallen in with simplistic functionalist ideas about government structure and process. Although as academicians we deride the early principle of administration separate from politics, we continue, both as academicians and as practitioners, to write and act as though they are separable.[12] We must take on the difficult task of educating ourselves and others to understand that politics, administration, and management are all integral parts of the governance process. This means that all have legitimate and interwoven, but still distinguishable, roles in governance.

We have all too often stepped back from claiming an appropriate role in governance, even when we knew that means and ends, facts and values, and administration and politics cannot be disentangled. We have also failed to develop a distinctive role *based on* their inextricable entanglement. Despite fear and anxiety and despite the fact that America's political culture currently denies our legitimacy in governance, we, as scholars and practitioners, need to believe in that legitimacy and stand up for our role in governing, for our professional standards, and for the citizens who depend on us.

Our confusion between management and governance is deeply embedded in our conventional wisdom, which places the president (or governor or strong mayor) in the role of corporate chief executive officer and which convinces us that a hierarchical decision-making and implementation structure is compatible with our constitutional form of government (Lane and Wamsley n.d.). This has served, to our detriment as academics, to differentiate the term "practice" from all of our other conceptualizations of public management or the public service. By relying on a definition of responsibility or accountability that measures performance of government agencies exclusively in terms of rationalist efficiency and effectiveness and by reifying techniques, procedures and measurement, we have lost our understanding of "practice," as Harmon (1995) uses the term. In addition, this leads us to see institutions of governance in ways that fail to differentiate them from social constructs of the market.

Harmon (1995) defines governance as a practice that enables a dialogue within which the community "cooperatively discover[s] what sorts of practices are worth engaging in" (195)—codetermines policy objectives and codetermines the means by which to reach them. The public servant, he goes on to say, should "be alert to the legal and political constraints on those practices; . . . make available relevant political knowledge to those engaged in practices; and, perhaps most important of all, . . . facilitate practice itself. That [multidimensional] role, which is both authoritative *and* enabling, pertains to public servants' relations with citizens who seek or require aid in redefining their life projects (and thus, their practices) as well as to relations with colleagues in creating and sustaining worthwhile organizational practices" (195). In this view, the institutional support of some practices and not others acts as a bridge connecting individual self-development with the quest for the collective good.

This relationship between individual self-development and collective good is the key to understanding active citizenship. Public administration has had great difficulty with the concept of citizenship and how it should relate to it, and public management has simply dealt with it by defining the citizen as a customer. The practices that are constitutive of organizational life, however, are carried on within a broader system of the evolving political and social community where meaning is collectively construed, and institutions of governance provide the meeting place wherein this activity is conducted.

March and Olsen (1995) see democratic governance as faith that meaningful dialogue can and does take place in the political and institutional life of the polity. Building on Smircich and Morgan (1982), they argue that "democratic governance involves managing those contests over meaning and building institutions that allow citizens to create, sustain, and change interpretations of reality in an ambiguous and uncertain world" (180). This, they add, makes it possible for citizens and officials to "construct a moral account of the good society, recognize appropriate tasks, ends, and forms of governance, and develop confidence in their mutual good spirit and capabilities for reason" (180–81). What is constructed is an environment where public administration and public management—where public service—can work to "evoke . . . human potential" and even "to occasionally transcend, renew, or recreate ourselves individually and collectively in ways that maintain democracy while fostering human development and fulfillment" (Wamsley 1996, 369). *Thus, governance, while including management, goes beyond management into the realm of a politics whose principal objective is the collective construction of meaning and value.*

Many students of both public administration and public and private management, in an attempt to eradicate partisanship, have tried to ignore politics. Perhaps because of its complexity and recondite nature, politics, as manifested in organizations and institutions, has eluded the functionalist lens of inquiry. Yet, if March and Olsen (1989) are right and there is no "invisible hand" adjusting our individual political preferences into something akin to the "public interest," we cannot afford to ignore the political consequences of institutions as extraneous to or as something we can conceptually exclude from our management of public organizations. We have to study and understand this troublesome territory. We have alluded to its intrusion into the study of management many times—describing management as the "science of muddling through" and as a process of "groping along" (Lindblom 1992; Behn 1988).

Seemingly, then, most of us recognize politics as the fox in the chicken coop of public policy administration, yet we continue to try to exclude it conceptually, and we fervently wish it would change its diet. As scholars and practitioners we acknowledge the presence of the fox but then proceed to write and act as though the fox is, and will remain, outside with only occasional if devastating incursions while we focus on our study of the chickens. Like the Cowardly Lion, we have not shown the courage to include politics fully in our study and, thereby, to face the ontological question of our purposes. We have learned a great deal about the routines and behaviors of the chickens in our bounded set, but not enough about foxes and how they affect and constrain the possibilities the chickens face or, perhaps of more importance, what the ends of farming (our practice of governance) should be.

Still, perhaps we can—and ought to try to—bring the fox more fully under our analytic lens. We should study not just the chickens, the farm, and the barnyard but the whole system that includes, as well, the habitat of the fox.

Recognizing better the interconnectedness of this ecology may provide the insight we need to bring politics, administration, and management into a harmony, or a state of dynamic tension that supports the life practices of citizens. Harmon (1995) argues that seeing politics only as an external control on administration damages the delicate relationship in this ecology by creating a barrier between citizens and public servants. He proposes, and we agree, that "if, in addition to its [currently prevailing] authoritative role in defining social constraints [for public servants], politics [which, in Harmon's conception, includes administration] were conceived as *the public process for generating knowledge enabling citizens to assess the risks and opportunities confronting them,* then it would likely seem far less controlling" (196, emphasis added) and would also provide for an appropriate use of policy analysis.

March and Olsen (1989) remind us as well that if politics can be seen as "building community and a sense of common identity within which decisions are made, [then] we [would] welcome the role of political institutions as agents in the construction of political interests and beliefs. . . . They [would be] sources of vitality in political life and coherence in political identity" (165). Instead, we all too often perceive politics and political institutions as the enemy to our rational processes of administration and view their effect on the operation of our public organizations as an unpleasant, if necessary, evil. However much we may fear and distrust political impingements on administration, we cannot build a fox-proof chicken coop. We need to find the courage inside ourselves and seek ways through institutions and practices to accept and value the presence of the fox and to achieve a meaningful and healthy balance within the wider system that encompasses not only chickens but also foxes.[13]

The Emerald City, Wherein the Wizard Rules

On being stranded in Oz, the man who assumed the role of the Wizard conned the local residents into believing him to be possessed of great powers of magic. He encouraged the citizens to rest their hopes in his powers of arcane expertise (much as have successive waves of government reformers since the Progressive Era). *To maintain the illusion of power and riches, he required that all persons within the city wear green-tinted glasses* (perhaps the lenses of "neutral competence") *so that what was in reality plain would appear glorious. The Wizard then surrounded himself with guards and was seldom seen again. His reputation of great power kept the idly curious away and only the determination of Dorothy and her companions gained them access. Each supplicant saw the Wizard alone. To each, the Wizard presented a different appearance—to one, a giant head* (the rigor of science, perhaps?); *to the next, a lovely lady* (representing the rewards of connection and relationship?); *then, a terrible beast* (the political fox?); *and finally, a ball of fire* (to frighten us, as Dorothy, away from the search for home?).

When faced with the prospect of dealing with the companions' requests, the Wizard imposed a condition—contain and destroy the Wicked Witch of the West. The Wizard, it may be recalled, wasn't really a powerful magician, he was merely an illusionist. He feared that one day the Witch would expose him for the humbug he was, revealing that the Emerald City was a fraud—a hollow capital for a hollow empire. The structure built by the Wizard could only be beautiful to those whose vision was distorted. In much the same way, our various iterations of government reform have been made to seem beautiful by the "wizards" working in PA and PM. If we look at our institutions of government without our "shades," what will we see?

The historic direction of administrative reform in the United States has consistently been toward greater instrumental rationality, grounded in an organizational ethos, and premised on the assumption (myth?) that we could keep politics out of the administrative process. It has taken public administration decades, but at last there is a sizable body of literature that challenges these premises and recognizes that government reorganization efforts are a partisan political game that uses a concern for good management only as camouflage (Wamsley and Dudley n.d.).

It has often been remarked in the years following Watergate that government—read that "bureaucracy"—has somehow failed, has grown too large, has become too entangled with special interests, is inefficient, is unresponsive, has taken on a life of its own, cannot be trusted, or impedes political and democratic process. Every important political campaign since Nixon's time has had as a theme—major or minor—the need to "tame the beast." Presidents and Congresses, each with their own spin, have taken steps to reform, to control, to reorganize, and to reinvent government. The message that political actors have absorbed, and have interpreted as originating from citizens, is that government—read that "bureaucracy"—must be "gotten off the backs" of the citizens. The issue is nebulous and purposely vague in definition. The characterization, largely inaccurate and oversimplified, has, therefore, proven recalcitrant, with more or different "reform" efforts required at each subsequent iteration. The ritual flagellation of this problem come election time has had two outcomes that, although seemingly contradictory, have produced similar deleterious effects. In the minds of some citizens and political elites, it seems to have reinforced the belief that there was, or should be, a politics–administration dichotomy. In the minds of these persons, blame for perceived or real government ineffectiveness must be borne by administrative agencies, and elected officials are absolved of responsibility or culpability. For other citizens and political elites, the constant refrain that "government is broke" has tarred both elected and nonelected officials with the same brush and has added significantly to the decline in the legitimacy of government in general.

The Clinton administration's movement to "reinvent" government, although different in some detail from reform efforts of the past, has enlisted the energy of many scholars identified with public management. Although there have been numerous positive accomplishments, the "reinvention" effort has ignored the lessons learned in streams of discourse within public administration and continued in the traditional quest for greater efficiency, economy, and control of process. These results are to be achieved by "slimming down" administrative agencies, reducing procedural "red tape," and, whenever possible, privatizing government services.

Whatever positive results may stem from current "reinvention" efforts, past reform efforts lead us to contend that ignoring the partisan game aspects of reinvention leaves public management vulnerable to partisan denigration and manipulation. We would argue that "reinvention," like reorganization and other reform efforts, leaves us as always with a government that resembles the Emerald City—it is beautiful only when viewed through colored glasses. Of more importance, the reinvention project's pursuit of efficiency, economy, and effectiveness and the further rationalization of public institutions is precisely the wrong direction for us to go in light of the role played by public institutions in enabling the practices of governance and citizenship. Seeing institutions (organizations) in such a purely instrumental light acts to erode the civic character and customs necessary for a flourishing democratic constitutional republic—and it undercuts the institutional support that can enable the personal development of citizens and facilitate their life projects—the appropriate ends of democratic governance.

As Sullivan (1995) describes them, institutions "are normative patterns that define purposes and practices, patterns embedded in and sanctioned by customs and law. They are patterns of social relationship that structure experience and shape character by assigning responsibility, demanding accountability, and providing the standards in terms of which each individual takes stock of his or her own life" (175). Institutions are not simply the mechanisms that permit "efficient political coalition-building and exchange" (March and Olsen 1995, 44). Rather, they provide the context for governance involving the development of identities, of capabilities, of meaningful accounts, and of adaptation of the polity (March and Olsen 1995, 45–46). They provide, in other words, the infrastructure that supports our common life in a democratic society.

If "reinvention" of government succeeds in its stated purposes, many positive outcomes may be produced—reduced cost of service provision, less waste, fewer public employees, an increased "simplicity" in the structure of the federal bureaucracy—but these will happen only at a price. Although management processes may be reduced, in many cases, to contract management, other purposes of government agencies will no longer be served. Blinded by false consciousness, we may fail to see that reinventing leaves us with many of the same problems but with fewer resources for dealing with them. Improved economy notwithstanding, we will have to pay dearly for reinvention as it diminishes the capacity of government institutions to support the practices of democracy and to enhance the life opportunities of citizens. Moreover, once the institutional base has been damaged or destroyed, the cost of rebuilding it will be dear indeed (Lane and Wolf 1990).

As we see it, PA and PM, by sustaining once again the organizational/ managerial ethos, will only delay the awareness of the need for institutionalism. The organizational/managerial ethos of efficiency and economy sees no place for public administrators or managers to be part of the policy process. As they are closed out of the policy-making loop, public servants become even *less* accountable for actual results. They become answerable principally for the outward trappings of "effective" management of programs (Harmon 1995, 186). As services are increasingly delivered by third parties and as citizens are regarded as customers, even this measure of accountability is diffused.

If the answer to our need for governance is not reinvention, and if it may possibly be found in institutionalism and an enhanced sense of community, what steps can we take without sacrificing either individual freedom or our constitutional form of government? Barber (1984) offers this prescription: "Community grows out of participation and at the same time makes participation possible; civic activity educates individuals how to think publicly as citizens even as citizenship informs civic activity with the required sense of publicness and justice. Politics becomes its own university, citizenship its own training, and participation its own tutor. Freedom is what comes out of this process, not what goes into it" (152). What he describes is a "politics of amateurs" that denies the privilege of the Wizard's "expertise" and has no place for green glasses. Public administrators and managers would find themselves in the position of enabling these amateurs in their practice of citizenship rather than of deciding how to provide what people need—a new role, but perhaps one that reduces the paradoxical nature of our government as we find it today.

Dorothy's Journey Home

The Wicked Witch is dead, and Dorothy's companions have found their brains, heart, and courage, but Dorothy is still far from Kansas. The Wizard plans to take her home in his hot-air balloon, but he accidentally takes off without her. The Scarecrow (now the ruler of the Emerald City), the Tin Woodsman (who has been adopted by the Witch's former slaves as their leader), and the Cowardly Lion (now truly the king of beasts) accompany Dorothy across Oz to find Glinda, the Good Witch of the South, in a last ditch effort to find home. Like the others, Dorothy already possesses the means to get home—the magic slippers she has worn since the beginning of her adventure have the power to transport her back to Kansas. She only needed the guidance and reassurance of a trusted colleague to be able to use them. Home is just three clicks of her heels away. The vision of community and institutional life discussed above is also within the grasp of PA and PM. It cannot be merely wished for, but must instead be worked for. First and foremost, however, we must be able to arrive at some level of agreement about what that vision entails. Can we see Kansas yet?

Our descriptions of institutions and governance, informed as they are by many voices, including that of communitarian thought and a vigorous renaissance in democratic theory, can be viewed as overly optimistic about the possibility for reclaiming practices through re-envisioning, not reinventing, government. We can only agree that our vision of the polity will be difficult to achieve—we are not sure we have the equivalent of the ruby slippers. The organizational/managerial ethos is deeply ingrained, and giving life to the metaphors of institution and community described above will require considerable courage, effort, and ingenuity—those characteristics that enabled Dorothy to dispose of the Wicked Witch. We believe, however, that the rewards inherent in enhancing the practices of citizenship and constitutional governance would compensate us for that effort and that the penalties for neglecting these practices may be higher than any of us would be willing to pay. We believe as well that the ability to realize these visions lies in an unrecognized strength within us.

Enriching our public space by providing support for our institutions—bringing reform that moves them toward dialogue and the creation of shared meaning—is an investment for our common future. Further marginalizing and rationalizing our institutions increases the fragmentation of our society and makes discourse leading to common action even less likely. For our society to sustain itself over time in a democratic, constitutional republic, we must make such investments in our civic infrastructure.

The hard truth is that the question of the legitimate role for public administration and public management in our constitutional democracy simply cannot be effectively addressed within the organizational/managerial ethos nor within the rationalist discourse in which we currently engage. To renew our democratic life, we must, as Sullivan (1995) admonishes us, "tak[e] responsibility for the well-being of our institutional structure" (180). By recognizing that our problems in government do not stem from a lack of rational action in our administrative agencies—and, rather, that they are already too rational—we will have taken a first step toward a solution that builds community. When we can see PA and PM as aspects of organizational life that facilitate and evoke—not direct or control—our public life, we will have taken the next step.

In the motion picture version of this story, Auntie Em's farm in Kansas—Dorothy's home—was depicted in black and white. The vivid Technicolor treatment of the dreamlike fantasy of Oz made a stunning contrast to the gray drabness and shadows associated with life in the "real world." This technique reinforced the fairy tale quality of the story, but it accomplished something else as well. The viewer is subtly reminded that the illusion can be more aesthetically pleasing than everyday reality. Its attractive quality can distract us from our proper purposes. Dorothy was sure she wanted to go home—Kansas represented the solid security of family, love, and community—and the illusion, however colorful and full of excitement, could not hold her back.

Reaching some agreement on what "Kansas" means for us requires that we cut through our conceptual confusion and assign administration and management—based on the ethos of efficiency—their appropriate role in governance—a role that continues to be significant in, but no longer dominates, our thinking. Taking off the glasses of false consciousness may initially disappoint us as the glittering glamour of the Emerald City is temporarily reduced, but a government of plain walls built on authentic relationships will be stronger and will suit our republic better than the illusion of emeralds ever did. If we can rid ourselves of the Wicked Witch, bypass the quackery of the Wizard, accept the value of theorizing and practical wisdom, recognize our power to evoke the strengths of all citizens and build community, and have the courage to claim an appropriate role in governing, we will not need to remain in Oz to enjoy exciting challenges and colorful scenery—we will be able to bring the vitality represented by the Technicolor transformation to our real-life Kansas through our own powers.

Notes

1. Anyone who looks at a *McGuffey Reader* from 1900 would probably agree. See Sullivan (1996, 134–40) for the story of the death by drowning of the boy who stopped to play at the pond on the way to school; the book also contains other moral warnings for youngsters.

2. This and all following paraphrases of parts of *The Wizard of Oz* are taken from Baum (1985). Descriptions of the journey through Oz as told by Baum are highlighted.

3. The reader should be advised at the outset that this chapter is directed both at those scholars in the public administration tradition and at those who identify with the stream of discourse called "public management." Despite the differences between these streams of discourse, we believe they have remarkably similar characteristics and problems. When we mention both (we designate them as PA and PM simply because PA historically preceded PM) we mean to refer to both. When we speak to one, but not to the other, it will be because we mean to refer specifically to that one and not to both.

4. Theories of management, both public and private, rest solidly on the conceptions of organization found in Taylor (1915), echoed in the writings of Gulick and Urwick (1937), and reinforced by Herbert Simon (1976). Organizations, and the management processes required to maintain them, are conceptualized as purposive, contractual, and infused with an instrumental calculus.

5. There has always been a significant but minority faction of public administration that never lost sight of the fact that what we are about principally is governance, not merely management. Apparently, public management has not yet developed such an articulate faction, nor is it likely to. This stream of public administration thought, characterized by White and McSwain (1990) as "traditionalist," included such scholars as Appleby, Long, Waldo, Kaufmann, Redford, Sayre, and Allison, who recognized that the coherence and sense of stability provided by institutions of governance cannot be reduced to management technique.

6. From Lindblom (1992) through Wamsley and Zald (1973), Harmon and Mayer (1986), Behn (1988), and Lynn (1993, 1994), public administration and public management scholars have recognized factors other than development of or reliance on *a* theory that explains what happens in public organizations. This is not to say that there is not a dominant ontology or conventional wisdom among both scholars and practitioners of both PA and PM. There is, and it has been relatively unchanged for decades. This dominant ontology assumes that the primary aim of administration or management is to maximize economy, efficiency, and effectiveness.

7. Purists will note that in the book, Dorothy's slippers were silver, not ruby. We guess MGM decided to make this small change in detail to make them showier, taking advantage of the Technicolor transition between Kansas and Oz.

8. The progressive movement, however, is characterized by a sense of both "eliteness"—its membership was largely professional and well educated—and "xenophobia"—fears that the increasing immigrant population and its connection with machine politics had, and would continue to have, a negative effect on American political processes. Neither of these characteristics supports the "democratic" and "citizen" elements associated with reform.

9. For an example of this, see Wamsley (1969).

10. Our loss of nurturing community is what Tocqueville (1990) foresaw and feared when he described America's fascination with equality of condition and the negative im-

plications of that for individualism. His prescription was simple—cherish and nurture associational life. "The free institutions which the inhabitants of the United States possess, and the political rights of which they make so much use, remind every citizen, in a thousand ways, that he lives in society" (2: 105). The health of today's institutions is uncertain, however, and the questionable direction that our rights talk has taken us should bring us to realize that we need to take action to preserve or reinvigorate associational life—that this is one of the purposes of government lost in our rush to reinvent.

11. See Arendt (1977). Arendt describes "public happiness" as something like the satisfaction citizens derive from participating in self-government. "Americans knew that public freedom consisted in having a share in public business, and that the activities connected with this business by no means constituted a burden but gave those who discharged them in public a feeling of happiness that they could acquire nowhere else" (119).

12. This battle has been waged for more than a century. Because the United States lacks a parliamentary system where elected legislators take up administrative roles, Wilson (1887) and Goodnow (1900) saw this as a thorny problem—one that we have come to know as the politics-administration dichotomy. We think that PA and PM have utterly failed to give alternative legitimating role conceptions.

13. One example of an egregious need for PA and PM to seize the initiative is the urgent necessity of fostering a modicum of understanding and trust between career administrators and politically appointed executives.

References

Arendt, Hannah. 1977. *On Revolution.* New York: Penguin Books.

Barber, Benjamin. 1984. *Strong Democracy: Participatory Politics for a New Age.* Berkeley, Calif.: University of California Press.

Baum, L. Frank. 1985. *The Wizard of Oz.* New York: Rand McNally/Childrens Press Choice.

Behn, Robert D. 1988. "Management by Groping Along." *Journal of Policy Analysis and Management* 7 (fall): 643–63.

———. 1995. "The Big Questions of Public Management." *Public Administration Review* 55, no. 4: 313–24.

Bozeman, Barry. 1993. "Theory, 'Wisdom,' and the Character of Knowledge in Public Management: A Critical View of the Theory-Practice Linkage." In *Public Management: The State of the Art,* edited by Barry Bozeman. San Francisco: Jossey-Bass.

Campbell, James. 1995. *Understanding John Dewey: Nature and Cooperative Intelligence.* Chicago, Ill.: Open Court.

Cook, Brian J. 1992. "The Representative Function of Bureaucracy: Public Administration in Constitutive Perspective." *Administration and Society* 23, no. 4: 403–29.

Dewey, John. 1954. *The Public and Its Problems.* Denver, Colo.: Alan Swallow.

———. 1958. *Experience and Nature.* 2d ed. New York: Dover Publications.

———. 1988. *The Later Works, 1929–1930.* Vol. 5. Edited by Jo Ann Boydston. Carbondale, Ill.: Southern Illinois University Press.

———. 1991. *The Later Works, 1935–1937.* Vol. 11. Edited by Jo Ann Boydston. Carbondale, Ill.: Southern Illinois University Press.

Douglas, Mary. 1986. *How Institutions Think.* Syracuse, N.Y.: Syracuse University Press.

Evans, Karen G. 1997a. "Reclaiming John Dewey: Democracy, Inquiry, Pragmatism, and Public Management." Paper presented at the Fourth National Public Management Research Conference, the University of Georgia, Athens, Georgia.

———. 1997b. "Imagining Anticipatory Government: A Speculative Essay on Quantum Theory and Visualization." *Administrative Theory and Praxis* 19, no. 3: 355–67.

Giddens, Anthony. 1984. *The Constitution of Society: Outline of the Theory of Structuration.* Berkeley, Calif.: University of California Press.

———. 1987. "Structuralism, Post-Structuralism and the Production of Culture." In *Social Theory Today,* edited by Anthony Giddens and Jonathan H. Turner. Stanford, Calif.: Stanford University Press.

Goodnow, Frank J. 1900. *Politics and Administration: A Study in Government.* New York: Russell & Russell.

Greider, William. 1992. *Who Will Tell the People?* New York: Simon and Schuster.

Gulick, Luther, and Lyndall Urwick, eds. 1937. *Papers on the Science of Administration.* New York: Institute of Public Administration.

Gutmann, A., and D. Thompson. 1996. *Democracy and Disagreement.* Cambridge, Mass.: Harvard University Press, Belknap Press.

Harmon, Michael M. 1995. *Responsibility as Paradox: A Critique of Rational Discourse on Government.* Thousand Oaks, Calif.: Sage.

Harmon, Michael M., and Richard T. Mayer. 1986. *Organization Theory for Public Administration.* Boston: Little, Brown.

Hummel, Ralph P. 1991. "Stories Managers Tell: Why They Are As Valid as Science." *Public Administration Review* 51, no. 1: 31–41.

Kofman, Fred, and Peter M. Senge. 1993. "Communities of Commitment: The Heart of Learning Organizations." *Organizational Dynamics* 72, no. 2: 5–23.

Lakeoff, George, and Mark Johnson. 1980. *Metaphors We Live By.* Chicago: University of Chicago Press.

Lane, Larry M., and Gary L. Wamsley. n.d. "Gulick's Presidency: Promise and Consequences." *International Journal of Public Administration.* In press.

Lane, Larry M., and James F. Wolf. 1990. *The Human Resource Crisis in the Public Sector.* Westport, Conn.: Quorum.

Lindblom, Charles E. 1992. "The Science of 'Muddling Through.'" *Public Administration Review,* 1959. Reprint, *Classics of Public Administration,* edited by Jay M. Shafritz and Albert C. Hyde. 3d ed. Pacific Grove, Calif.: Brooks/Cole.

Littlefield, Henry M. 1964. "The Wizard of Oz: Parable on Populism." *American Quarterly* (spring): 48–58.

Lynn, Laurence E., Jr. 1993. "Policy Achievement as a Collective Good: A Strategic Perspective on Managing Social Programs." In *Public Management: The State of the Art,* edited by Barry Bozeman. San Francisco: Jossey-Bass.

———. 1994. "Public Management Research: The Triumph of Art over Science." *Journal of Policy Analysis and Management* 13, no. 2: 231–59.

MacIntyre, Alasdair. 1984. *After Virtue: A Study in Moral Theory.* 2d ed. Notre Dame, Ind.: University of Notre Dame Press.

March, James G., and Johan P. Olsen. 1989. *Rediscovering Institutions: The Organizational Basis of Politics.* New York: Free Press.

———. 1995. *Democratic Governance.* New York: Free Press.

Newland, Chester A. 1994. "A Field of Strangers in Search of a Discipline: Separatism of Public Management Research from Public Administration." *Public Administration Review* 54, no. 6: 486–88.

Noordegraaf, Mirko. 1995. "Public Humanagement: Public Management Approaches and the Managerial Behavior of Civil Servants." Paper presented at the Third National Public Management Research Conference, University of Kansas, Lawrence, Kansas.

Rainey, Hal G. 1991. *Managing in the Public Sector.* San Francisco: Jossey-Bass.

———. 1993. "Important Research Questions." In *Public Management: The State of the Art,* edited by Barry Bozeman. San Francisco: Jossey-Bass.

Schmidt, Mary R. 1993. "Grout: Alternative Kinds of Knowledge and Why They Are Ignored." *Public Administration Review* 53, no. 6: 525–30.

Selznick, Philip. 1957. *Leadership in Administration: A Sociological Interpretation.* Berkeley, Calif.: University of California Press.

Simon, Herbert A. 1976. *Administrative Behavior: A Study of Decision-Making Processes in Administrative Organization.* 3d rev. ed. New York: Free Press.

Smircich, Linda, and Gareth Morgan. 1982. "Leadership: The Management of Meaning." *Journal of Applied Behavioral Science* 10, no. 3: 257–73.

Stivers, Camilla M. 1990. "Active Citizenship and Public Administration." In *Refounding Public Administration,* by Gary L. Wamsley, Robert N. Bacher, Charles T. Goodsell, Philip S. Kronenberg, John A. Rohr, Camilla M. Stivers, Orion F. White, and James F. Wolf. Newbury Park, Calif.: Sage.

———. 1996. "Refusing to Get It Right: Citizenship, Difference, and the Refounding Project." In *Refounding Democratic Public Administration: Modern Paradoxes, Postmodern Challenges,* edited by Gary L. Wamsley and James F. Wolf. Thousand Oaks, Calif.: Sage.

Stokes, Donald E. 1994. "The Changing World of the Public Executive." Paper presented at the Conference on Public Affairs and Management in the Twenty-First Century, School of Public Affairs, Baruch College, City University of New York.

Sullivan, Mark. 1996. *Our Times: America at the Birth of the Twentieth Century,* edited by Dan Rather. New York: Scribner.

Sullivan, William M. 1995. "Institutions as the Infrastructure of Democracy." In *New Communitarian Thinking: Persons, Virtues, Institutions, and Communities,* edited by Amitai Etzioni. Charlottesville, Va.: University Press of Virginia.

Taylor, Charles. 1995. "Liberal Politics and the Public Sphere." In *New Communitarian Thinking: Persons, Virtues, Institutions, and Communities,* edited by Amitai Etzioni. Charlottesville, Va.: University Press of Virginia.

Taylor, Frederick W. 1915. *The Principles of Scientific Management.* New York: Harper and Brothers.

Tocqueville, Alexis de. 1990. *Democracy in America.* Vols. 1 and 2. New York: Vintage Classics.

Wamsley, Gary L. 1969. *Selective Service and a Changing America.* Columbus, Ohio: Charles E. Merrill.

———. 1990. "The Agency Perspective: Public Administrators as Agential Leaders." In *Refounding Public Administration,* by Gary L. Wamsley, Robert N. Backer, Charles T. Goodsell, Philip S. Kronenberg, John A. Rohr, Camilla M. Stivers, Orion F. White and James F. Wolf. Newbury Park, Calif.: Sage.

———. 1996. "A Public Philosophy and Ontological Disclosure as the Basis for Normatively Grounded Theorizing in Public Administration." In *Refounding Democratic Public Administration: Modern Paradoxes and Postmodern Challenges,* edited by Gary L. Wamsley and James F. Wolf. Thousand Oaks, Calif.: Sage.

Wamsley, Gary L., and Larkin S. Dudley. n.d. "Reorganization to Reinvention: Sixty Years and We Still Don't Get It." In press. *International Journal of Public Administration.*

Wamsley, Gary L., and Mayer N. Zald. 1973. *The Political Economy of Public Organizations.* Lexington, Mass.: Lexington.

White, Orion F., Jr., and Cynthia J. McSwain. 1990. "The Phoenix Project: Raising a New Image of Public Administration from the Ashes of the Past." In *Images and Identities in Public Administration,* edited by Henry D. Kass and Bayard L. Catron. Newbury Park, Calif.: Sage.

Wilson, Woodrow. 1887. "The Study of Administration." *Political Science Quarterly* 2: 197–222.

6 | Assessing Public Management Reform with Internal Labor Market Theory
A Comparative Assessment of Change Implementation
Lois R. Wise and Per Stengård

Is Public Management Reform Potential or Realized?

A critical deficiency in the research regarding change implementation in the workplace is that it provides little evidence into just how much real change is being put into place (Osterman 1994). This lack of knowledge about the extent to which reform can be effected and the conditions under which change is likely to occur may generate unrealistic expectations on the one hand and perpetuate a false sense of futility on the other. It can be particularly costly in a period when governments are encouraging public agencies to embrace a new public management style and expend substantial amounts of resources to transform themselves into high-performance organizations.

Because public management reform places such a strong emphasis on human resources as a target for change, policies affecting personnel management provide a good opportunity for assessing the extent to which national government postures toward reform are real or rhetorical. Research suggests that efforts to implement organizational change may be impeded by various factors. Brunsson (1989) identifies two specific traps. One is in confusing organizational talk and decision statements with the actions they describe. The second involves confusing intentions, or, in his terminology, "organizational display," with real outcomes. Issued statements may reflect a desire to achieve policy consistency or some other political objective but do not automatically mean that organizations pursue these desires or fulfill these promises: "Observers might make the mistake of supposing that organizational statements and decisions agree with organizational actions, and that organizational decisions really have been or will be implemented. . . . Perceptions that put ideology and action on an equal footing certainly confirm traditional models of organizations, but they are likely to be poor reflections of reality. Talk and decisions are important in organizations, but they should be analyzed as autonomous activities" (231–32). Thus prior to any assessment of the impact of public management reforms on government performance, the critical question that must be answered is the extent to which proposed reforms have, in fact, been put into place.

This study explores the extent to which policies and promises for reform of national public bureaucracies are reflected in implemented changes. We will use the concept of internal labor market systems (ILMs) as a framework for a comparative analysis of two national government bureaucracies. This approach allows us to present evidence about change implementation on specific internal labor market components as well as to identify any evidence of change in the extent to which internal organizational forces rather than external market forces account for the pattern of human resource utilization in government. The study will in fact show substantial differences in the two cases with regard to the extent to which promised reforms were put into place; a fundamental shift is apparent in one bureaucracy's labor market system.

We proceed in this chapter with a brief explanation of the constructs and research approach, and then we present the reforms proposed in the two cases for the period studied (1983–1993). In the section following that one, we review evidence of reform implementation, and in the final section we discuss the implications of the research findings. The analysis will demonstrate that, as a consequence of reform implementation, Sweden moved from an internally driven labor market system to one with substantial influence from external market forces whereas the United States, although it has put some reforms into effect, continues to rely mainly on internal labor market systems for human resource management in the federal government.

Research Approach and Concepts

Internal labor market systems involve a system of formal and informal rules for determining employment relationships within an organization and provide a useful framework for studying the reform implementation process (Wise 1994a). In contrast with externally driven labor market systems, ILMs set the conditions for employment, compensation, job status, job rights, career progression, and so forth in isolation from market forces and based on the incentive system of a particular organization and the value it attaches to different employee characteristics (DiPrete 1989).

Large national civil service systems are characteristic of the type of organization that has historically featured well-developed internal labor market systems (Wise 1996). National civil service systems may offer employees unique job rights and other employment protections, they may be characterized by formal career progression paths, they may involve substantial investment in training and development, and they may establish compensation systems that do not parallel market systems for prevailing rates and salary development patterns.

ILMs serve different employer purposes, including fostering long-term employment relationships, capitalizing on investments in training and development, and perhaps limiting the strength of union activity (Soeter and Schwan 1990). Organizations may have multiple ILMs based on occupational groups or organizational structure. Similarly, the extent to which human resource decisions are exclusively based on internal labor market systems as opposed to some level of influence from the external market may vary from organization to organization as well as for different ILMs within the same organizational structure. To the extent that the current pattern of public management reforms attempts to make "government work like a business," successful implementation of reform should be associated with a weakening of ILMs or at least evidence of greater influence from external market forces on the way human resources are managed.

Using specific ILM components, this study attempts to assess the extent to which promised changes have occurred in government bureaucracies and the extent to which they are evident in internal labor market systems. It draws on evidence from two national cases: the Nordic country of Sweden and the United States of America. Sweden and the United States make an interesting pair of cases because they differ on a number of indicators that research suggests might be important in explaining why and how organizations transform themselves.

Factors related to organizational culture and size are features that distinguish the U.S. and Swedish central government agencies and that may impact their ability to put reforms into place. Sweden's smaller and midsized agencies might have an advantage in their ability to implement reform over the large federal agencies of the United States. To the extent that a strong union presence inhibits reform, the United States, with a relatively weak union movement at the federal level, would be advantaged over Sweden, where most public employees, including managers, are affiliated with a professional union. Research leads us to expect that Sweden, an export–dependent country, would be more successful in implementing reform than the United States, which is more domestically focused because Sweden's international orientation makes the need for change manifest among members of government, the trade union movement, and the work force at large (Osterman 1994). Finally, the administrative styles of consensus building and confrontation that distinguish Sweden and the United States may account for differences between the two countries in their ability to both enact and implement legislated reforms. The discussion now turns to the connection between public management reform and internal labor markets.

Debureaucratization of the public sector is one category of public management reform that is closely connected to internal labor market systems. This construct involves efforts to promote decentralization, greater flexibility, and flatter and leaner organizations and is linked to internal labor market components including job security systems, compensation systems, job status, and career progression.

Decentralization transmits authority for using human resources down to the level of line managers, giving them greater discretion in defining job structures and individual status. In this context, it affects both career progression and compensation. It might involve a changeover from a narrow-graded classification system to a broad-banded plan or away from a graded system altogether. Such a system would provide for substantially greater managerial discretion in determining how individual employees might be placed within the structure of an organization and put less importance on rules and regulations designed to protect employees' rights.

Debureaucratization activities also include reforms to make organizations flatter and leaner. In the context of ILMs, such an organizational restructuring might be reflected in formal changes in the rules and regulations governing job security, reductions in force, layoffs of permanent staff, or the reassignment of permanent personnel to other departments or ministries as well as to other levels of government. Public agencies might be reorganized, shut down, converted into public enterprises, or fully privatized. The discussion now turns to the two cases, Sweden and the United States.

Proposals and Policies for Reform in Two Cases

This section provides some general background information about the two cases so that the reform activities described can be put into context. Figures 1 and 2 summarize promised reforms and reform legislation pertaining to deregulation for each national case study. In the context of the current framework, we can say that at the beginning of the studied period, 1983, both Sweden and the United States had civil service systems where personnel actions and human resource utilization decisions were largely determined by internal labor market systems, but promised reforms had already begun to be articulated that would have the effect of introducing greater influence from the external market on human resource management activities. The two countries shared relatively strong job security systems (including retreat rights for

Figure 1. Activities and Legislation with Potential for Affecting
Debureaucratization in Sweden

1983   •Reestablishment of a ministry of public administration with responsibility for pursuing civil service reform.
1984   •Market supplements permitted for recruiting and retaining top employees.
1985   •Personnel Policy Bill brings forward interests of the employer and emphasizes decentralization; pay is connected to productivity and the standard for pay shifts from
seniority to skill; intra-departmental mobility promoted.
•New Public Administration Act put into effect. Emphasizes agency level goal steering
and "harmonization" of public/private sector personnel practices, professional
development for managers.
1986   •Administrative Procedure Act reduces red tape and waiting periods, the size of
government, and strengthens the importance of client service.
1987   •A Parliamentary Decision on Public Management and a Government Agency
Ordinance set guidelines for administrative reform.
•Possibility for agencies to offer cost savings based bonuses established.
1988   •New instructions for 200 agencies introduce decentralization process, focus on results
and long-term objectives, and increased autonomy and discretionary authority for
agency managers.
1989   •Reorganization and reinforcement of the leadership role of the Ministry of Public
Administration; more flexible system of wages and salaries introduced; more flexibility introduced into recruitment and mobility of senior executives.
1990   •Government announces a program (approved by Parliament in 1991) to reduce
national administration by 10% over three years.
•Implementation of a new class specification system as basis for civil service wage and
salary statistics to help individual agencies set payments and provide some equivalen-
cies with the private sector.
1991   •Ministry of Finance receives responsibility for central matters of public administration.
•Job Security Agreement establishes policy that a local authority in conjunction with
other institutions is responsible for employment security activities; employment
security activities should be carried out without close regulations or restrictions.
•Criteria developed to determine when a State company is suitable for privatization,
transformation, or closure.
1993   •Budget Bill promises to decrease total public spending by the equivalent of 5% of
GDP.
•New Law on Public Employment passed (in effect July 1994). Makes personnel
management more flexible by eliminating the notion of "appointment" as a relevant
employment concept, weakening the requirement for publicly announcing vacant
positions, and by removing numerous special rules and protections that applied to
state sector workers, for example in cases of reductions in force, layoffs, sickness, and
temporary assignments. Differences between public and private sector management
are minimized by this law.

Sources: OECD, *Public Service, 1993*; Maivor Sjölund, *Statens Lönepolitik*, 1989; Maivor Sjölund, "Transition in Government Pay Policies," 1994.

Figure 2. Activities and Legislation with Potential for Affecting
Debureaucratization in the U.S.

1984 •Performance Management and Recognition System establishes performance based
pay for middle managers.
•Private Sector Survey on Cost Control (Grace Commission)'s 2,400 recommendations
submitted to Congress promise cost saving of $424 billion in three years. Half of
savings attributed to correcting system failures and personnel mismanagement.
1986 •Launch of an extensive effort to improve the quality of government services and
products, thereby improving efficiency and productivity.
1987 •Public Law 100-202 expands circumstances when special pay rates can be used to
counter recruitment and retention problems.
1988 •U.S. OPM delegates to federal agencies authority for hiring highly qualified GS 11 or
higher employees at pay rates above the entry step.
•Great increase in the number of agencies having inspectors general who are
empowered to carry out audits and investigations, particularly of wasteful and
inefficient practices.
1989 •Major review across more than 65 departments and agencies of the adequacy of
management controls.
•Studies begun to identify actions to ensure that the government continues to hire and
retained skilled personnel.
•A Management by Objectives system established to allow the President and senior
officials to monitor and evaluate some 50 major programs and policies.
1990 •The President signs into law the Federal Employees Pay Comparability Act which
affects over 1.4 million General Schedule employees by establishing cost of living
localities for pay setting instead of using a national average. Law eliminates the GS
grade 11 restriction on hiring above the entry pay step. Law extends the use of pay
supplements based on geographic location. Authorizes agencies to pay up 25% of
salary to retain top workers.
•Congress enacts legislation to provide locality pay and monetary supplements for
Title 38 employees (PL 101-366).
1991 •Increased emphasis assigned to measurement of program performance; renewed focus
on improving quality of government services and products.
•OMB asks federal agencies to provide cost/benefit data for all significant regulations,
thereby increasing the number of rules covered from about 80 to 500 per year.
1992 •Government Performance and Results Act enacted with requirements including
agency preparation of annual performance goal plans and reporting actual performance against goals.
1993 •New administration launches National Performance Review and sets goal of cutting
100,000 positions and reducing White House staff 25%.
•President's Council on Competitiveness, responsible for reviewing regulatory issues
bearing on competitiveness, abolished.
•Government Performance and Results Act passed by Congress, requires that federal
agencies set organizational, define goal measures, and report performances in
achieving goals by 1999. Enables the Director of OMB to approve waivers to
enhance managerial flexibility by allowing managers to dispense with administrative
rules that decrease efficiency.

Sources: OECD, *Public Service, 1993*; U.S. General Accounting Office, 1990b, 1994a, 1994b, 1995.

civil servants), emphasized career employment, had defined job structures and career ladders, defined organizational status and pay on the basis of position, had narrow graded classification systems, and used centrally determined fixed step pay schedules to determine compensation levels.

The Swedish Case

Sweden has a parliamentary system of government and a strong labor union movement. The relatively small ministries employ between 80 and 250 people each and have responsibility for formulating policy and legislation. Sweden can be characterized as a consensus-oriented society, and this quality affects both the relationship between the administration and parliament as well as management practices within organizations. Also characteristic of Sweden is a tendency to install certain generally accepted reforms informally and subsequently create or change legislative codes to provide a formal legal basis for these practices. The bulk of the state's public service is found in about three hundred national agencies that engaged about 8.8 percent of the national work force in 1993. In 1983 central government employees represented 11.1 percent of the total work force. Public management reforms have been supported by parties of the left, right, and center. These reforms represent a fundamental shift in public policy and management practice.

Although characterized as ad hoc (Premfors 1991), contemporary public management reform can be traced to the 1970s. For example, in 1977 an executive pay board was established to develop and promote individually based pay for top civil servants, and these executives were removed from the collective bargaining process (Gustafsson 1990, 31). In 1978, 1 percent of the centrally bargained pay bill was set aside for negotiations at the agency level. This agreement was important on two counts. It marked the beginning of the end of the direct relationship between position status and pay level in Sweden. Second, this was the first step toward providing managers discretion in allocating money from the central wage agreement, and the amount set aside grew steadily thereafter. By the end of the next decade, individualized pay was broadly applied to the civil service.

The 1980s were characterized by activities to decentralize the public bureaucracy, enhance opportunities for democratic responsiveness, and provide for greater flexibility in pay administration. Public sector reform was a priority of the reseated Social Democrat government, and the creation of a Ministry of Public Administration in 1983 as a center in driving administrative reforms into practice marked the start of a period focusing on reorganization and transformation (Premfors 1991).[1]

The 1990s have been marked by activities to "harmonize" public and private sector employment conditions. These efforts include attempting to transform public agencies into shareholding companies and allowing them to use private sector rules for managing resources. The 1990s are also marked by efforts to make public management more flexible, to reduce the size of the state sector, and to increase the level of equality between the sexes. The general direction of reform has not changed under the minority Social Democrat government formed in 1994 and reorganized in 1996.[2] Legislation affecting debureaucratization for this period in Sweden are highlighted in figure 1.

The U.S. Case

The United States government is a federal system, and, relative to other nations, the central bureaucracy is relatively small. Labor unions are relatively weak, and pay for most federal employees is not subject to collective bargaining. Relations between the U.S. Congress and the administration can typically be characterized as confrontational. The Office of Personnel Management (OPM) is the central agency responsible for human resource management policy at the federal level, conducting about 60 percent of the recruitment and examination activities. Remaining responsibilities are delegated to agency and department heads by OPM. OPM prescribes specific standards and procedures that must be followed in carrying out human resource management tasks, and it also often requires that proposals and individual actions be submitted for its approval.

In 1993 federal civilian employment involved about 2.5 percent of the U.S. work force; in 1983 it was 2.9 percent of the work force (U.S. Office of Personnel Management 1994). Activities and legislation addressing debureaucratization in the United States are highlighted in figure 2. Public management reforms have been supported by presidents of both political parties.

Demands for a more effective and efficient public service began to dominate the public debate in the 1970s. The Civil Service Reform Act of 1978 redefined the notion of merit in terms of performance and efficiency and marked an effort to reshape the federal civil service and to bring private sector management principles into the civil service. Under the provisions of this legislation, experiments in more flexible pay systems, including broad banding, were permitted in designated demonstration agencies.

The 1980s were marked by the creation of numerous study commissions to improve government efficiency. In 1982 President Reagan established one, popularly known as the Grace Commission, to figure out how government could be made to work like a business. In 1984, the Grace Commission produced an extensive list of recommendations addressing public management reform, but the report, although much discussed, had little impact on actual practice (Paul 1996). Other initiatives to improve efficiency and effectiveness were launched during the same decade.

Some concrete steps toward debureaucratization were taken during the 1980s. In 1988, the U.S. Office of Personnel Management enhanced flexibility in pay setting by allowing federal agencies to offer pay rates above the established entry level for employees at the GS-11 level or higher. Also, by 1989 the number of payroll systems for federal employees had been reduced from 132 to 53.

The 1990s have been marked by continued discussion and plans for reforming and downsizing government and by some legislation to initiate reform. In terms of plans for change, the National Performance Review (1993), presented by Vice-President Gore, and the proposals subsequently drawn from it and put forward to Congress by the White House continue to reflect the goal of adapting private sector management practices to make government more flexible and less encumbered by rules and regulations and to reduce the size of the federal work force. As part of its presidential campaign message, the Clinton administration promised to reduce the size of the federal bureaucracy by 100,000 civil service jobs. As part of Gore's National Performance Review, the job reduction goal was increased to 252,000. Under congressional mandate the administration must eliminate a total of 272,900 jobs between 1993 and the end of 1999.

In the area of pay administration, the passage of the Federal Employees Pay Comparability Act in 1990 has important potential for debureaucratization in that it eliminates the GS-11 grade level restriction on hiring employees above the entry pay level and authorizes managers to offer up to 25 percent of salary to retain a highly valued General Schedule employee. Recruitment bonuses may also be offered. Similarly, geographic supplements and monetary supplements for recruitment and retention were authorized for other federal employees covered under Title 38 of the U.S. Code.

Reform Implementation

In order to assess the extent to which proposed reforms have changed internal labor markets in Sweden and the United States, we will look at three ILM components. These are systems and rules affecting compensation, job security, and deployment and staffing patterns.

Compensation

Both Sweden and the United States took steps to transfer certain authority for compensation policy from the central government to the agencies. In the U.S. case, the passage of the Civil Service Reform Act of 1978 provided agencies the opportunity to experiment with broad-banded pay systems that collapsed the 15-grade white-collar pay schedule into six or less broad bands to enable managers in these agencies more flexibility in setting pay rates within the defined bands and more discretion in assigning employees to different tasks. These experiments are generally judged successful (Ban 1992) and are still in place, but wide application of broad banding has not been authorized by Congress.

The U.S. Office of Personnel Management delegated authority to the agencies for hiring qualified employees above the entry step, first at the GS–11 level or above and later, under the Federal Employees Pay Comparability Act, for all GS employees. The same act also provided for one-time recruitment bonuses as an alternative to permanent salary supplements. The use of special pay allowances grew dramatically during the second half of the 1980s and signaled a need for reforms in compensation policy, including greater flexibility and market parity. Whereas 3 percent or less of the GS work force received any pay supplement before 1985, by the end of the decade 14 percent of the GS work force received one or more special pay supplements designed to enhance recruitment or retention of valued employees (Wise and Barry 1996).

Sweden abolished[3] its narrow 34-grade pay schedule and switched to a completely ungraded agency-based model in 1990. Individual pay was adopted after the introduction of other measures to make pay setting more flexible, including broader pay bands, market-based supplements, and other special supplements and allowances (Wise 1994b). Because of the extensive number of exceptions and special provisions, support for the existing "system" collapsed, and individual pay was seen as a solution to the problem of a system that lacked any semblance of internal alignment and was under criticism for being dysfunctional.

The portion of the pay package at the discretion of local managers increased slowly. In the mid-1980s, steps to individualize pay through special supplements or pay bonuses were also gaining popularity in Sweden (Ahlén 1989; Sjölund 1989). Beginning in 1984, pay could be augmented through market supplements designed to make government more competitive with other employers (Sjölund 1987, 1989). The popularity of these rewards increased yearly in the state sector but with considerable variation among functional areas. Market supplements were abolished in 1989 with the advent of individualized pay. As in the U.S. case, these market supplements were intended to enhance recruitment and retention. Sweden also used locality pay to provide an incentive for workers to accept jobs in arctic regions, but these involved a relatively small portion of the civil service. Market supplements grew

rapidly in popularity and by the end of the decade were thought to have eliminated any semblance of internal alignment. The result was that the system of
position-based pay using fixed rate step increases was abandoned. Central bargaining between the government's representative, the Swedish Agency for
Government Employers, and central trade union federations provides the
framework for pay setting for occupational groups and professional levels, but
individual variations from these rates are now substantial. Use of individualized pay has grown rapidly in national government and the private sector.

Sweden does not have a pay-for-performance compensation system,
which directly links some measure of output with a commensurate pay increase.[4] There is no custom of formal performance evaluation, and the use of
individual performance rating scores is anathema to most Swedes. The system
of individualized pay can be more appropriately described as one based on
contribution. Contributions include work results as well as the skills, competencies, flexibility, and market value an individual brings to an organization.[5]

Job Security

The debureaucratization reform of flatter and leaner organizations involves staff reductions as well as efforts to reduce the layers of organizational
hierarchy. Changes in personnel levels are associated with revisions in personnel rules such as those affecting job security and reductions in force or redun-
dancies. Although rhetoric in both countries emphasized reduction in the size
of the central government work force, quite different approaches to staff reduction were taken in the two cases. Differences between the U.S. and Sweden
become apparent when similar data are presented.

U.S. Strategy for Staff Reductions

The United States has taken an essentially passive approach to reductions
in force. This partly reflects a belief that, in the long run, attrition is more
cost-effective than buyouts. Sweden has pursued a more active policy.

The policy of attrition to reduce the size of the U.S. federal work force is
apparent in turnover statistics from 1982 to 1993 that show the different categories or reasons for separation from the federal government. As the data in
table 1 indicate, total separations for white-collar (GS) employees were lower
during the first parts of the 1990s than during the 1980s, with the highest level
in 1990 at 7.5 percent of the work force. For blue-collar (Federal Wage System [FWS]) employees, the 1993 rate was the highest level, when 8.3 percent
of the work force left federal employment. Information is given for four categories of turnover: resignations, retirements, discharges, and reductions in
force. Retirements increased for both blue- and white-collar workers in 1993,

Table 1. Turnover Rates as a Percentage of Total Employment for U.S. Federal White- and Blue-Collar Employees, FY 1982–FY 1993

	Fiscal Year											
Separation	1982	1983	1984	1985	1986	1987	1988	1989	1990	1991	1992	1993
Total separations												
GS	8.1	7.7	8.0	8.5	8.8	8.4	8.8	8.0	7.5	6.5	5.2	6.5
FWS	7.3	7.2	7.2	7.6	7.8	7.6	8.5	7.2	6.8	7.4	5.2	8.3
Resignations (quits)												
GS	4.7	4.4	4.9	5.1	5.2	4.9	5.1	4.9	4.5	3.5	3.0	2.9
FWS	2.2	2.1	2.5	2.7	2.5	2.4	2.5	2.6	2.4	1.8	1.5	1.8
Retirements												
GS	2.3	2.5	2.4	2.5	2.8	2.4	2.8	2.2	2.2	2.2	1.5	2.8
FWS	3.8	3.9	3.6	3.7	3.9	3.7	4.6	3.3	2.9	3.2	1.9	5.5
Discharges												
GS	NA	0.3	0.3	0.3	0.4	0.4	0.5	0.5	0.5	0.4	0.4	0.3
FWS	NA	0.4	0.5	0.5	0.6	0.5	0.6	0.6	0.7	0.6	0.6	0.6
Reductions in force												
GS	NA	0.1	0.1	0.1	0.3	0.1	0.1	0.1	0.1	0.1	0.1	0.2
FWS	NA	0.2	0.2	0.2	0.1	0.4	0.3	0.1	0.2	1.3	0.6	0.3

Sources: U.S. Merit Systems Protection Board, *Federal Blue Collar Employees: A Workforce in Transition;* U.S. Office of Personnel Management, *The Fact Book* (1995); and unpublished data, U.S. Office of Personnel Management, Office of Workforce Statistics.

GS, General Schedule; FWS, Federal Wage System.

reflecting federal policy to induce early retirement.[6] Reductions in force were highest in 1991 for blue-collar workers and declined thereafter. Reductions in force increased by .1 percent of the white-collar work force in 1993. Further reductions in force occurred between 1994 and 1995, the great majority of which were separations from the Department of Defense (U.S. Office of Personnel Management 1997).[7] The overall rate of separation, however, declined in 1996.

Blue-collar or FWS employment underwent significant reductions in force during the last two decades, with a work force loss of about one-third from 1970 to 1989. The rate of reductions accelerated after fiscal year 1989 when the Department of Defense initiated major cutbacks in staffing and a system-wide reorganization. In the more recent period, higher grade positions began to experience job loss as part of this broad downsizing effort.

Overall, as table 2 indicates, changes in employment levels for U.S. federal employees were negligible from 1985 to 1993, with a .2 percent overall reduction. Reductions in employment levels amounted to only .6 percent for the executive branch and 1.3 percent for the legislative branch of government. For

Table 2. Employment Levels for U.S. Federal Civilian Employees by Category, 1985 to 1993

| | Employment Levels | | Change 1985–93 | |
			N	%
Category	1985	1993		
Executive branch	2,963,500	2,947,100	−16,400	−.6
Defense	1,084,500	921,200	−163,300	−15.1
U.S. Postal Service	750,000	790,300	+40,300	+5.4
Legislative branch	38,800	38,300	−500	−1.3
Judicial branch	18,200	28,100	+9,900	+54.5
Total	3,020,500	3,013,500	−7,000	−.2

Source: U.S. Office of Personnel Management, *The Fact Book* (1994), 5.

the judicial branch, a substantial increase of 54.5 percent occurred between 1985 and 1993. Within the Postal Service, a reduction of about 5 percent occurred, but the largest reduction in force involved the Department of Defense, which lowered its staffing level by 163,300, or 15 percent.

According to the same source, more substantial activity to reduce the size of the national government happened after 1993. Federal civilian employment was about 1.5 percent smaller in 1995 than in 1993 and about 3.9 percent smaller in 1996 than it was in 1985. By category, reductions were reported for the executive and legislative branches and the Department of Defense. Defense employment in 1996 was about 26.6 percent smaller than it was in 1985. Expansion of employment levels, however, occurred for the Postal Service and judicial branch (U.S. Office of Personnel Management 1997).

Sweden's Strategy for Staff Reduction

Activities to create a flatter and leaner central government bureaucracy in Sweden have impacted agencies in three ways: some authorities have been closed down or moved to other sectors; some have been reorganized and consolidated; and still others have been converted into public enterprises or joint stock companies.[8] Sweden's efforts for the period studied are substantially greater, in relative terms, than those of the United States.

Table 3 breaks the central government work force into four main categories and compares employment levels in 1985 and 1993. Overall, staff reductions cut one in four employees from the state sector work force. Cutbacks in staffing levels in the state sector have been particularly significant among those working in public corporations, but about one in ten of those working in the general categories of Public Administration and Defense was eliminated during this period. Of the four categories given, three show reductions in the

Table 3. Employment Levels for Swedish Government Employees by Category, 1985 to 1993

	Employment Levels		Change 1985–93 N	Change 1985–93 %
Category	1985	1993	N	%
Public administration (including executive, legislative, and judicial branches)	139,954	128,217	-11,737	-8.4
Defense	43,877	38,991	-4,886	-11.1
Public corporation	164,085	79,684	-84,401	-51.4
Upper education	40,534	43,694	3,160	7.8
Total	388,450	290,586	-97,864	-25.2

Source: Swedish Agency for Government Employers, unpublished data. These data exclude those over 64 years of age, those working under special labor market employment policies, and those employed less than 40 percent of full-time hours. The data include employees in Sjöfärtsverket and Banverket in the 1993 public administration category.

number of employees from 1985 to 1993. In the general area of Public Administration, 11,737 employees were removed, representing a reduction of 8.4 percent. In Defense, 4,886 fewer people were employed, representing a reduction of 11.1 percent.

Downsizing in public corporations reduced employment levels in the state sector by about half (51.4 percent). About eighty-four thousand employees were affected by cutbacks and activities putting their jobs under private jurisdiction and private sector agreements. Upper Education, including colleges, universities, and upper-level technical schools, was the only category that shows evidence of growth, with an increase of 3,160 employees, or 7.8 percent, between 1985 and 1993. Note, in comparison, that relatively few employees in this occupational group are part of the central government work force in the United States. Overall, downsizing efforts in the state sector reduced the work force by 97,864 employees, or 25 percent, between 1985 and 1993. Although not quite as substantial, reductions in force continued in 1994 and 1995, eliminating about sixty-three thousand more employees for the central government. Employment levels continued to decline in all categories except Upper Education. The central government work force was about 42 percent smaller in 1995 than it was in 1985 (Statistics Sweden 1997).

Changes in both job security rights and the options available to employees whose positions were terminated under the State Agreement on Job Security of 1990 may have facilitated staffing changes. On the one hand, it is easier for managers to remove employees, and on the other, managers no longer have any responsibility to accommodate employees displaced from other authorities. Previously, the system focused on finding new jobs for displaced workers within the central government.

The Job Security Foundation was established in April of 1990 when the new job security agreement became effective. It attempts to assist employees before, during, and after termination by collaborating with a relevant employer to find alternative employment options for the worker within the labor market at large (including self-employment and the private sector) and to soften the economic blow of transfer or termination.

In Sweden, more than three thousand jobs were eliminated by agency closings and transfers to other sectors. As of September 1993, twelve agencies, ranging in size from 10 employees to 730, were affected, with 100 percent of staff eliminated from government employment rosters. Among these agencies was the State Institute for Personnel Development (SIPU).

About 33,620 jobs in the Swedish national government were cut in agencies that were reorganized or consolidated. These reductions represented cutbacks in staff size from 3 percent in the Labor Market Authority to 56 percent in the National Education Authorities. Some reorganizations had a substantial impact on the size of the central government. The National Social Insurance Board was reorganized, producing a staff cutback of 30 percent. Another relatively large staff reduction occurred in the National Board of Social Welfare, which reduced staffing levels by 26 percent. About sixty-three hundred jobs were cut from Sweden Post, representing an 11 percent reduction in staff. Reorganization at the National Railway Board cut almost fourteen thousand jobs from its rosters.

Twelve national agencies were converted to public enterprises or limited companies during the study period, but most of the action occurred in the 1990s.[9] Overall, these conversions represented a transfer of more than seventy-one thousand real jobs between 1985 and 1993, and further transfers to the private sector occurred in 1994 and 1995. The most substantial of all these conversions involved the Sweden Post in 1994 (which had been recently reorganized). Privatization of the postal service moved about fifty thousand people into the private sector and eliminated another five thousand real jobs (Statistics Sweden 1997; Olsson 1995). Among the converted authorities involving more than four thousand employees were the agencies for the National Forest Enterprise and Sweden's National Power Board. In addition, two-thirds of Sweden's National Employment Training Authority was privatized, representing a transfer of about four thousand jobs into the private sector.[10]

Deployment and Staffing

The United States and Sweden differ sharply in practices related to deployment and staffing. In the U.S. case, a central authority, OPM, continues to regulate agency practices in the area of staffing out deployment, including posting, testing, recruitment, and promotion. Peters and Savoie (1996) conclude that despite much discussion of reform, OPM, like other federal regulatory agencies (Office of Management and Budget, General Services Administration), remains fundamentally the same in its posture toward other agencies: they "are still much in the business of imposing central policy and management controls" (28).

Deployment and staffing decisions for General Schedule federal employees are largely position based. Job content as defined in a formal position description provides the basis for criteria related to selection, performance appraisal, and promotion. Job status is determined by the content of the job regardless of any special qualities an individual might be able to contribute to an organization. The ideal is to perform these activities in an "incumbent-neutral context." Opportunities for promotion and reassignment are defined by the existing positions within an organization, and the number of positions may be regulated by a congressional committee. Efforts to upgrade or combine positions are normally approved by the Office of Personnel Management.

Important progress in achieving greater flexibility in staffing has occurred, however. The authority to hire employees directly was expanded under the Civil Service Reform Act of 1978, and the use of direct hire as opposed to hiring from a central register based on a competitive exam process increased to become the third most common hiring method by 1989 (U.S. General Accounting Office 1990a). OPM establishes specific criteria regarding when direct hiring can be applied to recruit individuals with unusually rare or unique qualifications.

Sweden moved from a rank-in-position to a rank-in-person system during the first part of the 1990s, with the official elimination of the notion of appointment or post in 1994. Departure from this terminology signaled the switch from a system based on organizational status and position to one based on contribution and performance (Wise 1994b). It also marks the final end of the concept of guaranteed or permanent employment which was seen as incompatible with policies to reduce the size of the public sector and enhance flexibility.

Decisions related to recruitment, training, and promotion have been fully decentralized. There is no central regulatory authority with the capacity to approve or deny agency decisions related to staffing and deployment. Formal performance evaluation ratings are uncommon in the civil service, and formal tests are not used for selection or promotion. There is no formal career system with clear steps of progression because the grade scale has been abolished. Career development is a more individualized process that depends on the initiative of an individual and his or her supervisor to identify existing opportunities to expand work complexity and demands.

Implications

These findings indicate significant differences in the pattern of public management reform implemented in the two cases studied and provide evidence of clear differences between two national civil services systems in the structure of internal labor market systems. In the U.S. case, despite discussion of reform, the internal labor market remains the primary determinant of employment conditions for civil servants. Decisions related to recruitment and promotion remain controlled by or supervised by the central personnel authority, OPM. Job security and career systems remain intact, and civil servants continue to enjoy other protections that do not exist for many private sector employees. Moreover, although the compensation structure was converted from a national pay schedule to locality-based pay, the pay structure itself is still centrally determined with fixed rates and relatively narrow grades. We can describe the U.S. ILM as one with a strong specialized personnel function. The Swedish case, however, demonstrates more evidence of change. The Swedish civil service can be described as one where personnel tasks have become a part of the general management function. It is also an environment that values employee flexibility and reinforces key elements of organizational culture as a way of integrating employees into the organization.

The evidence presented here makes a contribution to the literature regarding the amount and type of reforms that are put into place and their implications for ILMs. In the area of debureaucratization, the ILM structure in the Swedish central government was made substantially more flexible, and authority was decentralized to line managers. The limited context of the two case studies suggests some factors that might be worth pursuing to understand why some governments are able to put public management reforms into place quicker and more effectively than others.

In the United States, decentralization, flexibility, and leaner organizations were, for the most part, still at the discussion stage at the end of 1993. Major reform activities did not get under way until 1994. Legislation to enact change was initiated in 1994 and 1995. In contrast, by 1993 the Swedish central government, which had in relative terms a much larger central government work force, had already been substantially decentralized and downsized through active rather than passive measures to remove employees and positions from the state rosters. Flexibility had also been increased by the removal of a graded pay structure and the introduction of individualized pay within a collective bargaining framework. Differences between ILMs in the national government and private sector had been substantially removed.

It would be easy to discount the level of change that has occurred in Sweden based on its substantially larger national government sector and the assumed greater potential for change. Such an approach, however, would fail to digest the significance of the scope of change, for example a staff reduction of 25 percent from 1983 to 1993 in the national government in Sweden relative to .2 percent in the United States during the same time period.[11] It would also fail to take into account the profound shift in thinking about the role of government and employment rights in a worker-oriented society. The argument put forward here is that the changes in ILM systems that have occurred in Sweden represent a true paradigm shift.

In comparing the two situations, the U.S. case seems to be the one where organizational talk is largely detached from action and where statements for reform reflect a desire to achieve policy consistency more than action. The Swedish case, however, seems to have converted talk and promises for reform into action. Movement toward reform has been steadily pursued by Social Democrat and Moderate-led governments. If Peters and Savoie (1996, 325) are correct in describing the lack of reform implementation in the United States as a failure of political will, then perhaps it is appropriate to judge the Swedish case as one where political will succeeded.

Decentralization of responsibility from a central personnel authority to the agencies themselves, consolidation, and integration of agencies reconfigure the prevailing set of rules and norms that determine status, earnings, and job security in public organizations. The transitions under way provide greater opportunities for discretion among managers and can also be seen as creating new opportunities for growth and development for employees while at the same time redefining and weakening rights for job security and tenure. The consequences of reconfiguring ILMs are apparent in many different aspects of human resource management. Use of the construct provides some insight into the extent to which significant change was put into place in a defined period and the way ILMs themselves can be transformed in innovative organizations.

Some important questions are left begging by this effort. First, we do not know why governments differ in their capacity to link organizational talk with action. Second, and more important, we do not know whether the changes observed have improved or will improve the quality of public services or the effectiveness of central government agencies (Frederickson 1996; Premfors 1998). Investigation of these important questions is left to future research.

Notes

1. The ministry was phased out in 1996. Central responsibility for reform policy initiative now resides in the prime minister's office and the Ministry of Finance.

2. Some movement toward less discretion became evident in the 1990s when, like other European countries, Sweden began to view job evaluation as a solution to the male-female wage differential. A few national authorities put different forms of job evaluation into place around the mid-1990s. These systems can be described as broad-banded mixed systems based on both rank in person and position. In a collective bargaining system these rankings are one element taken into consideration when deciding the pay range for a particular occupational group. Individual differentials remain at the discretion of the local manager.

3. Exceptions include university lecturers, judges, and some blue-collar workers who are still on formal pay scales.

4. There are some exceptions, particularly in public corporations and public enterprises where gainsharing has been applied (see Sjölund 1994). Distributions to individuals are typically based on hours worked or other objective measures.

5. According to survey data compiled by these authors, about 3 percent of all central government employees report that they receive some form of variable pay, but 97 percent of all managers say they use individualized pay.

6. Congress passed a special "buyout" law in the spring of 1994 that offers $25,000 to each employee who takes early retirement or resigns from the federal government through March 1995. In 1994 more than fifteen thousand workers from different agencies accepted that option. Special provisions were made for the Department of Defense, extending the buyout option until the end of 1999.

7. According to the National Performance Review Status Report, issued in September 1994, activities in the area of debureaucratization are found at the Departments of Labor, Agriculture, and Housing and Urban Development, as well as in certain authorities including the Federal Emergency Management Agency, Customs, Bureau of Reclamation, Social Security Administration, Small Business Administration, and the Federal Bureau of Investigation. According to the status report, seventy-one thousand full-time equivalent positions were eliminated through buyouts and other actions as of September 1994. The U.S. Office of Personnel Management cites a cutback of 102,500 employees during fiscal year 1994. As the U.S. General Accounting Office (1994b) points out, however, during the same period, other agencies including Justice and EPA, were expected to increase their staffing levels (13).

8. The Swedish Agency for Government Employers excludes in its statistics jobs

funded under special labor market programs, jobs involving less than 40 percent of full-time working hours, and jobs occupied by persons over 65 years of age.

9. Privatization of Swedish Telecom, which occurred between 1993 and 1994, took close to forty-four thousand employees off central government rosters.

10. Swedish Agency for Government Employers *(Arbetsgivarverket),* unpublished data. According to Statistics Sweden, for the period 1985–1995 more than 150,000 state jobs were moved out of the public sector.

11. For the period 1985–1995, Sweden experienced reductions in total employment of about 42.0 percent relative to 3.9 percent for the United States in the same period.

References

Ahlén, Kristina. 1989. "Swedish Collective Bargaining under Pressure: Inter Union Rivalry and Incomes Policies." *British Journal of Industrial Relations* 27: 330–46.

Ban, C. 1992. "Research and Demonstration under CRSA: Is Innovation Possible?" In *The Promise and Paradox of Civil Service Reform,* edited by P. W. Ingraham and D. H. Rosenbloom. Pittsburgh: University of Pittsburgh Press.

Brunsson, Nils. 1989. *The Organization of Hypocrisy: Talk, Decisions, and Actions in Organizations.* New York: Wiley.

DiPrete, T. A. 1989. *The Bureaucratic Labor Market: The Case of the Federal Civil Service.* New York: Plenum Press.

Frederickson, H. G. 1996. "Comparing the Reinventing Government Movement with New Public Administration." *Public Administration Review,* 56, no. 3: 263–70.

Gustafsson, Lennart. 1990. "Promoting Flexibility through Pay Policy: Experience in Swedish National Administration." In *Flexible Personnel Management in the Public Service,* OECD. Paris: OECD.

National Performance Review. 1993. *From Red Tape to Results: Creating a Government That Works Better and Costs Less.* Washington, D.C.: U.S. Government Printing Office.

OECD. 1993. *Public Service, 1993.* Paris: OECD.

Olsson, Hans. 1995. "Flera hundra postkontor i fara." *Dagens Nyheter,* February 4, 1995, p. 1.

Osterman, P. 1994. "How Common Is Workplace Transformation and Who Adopts It?" *Industrial and Labor Relations Review* 47, no. 2 (January): 173–87.

Paul, Ezra. 1996. "Comparing the Grace and Gore Commissions." Paper presented at the Annual Meeting of the American Political Science Association, San Francisco.

Peters, B. G., and D. Savoie. 1996. "Managing Incoherence: The Coordination and Empowerment Conundrum." *Public Administration Review* 56, no. 3: 281–89.

Premfors, R. 1991. "The 'Swedish Model' and Public Sector Reform." *West European Politics* 14: 83–95.

———. 1998. "Reshaping the Democratic State: Swedish Experience in Comparative Perspective." *Public Administration* 76 (spring).

Sjölund, M. 1987. *Statens Kaka, Lönepolitik i Förändring* [The State's Cake: Pay Policy in Transition]. Stockholm: Almänna Förlaget.

———. 1989. *Statens Lönepolitik, 1977–1988* [The State's Pay Policy, 1977–1988]. Stockholm: Almänna Förlaget.

———. 1994. "Transition in Government Pay Policies, Symposium on Transitions in Public Administration." *International Journal of Public Administration* 17, no. 10: 1907–35.

Soeter, Joseph L., and Rolf Schwan. 1990. "Towards an Empirical Assessment of Internal Labor Market Configurations." *International Journal of Human Resource Management* 1, no. 1 (June): 271–87.

Statistics Sweden (SCB). 1997. *Statistical Yearbook Orebro.* Stockholm: Statistics Sweden.

U.S. General Accounting Office. 1990a. *Federal Recruiting and Hiring: Making Government Jobs Attractive to Prospective Employees.* Washington, D.C.: U.S. General Accounting Office.

———. 1990b. *Federal Pay: Special Rates, Effect on Recruitment and Retention for Selected Clerical Occupations.* Washington, D.C.: U.S. General Accounting Office.

———. 1994a. *Management Reforms.* Washington, D.C.: U.S. General Accounting Office.

———. 1994b. *Improving Government.* Washington, D.C.: U.S. General Accounting Office.

———. 1995. *Government Reform: GAO's Comments of the National Performance Review.* Washington, D.C.: U.S. General Accounting Office.

U.S. Merit Systems Protection Board. 1992. Federal Blue Collar Employees: A Workforce in Transition. Washington, D.C.: U.S. Merit Systems Protection Board.

U.S. Office of Personnel Management. 1994. *The Fact Book.* Washington, D.C.: U.S. Office of Personnel Management.

———. 1995. *The Fact Book.* Washington, D.C.: U.S. Office of Personnel Management.

———. 1997. *The Fact Book.* Washington, D.C.: U.S. Office of Personnel Management.

Wise, L. R., and Maureen Barry. 1996. "Discretion in Pay Setting: Greater Flexibility or More Discrimination?" Paper presented at the Annual Meeting of the American Political Science Association, San Francisco.

Wise, Lois Recascino. 1994a. "Rethinking Public Employment Structures and Strategies." In *New Paradigms for Government,* edited by Patricia W. Ingraham and Barbara Romzek. San Francisco: Jossey-Bass.

———. 1994b. "Implementing Pay Reform in the Public Sector: Different Approaches to Flexible Pay in Sweden and the U.S." *International Journal of Public Administration* 17, no. 10: 1937–59.

———. 1996. "Internal Labor Markets." In *Civil Service Systems in Comparative Perspective,* edited by J. L. Perry and T. Toonen. Bloomington, Ind.: Indiana University Press.

7 | Good Budgetary Decision Processes
Patrick D. Larkey and Erik A. Devereux

The budget should be balanced, the Treasury should be refilled, public debt should be reduced, the arrogance of officialdom should be tempered and controlled, and the assistance to foreign lands should be curtailed lest Rome become bankrupt.
— Marcus Tullius Cicero (63 B.C.)[1]

SOUND FAMILIAR? Budget problems are indeed venerable. So also, it seems, are the norms for budgetary outcomes such as balance, cash surpluses, debt reduction, and expenditure patterns such as less foreign aid. Unfortunately, except for the "arrogant officials"—surely Cicero's political rivals—who should be "tempered and controlled," there is nothing in Cicero's statement about how to achieve an improved budgetary decision process.

This chapter looks, in an abbreviated and highly selective way, at both the history of and the prospects for reforming budgetary decision processes. Few government, indeed human, activities have been reformed more often than budgetary decision processes. In the past century there has never been a shortage of new decision technologies or reform proposals. We should be getting better at government budgeting. Alas, things seem to be getting worse.

Past and proposed reforms fail because they fail to alter underlying incentives for the primary participants, bureaucrats and politicians, and for the ultimate stakeholders, citizens. Reforms to increase political attention in budget deliberations to the substantive effectiveness and efficiency of government programs have not stopped politicians from making decisions on the basis of immediate distributional effects on their constituencies or ideological defensibility or political advantage. Reforms to increase the active participation of citizens in deliberations by improving information and opening the decision processes have had no discernible impact on the proportion of uninformed and uninvolved citizens. Reforms such as balanced budget amendments and audit requirements that seek to control behaviors externally are subverted by the boundless ingenuity and audacity of those we would control.

This chapter offers a set of reforms to budgetary decision processes that would alter the incentives and the nature of budgetary decision making profoundly. These reform proposals are politically neither correct nor feasible.

166

They should, however, provoke thought about what it might take to improve budgetary decision processes fundamentally.

The Reform Experience

When Dr. Johnson defined patriotism as the last refuge of a scoundrel, he ignored the enormous possibilities of the word reform.

—Senator Roscoe Conkling

For this abbreviated, selective history there are five classes of reforms. First, there are the *rationalizing* reforms that emphasize enhanced analysis and reason. Second, there are *ad hoc norms* such as balance and annularity that have been evolving over the last 150 years or so in Western democracies and have been expressed in a variety of administrative reforms. Third, there are *democratizing* reforms that seek to open the decision processes to inform and involve citizens better. Fourth, there are *power shifting* reforms such as line-item vetoes that adjust authority and responsibility for budgeting, particularly between executives and legislatures. Fifth, there are *control* reforms such as auditing, tax limitations, and balanced budget amendments that attempt to impose external constraints on decisional behaviors.

Rationalizing

An idea isn't responsible for the people who believe in it.

—Don Marquis

Just three decades ago budgeting was widely believed to be the primary instrument through which governments would finally be perfected. Through the wondrous technology of Planning, Programming, Budgeting Systems (PPBS) we would achieve and maintain an optimal level of government and mix of programs putting government, at long last, on a rational basis. PPBS was the culmination of several decades of work on budgeting, attempting to develop "a theory for deciding to allocate X dollars to Activity A instead of allocating them to Activity B, or instead of allowing the taxpayer to use the money for his individual purposes" (Key 1940; Lewis 1952). PPBS had predecessors (performance budgeting and program budgeting) and successors (management by objectives and zero-base budgeting), but it was the only complete and logically consistent description of how we might go about addressing Key's question on allocating X to A or B. It is as close as academe has come to a coherent, albeit infeasible, theory of what constitutes good budgetary outcomes and good budgetary decision processes. The good, indeed optimal, budgetary outcome is one in which no public expenditure is made if the equivalent amount utilized in the private sector would yield a higher rate of return. The good processes were the elaborate analytic and reconciliation procedures developed in PPBS for analyzing, arraying, and selecting alternatives.

In the economic view, the essential budgeting problem is allocating scarce resources, and the essential basis of deciding the allocation is in terms of maximizing the value in a chosen set among all possible sets. PPBS, and all other systems that emphasize the allocative function of budgets and stress deciding on the basis of purpose, are very attractive normatively. This is obviously the way we should be deciding. It is the rational way . . . and we should all obviously aspire to be rational or, at least, appear to be rational. Aaron Wildavsky told us early, eloquently, and often that PPBS was cognitively and politically infeasible.[2] He was correct.

The normative approach to budgeting inspired by neoclassical microeconomic theory has much in common with Will Rogers's proposed solution to the U-boat problem in World War II. He maintained that the solution was quite simple: Bring the Atlantic to a slow boil and then skim the U-boats off the surface. When pressed on how to do this he responded that he was a big idea man and that someone else would have to work out the details. The "details" provided for budgeting—benefit-cost analysis, multi-year costing, program memoranda, and so on—proved grossly inadequate to the practical budgeting task even in the Department of Defense, where it all started.

All of the reforms inspired by the economic perspective over the last fifty-five years, since V. O. Keys's (1940) pessimistic but effective articulation of the economic perspective on budgeting, have failed but have never been totally abandoned. The normative attractiveness of some form of "rational" budgeting is just overwhelming, and the notions are continually being reinvented and reapplied. The Clinton/Gore National Performance Review attempts to resurrect performance budgeting with their "mission-driven, results-oriented" budgeting (Thompson 1994).

Performance budgeting had its first life in 1949 from the first Hoover Commission, which called for the adoption of a "performance budget": "We recommend that the whole budgetary concept of the Federal government should be refashioned by the adoption of a budget based upon functions, activities, and projects, this we designate a performance budget. Such an approach would focus attention upon the general character and relative importance of the work to be done, or upon the service to be rendered, rather than upon the things to be acquired, such as personal services, supplies, equipment, and so on. These latter objects are, after all, only the means to an end. The all important thing in budgeting is the work or the service to be accomplished, and what that work or service will cost" (U.S. Commission on the Organization of the Executive Branch 1949, 8).

Although performance budgeting is much less ambitious than PPBS, there have been myriad failures in applying its concepts in real governments at all levels over the past fifty years, and there is no reason to think that the latest instantiation will be more successful. Thompson (1994) makes some useful suggestions on how to improve the performance budgeting experience this time around.

What do we mean when we say that a budget reform such as performance budgeting or PPBS has "failed"? The easy argument is that the organizations that once embraced a reform with great enthusiasm no longer claim that the reform exists, was completed, or is in progress. A tougher test is impact. The first step is in identifying impact: Did the reform change the levels of revenue and the allocation patterns? This test requires analysis of the counterfactual: What would levels of revenue and allocation patterns have been without the reform? (Larkey 1979). To our knowledge there are no rigorous empirical tests that have shown a significant impact of budget reforms. Yet a tougher test is: Did the reform improve either budgetary outcomes or the processes? To do this test you would first have to establish changes with the counterfactual analysis and then somehow show that the process characteristics and/or outcomes before the reform are inferior to those after the reform. The direct examination of the economist's Valhalla, where the budget outcomes are optimal in the rate-of-return sense, is obviously impractical because it requires rate-of-return calculations for *all* possible spending alternatives in the public and private sectors. Moreover, we must do this prospectively in forecasts of the consequences because post hoc evaluations, however carefully done, are not of much direct value in the decision making.

For the economically inspired reforms we can safely say that their salutary effects have not been demonstrated in spite of some very serious attempts, and with few exceptions, notably the Department of Defense, most of the organizational forms have been abandoned.

The economic reforms not only have failed to make budgeting better; they also may have made it worse by focusing attention on the systematic, comprehensive, and simultaneous comparison of all possible alternative taxing and spending programs. This is a task that we cannot do at all well primarily because of our inabilities in commensurately valuing dissimilar things and in forecasting the consequences of one action versus another. The economic perspective and the analysis that we can do just breeds dissatisfaction with our budget choices with no clear guidance on how to make better choices.

The economic, rationalizing perspective was a point of departure rather than a culmination of the long history of attempting to improve government budgetary processes. Other classes of reform have evolved piecemeal without benefit (or burden) of a coherent theoretical vision.

The rationalizing reforms do not acknowledge and work around some fundamental, inherent limitations on what we know and what we can know in the near term at reasonable cost. In the budget reform business there has always been too much pretense that we can know the effects of adopting policy A versus policy B. The reality is that the effects of A or B depend on poorly understood causal mechanisms and conditions that are not easily forecast. The difficulty is compounded because the research that would improve our understanding of the causal mechanisms or improve our forecasts of base conditions is usually infeasible intellectually, politically, or both.

If there have been improvements in our base understanding of the effects of one policy versus another over the past twenty or thirty years, the changes have been imperceptible. What would be the effects of massive cuts in capital gains taxes on economic growth, rates of employment, and the distribution of income and wealth? How would we ever know the effects even after the fact in a global, rapidly changing world?

Ad Hoc Norms

> *Idealism increases in direct proportion to one's distance from the problem.*
> —John Galsworthy

In his second edition of *The Politics of the Budgetary Process* (1974), the late Aaron Wildavsky wrote an interesting "Prologue Transformation of Budgetary Norms" in which he despaired at the demise of the traditional budgetary norms—annularity, balance, and comprehensiveness—with no new set of norms in sight. These norms are a subset of the norms from the European school of budgeting at the end of the nineteenth century (Sundelson 1935; Burkhead 1956). These norms, although invariably ad hoc because of the absence of any underlying normative theory, have practical import primarily as criteria for thinking more systematically about the design of budgetary decision processes. The most ambitious and interesting recent attempt to posit norms for the U.S. federal budgetary process is in the work of Roy Meyers (1996). He offers ten "standards" arguing that "a budget process should be: comprehensive, honest, perceptive, constrained, judgmental, cooperative, timely, accessible, accountable, and responsive" (171).

There are two main difficulties in applying Meyers's criteria or anyone else's to the task of designing budgetary decision processes. First, the criteria are inevitably ambiguous and can be operationalized in several different ways. For example, Meyers's "responsive" criterion is for a budget process that "adopts policies that match public preferences." Second, some of the criteria invariably conflict and must be traded off in any application to a real decision process. For example, it is hard to design a decision process that is simultaneously timely and responsive or judgmental and cooperative.

A more general difficulty is the large set of possible standards, norms, or criteria and the inevitable normative disagreements absent a coherent theory. There is a real danger that anyone's list will read like the features in the Boy Scout's motto: trustworthy, loyal, obedient, cheerful. . . . Our tentative list contains just six items:

1. Conditional, Approximate Balance

> *I'm working as hard as I can to get my life and my cash to run out at the same time.*
> *If I can just die after lunch Tuesday, everything will be fine.*
>
> —Doug Sanders

Budgets should approximately balance over several years. Balancing a budget is far from unequivocally good (Burkhead 1956; Lehan 1981), particularly when capital and operating are mixed, as with the U.S. federal government, or when there is an overriding social crisis, such as a war or depression, that gives priority to expenditure over balance. Yet, absent crises and if capital projects are handled separately so as to somewhat match the distribution of cost burdens with beneficiaries, target balance in the operating accounts provides a necessary discipline. *A good budgetary decision process is balanced approximately and conditionally.*

2. Decisional Efficiency
   Budget processes should be efficient in the time and effort they require for decisions. Budgeting presently consumes too much time and attention of elected officials to no good end. The quality of the outcomes does not depend on the intensity of the ideological competition; indeed, the opposite is probably true. Politicians posture for personal political ambitions in the endless partisan and ideological bickering that has become budgeting. *A good budgetary decision process minimizes conflict specifically and transaction costs generally where the conflict and costs contribute nothing to the substantive quality of the decisions.*

3. Feasible Comparisons
   Budget processes should foster healthy competition among different values. The norm of conscious, comprehensive, and simultaneous comparison of alternative budget programs is infeasible. Incremental decision practices too often suppress competing values to assure decisions and continuity in governance. *A good budgetary decision process will stimulate feasible comparisons by stimulating competition or cooperation, as appropriate, among agencies for solving particular problems.*

4. Uncertainty and Flexibility

Budget processes too often freeze public production functions by specifying in such detail what resources agencies will have available to solve problems that the managers are left with almost no flexibility in what resources they use and how they deploy them in dynamic policy environments. *A good budgetary decision process will acknowledge that we live in an uncertain world and pass along sufficient discretion in the allocation process so that properly motivated and trained government employees can exercise their best judgment in adapting to facts as those become known during an allocation period.*

5. Stability

Thorough substantive review of each program and element is not possible in each budget period. Program management often benefits from some stability in financial support. It is hard to motivate employees to perform on program tasks when their jobs are perpetually up for grabs. Proposing the abolition of departments and programs happens much more often for purely political reasons than for any substantive reasons. *A good budgetary decision process will provide for a balance between the frequency and intensity of program review and the managerial need for stability.*

6. Multiple Budgets

Most moderately complex government organizations require several budgets for several purposes: management, planning, and control. Trying to do everything with a single set of accounts and a single document often harms the whole enterprise (Thompson 1994). *The traditional comprehensiveness norm has outlived its usefulness. A good budgetary decision process will explicitly recognize the need for different budgets for different purposes.*

The U.S. federal budgetary decision process clearly falls short on all six norms, however operationalized.

The ad hoc norms approach to reforming budgetary decision processes is worthy of much greater academic effort. Perhaps we can achieve a more coherent, consensual process theory for budgeting.

Democratizing

> *The notion that legislation becomes more expert because of prolonged public discussion of proposed measures is an illusion which follows the notion that public debate is addressed to a thinking man through whose decisions organizations have group free will. All prolonged public discussions of any measure can do is to reconcile conflicts and get people used to the general ideal which the measure represents.*
>
> —Thurman Arnold, *The Folklore of Capitalism*

In the business of reforming the American national government, it is taken as axiomatic that almost anything you can do to open up the government's deliberative processes and to educate and inform the citizenry about governing is a good thing. With few tolerable exceptions (e.g., national security), open government and informed citizens should, according to many would-be reformers, lead to both a more controllable, accountable government and more equitable, efficient, and effective government outcomes.[3]

Over the last twenty-five years there has been a cascade of reforms to increase the openness of government deliberations at all levels, much of it under the rubrics of "sunshine" or "freedom of information." Upon taking control of the House of Representatives in 1994, Republican leaders announced with great fanfare that all nonclassified committee hearings and markup sessions would be open to public view and, in many cases, televised. Aggressive media have taken advantage of their eased access to officials and officialdom; we now live in a virtual torrent of information about the day-by-day, blow-by-blow proceedings of government. Two C-Span channels; routine news coverage by national newspapers, networks, and regular cable shows; aggressive investigative reporting by the print and broadcast media; a myriad of sites for politics on the World Wide Web; a veritable blizzard of talk radio programs; and many other sources have made it possible for each of us to learn much more about the daily activities of government than we ever wanted to know.

In the case of the budget process, the effects of increased openness are, at best, disappointing and, at worst, catastrophic. On the one hand, the citizens are not obviously better informed and, as measured by a spate of recent polls, have become increasingly cynical about the policy process and its outcomes. The public is more dissatisfied with, and distrustful of, politicians and government than ever before; the voters decidedly do not believe that the government's budget is more accountable and responsive after decades of increased openness. On the other hand, budget outcomes in this era of openness are not obviously more equitable, efficient, and effective. Quite the contrary, openness reforms have coincided with huge structural deficits, a clear unwillingness by the key political leaders of the day to face up to the hard choices before them, and a series of policies that put the blame for the crisis on the poor and the newly immigrated (two groups that conveniently tend not to vote).

A fundamental concern is the lack of recognition by advocates of openness that the logic of democratic accountability and responsiveness often has little to do with the outcomes of the policy process. The notion of accountability in a representative democracy is remarkably simple. We hold some preferences on both policy and process. We observe what our elected representatives are doing and compare their *efforts* (and not the final outcomes) to our preferences. If the comparison yields differences greater than the differences between our preferences and the believable promises of the opposition, we replace the representative; otherwise, we support the person again and perhaps communicate with the individual about how he or she can better represent our interests.

In this scheme politics has a logic and progression. Government is governed by our preferences. Each succeeding generation of representatives, assuming some availability of candidates, should be better than the previous one. Government should be getting better. We should be increasingly happy with the government's performance. We are not.

To understand better the source of this conundrum, consider the following simple example. Suppose that a democratic government is considering two budget proposals, A and B, for the next fiscal year, with all deliberations completely open to public inspection. Also suppose that budget B is "better" than budget A according to any of the criteria discussed previously (e.g., B is in conditional approximate balance, A is not; or B is an elegant PPBS solution, A is an *ad hoc* collection of poorly analyzed proposals). To add spice to the stew, imagine as well that budget A proposes lower taxes and more spending whereas budget B proposes higher taxes and less spending. In this instance the citizenry, for whatever reason, might prefer either A or B, and the government, also for a variety of reasons, might choose either A or B. Now examine the implications for both the financial viability and the political success of the government, depending on how these preferences and choices intersect.

Citizens desire budget B, government chooses budget B. This "ideal scenario" of course is what we would like to achieve. The citizens seem to be sufficiently informed to desire the policy that contributes to the financial viability of their nation, and the government follows their preferences. We conclude that this political system is responsive and that democracy works. We have a parade and call it a day.

Citizens desire budget A, government chooses A. This is the GIGO ("Garbage In, Garbage Out") scenario. For whatever reasons or lack thereof, the citizens desire the worse budget, and the government obliges. Observe that in terms of responsiveness this scenario is indistinguishable from the ideal case! Again, we have a parade to celebrate democracy. Unfortunately, this country also may be on the way to financial ruin even as the drums, bugles, and batons complete their triumphant procession on Main Street.

Citizens desire B, government chooses A. This is the "rascals scenario" (as in, "throw the rascals out") that emphasizes the true meaning of accountability. The government makes a poor choice, and, if accountability exists, the government is then punished by the citizens. We hope the next government learns from the experience and makes better choices. When this happens, we chalk up another victory for a democracy that can also achieve financial viability. (Naturally, there is the possibility that the government is not punished for violating the desires of the citizens—a scenario we might label "stupid is as stupid does.")

Citizens desire A, government chooses B. This "martyr scenario" reveals a dark underside of democratic accountability. Here it is likely that the citizens will punish the government for doing something such as raising taxes and cutting spending in order to end a decade of ballooning structural deficits.[4] Observe that, in terms of accountability, this is identical to the rascals scenario! Yet if the next government "learns" from the experience of its predecessor, then the country again may be parading triumphantly off to financial ruin.

This exercise highlights the major flaws in all efforts to improve the budget process through openness and accountability. These attributes of democracy over time can easily yield a succession of bad yet popular choices by government. Politicians know that they will rarely find themselves immersed in the ideal scenario if, for example, a clear majority wants simultaneously lower taxes, higher expenditures, and a balanced budget.[5] Given such intractable preferences, politicians in a democracy would be rational to prefer the GIGO scenario to either the rascals scenario or, heaven help them, the martyr scenario. In fact, it is not even clear that rational politicians would prefer the ideal scenario if the choices made within that framework contributed to a hectic and unrewarding lifestyle.[6]

The exercise also highlights a questionable assumption behind all openness reforms, namely, that the citizens actually would know beyond a shadow of a doubt who is responsible for making both popular and unpopular choices. The policy process, however, rarely allows a fair determination of responsibility. Quick: Who is responsible for the trillions of dollars of accumulated debt of the United States? Was it Jimmy Carter (who approved the indexation of income tax brackets), Arthur Laffer (the father of supply-side economics), Ronald Reagan (the Great Communicator who sold the package of lower taxes and more spending), David Stockman (who managed the actual sale of the package to the Congress), the CEOs of various Fortune 500 companies (who besieged Congress in 1981 to pass the package), Tip O'Neill (who arranged for Democratic members of the House to support Reagan's budget in exchange for even more tax cuts and spending measures), or Bob Dole (who went along with it all despite strong reservations)? All of these persons and more share some responsibility for the 1981 budget that began the rapid accumulation of debt. All the openness in the world would not facilitate accurate and precise assessments of who should be rewarded and punished in this important case. In a similar way, the rascals and martyr scenarios easily could devolve into the unfair punishment of those not to blame or unfair rewarding of those not deserving of credit.

A fascinating paradox is that openness in the process actually facilitates the dynamics behind all of the nonideal budgeting scenarios. Two hallmarks of the openness movement in law and legislative procedures are the requirements that (1) most, if not all, meetings at which the public's business are discussed be open to the public and that (2) all votes by elected officials be recorded so that individual positions are ascertainable. Without these two features, budgetary decision makers actually might make hard choices and then package the final product for public approval. With these two features, combined with essential political factors, a variety of morbid symptoms characterize the process.

Such openness provides strong incentives for participants to perform for attributional effect rather than conduct any real business. It greatly increases the stakes of taking a position against specific interests in favor of broader interests. In fact, the news media and special interests are the primary beneficiaries of increased openness because the resulting information is closely tied to their livelihoods.[7] The requirements probably do not prevent closed meetings to discuss the public's business; they just make it likely that only the scoundrels are there. The requirements have not eliminated the worst forms of collusion, e.g., logrolling, because most politicians have remarkable abilities to cloak any position or vote in terms of the broader public interest, and tacit collusion is easy. Since the governing processes were opened, there has not been any observable movement toward eliminating foolish policies.

The increased volume of information due to openness reforms aggravates the public's overload problem. There was always too much to which to attend. Now we have endless data about the processes of deliberation (if it is not open, descriptions are leaked) and about the personal lives of public figures—even sworn affidavits describing physical features of the president of the United States that can only be corroborated by intimates and those who showered with him in high school gym class. The media tend to stress the titillation factor over substantive insights because it is good marketing; as John Frohnmayer, former chairman of the National Endowment for the Arts noted in the *New York Times* on April 18, 1993, "Congress received more mail in 1990 on the Arts Endowment, which cost each citizen 68 cents for everything we did, than on the savings and loan scandal, which will cost each of us at least $2,000." The political opponents sift the data closely looking for any bit that might stir controversy.

The extended nasty flap in the fall of 1994 over the leaked memo from Alice Rivlin, director of the Office of Management and Budget (the memo outlined a variety of options, some politically unpalatable and infeasible, for addressing further the deficit problem), is a good example of how highly charged and dysfunctional the current political environment is. If it becomes impossible even to lay out and discuss options, the decision-making process becomes sterile. Another somewhat fallacious assumption behind the openness reforms is that responsible use will be made of the resulting access and information. Uses of the information for partisan advantage or for ratings are commonplace, and it is foolish to believe that these uses will ever go away. The public's task of sorting all this out and deciding what to believe, assuming they take the normative chore of being informed citizens seriously, is somewhere between formidable and impossible.

In criticizing the purpose and effects of democratizing reforms we certainly do not want to deny their base appeal. Surely part of the rationale is that governments, unlike businesses in competitive markets, have no natural checks on their exercise of power and that only close, critical scrutiny by an informed public can prevent or discover and punish abuses of power. There is good reason to doubt that closed meetings necessarily will find the public interest; indeed, the parochial interests of the participants will too often predominate. Public meetings, on the other hand, force participants to defend (rationalize) their position in terms of the broader public interest rather than crass parochial interests.

Nevertheless, the success of openness and other democratizing reforms in the budget process hinges on developments that are highly unlikely to occur now or in the future. We emphasize only a few of these here: (1) the public must be highly educated on budgetary matters and focused entirely on outcome rather than process; (2) the public also must be highly organized in order to counter the investments of time and other resources constantly being made by special interests; (3) the incentives for key decision makers must be conditioned on public approval of *outcomes;* and (4) the choices of all actors in the process must be immune from the day-to-day tussles of modern politics under the constant glare of media attention. Those who would court these occurrences surely deserve recognition for their faith in the miraculous.

Power Shifting

> *The essence of a free government consists in an effectual control of rivalries.*
> —John Adams

From the restrictions on "scutages and aid" in the Magna Carta in 1217 to the creation of the republic following the French Revolution, the earliest reform attempts in this "modern" era were concerned with gaining some popular control over sovereigns.[8] This move to popular control began with avoiding capricious and burdensome taxes to control over expenditures (Burkhead 1956). Once legislatures had achieved a high degree of control over expenditures a new problem emerged. The legislatures appeared to have an insatiable appetite for spending money, little taste for raising it if unpopular measures were required to do so, and no ability to reconcile expenditures across separate appropriation groups with available revenues. This problem led directly, albeit slowly, to the creation and adoption of executive budgets in 1921 for the U.S. federal government, a move that centralized budgeting and shifted some power from the legislatures to the executives.

Over the last twenty years there has been a pronounced transfer, particularly at the federal level, of budgetary power from the executive to the legislature. The main lesson from these power-shifting reforms is that the essential problems with the budgetary decision process do not stem from the distribution of power.

The contemporary power-shifting reforms, such as the recently passed presidential line-item veto and the various balanced budget amendment proposals, may not have much effect. The line-item veto law will succeed only in adding another layer of complexity to an already overly complex game. The proposers will be able to blunt the veto threat to their pet line items through careful packaging. Also, although the line-item veto would strengthen the hand of the president, the extent of strengthening depends on how the law is written and might merely make the president the ultimate logroller.[9]

The balanced budget amendment proposals represent another form of power shifting. Power would shift from fallible human beings in the legislature and the executive to the balance norm defined and required in law. The amendment most likely to pass will, like the Gramm-Rudman law, be defeatable by various legislative sleights of hand. If not, the amendment may become a pretext and political cover for eviscerating defense and entitlement programs in an era when it may prove impossible to achieve super majorities required for tax increases. At last, a power-shifting reform with real effects on revenue and allocation patterns! Unfortunately, most of the effects will be perverse, as we find ourselves unprepared for the next significant occasion requiring military force and a growing penurious segment of the population.

Control

> To be governed is to be, at every operation, every transaction, noted, counted, registered, taxed, stamped, measured, numbered, assessed, licensed, authorized, admonished, prevented, forbidden, reformed, corrected, punished.
>
> —Proudhon

The most popular budget reforms historically are controls. Controls are always the easiest politically because they purportedly address the problems of fraud, waste, and abuse in the handling of public money. We have auditors auditing the auditors who audit the auditors, all overseen by legislators looking for political advantage and a sporadically attentive public. We have appropriations at such a fine-grained level of detail in an uncertain world that the budget becomes a great engine of endless complex adjustments, ineffective programs, and noncompliance.

Ironically, the transaction costs associated with elaborate controls to prevent fraud, waste, and abuse doom government to inefficiency; the control costs greatly exceed the amounts prevented plus the amounts found and recovered. In many areas, such as contracting, the controls are less than fully effective. For example, when a firm is convicted of defrauding the government and is forced to pay a fine, the government cannot hold this against them in considering their bids on subsequent government contracts; if the miscreants meet the specifications and have the low bid, the government must do business with them.

The essential lesson from experience with control reforms is that we need a lot fewer of them. Controls provide legislators with endless opportunities to find fault and grandstand politically, but they cost a lot directly and seriously disrupt much legitimate government business in the name of finding and preventing a much smaller proportion of illegitimate business. Many of the best potential suppliers for government at all levels will simply not take on government business because of the hassle, or, if they do, they charge governments a significant premium on what they charge their corporate customers for the same commodities. The corporate customers require much less nonsensical paperwork, decide and pay expeditiously, and do not send armies of inspectors around to monitor supplier behavior in performing the contracts.

Effective Reforms

Man must sit in chair with mouth open for very long time before roast duck fly in.
—Chinese proverb

Budget processes and outcomes are not obviously getting better. Government budget problems are not amenable to any stable, enduring solution because of the inherent complexities and dynamics in preparing and executing government budgets. Budget problems are highly interdependent temporally; the problems for current officials are driven to a very great extent by the actions (transgressions?) of former officials. The incentives to tax less and spend more in the here and now are almost always stronger than the incentives to abide by the abstract canons of good financial practice. The future consequences of current financial decisions are both ambiguous and uncertain. Budget decisions invite the most bitter bureaucratic and political rivalries.

So long as the incentives for the individual participants, notably the elected and appointed officials, remain the same, not much will change about budgetary decisions. As things now stand, individuals cannot, with rare exceptions, be held accountable for the characteristics of the budget process or for the quality of budget outcomes. Following are a few "modest proposals," in something of a Swiftian spirit, that would, if adopted, make a considerable difference in budgetary process and outcomes.

Improving the Signal-to-Noise Ratio

Better make it four; I don't think I can eat eight.
—Yogi Berra after having ordered a pizza and being
asked if he wanted it cut into four or eight pieces.

There has always been a lot of funny figuring in Washington and in many of our larger state and city governments. There is, however, much too much time and effort wasted in federal budgeting in recent years arguing about numbers and assumptions. For a while, perhaps its first ten years of life, the Congressional Budget Office (CBO) was a welcome source of nonpartisan numbers for use in the budgeting process. CBO was a reality check on the Office of Management and Budget (OMB), which has become increasingly partisan over the years—professional norms for data integrity from OMB reached a nadir in the David Stockman era when he confessed to a level of perfidy that shocked many outsiders; the insiders were only shocked that he would confess such common, but ethically questionable, practices to a journalist. Unfortunately, CBO is increasingly politicized, and the budget process is currently plagued by endless, acrimonious disagreements over which are the proper baselines and deflators in preparing estimates. The situation with different political parties controlling the Congress and the presidency clearly fuels Pyrrhic battles over technical details that are wasteful of scarce political attention and unfathomable to all but the most inside insiders. The circumstance where one party controls both Congress and the presidency might be even more dangerous to the country because the only contesting assumptions and numbers will have to come from think tanks that do not have the same resources available as OMB and CBO.

We need an independent, nonpartisan source of numbers and assumptions. This organization, probably new, should be fully insulated from political vicissitudes. The membership should be selected on the basis of technical competence. The organization's reporting should be public. Its budget should be determined by formula, e.g., the organization's annual budget is a fixed percentage of the prior year's outlays for OMB plus CBO, and not subject to annual review. The organization's leadership should enjoy tenure and protections comparable to those of the comptroller general.

The technical cacophony is neither necessary nor useful except to those who would play games in the budget struggles. Superior technical virtuosity and an absence of conscience in exercising that skill is a poor basis for deciding budget issues. The various contestants in the budget process would be required to use the new organization's estimates and assumptions in evaluating ("scoring") their policy positions. Until we get beyond having to decide which of two liars—more politely, spin doctors—is more accurate, the substantive quality of budget debates simply cannot improve.

Improving People Quality

The trouble with the rat race is that even if you win, you're still a rat.
—Lily Tomlin

In the spirit of democratizing reforms, something should be done to improve the selection of people for public responsibility, particularly elected officials with financial management responsibility. The media are diligent, but the information they provide us about electoral candidates is uneven and almost always far short of the information generated about proposed political appointees in confirmation processes. In the late twentieth century we are more likely to get good information about candidates' romantic proclivities, how they paid their maids, and their public-speaking abilities than about their substantive abilities to perform in whatever office they seek.

Electoral candidates should be required to provide the same level of information about their background as an applicant for a GS–11 position requiring a top secret security clearance. This would give the press a head start. Furthermore, we should require some sort of basic examination of elemental knowledge and skills, including financial skills. There would be no passing "grade," just an examination with the results openly reported. An ancillary benefit would be the new market for higher education in general and for those who teach budgeting and financial management in particular.

Pay and Performance

They tell a story about a Hollywood agent's young son who asked his father what the word "integrity" meant. "Let me give you an example, son. Let's say Kirk Douglas sent me a check for the agency's commission on the new picture we got for him. And let's say a few days later his business manager sends me another check in error for the same commission. Integrity is whether or not I tell my partner."
—Tony Randall and Michael Mindlin, *Which Reminds Me*

It is easy to devise reforms that will make the norms for budgetary processes personally meaningful for individuals. If all we cared about was balancing the budget, for example, we might make the salaries of members of Congress and of everyone in the executive branch at or above the grade of GS–15 directly dependent on their success in controlling the deficit. The simplest formula for their compensation in year *t* might be:

$$\text{Actual Pay}_t = \text{Salary}_t \times (\text{Total Revenue}_t \, / \, \text{Total Expenditures}_t)$$

In this scheme, deficits reduce the salaries; exact balance yields exact salaries; and surpluses increase salaries. If, for example, revenues were 85 percent of expenditures—one form of 15 percent deficit—the Actual Pay would represent 85 percent of the Salary.[10] The formula is easily rewritten so that only a portion of the compensation would be at risk and that at reasonable levels, for example:

$$\text{Actual Pay}_t = .75(\text{Salary}_t) + [.25(\text{Salary}_t) \times$$
$$(\text{Total Revenue}_t \, / \, \text{Total Expenditures}_t)]$$

This formula would have an immediate and profound impact on budget balancing behavior, but it is obviously inadequate because it introduces several new improper incentives; raising more revenue and spending less without regard to the effects on values other than balance would have a direct salutary effect on individual compensation. Clearly, we care about much more than simple balance in the current accounts. We might, for example, want a revenue system and outlays that improve our standard of living measured in after-tax disposable income, lower the rates of unemployment, increase GNP, reduce the overall trade deficit, and stabilize the currency. The measures should all be benchmarked over time and against a select set of other industrialized nations; this keeps the focus on the competition and separates some of the uncontrollables. Each of these factors could be defined so that 1.0 would represent acceptable performance, more superior performance, and less inadequate performance. It might also make sense to extend this payment scheme into the retirement plan so that all officials have an incentive on their watch to behave responsibly for the long term and to ensure that their successors are capable of protecting their retirement.

Many politicians, particularly conservative politicians, believe strongly in the virtues of tying pay to performance. They believe that this linkage happens automatically in free markets and that its absence in government is a major reason why government's performance is usually inferior to private sector performance. What better place to start in remedying this problem than at the top?

A Little Darkness and Collective Responsibility

No individual raindrop ever considers itself responsible for the flood.
—Anonymous

Another source of problems—described in some detail in the "Democratizing" section above—is the incentives for individual legislators with political ambitions to spend more time on pointless public relations and in managing the public's attributions about their relationship to particular issues and actions than in seriously striving to solve the nation's problems. There is a long-standing situation where a majority of the American electorate despise Congress as a collectivity but like their own representative. Arnold (1990) discusses the importance of the "chain of traceability" for members of Congress. Their decisional behavior is one thing when it can be linked to effects and something else when it cannot.

A simple reform with profound implications for budgetary processes would be to close all deliberative hearings to everyone but members and full-time staff and have all secret votes. Members would be free to claim or imply whatever they choose as to their positions in the deliberations and their opinions of the results. There would be no record of individual activity. Members would have neither the need nor the opportunity to posture for their various constituencies amid unrecorded deliberations, only outside deliberations.

This reform had several effects. The closed hearings and secret votes would thoroughly disrupt the processes through which special interests now work. Indeed, the lobbyists have benefited much more than average citizens from openness reforms; the special interests are the only groups with sufficiently strong incentives actually to attend laborious markup sessions and to keep close track of votes. Because members of Congress would not be able to differentiate themselves from the collectivity as easily, they would have much stronger incentives to work hard for sensible, defensible collective decisions.

Territorial Competitions

Burke got his ass sent packing home.
—Congressman Ronald Coleman in the *Economist,* June 27,
1992, responding to someone noting that Edmund Burke
said a representative should exercise his own opinion

Another source of incentives problems is that the founding fathers structured a perpetual political competition among opposing values where the basis, geography, has no inherent virtue. Territoriality in animal communities often makes evolutionary sense; the opportunities to eat and procreate are often associated with particular territories, and so competitions over territory have real meaning. The geographical basis of political competition in the United States increasingly serves no useful purpose. Competitive modes of organization are useful when they motivate the competitors (e.g., firms or politicians) to produce more value for the arbiters of the competition (e.g., consumers and voters). Where the production virtues and the rewards are tightly coupled and the production units are reliably motivated by self-interest, we have two hundred years of theoretical results from economists indicating that competition is the superior form of organization in terms of the total value produced. These results are not relevant to the government where production virtues and rewards have little relationship.

Let us consider a simple, not so hypothetical, example. The air force decides to change one of the aircraft that it uses in primary flight training. The new trainer offers substantial improvements over the trainer that has long been used to train new pilots. The old trainer has been produced at a plant on Long Island, New York, where it is a mainstay of the local economy. Under the current political arrangement that allows large, persistent geographic imbalances in benefits from the federal trough, the political competition centers on the economic benefits to the two constituencies rather than the substantive intent of the flight training program. The production virtues associated with the program are positively harmed by the geographical basis of the competition. If the ultimate decision is to stay with the old trainer, the primary cost is pilots who are not trained as well as they should be. Even if the ultimate decision is to acquire the new trainer, the competitive process produces costs. There are improper signals to the contractors and contractees: geographic politics is more important than substance. There may also be costs in the form of compensating inefficiencies to the losing geographic unit. In either case, there are substantial costs in the political attention spent on geographical infighting rather than on more salutary issues. The 1995 discussions of the B-2 and the Seawolf submarines provide further examples of the triumph of geographic politics over the substantive effectiveness of programs.

There are no long-term members of Congress who routinely focus on the substantive program issues at the expense of "crass" constituency issues. One approach to removing the irrational competition would be to create a set of accounts that show the flows of federal money to and from congressional districts. The collections and disbursements will be categorized and weighted differentially. A dollar of income tax paid from the district will count differently than a dollar of apportioned corporate income tax paid. A dollar in a grant to a local government will count differently than a dollar of direct assistance to an individual. The weights can be devised to accomplish a variety of social goals, particularly redistributional goals. The output of the accounts would be an index number for each congressional district of the net impact of federal revenue collections and expenditures. The law would require the books to be balanced on a moving average basis every three to five years. Rather than make the adjustments directly in programs, it would be better to utilize a set of compensatory tax credits or grants for relief to districts that are losers on the accounts.

This system would take many of the irrational competitive incentives out of the congressional system—why have we ever considered it healthy for members to compete for the affection of their constituents on the basis of how well they do relative to other members in bringing home the bacon for their district? This system would give members at least some opportunity to redirect their attention from protecting shares of existing pork and seeking new pork regardless of its form to concerns about the "best pork" for their constituents.

The competition for financial advantage from the activities of the U.S. federal government would be one that cannot be won on a geographical basis. The numbers to implement the system are (or should be) available routinely from the Internal Revenue Service and the Office of Management and Budget. The computations required would be no more difficult than those associated with the late, sometimes lamented, general revenue sharing program.

The Bottom Line

All progress is based upon a universal innate desire of every organism to live beyond its income.

—Samuel Butler

We have several hundred years experience in attempting to reform budget processes. There have been many more reform failures than successes. It is important to begin learning from the rich failure experiences and quit recycling the same failed ideas in ways that assure that they will fail again.

The economic perspective has been, at best, a mixed blessing. It is a glimpse of unattainable perfection and a set of tools that have changed the language in which the arguments are made but not the arguments. The traditional norms face difficulty because times have changed and because they lack any theoretical basis; devising new norms for budgetary processes, norms with some grounding in a boundedly rational theory of decision making, is important. The democratizing reforms have failed because they are founded on models of how people *should* behave rather than how they *can* and *do* behave. The power-shifting reforms fail because power is still shared and because the underlying incentives for those holding power remain unchanged. The control reforms fail because they attempt to control the uncontrollable and carry their own enormous costs.

Budgeting and budget reform are much too important to leave to the politicians, to those with unshakable commitments to disproven theories, and to the next generation of public servants who will undertake to solve problems in much the same way as past generations attempted to solve them with no benefit of their failure experiences.

Historical reforms have failed to solve the problems with the budget process primarily because they have failed to address the underlying source of the problems, the incentives for the participants. The "modest proposals" are not apt to garner much immediate support. They do, however, suggest a different problem diagnosis, which in turn suggests a different path to solution.

Notes

1. The original Latin text is not at hand, but the translation should probably be "accounts" rather than "budget." "Budget" is from the French baguette, little bag, or peddlar's pack, in which the chancellor of the exchequer kept his papers. The French adopted the term in about 1814 (Dowell, cited in Adams 1898).

2. Herbert Simon's role is interesting. In his work with Clarence Ridley and in his dissertation, which became *Administrative Behavior* (1945), Simon did more than anyone else to bring the economic perspective to the issues, including budgeting, of government organizations. Both Key (1940) and Lewis (1952) rely on Simon's work. Then Simon became the earliest and most ardent critic of the rational model of decision making. By the time PPBS came along, Simon was deeply into creating cognitive science as an alternative descriptive theory of how individuals do make decisions. Key, Lewis, and, eventually, Aaron Wildavsky were skeptical of the practicality of the economic approach to budgeting and based their skepticism to a great extent on Simon's criticisms of rational models as descriptive theories of decision making.

3. Note, however, that the framers of the Constitution were both deeply suspicious of popular control and operated in a technological environment that did not allow for rapid long-distance communication. Consequently, their original design for the U.S. government included just one element—the House of Representatives—that featured direct public choice of political leaders. In keeping with English tradition, the framers gave the House unique responsibility for raising revenue but no special voice in setting expenditures.

4. Those who doubt the realism of this scenario might revisit the promises by H. Ross Perot to serve only one term if elected president. Perot is probably aware that he will not be asked back if he administers his cure for what ails America.

5. The key, of course, is to eliminate the inefficiencies in fraud, waste, and abuse. Unfortunately, to get the magnitudes of savings required to balance budgets requires defining entire programs, including entitlements, as "waste."

6. The great budget battles of 1995 and 1996 between President Clinton and the Republican-controlled Congress resulted in a large number of retirements by members of the House and Senate. Many of them spoke directly of the grimness of legislative life now that balanced budgets were to be the central objective of the process.

7. It is not average citizens who sit through lengthy, complicated markups but the vested special interests and reporters. Ironically, in opening up the processes we have made it much easier for the well-funded, well-organized special interests to dominate the public interest—all in the name of improving democracy!

8. Burkhead (1956) provides an excellent brief history of modern budgeting. Parnell (1968) is a fascinating early history of the attempt to regularize the financial functions of Britain. Bolles (1969) is excellent on budgeting prior to the advent of the "executive budget." Lehan (1981) provides a useful historical perspective. Sundelson (1935) provides an outstanding review of the European school's norms for budgeting. Downs and Larkey (1986) critically review a few modern attempts at budget reform.

9. There are more effective forms of line-item veto, such as the one wielded by the governor of Wisconsin.

10. The problems in defining terms and specifying time lags or payment schemes that would smooth the payments are manageable.

References

Adams, Henry Carter. 1898. *The Science of Finance.* New York: Henry Holt.

Arnold, Doug. 1990. *The Logic for Congressional Action.* New Haven, Conn.: Yale University Press.

Bolles, Albert S. 1969. *The Financial History of the United States from 1861 to 1885.* Vols. 1–3. New York: Appleton, 1894. Reprint, New York: Augustus M. Kelley.

Burkhead, Jesse. 1956. *Government Budgeting.* New York: John Wiley and Sons.

Downs, George W., and Patrick Larkey. 1986. *The Search for Government Efficiency: From Hubris to Helplessness.* Philadelphia: Temple University Press.

Key, V. O. Jr. 1940. "The Lack of a Budgetary Theory." *American Political Science Review* 24 (December): 1137–44.

Larkey, Patrick D. 1979. *Evaluating Public Programs: The Impact of General Revenue Sharing on Municipal Government.* Princeton, N.J.: Princeton University Press.

Lehan, Edward A. 1981. *Simplified Governmental Budgeting.* Chicago: Municipal Finance Officers Association.

Lewis, Verne B. 1952. "Toward a Theory of Budgeting." *Public Administration Review* 12 (winter): 42–54.

Meyers, Roy. 1996. "Is There a Key to the Normative Budgeting Lock?" *Policy Sciences* 29 (August): 171–89.

Parnell, Henry. 1968. *On Financial Reform,* 1831. Reprint, New York: Augustus M. Kelley.

Simon, Herbert. 1945. *Administrative Behavior.* New York: Free Press.

Sundelson, J. Wilner. 1935. "Budgetary Principles." *Political Science Quarterly* 1, no. 2.

Thompson, Fred. 1994. "Mission-Driven, Results-oriented Budgeting: Fiscal Administration and the New Public Management." *Public Budgeting and Finance* 14 (fall): 90–105.

U.S. Commission on the Organization of the Executive Branch of the Government. 1949. *Budgeting and Accounting.* Report to the Congress. Washington, D.C.: U.S. Government Printing Office.

Wildavsky, Aaron. 1974. *The Politics of the Budgetary Process.* 2d ed. Boston: Little, Brown.

8 | Implementing Mission–Driven, Results-Oriented Budgeting

Fred Thompson and Carol K. Johansen

ThEsE ARE EXCITING times, although not easy ones, for public managers and for students of public management. The conduct of the public's business is undergoing a sea change. This seems to be a worldwide phenomenon—not merely with respect to the fact of change, but in its content as well (Borins 1994; National Performance Review 1993; Reschenthaler and Thompson 1996; Schedler 1995; Trebilcock 1994; World Bank 1995). The new public management reformers call for the decentralization of the management and delivery of services, improved service quality, a relentless emphasis on customer satisfaction, and a "bold use of market-like mechanisms for those parts of the public sector that cannot be transferred directly into private ownership" (Pollitt 1993, 180).

This chapter is concerned with one of those marketlike mechanisms, outcome budgeting, or, to use the National Performance Review's terminology, mission-driven, results-oriented budgets. Outcome budgeting involves a wholesale transfer of state-of-the art financial management concepts, practices, and processes from the private sector to the public. It means that budget formulation in the public sector ought to be more like private sector capital budgeting and that budget execution ought to be more like private sector responsibility budgeting. In this chapter we will explain what these claims mean and show how outcome budgeting could be implemented by the federal government of the United States.

Capital Budgeting Fundamentals

In the private sector, budgeting starts with cost-benefit analysis. Financial theory teaches that, in the presence of a capital market where funds can be obtained at a price, the welfare of an entity's stakeholders—a firm's stockholders, a not-for-profit's clients, a jurisdiction's citizens—will be maximized by the implementation of all policy choices that generate positive net present values. This means, in part, that the timing of cash flows—future benefits or costs—

accruing from the policy choice is generally of no importance, so long as benefits or costs are properly discounted.

This conclusion follows from the separation principle, often called Fisher separation, after its formulator, Irving Fisher. This principle states that an entity's operating decisions should be independent of the personal consumption decisions of its stakeholders. Where the entity maximizes net wealth, individual stakeholders can maximize utility by borrowing against this wealth or lending it, thereby timing cash flows to match their personal consumption preferences.

Many students of financial economics further assert that an entity's capital budgeting decisions should also be independent of the source of financing. This view is associated with the work of Nobel laureates Franco Modigliani and Merton Miller and derives from two distinct inferences: (1) the law of one price, which says that, owing to the possibility of "homemade leverage" or "arbitrage" by investors, two similar assets must have the same price (i.e., must be priced to yield the same expected rate of return); (2) the irrelevance of capital structure, which says that under certain conditions, an entity's value will be the same regardless of whether it finances its activities with debt or equity—this conclusion is easily extended to debt and taxes (Gordon and Slemrod 1983, 1986; Gordon and Metcalf 1991; Choate and Thompson 1996).

The basic thrust of this logic is that budgetary decisions should be governed by the cost-benefit rule: "say yes whenever benefits exceed costs." There is only one basic caveat to this rule. Delay may be justified when it will provide additional information about the true costs or benefits of a decision. As Avinash Dixit and Robert Pindyck (1994) explain, holding a decision opportunity that can be postponed is analogous to holding a call option; it gives you the right but not the obligation to exercise it at a future time. When an entity makes an irreversible decision, it "kills" its option to decide. That means that it sacrifices the possibility that waiting would provide information affecting the desirability or timing of the decision. This "opportunity cost" (lost option value) should be included as part of the cost of the decision. Hence, where decisions are both irreversible and can be postponed, the net present value rule should be amended to read: say yes whenever benefits exceed costs by an amount equal to keeping the option alive.

Budget Processes

The institutional arrangements through which budgets are formulated and resource allocation decisions are made in the private sector are often analogous to the authorization/appropriations processes of the federal government of the

United States. Indeed, Donaldson Brown, former chief financial officer of the General Motors Corporation, explicitly referenced the authorization/appropriations processes of the federal government when he created the first modern procedure for the allocation of capital funds between corporate divisions in 1923. Under Brown's system, appropriation requests had to include detailed plans of the buildings, equipment, and materials required; the capital needed; and the benefits to be achieved from an appropriation. A general manager's signature was sufficient authorization for a request below a certain amount. All very large projects, however, were subject to review by the appropriations committee and required the approval of both the executive committee and the finance committee (Chandler 1962, 146–47).

Prior to 1981, when the General Electric Corporation restructured and decentralized operations, resource allocation at GE followed a similar procedure. First came strategic planning, which authorized organizational units to undertake various projects. This process produced tentative income targets for each business unit and allocations of capital from corporate headquarters to sectors, sectors to strategic business units, and strategic business units to divisions. Commitment was provided in the next step of the resource allocation process, which authorized sponsoring managers to encumber funds to carry out initiatives. Division managers could appropriate up to $1 million for each initiative, sector executives $6 million, and the CEO $20 million; larger amounts had to be appropriated by the board of directors. The appropriator was supposed to ascertain that the strategic purpose behind the initiative was valid and then determine that the proposed initiative was optimally designed for its purpose (Anthony and Govindarajan 1995). Traditionally, detailed appropriation requests have served as operating budgets for capital projects in business—i.e, as a starting point for project control and variance analysis.

Differences between Capital Budgeting Processes in Business and Government

Despite certain similarities, the differences between budget formulation in the private sector and governmental budgeting are often great and in several respects decisive. In the first place, most private entities employ multiple budgets: capital budgets, operating budgets, and cash budgets. Private sector capital budgeting is concerned only with decisions that have significant future consequences. Its time horizon is the life of the decision; its focus is the discounted net present value of the decision alternative. It is always distinguished from operating budgeting, which is concerned with motivating managers to serve the organization. In the operating budget, the relevant time horizon is the operational cycle of the administrative unit in question, perhaps a month or even a week in the case of cost and revenue centers and usually longer where investment and profit centers are concerned. Operating budgets focus on the performance of the administrative unit, the outputs produced, and the resources consumed—where possible these are all measured in current dollars. Cash budgeting is concerned with providing liquidity, when needed, at a minimum cost. Most governments try to make one process do the work of three. Not surprisingly, that process usually fails to do any one thing very well. What governments do best is liquidity management, although, paradoxically, liquidity is rarely a serious concern to most national governments.

Second, private sector capital budgeting is selective. It is usually concerned only with new initiatives and then only with changes in operations that are expected to yield benefits for longer than a year. Despite powerful inclinations to incrementalism, governmental budgeting tries to be comprehensive. All planned asset acquisitions, including current assets as well as long-term assets, are typically included under the appropriations/authorization process.

Third, private sector capital budgeting tends to be a continuous process. Most well-managed firms always have a variety of initiatives under development. The decision to go ahead with an initiative is usually made only once, when the initiative is ripe, and is usually reconsidered only if it turns sour. In contrast, budgeting in the government tends to be repetitive—most appropriations are reconsidered annually on the basis of a rigid schedule.

Fourth, an initiative's sponsor or champion within the organization is usually given the authority and the responsibility for implementing it. In government the new initiative's champion is seldom assigned responsibility for its implementation; instead, that responsibility is usually given to someone else, sometimes even in an entirely different department (see Bower 1970).

Another difference is that the objective of capital budgeting in the private sector is the identification of options with positive net present values because, in the absence of real limits on the availability of cash or managerial attention, the welfare of a firm's shareholders will be maximized by the implementation of all projects offering positive net present values. Although many government decisions are informed by cost-benefit and cost-effectiveness analysis (in the United States, federal water and power and state construction projects have long been required to pass a benefit-cost test; Congress has recently imposed similar requirements on mandates; and federal loan guarantee and insurance programs are funded in present value terms), appropriations requests rarely show all the future implications of current decisions in present value terms. For example, in the United States, the federal government routinely reduces current outlays by delaying major acquisitions and maintenance efforts, often thereby increasing discounted costs 60 percent or more. This irrational policy is justified by the need to reduce the deficit and, thereby, avoid borrowing at interest rates of 7 percent (or less at present).

The biggest difference, however, between budget authority in most governments and the capital budgets approved by top management in the private sector lies in their relationship to operating budgets.

Government Budgeting and Operational Budgeting

In the private sector, operating budgets are management control devices. They are a means of motivating managers to serve the policies and purposes of the organizations to which they belong. In the private sector, management control is not primarily a process for detecting and correcting unintentional performance errors and intentional irregularities, such as theft or misuse of resources. In operating-budget formulation, an organization's commitments, the results of all past capital budgeting decisions, are converted into terms that correspond to the sphere of responsibility of administrative units and their managers. In budget execution, operations are monitored and subordinate managers evaluated and rewarded.

The budgeting systems of some governments do this. Nevertheless, there are critical differences between programming and budgeting in most governments and standard practices in well-run firms: operational budgets in government tend to be highly detailed spending or resource-acquisition plans, which must be scrupulously executed just as they were approved; in contrast, operating budgets in the private sector are usually sparing of detail, often consisting of no more than a handful of quantitative performance standards.

This difference reflects the efforts made by firms to delegate authority and responsibility down into their organizations. Delegation of authority means giving departmental managers the maximum feasible authority needed to make their units productive—or, in the alternative, subjecting them to a minimum of constraints. Hence, delegation of authority requires operating budgets to be stripped to the minimum needed to motivate and inspire subordinates. Ideally the operating budget of an organization would contain a single number or performance target (e.g., a sales quota, a unit cost standard, or a profit or return-on-investment target) for each administrative unit.

Responsibility budgeting is the most common approach to operational budgeting used by well-managed private organizations. The fundamental construct of responsibility budgeting is an account (or control) structure that is oriented toward responsibility centers. A responsibility center is an administrative unit headed by a manager who is responsible for its actions. Responsibility centers have purposes or objectives, and they use inputs (resources) to produce outputs (goods or services). The outputs of a well-designed responsibility center will be closely related to its objectives.

Responsibility centers are usually classified according to two dimensions: (1) the integration dimension—i.e., the relationship between the responsibility center's objectives and the overall purposes and policies of the organization; and (2) the decentralization dimension—i.e., the amount of authority delegated to responsibility managers, measured in terms of their discretion to acquire and use assets.

On the first dimension, a responsibility center can be either a mission center or a support center. The output of a mission center contributes directly to the organization's objectives. The output of a support center is an input to another responsibility center in the organization, either another support center or a mission center. On the decentralization dimension, discretionary expense centers, the bureaucratic norm, are found at one extreme and profit and investment centers at the other. A support center may be either an expense center or a profit center. If the latter, its profit is the difference between its expenses and "revenue" from "selling" its services to other responsibility centers.[1] Both profit and investment centers are usually free to borrow, and investment centers are also free to make decisions about plant and equipment, new products, and other issues that are significant to the long-run performance of the organization.

In the context of responsibility budgeting, budget execution means monitoring a responsibility center's performance in terms of the target specified and rewarding its manager accordingly. Responsibility centers coordinate their activities via a process of mutual accommodation. Effective delegation of authority is possible in the private sector in part because capital budgeting and operational budgeting are treated as related but distinct processes. An organization's operating budgets must reflect its long-term commitments. Thus, a decision to invest resources in a new initiative should be reflected in the operating budgets of all the responsibility centers affected. The process by which commitments are reflected in operating budgets is called programming or, in the case of discrete multiperiod projects, project budgeting. In programming, operating budgets are revised to reflect the benefit and cost flows that justified the decision to go ahead with a new initiative in the first place. Increases in performance expected of each administrative unit or responsibility center are specified, targets are revised to take account of anticipated improvements, and responsibility for realizing them is assigned.

Again, government budgeting often reflects the form but not the content of private sector capital and operating budgets. The U.S. Department of Defense's Planning, Programming, Budgeting System, for example, starts with strategic plans. These are then broken down by function into broad missions (e.g., strategic retaliatory forces) and are then further subdivided into hundreds of subprograms or program elements. Next comes the identification of program alternatives, forecasting and evaluating the consequences of program alternatives, and deciding which program alternatives to carry out. This exercise produces a plan detailing both continuing programmatic commitments (the "base") and new commitments ("increments" or "decrements") in terms of force structure (including sizes and types of forces) and readiness levels, inventories and logistical capabilities, and the development of new weapons and support systems. The consequences of the DOD's programmatic decisions are estimated in terms of the kind, amount, and timing of all assets to be acquired, including personnel services as well as plant, equipment, and supplies, to be funded for each program package (assuming no change in commitments) during the next six-year period. These acquisition plans are expressed in terms of current dollars and arrayed by military department, object of expenditure, and function. This constitutes the financial management portion of the Future Year Defense Plan, the first year of which is the Department of Defense's budget proposal (Jones 1991).

Even in the U.S. Department of Defense, however, government budgets do not really distinguish between deciding what to do and actually doing it. What Congress decides is what is supposed to be done—budgets are supposed to be executed the way they are enacted. For the most part, operating managers within the federal government may do only what their budget says they can do: buy things, e.g., personnel services, materials and supplies, long-lived plant and equipment. Their budgets focus exclusively on assets to be acquired by individual administrative units and on the timing of those acquisitions—on objects of expenditure or line items rather than performance targets, on many inputs rather than a few critical outputs or results. In other words, most operating managers in the federal government are treated like the managers of discretionary expense centers; they have no real authority to acquire or use assets; without this authority, they cannot be held responsible for the financial performance of the administrative units they nominally head.

Historical Development

That there are great differences between the budgetary process in government and the way capital and operating budgeting are done in the private sector is hardly surprising. Governmental financial management has always been sui generis. In the English-speaking world, its roots are to be found in a procedure that was established in the twelfth century involving a teller, a tally cutter, an auditor, a clerk of the pells, a scriptor tallier, and several chamberlains, and survived more or less intact until 1826. Object-of-expenditure appropriation and accounting was introduced in 1666 to prevent Charles II from spending money from the navy allocation on his mistresses. This system, which has come to be known as fund accounting and which was evidently inspired by the pigeonhole design of the rolltop desk (or bureau), assumed its present form in 1689. Thus fund accounting dates from a time when double-entry bookkeeping was generally unknown, few gentlemen knew Arabic numbers, and financial transactions involved an exchange of hard coins (specie) or personal IOUs.

This system was revised in 1829, but at that time the recommendations of the accounting profession were rejected in favor of the civil servants', which were against double entry and the shift from a cash to an accrual basis of accounts and which left intact the previous confusion between the balance sheet and the income statement and current and long-term assets and liabilities. Also during the nineteenth century, the English-speaking world adopted French budgetary norms—comprehensiveness, exclusivity, repetition, and annuality, which had already been introduced to most of the European continent along with other aspects of bureaucratic rationality by Napoleon's armies.

The United States was a laggard in this area. Most of its financial management practices were improvised from whatever was at hand to deal with problems or needs as they arose. The result was neither pretty nor systematic, but on balance worked fairly well. The Progressives changed all this. As Irene Rubin (1993) explains, progressive officials and academics, those who favored expansionary, activist government, invented or imported modern public budgeting in the United States. The reformers were generally committed to making procedures more orderly and increasing executive authority. They were not really interested in business practice, and business played almost no role in providing examples for government to follow, although business leaders often supported budget reform and funded its study and implementation.

Even where business and government use similar terms they often refer to different things. For example, many state and local jurisdictions remove large-scale, lumpy investments in plant and equipment (highway construction, waste-management facilities, public housing, educational facilities, hospitals, and so on) from their operating accounts/budgets to a plant or fixed assets fund/capital budget. Often they borrow the cash used to make these investments and match repayment of principal and interest payments to the life of the asset. These payments are then charged to the operating fund. Lacking economically sound opportunity cost measures, these principal and interest payments more or less satisfactorily measure the consumption of the asset. Certainly, they are no less satisfactory than the straight-line depreciation schedules businesses often use for their general purpose financial statements and, in some cases, their cost accounts. Nevertheless, this procedure turns capital budgeting practice on its head, i.e., instead of converting future flows of benefits and costs to present values, large, lumpy current outlays are converted into a stream of future payments.

In fact, differences between the institutional arrangements through which capital budgeting decisions are made in government and in business were probably never greater than they are in the United States right now. This is the case for two reasons. First, business has reduced its reliance on tight capital controls. Businesses used to believe that capital was their most valuable asset and that the chief task of top management was allocating it to productive uses; now most realize that their most precious resource is knowledge and that management's most important job is ensuring that knowledge is generated widely and used efficiently. As Jack Welch, chairman of General Electric recently explained, the centralized capital budgeting procedures it once used were "right for the 1970s, a growing handicap in the 1980s, and would have been a ticket to the boneyard in the 1990s."

Second, in the 1973 Budget Impoundment and Control Act, Congress adopted the defunct Keynesian economics of the 1967 report of the President's Commission on Budget Concepts and now gives as much weight to outlays as to budget authority and sets ceilings (top lines) on both obligational authority and outlays (Doyle and McCaffery 1991). This is deplorable because outlays have little real economic significance except insofar as the sources of government financing or the timing of payments influence long-term considerations arising from the level of savings or private sector investment.

In the meantime, other countries looked to private sector practices. Indeed, Christopher Pollitt (1993, 52–58) traces the etiology of the new public management back to the Financial Management Initiative of the Thatcher government in the United Kingdom, which was announced May 17, 1982. The Financial Management Initiative called for a radical change in the internal structure and operations of government agencies designed to mimic private sector budgeting and accounting practices. Objectives were to be assigned to "responsibility centers," within which costs would be systematically identified to enable those responsible for meeting particular objectives to be held accountable for the cost of the resources they were consuming. Costs were to be measured on an accrual basis (i.e., matching resources consumed to services delivered) and include not only the direct costs of service delivery but apportioned overheads as well.[2] Managers were to be given considerable discretion to control costs and outputs. Following the launch of the Financial Management Initiative in Great Britain, other governments—Australia, Canada, Denmark, Finland, and Sweden—have experimented with outcome budgeting and responsibility accounting. None, however, has moved as far or as fast as New Zealand.

Most of the external attention given to New Zealand's public management reforms has focused on its efforts to improve the quality of external financial reporting practices: the adoption of accrual accounting and reporting on performance. New Zealand was the first country to publish a rational set of government accounts that includes a balance sheet of its assets and liabilities and an accrual-based operating statement of income and expenses. Yet the changes made in the structure of the government of New Zealand designed to promote effective resource use and investment are even more significant than are the changes in its financial reporting practices (the following is based on Scott, Bushnell, and Sallee 1990). First of all, New Zealand's Parliament privatized everything that was not part of the "core public sector." The residual "core public sector" now includes a mix of policy, regulatory, and operational functions: military services; policing and justice services; social services such as health, education, and the administration of benefit payments; research and development; property assessment; and other financial services.

Second, Parliament redefined the relationship between it and the heads of government agencies. Agency heads lost their permanent tenure and are now known generically as "chief executives." They are appointed for fixed terms of up to five years, with the possibility of reappointment. Each works to a specific contract, the conditions of which are negotiated with the State Services Commission and approved by the prime minister. The State Services Commission also monitors and assesses executive performance. Remuneration levels are directly tied to performance assessment.

Third, Parliament changed the way it appropriates funds for use by the remaining government agencies. It has tried to link appropriation to performance, allowing Parliament to control the level of resource use and the purposes to which resources are put but, at the same time, providing greater flexibility for agency heads. The basis of appropriation depends on the agency's ability to supply adequate information about its performance. Three modes of appropriation are possible, recognizing that some agencies provide goods and services that are more "commercial" or "contestable" than others.

All agencies started out in Mode A, but most have now progressed either to Mode B or C. Under Mode A, agencies are still treated as discretionary cost centers. Parliament appropriates funds for the purchase of resources. Indeed, the only change from budget process in effect before 1989 (or, for that matter, the budgets used by most jurisdictions throughout the world) is that separate appropriations were provided for expenditures for plant and equipment. This mode remained in force until the agency developed a satisfactory accrual accounting system and identified its outputs, both of which are needed for performance assessment.

Under Mode B, agencies are treated like expense or quasi-profit centers. This mode is designed for agencies that supply traditional, noncontestable governmental services: the central control agencies, including the State Services Commission, most regulatory and police functions, and some justice services, i.e., policy agencies and activities that include an element of compulsion for the buyer. Under this mode, Parliament appropriates funds retrospectively to reimburse agencies for expenses incurred in producing outputs during the period covered by the contract, whether for the government or third parties. Expenses are measured on an accrual basis; they include depreciation but exclude taxes and the return on funds employed. Changes in the agency's net asset holdings are also explicitly appropriated.

Under Mode C, agencies are treated like investment centers. Appropriations pay for the outputs produced by the agency and for any changes in the agency's net assets. Agencies in Mode C are required to pay interest, taxes, and dividends and must establish a capital structure. The agency is set up in a competitively neutral manner so that its performance can be assessed by comparison with firms in the private sector. The price paid for the outputs supplied the agency is supposed to approximate the "fair market price." In general, this means that the agency must show that it is receiving no more than the next best alternative supplier would receive for providing the outputs. Under Mode C agencies are similar to state-owned enterprises, but they are not permitted to borrow on their own behalf or to invest outside their own businesses.

Each month, each agency reports on its financial position and cash flows and resource usages and revenue by output. Variances are calculated and explanations provided. Under both modes B and C, managers are free to make some decisions (under C primarily) about investments in plant and equipment. The fact that their financial performance is one of the main bases on which their performance is assessed helps to insure that those decisions will be sound.

Government's key capital budgeting decisions remain firmly in the hands of Parliament, however. The decisions that have the most significant future consequences for the government of New Zealand's stakeholders are clearly those that have to do with the kind, quantity, and quality of service provided by the citizenry. Under the existing system of appropriations and financial reporting, those issues must be explicitly confronted when the cabinet enters into long-term contracts with agencies, state-owned enterprises, and firms to deliver service outputs, and its consequent liabilities must be stated in present value terms. The fiscal outcomes of the government of New Zealand's decision-making processes are truly both mission driven and results oriented.

Implementing Mission-Driven, Results-Oriented Budgets in the United States

Although the components of outcome budgeting were invented in the United States and it influenced the now defunct Defense Management Report Initiatives of the Bush/Cheney era in the Department of Defense, and arguably the content of both the Chief Financial Officers Act and the National Performance Review's call for mission-driven, results-oriented budgets as well (Organization for Economic Co-operation and Development 1995, 230), it has had little or no practical effect in this country. This fact has led many students of the expenditure process to conclude that outcome budgeting is most appropriate where power is concentrated in the hands of a single branch of government (Parliament or a city manager, for example), which can provide the clear signals to agencies that outcome budgeting requires, and a few to reject altogether the notion that outcome budgeting can be reconciled with the American federal legislative budgetary process.

Can the kind of arms-length, quasi transfer-pricing mechanism adopted in New Zealand under modes B and C be adapted to the realities of congressional power, or is it necessary to transform Congress to give meaning to the mission-driven, results-oriented budget concept? That a number of states have experimented with mechanisms such as New Zealand's suggests that the American form of government, with its separation of powers, is not inherently inimical to the adoption of businesslike budgeting practices (see Barzelay 1992). Indeed, it is possible that Congress could allow enough flexibility to make it work merely by increasing agency discretion to transfer budget authority between lines and through time, by treating budget authority as permissive (i.e., permitting, but not requiring, the obligation of funds), and by restricting its propensity to fund long-term investment programs on a one-year-at-a-time basis.

Robert Anthony (1990), for example, argues that this could be done by dividing the United States budget into an operating portion and a capital portion, much like some state and local budgets. The operating budget would be appropriated annually or biannually and would be expressed in terms of the amount of expenses authorized for the period in question. The capital budget would be directed to the acquisition of long-lived assets and would in essence be unchanged from existing provisions of obligational authority.

Anthony recognizes that responsibility centers cannot possibly meet all of their needs using spot-market transactions. They frequently need to enter into long-term, exclusive relationships with outside suppliers, and support centers have to make long-term commitments, involving highly specific assets, to supply other support and mission centers within government. Regardless of how mission centers obtain the use of long-term assets, directly from an outside supplier or indirectly through a support center, their employment will give rise to discrepancies between obligations, outlays, and consumption. The use of long-term assets and inventory depletion also gives rise to intertemporal spill-overs from one budget period to the next and, therefore, discrepancies between operating budget accounts and the Treasury's cash account. Reconciling these discrepancies under Anthony's proposal would necessitate the creation of an additional annual (or biannual) appropriation for changes in working capital. Presumably too, Anthony would have Congress set up a capital fund to provide both mission centers and their suppliers in government with financing for the acquisition of long-term capital assets.

Elsewhere, however, one of us has argued that it is possible to go still further toward making congressional budgeting like capital budgeting in benchmark businesses: i.e., permissive, continuous, and selective (Thompson 1994). What this means is that congressional budgeting should focus on all of the cash flows that ensue from its programmatic decisions (operating expenditures and transfers as well as acquisitions and construction) and should do so for the life of the decision, not just the cash flows that occur in the initial fiscal year. New obligational authority should be expressed in terms of the discounted present values of those cash flows. Congress would also deemphasize the budget resolution, with its fixation on outlays, and reemphasize obligational authority. The core of congressional power lies in its authority to decide to go ahead with a program, activity, or acquisition, which is what the authorization/appropriations process has always been about. Its next step would be to throw away the comprehensive, annual executive budget. Executive branch agencies should be permitted to come forward at any time with proposals to change the scope, level, or timing of their operations.

Congress should consider proposals to try something new as soon as they are ready to be considered, but consider them only once. Once a project has been approved by Congress, it should be reconsidered only if circumstances change or the project goes bad. This means that obligational authority should be granted for the life of the project and should reflect the discounted present value of the project's cash flows. Standing appropriations should be continuously adjusted to reflect these important decisions.

Congress currently takes about the right approach to providing budget authority for the acquisition of long-lived assets, although the system of one-year-at-a-time authorization and appropriation that Congress has adopted in recent years is inimical to sound project management. Nevertheless, where plant and equipment are concerned, current costs are present values. In contrast, where ongoing activities are concerned, current costs greatly understate government's actual obligations.

The third step would be to make legislative budgeting more selective—this means that most federal budgeting would be more like the current process of authorization and appropriation for social security. Congressional budgeting should focus only on significant changes in operations, activities, and investments in fixed assets. Otherwise, congressional attention should not be necessary.

Most government departments/responsibility centers should probably operate under permanent authority. They should have to seek budget authority from Congress only when they wanted to make changes with significant future consequences and, then, only if the changes increased the Treasury's liabilities. If Congress wanted to reduce spending, it would have to enact programmatic changes that reduced permanent appropriations (although performance-based spending cuts could be built into those appropriations).

Under this approach, most departments would still have to obtain congressional authorization to make major new investments or changes in their corpus. Moreover, Congress would probably still reconsider funding levels for research and development on an annual or biannual basis. Aside from these exceptions, however, all new obligational authority would be expressed in terms of discounted net cash flows—which would dramatically change congressional authorizations and appropriations for operating purposes. Congress would probably also have to acknowledge formally that obligational authority is permissive rather than mandatory.

Fiscal control under this approach to congressional budgeting would remain more or less as it is now. Presumably, the Office of Management and Budget's monthly apportionments to responsibility centers would remain at constant levels so long as Congress did not increase (or reduce) their budget authority. In addition, the Treasury should probably be authorized to buy and sell notes on behalf of agencies to provide it with short-term liquidity and to match cash inflows with the actual pattern of cash outflows.

There really is nothing new about any of these proposals. In essence they merely would restore the congressional budget process that existed prior to the passage of the Budget Act in 1921, which established a comprehensive, annual executive budget for the federal government, created what has become the Office of Management and Budget, and at the same time, restricted congressional power. Many of the constraints that Congress has built into the existing budget process can be interpreted as efforts to overcome those restrictions and to escape the procrustean bed imposed by the comprehensive, annual executive budget (maybe because a comprehensive, annual executive budget was a bad idea to begin with or maybe because it has now outlived whatever usefulness it once might have had).

In any case, congressional budgeting used to be a lot more like private sector capital budgeting than it is now. It was once permissive, continuous, and selective, rather than comprehensive and repetitive. Indeed, looking at policy choices in present value terms is the only real difference between the congressional budget process that existed prior to the Budget Act and private sector capital budgeting. Yet even appropriating on a present value basis has a clear precedent in the congressional budgetary process. Congress currently funds the federal government's loan guarantee and insurance programs in precisely that manner. Perhaps the time has now come to make congressional budgeting more like private sector capital budgeting.

Notes

1. "Selling" is in quotation marks here because the organization as a whole has not sold anything to an outside party. Rather, the responsibility center providing the service records revenue in its accounts, and the center receiving the service records an expense. Both revenue and expense cancel out when the organization consolidates its books. Money rarely changes hands in interdivisional transfer pricing, and responsibility centers do not get to keep "their" profits. Only the organization as a whole earns a profit, and selling to and buying from outsiders are the only activities that can generate real profits or losses for the organization.

2. Accrual accounting provides a more accurate picture of a government's financial position because it keeps track of the changing value of assets and liabilities. Capital investment is depreciated over the life of the asset rather than being written off in the year when the money is spent, as is done under cash accounting. Likewise, future pension obligations count as a liability. All of these changes have helped to bring New Zealand financial reports into line with present value calculations.

References

Anthony, Robert N. 1990. "The AICPA's Proposal for Federal Accounting Reform: It Should Focus on the Budget System, Not the Accounting System." *Management Accounting* 72, no. 1 (July): 48–52.

Anthony, Robert N., and Vijay Govindarajan. 1995. *Management Control Systems.* 8th ed. Chicago: Irwin.

Barzelay, Michael. 1992. *Breaking through Bureaucracy: A New Vision for Managing in Government*. Berkeley, Calif.: University of California Press.

Borins, Sanford. 1994. "Government in Transition: A New Paradigm in Public Administration." *A Report on the Inaugural Conference of the Commonwealth Association for Public Administration and Management*. Toronto: CAPAM.

Bower, Joseph L. 1970. *Managing the Resource Allocation Process: A Study of Corporate Planning and Investment*. Boston: Harvard Business School Division of Research.

Chandler, Alfred D. 1962. *Strategy and Structure: Chapters in the History of Industrial Enterprise*. Cambridge, Mass.: MIT Press.

Choate, G. Marc, and Fred Thompson. 1996. "Debt and Taxes." In *Handbook of Debt Management,* edited by Gerald J. Miller. New York: Marcel Dekker.

Dixit, Avinash K., and Robert S. Pindyck. 1994. *Investment under Uncertainty*. Princeton, N.J.: Princeton University Press.

Doyle, R., and J. McCaffery, 1991. "The Budget Enforcement Act of 1990: The Path to No Fault Budgeting." *Public Budgeting and Finance* 11, no. 1 (spring): 25–40.

Gordon, Roger H., and Gilbert E. Metcalf. 1991. "Do Tax-Exempt Bonds Really Subsidize Municipal Capital?" *National Tax Journal* 44, no. 4 (December): 71–79.

Gordon, Roger H., and Joel Slemrod. 1983. "A General Equilibrium Simulation Study of Subsidies to Municipal Expenditures." *Journal of Finance* 38, no. 2 (May): 585–94.

——. 1986. "An Empirical Examination of Municipal Financial Policy." In *Studies in State and Local Public Finance,* edited by Harvey S. Rosen. Chicago: University of Chicago Press.

Jones, L. R. 1991. "Policy Development, Planning, and Resource Allocation in the Department of Defense." *Public Budgeting and Finance* 11, no. 3 (fall): 15–27.

National Performance Review. 1993. *From Red Tape to Results: Creating a Government That Works Better and Costs Less*. Washington, D.C.: U.S. Government Printing Office.

Organization for Economic Co-operation and Development. 1995. *Budgeting for Results: Perspectives on Public Expenditure Management*. Paris: Organization for Economic Co-operation and Development.

Pollitt, Christopher. 1993. *Managerialism and the Public Services: Cuts or Cultural Change in the 1990s?* 2d ed. Cambridge, Mass.: Basil Blackwell.

Reschenthaler, G. B., and Fred Thompson. 1996. "The Information Revolution and the New Public Management." *Journal of Public Administration Research and Theory* 6, no. 1: 125–44.

Rubin, Irene S. 1993. "Who Invented Budgeting in the United States?" *Public Administration Review* 53, no. 5 (Sept./Oct.): 438–44.

Schedler, K. 1995. *Ansatze einer Wirkungsorientirten Verwaltungsfuhrung: Von der Idee des New Public Managements (NPM) zum konkreten Gestaltungsmodell*. Bern: Verlag Paul Haupt.

Scott, G., P. Bushnell, and N. Sallee. 1990. "Reform of the Core Public Sector: The New Zealand Experience." *Public Sector* 13, no. 3: 11–24.

Thompson, Fred. 1994. "Mission-Driven, Results-Oriented Budgeting: Financial Administration and the New Public Management." *Public Budgeting and Finance* 14, no. 3 (fall): 90–105.

Trebilcock, Michael J. 1994. *The Prospects for Reinventing Government.* Toronto: C. D. Howe Institute.

World Bank. 1995. *Bureaucrats in Business: The Economics and Politics of Government Ownership.* New York: Oxford University Press.

The Management of
III Innovation and Reform
Organizational and Bureaucratic Factors

THE MANAGEMENT OF government reform necessarily entails attention to the organizations that deliver public services and the relationship between those organizations and the nature and structure of the public bureaucracy. Many components of the National Performance Review (NPR) are aimed at transforming the orientations and behaviors of individual representatives of government. Those individual representatives, however, function primarily within organizations—organizations that differ significantly in scope, mission, culture, size, etc. Moe (1994) reminds us that "the natural basis for understanding public bureaucracy is organization theory" (17). The chapters in this section provide insights into how and why some organizations—and, consequently, members of those organizations—might be more apt to innovate, to embrace reform successfully, and to provide incentives for individual members of the public bureaucracy to act as agents for reform. In short, the authors search for the determinants of organizational change and reform.

Patricia W. Ingraham and Vernon Dale Jones examine the impact of "reinvention" related organizational changes on the roles of federal public managers, with a focus on middle managers. They highlight the crucial contributions of middle managers to effective organizational change. These managers serve as "information conduits," providing the link between the change initiated by organizational leaders and employees in lower organizational levels. Early federal reinvention efforts were often synonymous with downsizing, and middle managers were primary targets of downsizing efforts. Yet they were expected to participate in—indeed to facilitate—NPR and related downsizing efforts.

The authors explored organizational changes in four federal agencies, focusing on the roles of middle managers and executives in the management of change. They identified key transformations in those roles. Managers, both executive and middle, are increasingly shifting from employee direction to "team" leadership. Their new roles require them to relinquish some authority, to focus more on facilitation and communication, and to devote increasing amounts of time to human resources management, often at the expense of work in their areas of technical expertise. Most important, the relationships between executive and middle managers have undergone significant changes. Ingraham and Jones formulate a theoretical model that explains the parameters of this new relationship. The management of organizational change requires substantial communication and cooperation between executive and middle managers, with executives managing change and middle managers playing the vital implementation role. These changes have posed difficult challenges to both executive and middle managers, but middle managers feel particularly ill-equipped to adapt to their new roles, and they remain skeptical about the ultimate outcome of "reinvention." The authors conclude that reformers must pay closer attention to the importance of middle managers in effecting successful reform.

Marcia K. Meyers and Nara Dillon examine the implementation of a state-level welfare reform in California, concluding that "promises to transform welfare programs had not been realized on the front lines of service delivery." Their research explores the determinants of "street level" implementation failure, focusing on organizational and bureaucratic factors. Meyers and Dillon note that the "success or failure of *policy* reform will often depend on the success or failure of *organizational* reform" and that although public policy analysts typically concentrate on policy inputs and outputs, they often neglect the crucial intervening variable—namely, the organization charged with implementing the reform.

The authors focus on the intervening organizational structure and leadership factors that affected the motivation of street-level welfare workers to implement the reforms. Structural factors included ineffective incentive systems for frontline workers (including inadequate resources) and a gap between the "mechanics" of the reforms and its goals. Viewed in terms of leadership factors, the implementation failure stemmed from the failure of policy makers to "exercise leadership in communicating the goals" of the reforms. This latter dynamic may be rooted in political conflict: the authors suggest that because of the highly charged nature of the political context for California's reforms, "unresolved policy conflicts" may have been "passed from the political to the administrative arenas." One consequence is that program managers and street-level workers responded by implementing the "letter" of the reforms, but not their "spirit." Policy leadership failed to reorient managers and workers from their highly instrumental approach to client services (i.e., emphasizing eligibility determination, compliance with program requirements, timely and accurate paperwork) to one that stressed the facilitation and encouragement of client self-sufficiency. Thus, the reforms were hampered by features inherent in the organizations responsible for managing those reforms and by the signals sent to those organizations by policy leaders.

The NPR emphasizes the importance of entrepreneurial activity in government. Government entrepreneurs are seen as models; they incorporate effective market mechanisms to improve government service delivery and to enhance its efficiency. In their chapter, Eric Welch and Stuart Bretschneider construct and test a theoretical model that estimates the impact of several organizational characteristics on the probability of such governmental entrepreneurship. Their analysis is based on *contracting in* activity in county governments. Contracting in occurs when government agencies sell their services or resources for profit—typically to other governmental organizations but also to private firms.

Welch and Bretschneider view the government organization as one that responds to an external environment (fiscal stress and social values) and to its own internal environment. They identify several key internal organizational features, including organizational culture, internal fiscal stress, management control and authority structures, the extent of bureaucratization in the organization, and the technological complexity of the agency's major tasks. Their model estimates the effects of these features on two sets of potential entrepreneurs within government organizations: information service managers and program managers. They conclude that larger, more specialized government agencies and those with larger information services units are associated with a greater probability of contracting in. In addition, they note differences in the responses of program managers and information service managers to organizational factors, indicating that entrepreneurial incentives for these two sets of public managers differ substantially.

Clearly, the authors of these chapters recognize that organizational change and adaptation is complex, difficult, and hardly free of "pain." Notwithstanding more optimistic prognoses for the capacity of organizations to change (Barzelay 1992; Osborne and Gaebler 1992), these chapters suggest that, in fact, government reform generates different responses within different levels and functions of the organization and that "reinvention" requires significant—often overwhelming—effort on the part of public managers.

References

Barzelay, Michael. 1992. *Breaking through Bureaucracy: A New Vision for Managing Government.* Berkeley, Calif.: University of California Press.

Moe, Terry. 1994. "Integrating Politics and Organizations: Positive Theory and Public Administration." *Journal of Public Administration Research and Theory* 4, no. 1 (January): 17–25.

Osborne, David, and Ted Gaebler. 1992. *Reinventing Government: How the Entrepreneurial Spirit Is Transforming the Public Sector.* Reading, Mass.: Addison-Wesley.

9 The Pain of Organizational Change
Managing Reinvention
Patricia W. Ingraham and Vernon Dale Jones

T HE FEDERAL GOVERNMENT is experiencing a storm of organizational change. Furthermore, the winds of change are not expected to subside anytime soon. Public organizations, like private sector organizations, are undergoing dramatic changes emanating from turbulent political and economic environments, radical internal transformations, and fundamental paradigm shifts for management and leadership (Barzelay 1992; Daft and Lewin 1993; Ingraham, Romzek, and Associates 1994). The changes center on organizational processes, systems, and structures. The organizational changes have perhaps been most difficult, challenging, and painful for federal employees, who are enduring budget cuts, reinvention, and downsizing. Other levels of government are feeling the pain as well.

Greater understanding of organizations in the context of change leads to opportunities for enhancing organizational performance (Druckman, Singer, and Van Cott 1997). Public management scholars recognize the need to devote attention to the reality and implications of current organizational change (Rainey 1997). This chapter presents the results of empirical research undertaken to investigate the nature of new forms of organizational change and how federal government executives and middle managers contend with it. It is based on research conducted in national and field offices during the mid-1990s. The findings are based on personal interviews, performance management surveys, and focus groups.

Reinventing Government as Organizational Change

The Clinton administration's National Performance Review (NPR) initiative is intended to create historic and revolutionary changes: to redesign, reinvent, and reinvigorate the federal government (National Performance Review 1993; Relyea 1993). More popularly known as "reinventing government," the NPR is intended to change and reform the federal bureaucracy's operations and culture to result in a more efficient and less expensive government. More than four years have passed since the September 1993 release of the NPR report. That report unveiled the plan to "begin a decade-long process of reinvention" (National Performance Review 1993, 9). During this time, both the scope and strength of the impetus for change expanded. The American public continues to have a strong appetite for criticizing government. The Republican-controlled Congress wants to extend reform to new extremes. In addition, the Clinton Administration recognizes political advantages by keeping reinvention moving forward. Indeed, the Clinton administration now seeks to analyze *what* government should do, not *how* it should do it.

The reinvention of government is clearly prescriptive: government should have an entrepreneurial spirit, a "steering, not rowing" focus (Osborne and Gaebler 1992). The first NPR provided the direction for "*how* government should work" (National Performance Review 1993, ii). Primary elements included changing government control, procurement, and personnel systems; management structures; organizational size; and the culture of the bureaucracy. At the same time, federal agencies have implemented—or are implementing—numerous initiatives aimed at achieving improved performance and lasting change: reinvention laboratories, reengineering, restructuring, redesigning, streamlining, downsizing, delayering, teaming, employee empowerment, and customer orientation. There is enough organizational change going around to ensure that no agency or federal employee is immune to it. Clearly, all this change is unsettling for federal workers, as well as for public management scholars, because it is "complex, occasionally contradictory, often far beyond existing public management theory, and sometimes in advance of anything written down" (Kettl 1995, 32–33).

Theoretical Shortfalls of Reinventing Government

Some public management scholars find theoretical faults with reinventing government. Seidman (1993) notes that reinventing government principles "are little more than restatements of conventional wisdom" with ideas that "are something old, mostly borrowed and nothing new" (32). Moe (1994) states that "there is little theoretical discussion with the theory being simply assumed within the recommendations" of the NPR (111). He argues that the NPR's proclivity for placing "economically based values over legally based values" creates serious democratic accountability problems (114). In addition, Thompson and Jones (1995) assert that "the atheoretical nature of the NPR report is readily apparent" (183) and that NPR implementation issues reflect tensions "implicit in NPR that can be traced to the absence of a coherent theoretical base" (190). More recently, Light (1997) asserts that reinventing government compounds government mismanagement because there is too much management reform in government. Also, Pfiffner (1997) presents some of the more salient scholarly and practical critiques of the NPR.

Although he agrees with many of those criticisms, Kettl (1995) also identifies two other important aspects related to theoretical shortfalls. First, existing administrative theory does not help solve the current performance problems of the government. This is because the traditional administrative theories are based on outdated views of administrative conditions. Second, administrative theory lags far behind administrative practices used by managers in their changing environments. Consequently, it is *necessary* for reinventing government to ignore prevailing theories.

Federal Executives and Middle Managers in Reinvention

The research reported in this chapter responds by attempting to advance theory associated with managing change in federal government agencies. The approach examines the experiences of federal Senior Executive Service (SES) members and middle managers who are in the center of this recent wave of change. From this, a theoretical model is developed to explain the changing relationship between executives and middle managers and their respective roles in managing complex waves of organizational change.

The Civil Service Act of 1978 (Public Law 95-454) created the SES to lead and manage the myriad diverse and complex government programs. The majority of the approximately seventy-five hundred SES positions are supervisory and managerial although some are scientific and professional. Leadership and management competencies of SES civil servants are "essential to effective governance, particularly during a period of fundamental change in government's structure and operations" (Sanders 1994, 234–35). If reinvention of the government is to succeed, contributions of SES professionals—the professional "leaders" of the federal government—are vital to the change process.

Less recognized is the critical role that middle managers play in reinvention. Indeed, from the outset, middle managers have been a target of the reinventing government movement. A major goal of the NPR is to reduce the executive branch civilian, nonpostal work force by 272,900 employees by the close of fiscal year 1999. That figure was reached by a three-step process consisting of presidential Executive Order 12839 of February 10, 1993, which called for a reduction of 100,000 positions; a presidential memorandum titled "Streamlining the Bureaucracy" and dated September 11, 1993, which provided direction for cutting 252,000 personnel as recommended in the NPR report; and congressional legislation in March 1994 that increased the number to 272,900 employees. Of the total number of employees slated to be reduced, "the Administration wants to get rid of roughly 140,000 supervisors, managers and SESers" (Shoop 1994a, 11).

Consequently, across the government, federal managers believe that reinventing government is synonymous with cutting middle managers in order to improve efficiency and save costs. According to Kettl (1995), "Virtually everyone who could potentially be considered a 'middle manager' felt threatened by the NPR" (27). For middle managers, however, the threats go beyond the fear of losing their jobs. Even if they survive downsizing, their jobs are significantly changed as a result of greater spans of control, new work processes, less budget and personnel resources, the introduction of teams, subordinates with greater empowerment, new organizational cultures, redesigned and restructured agencies, higher expectations, reduced upward mobility, and significantly reduced job security.

Middle managers, like the federal executives who are their superiors, are integral to effective government operations and successful change implementation. Mintzberg (1973) concluded that all managerial work can be described in terms of ten observable roles: figurehead, liaison, and leader (interpersonal roles); monitor, disseminator, and spokesman (information roles); and entrepreneur, disturbance handler, resource allocator, and negotiator (decisional roles). Of these, the roles of liaison, disseminator, disturbance handler, and negotiator are traditionally midmanagement functions: they are central to the effective management of change. Colvard (1994) explains: "Connecting is the process of converting policy-level strategic decisions into executable tactics. This is the role of what is commonly called middle management. . . . Vertical middle management is the connecting link between broader conceptual levels and execution-specific levels in an organization. Horizontal middle management provides administrative expertise outside the main line of business. . . . Middle management in both forms is critically important. . . . Middle management, done properly, is much more. It involves translation and judgment" (57). Kettl (1995) adds: "Middle managers play a critical role in the reinvention effort. They occupy the key positions throughout government that determine how well programs work. They are the project managers, branch chiefs, and section heads who shape programs and the behavior of their agencies. They model the behavior for their subordinates" (28).

In sum, *both* federal government executives and middle managers play a key role in change. They are strategy, change, and information conduits. They manage different, but equally important, levels of organizational change. They can make reinventing government work, or they can inhibit it in important ways. In the research reported here, middle managers are at the General Schedule (GS) 14 and 15 grade levels of civil service. According to the U.S.

Office of Personnel Management, in March 1994, GS-14 employees comprised 5.8 percent of the full-time General Schedule civilian work force and had an average of 19.9 years of service. GS-15 civil servants made up 2.7 percent of full-time General Schedule employees and worked an average of 22.2 years for the federal government.

Overview of the Research

The research, which was conducted in federal departments and agencies, illustrates the widespread organizational change due to effort to reinvent government and to downsize. Our interest was the relationship between executives and middle managers in these change processes. First, research results on reinvention from the perspective of downsizing in the Defense Logistics Agency, the Bureau of Reclamation, and the Food and Drug Administration are presented. Findings from another government agency, whose members were guaranteed confidentiality, supplement these cases. The findings center on changing structures, changing roles, and issues for the new relationship between executive and midlevel management and, to some extent, between central and field offices. We present a theoretical model to explain the roles of executives and middle managers in managing organizational change. Finally, we conclude with implications and new research questions.

Methodology

The research uses a multiple-case design in which eight criteria were used to select three agencies and ensure sufficient stratification. The Defense Logistics Agency (Department of Defense), the Bureau of Reclamation (Department of the Interior), and the Food and Drug Administration (Department of Health and Human Services) served as the case agencies. The primary data collection methods included interviews and documentation reviews. Research was conducted at offices of field and headquarters sites in the Washington, D.C., area, Philadelphia, and Denver.

Respondents included twenty-three SES executives and seven middle managers at the GS-14 and GS-15 grades. The SES officials were interviewed in September and October 1994, and the mean interview time was one hour and thirty-three minutes. For SES members, the mean total years of federal civil service was 25.2 years, and the mean number of years employed by their current agencies was 16.2 years. The middle managers were interviewed in a follow-on phase in July 1995, and the mean interview time was one hour. For middle managers, the mean total years of federal employment was 27.0 years, and the mean number of years with their current agencies was 17.0 years. SES leaders were interviewed because of their experience and knowledge in carrying out change direction from agency top leaders and supervisors and in interacting with middle managers. In addition, middle managers were interviewed in order to obtain directly data about middle manager involvement with downsizing and other organizational change. The findings from the anonymous agency are based on entire-population national and field performance management surveys conducted in 1994 and 1995.

Downsizing Federal Agencies

For many involved in reinventing government, downsizing quickly became the defining activity. Because reducing bureaucracy, agencies, and employees leads to reduced costs and visible results, downsizing became the core of reinventing government for both the White House and the Congress. Downsizing is described as the "centerpiece of the performance review" (Shoop 1994b, 19) and the "keystone of the cost savings" (Kettl 1995, 17). Major targets of downsizing were midlevel managers and "overhead control" positions: personnel, budget, and financial management.

Not surprisingly, many middle managers have reacted to the downsizing with disillusionment. On the one hand, they support improving government and reducing its costs; they accept their responsibility for implementing changes. On the other hand, they are targets of that change and are deeply concerned about being faulted for ills of our government (Shoop 1993; Kam and Shaw 1994; Kettl 1994; McCarthy 1994).

The Defense Logistics Agency

The Defense Logistics Agency (DLA) has a worldwide logistics and contract management mission to provide expertise, support, and services to the Department of Defense (DOD) and the army, navy, and air force departments. Established in 1962, the DLA provides supplies to the military services and supports their acquisition of weapons and other materiel. The DLA performs and is organized around three primary functions that comprise the agency's core logistics mission: supply, distribution, and contract administration services (or acquisition).

The end of the cold war, coupled with national fiscal problems, has led to significant DOD reductions in force and budget levels. Because the DLA's mission is central to military operations, defense reductions have had considerable impact on the DLA. At least six major related events over the past eight years have resulted in organizational changes for the DLA. First, the Bush administration's Defense Management Review (DMR) report in July 1989 established businesslike practices and consolidations to achieve improved efficiencies, reduce infrastructure, and realize monetary savings. Second, Congress legislated downsizing of U.S. military forces and civilian employees with the National Defense Authorization Act for Fiscal Year 1991. Third, since 1988, the Base Realignment and Closure (BRAC) Commission has closed and realigned bases and installations. As a result of the BRAC process, DLA operations at some locations were consolidated, transferred, or terminated. Fourth, the previous three events drove business, management, and systems changes or "reengineering" changes throughout the DLA. Fifth, expansion of DLA functions from DMR decisions, along with budget cuts and the personnel drawdown, forced the DLA to reexamine its organization. Consequently, the DLA restructured its headquarters in March 1993; it will continue to restructure some of its field organizations through reorganizations and mergers. Sixth, the DLA volunteered and was designated in January 1994 to be a pilot project for the 1993 Government Performance and Results Act (GPRA) from 1994 to 1996. All of these events combined to put DLA on a downsizing track well before the Clinton administration's reinventing government initiative.

Since 1992, DLA employee figures have dropped each year. During fiscal year 1993, the total figure declined to 61,040. By the end of fiscal year 1994, the number was down to 56,715. Further reductions resulted in 51,930 employees at the end of fiscal year 1995 and 48,663 at the end of fiscal year 1996. Reductions are expected to continue in future years and reach approximately 47,312 employees at the end of fiscal year 1997 and 41,718 by year-end 2000.

The Bureau of Reclamation

The Reclamation Act of 1902 created the Reclamation Service to administer the reclamation of arid and semiarid lands in western states. The service quickly established a respected reputation for constructing large dams and canals for agricultural irrigation. Renamed the Bureau of Reclamation (BOR) in 1923, the agency expanded its programs by the 1930s to include hydroelectric power generation, storage and delivery of safe municipal water supplies, and flood control. After that, the BOR's mission grew to include many other interrelated functions and projects: provision of industrial water supplies, improvement and protection of water quality, salinity control, river navigation, river regulation and control, fish and wildlife enhancement, recreation, conservation, environmental enhancement, and research on water-related activities.

In the past three decades, several trends pushed the BOR away from water resources development and toward water resources management. The environmental movement, multiple constituent groups, changing public values and competing interests regarding water and its use, and a diminishing number and scope of construction projects combined to influence the BOR. These trends led the BOR to the conclusion that it must focus on water resources management. Not until the late 1980s, however, did the BOR finally take concrete steps to change its organization and focus.

From 1987 to 1993, the BOR began to move away from its strong construction and engineering culture. In 1993, the Clinton appointee as commissioner, Dan Beard, was determined to commit the agency finally to making the transition from a water resources development agency to a water resources management agency. A team of midlevel employees from across the BOR issued the *Report of the Commissioner's Program and Organization Review Team (CPORT)* in August 1993. This was followed in November 1993 by *Blueprint for Reform: The Commissioner's Plan for Reinventing Reclamation.* The agency has since been implementing the numerous organizational changes associated with its new mission: reduction of bureaucracy, duplication, and inefficiencies and elimination of unnecessary internal reviews, excessive management oversight, and costly organizational layering. Other initiatives to transform the agency include bureauwide reorganizations and realignments, substantial delegation of authority to field offices, and organizational culture change efforts. All of this is being accomplished along with personnel reductions. In effect, the NPR was used as the change mechanism to get the BOR, finally and completely, to transform its mission, organization, and culture while downsizing.

At the end of fiscal year 1993, the total number of BOR employees was 7,929. During fiscal year 1994, the number decreased by 1,274 or 16.1 percent for a year-end total of 6,655. Between fiscal years 1993 and 1996, the work force was reduced by approximately 21.8 percent to a level of 6,200 where it has remained since.

The Food and Drug Administration

The Food and Drug Administration (FDA) was established in 1927 as a consumer protection agency that regulates a wide variety of products. The mission of the FDA is to enforce laws to ensure public health is protected against impure and unsafe foods, drugs, and cosmetics; unsafe medical devices; and unsafe radiation-emitting products, as well as to ensure that these products are truthfully and informatively labeled.

The FDA faces the dilemma of being required to increase and decrease its personnel simultaneously. On the one hand, the agency must comply with the NPR mandate to reduce its employment levels; on the other hand, user fee legislation requires the FDA to add employees to expedite work processes. The Prescription Drug User Fee Act of 1992 (PDUFA) (Public Law 102-571) permits the FDA to collect fees from industry to augment FDA resources. The purpose of the act is to increase personnel devoted to expediting the drug review and approval process within specified time periods.

Total FDA employment was 9,378 at the end of fiscal year 1993, increased to 9,691 at the end of fiscal year 1994, dropped slightly to 9,570 at the end of fiscal year 1995, reached 9,397 at the end of fiscal year 1996, and stood at 9,358 midway through fiscal year 1997. Total employment is expected to level off to 9,338 at the end of fiscal year 1997 and remain at that level through the year 2000.

For the FDA, downsizing requirements are contradictory to user fee program requirements. These unique circumstances point out that applying the NPR downsizing mandate equally across the government does not account for important differences among agencies. A similar case exists at the anonymous agency; while midlevel employees are targeted for reduction, technical specialists and some additional managers are being hired at the same level to manage redesigned and decentralized work processes and responsibilities better.

Summary of Downsizing Processes for Case Agencies

The downsizing processes of the DLA, BOR, and FDA are summarized in two tables. These tables reveal similarities as well as differences among the three case agencies. Table 1 shows the results of a comparison of environmental change factors influencing the downsizing processes of the agencies. Political, economic, social, and technical factors in the external environment of the agencies affect how they downsize. Each agency faces a different combination of environmental factors that create the context for downsizing and that influence the downsizing process. Two factors, the budget deficit and reinventing government, affect all three agencies.

Table 2 provides greater insight into how the factors in Table 1 affect the downsizing processes of the agencies in the study. Table 2 displays the results of a comparison of characteristics of the agencies' downsizing processes. The table is a six-by-three matrix containing descriptors in six categories among the three agencies. First, regarding the direction of change that external environmental factors cause, the DLA and BOR are driven consistently toward downsizing, but the FDA experiences factors that result in the contradictory incentives to both grow and downsize. Second, downsizing is difficult for each agency, but each agency has a different type of difficulty. The type of difficulty for the DLA is "direct" in that the majority of the difficulty is generally derived from factors pointing the agency toward downsizing. The BOR has "complex" difficulty because it is changing its mission at the same time that it is downsizing. The FDA also has "complex" difficulty because it is simultane-

Table 1. Comparison of Environmental Change Factors Influencing the Downsizing Process

	DLA	BOR	FDA
Political	End of the cold war		User fee legislation
	Reinventing government (NPR)	Reinventing government (NPR)	Reinventing government (NPR)
Economic	Budget deficit	Budget deficit	Budget deficit
	Infrastructure reduction	Budget decline for dam construction	
	Reinventing government (NPR)	Reinventing government (NPR)	Reinventing government (NPR)
Social		Changing social values	
		Competing public interests	
Technical			Growth and complexity of products
			Growth and complexity of scientific review

DLA, Defense Logistics Agency; *BOR*, Bureau of Reclamation; *FDA*, Food and Drug Administration; *NPR*, National Performance Review.

ously growing and downsizing. Third, regarding the extent of the downsizing process, it is "extensive" in the DLA and BOR. These agencies experienced aggressive process changes and high attrition rates in recent years. Meanwhile, FDA downsizing is classified as "minimal" because its net personnel reduction is small and because its process changes are not widespread.

Fourth, for type of downsizing, each agency is characterized differently. The DLA's downsizing is labeled "antecedent" because that agency started downsizing a few years before other agencies in the federal government. As a result, the DLA and other DOD organizations share valuable guidance and lessons learned with civilian agencies. The BOR receives the title "archetypic" because it serves as a prototype for how agencies can reinvent and downsize comprehensively. The FDA is called "discrepant" because the agency has unusual circumstances requiring it simultaneously to grow and downsize. Fifth,

Table 2. Comparison of Characteristics of the Downsizing Process

	DLA	BOR	FDA
Direction of change	Consistent: downsizing	Consistent: downsizing	Contradictory: growth and downsizing
Type of difficulty	Direct: downsizing	Complex: new mission and downsizing	Complex: growth and downsizing
Extent of down-sizing process	Extensive	Extensive	Minimal
Type of down-sizing	Antecedent	Archetypic	Discrepant
Predominant feature of downsizing	Continuation of earlier changes	Central to transforming agency	Contradictory to concurrent growth
Downsizing experience	Challenging, difficult, painful	Challenging, difficult, painful	Challenging, difficult, painful

DLA, Defense Logistics Agency; *BOR,* Bureau of Reclamation; *FDA,* Food and Drug Administration.

the predominant feature of downsizing for each agency is consistent with the other characterizations. What stands out is that the DLA's downsizing is a continuation of past organizational changes, the BOR's downsizing is a central part of its mission transformation, and the FDA's downsizing is contradictory to its concurrent growth mandate. Finally, the downsizing experience for each agency is challenging, difficult, and painful regardless of the unique circumstances of each agency.

In addition, the study identified three core components of downsizing as organizational change: process changes, personnel reduction strategies, and organizational reorientations. Process changes include reengineering, redesigning, restructuring, and streamlining actions that change organizational work processes; reduce functions, hierarchical levels, and units; realign functional activities; and maximize value-added steps. Personnel reduction strategies include buyouts, early retirements, and reductions-in-force. Both of these change processes contribute to organizational reorientations that are the creation of a new mission, a change in culture, the use of benchmarking and best practices, or other new ways of operating.

The research in our study clearly shows that downsizing consists of many levels of change that occur simultaneously. Although innovations such as teams have been introduced, both to guide the change and to support it, managing the change remains a multileveled process as well. The communication and linking function traditionally performed by the middle manager level of the organization is fundamental to communicating the purpose, progress, and likely impact of the change to employees in the lower levels of the organization. In the anonymous agency studied, where the political leadership took reinvention at its word and cut out middle management early in the change process, morale plummeted, communication was blocked or distorted, and the middle managers, though still on the job, "checked out," as one put it.

The Changing Relationship between Executives and Middle Managers

Reinventing government and the multiple organizational changes it brings are affecting the relationship between executives and middle managers. Clearly, changing structures in the workplace affect the relationship. In addition, roles are changing in ways that create the need for new skills and abilities; many executives and middle managers are not comfortable with these new demands. This was particularly true in the agencies we studied whose mission had been defined in technical terms and that had relied heavily on technical experts in its work force. Those experts had, of course, been promoted into management positions and had become agency leaders. The new demands for interpersonal and communication skills were an ill fit in this context.

Changing Structures

The most obvious organizational changes are those altering the structure of the workplace. A reduction in managers equates to a reduction in organizational hierarchy. A concomitant change is the movement toward greater empowerment of employees in field-level and lower-level organizations. Finally, in order to maintain productivity and accomplish their missions while undergoing these changes, agencies are turning to teaming arrangements among employees. Teams are now common in the DLA, the BOR, and the anonymous agency. The BOR has experienced the most extensive set of structural changes discussed above.

Changing Roles

There are several key changes in the roles of executives and middle managers; these are a direct result of the changing structures in the agencies. First, both levels of managers are experiencing a shift from being primarily "directors" or "chiefs" to being primarily "team leaders." Table 3 shows the changes in middle manager position titles in the three central organizations within the Bureau of Reclamation. Not only is it clear that the emphasis is on teams and

Table 3. Changes in Position Titles in the Bureau of Reclamation

Organization	Old Position Title	New Position Title
Management Services Office	Director (SES)	Director (SES)
	Division Chiefs (GS-15)	Leaders (GS-14/15)
	Branch Chiefs (GS-14)	Group Leaders (GS-14)
	Section Heads (GS-12/13)	Team Leaders (GS-12/13)
Technical Service Center	Director (SES)	Director (SES)
	Division Chiefs (GS-15)	Leadership Team Members (GS-15)
	Branch Chiefs (GS-14)	Work Group Managers (GS-14)
	Section Heads (GS-14)	Team Leaders (GS-13)
	Unit Heads (GS-13)	
Human Resources Office	Director (SES)	Director (SES)
	Division Chiefs (GS-15)	Deputy Director (GS-15)
	Deputy Division Chiefs (GS-14)	Group Leaders (GS-12/13/14)
	Branch Chiefs (GS-14)	
		-Two groups with GS-14 leaders -Threee groups with equal GS-12/13/14 members -One group with rotating GS-12/13/14 leaders

SES, Senior Executive Service; *GS*, General Schedule.

work groups, but it is also evident that managerial layers are eliminated. Another change includes the devolution of authority and responsibility from the central office to the field. The "control" function of central offices is being diminished or eliminated; the whole nature of central office work is being redefined.

Second, in their new roles as team leaders or group managers, executives and middle managers are expected to focus on facilitating and communicating. This requires the voluntary loosening—or abolition—of traditional managerial prerogatives and authority and the creation of new, nonhierarchical patterns of communication.

Third, executives and middle managers are finding that their positions require less technical expertise and more human resources management. In the BOR, executives consider the placement of middle managers with greater human resources skills to be a positive aspect of realignments. Some middle managers in that same agency, however, regret the "erosion" of their technical expertise due to increased time spent on human resources issues. One middle manager in the BOR estimated that his ratio of technical to managerial work changed from 80/20 to 5/95.

In the anonymous agency, this new emphasis was one of the most painful parts of the change process. Because, as noted earlier, the team activities were essentially created without managerial participation, the demand for better communication and improved interpersonal skills came like a "bolt out of the blue." Middle managers and executives went into denial. One manager summed up with the response: "Why should I do that [talk to employees]?" he asked. "That's not what I do well."

Finally, the role of leadership, and the relationship of the "leaders" to the middle managers of the organizations, are being redefined and reexamined. While we encountered many discussions of organizational visions and new organizational missions, we also encountered top executives who did not understand these processes and who were reluctant—at best—to involve lower-level managers and employees in such strategic activities. The critical role of career leadership in effective change is underscored by this point. In those cases in which the top career leaders have not bought into the change and created a managerial culture for change, the exit of Clinton administration political appointees is likely to be accompanied by the exit of reinvention initiatives.

Issues for the New Relationship

The magnitude of change for federal agencies being reinvented is enormous. Changing structures and roles for executives and middle managers result in greater challenges for these civil service professionals. A new relationship is forming between executives and middle managers and between them and their employees. The new relationship between executives and middle managers requires that both groups recognize changes in the workplace environment, establish new managerial practices, and work jointly to accomplish agency objectives. The research discovered these major issues for the new relationship:

1. *Middle managers are still important.* Middle managers serve important linking and communication functions in changing organizations. They are being asked to perform these functions while facing dramatically uncertain futures.
2. *Middle managers and executives need new skills to be effective in the new organizations.* The skills valued and developed by the civil service system are not the same skills required to manage change effectively.
3. *Organizational vision must be jointly established.* Organizations going through turbulent change must know where they are headed. Executives will better enable middle managers to help achieve organizational objectives if executives first establish a relationship in which cooperation and joint problem solving and decision making is possible.
4. *Communication is a problem.* One of the most prevalent issues to emerge was the requirement for executives and middle managers to increase communication. Agencies in change are better managed when their leaders and middle managers increase the level of communication with each other and with subordinates. Communicating the vision of executives to employees can be the most important communication item.
5. *Giving up power and control is difficult and is not rewarded in a risk-adverse system.* In agencies that have downsized, delayered, reengineered, restructured, redesigned, and streamlined, executives and middle managers must learn to give up power and control. If agencies are truly to empower employees and operate teams, it is essential that executives and middle managers let go of the previous hierarchical ways of doing business. Some of the interviewees in the studies admitted that some executives and middle managers talk about empowerment and teams but remain directive in their styles while not giving up power and control.
6. *Defining accountability mechanisms is hard.* In order for organizations to operate effectively, it is imperative that roles, responsibilities, and accountability mechanisms be redefined. The issue with some of the new structures—teams, for example—is that middle managers and executives remain accountable for the operations of their offices and programs. We did not find a case in which there was a clear understanding of how accountability and responsibility for performance "worked" in the new settings.
7. *A significant need exists for coaching and mentoring.* One of the strongest findings in the research was a new role for executives and middle managers,

which consists of coaching and mentoring subordinates. Because workplaces are enveloped in change and there is enormous uncertainty—as well as considerable fear—executives need to provide coaching and mentoring to middle managers. Likewise, middle managers are called on to coach and mentor employees who work for them. There is little in the traditional civil service backgrounds of most of these managers and executives that allows them to be comfortable in these roles. Both executives and middle managers informed us, however, that sensitivity to and empathy for workers experiencing very high levels of stress in the organization were important parts of effectively managing change.

8. *Throughout the change, trust must be maintained.* With change occurring so rapidly and at so many levels of the organization, understanding it is difficult for middle managers and other employees. Trust in the executives is essential to navigating the turbulence effectively. For two of the agencies we studied, the absence of trust by middle managers in executives resulted in serious complications in the change process; in one of those agencies, it may have derailed it.

9. *Workloads will change, and this must be acknowledged.* The need for executives and middle managers to make workload adjustments was a key finding. Middle managers and the employees who work for them experience workload increases that lead to increased anxiety. Although some workloads and functions are reduced or eliminated in some places, the norm is that decisions are not made about what work will no longer be performed. The consequence is that excessive work is expected to be performed by fewer remaining middle managers and employees, who suffer enormous anxiety over those circumstances.

10. *Work force needs for the future must be considered.* Both executives and middle managers expressed concerns about work force capabilities and outcomes after the change subsides. They are concerned about loss of experienced personnel, work skills imbalances, lack of resources and flexibility, gaps in necessary experience, and the need for reorientation training, education, tools, and techniques.

A Theoretical Model

These issues suggest not only changing responsibilities but also a relationship that is substantially different from that found in traditional federal hierarchies. Figure 1 displays a theoretical model of the relationship between executives and middle managers in federal government agencies. In this model, top leaders—usually political executives but sometimes a combination of political and career leaders—shape the broad parameters of change for agencies.

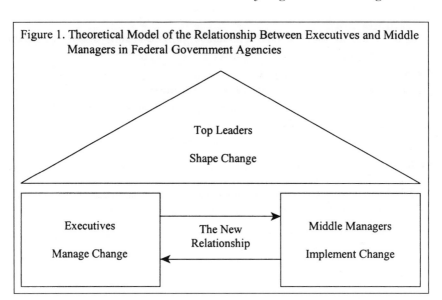

Figure 1. Theoretical Model of the Relationship Between Executives and Middle Managers in Federal Government Agencies

Executives, in partnership with middle managers and teams, create the new processes and structures for managing change. Middle managers, in their new roles as facilitators and communicators, implement change and maintain performance.

The model suggests that the new relationship between executives and middle managers consists of a pattern of exchange between the two groups. The new relationship requires executives and middle managers to take all of the actions described in the previous section, but they must also maintain the long view of the change activities and develop the personal and organizational skills necessary to adapt to it and manage it effectively.

Conclusion

Agencies can expect what one middle manager called "permanent white-water change" in the foreseeable future. Organizational change associated with reinventing government, budget cuts, and changes yet unforeseen will continue. The new skills and abilities discussed in this chapter and the new relationship emerging will be key to long-term success.

The questions that remain are equally important, however. There is a lingering concern that the current changes have decimated both banks of expertise and institutional capacity. Not enough is currently known about where the cuts have taken their greatest toll; that will need to be closely monitored. At the same time, the assumption that middle managers are expendable must continue to be questioned. This research supports the view that middle managers play an important role in organizational change. If middle managers are "let go," how will the linking function be carried out? Finally, all the changes described here have occurred without significant reform of the base management and support systems in the federal government. Can these changes endure without those changes?

Note

The views in this chapter are those of the authors and do not reflect the official policy or position of the Department of Defense or the U.S. government.

References

Barzelay, Michael. 1992. *Breaking through Bureaucracy: A New Vision for Managing in Government*. Berkeley, Calif.: University of California Press.

Colvard, James E. 1994. "In Defense of Middle Management." *Government Executive* 26, no. 5 (May): 57–58.

Daft, Richard L., and Arie Y. Lewin. 1993. "Where Are the Theories for the 'New' Organizational Forms? An Editorial Essay." *Organization Science* 4, no. 4 (November): i–vi.

Druckman, Daniel, Jerome E. Singer, and Harold Van Cott. 1997. *Enhancing Organizational Performance*. Washington, D.C.: National Academy Press.

Ingraham, Patricia W., Barbara S. Romzek, and Associates. 1994. *New Paradigms for Government: Issues for the Changing Public Service*. San Francisco: Jossey-Bass.

Kam, Allan J., and Jerry G. Shaw. 1994. "Managers and Top Professionals Band Together." *Public Manager* 22, no. 4 (winter): 7–10.

Kettl, Donald F. 1994. *Reinventing Government? Appraising the National Performance Review*. CPM Report 94-2. Washington, D.C.: Brookings Institution.

———. 1995. "Building Lasting Reform: Enduring Questions, Missing Answers." In *Inside the Reinvention Machine: Appraising Governmental Reform,* edited by Donald F. Kettl and John J. DiIulio, Jr.. Washington, D.C.: Brookings Institution.

Light, Paul C. 1997. *The Tides of Reform: Making Government Work, 1945–1995*. New Haven, Conn.: Yale University Press.

McCarthy, Eugene Michael. 1994. "The Elusive 252,000 or a Layman's Guide to Government Downsizing." *Classifiers' Column* (March/April): 2–6.

Mintzberg, Henry. 1973. *The Nature of Managerial Work*. Englewood Cliffs, N.J.: Prentice Hall, Inc.

Moe, Ronald C. 1994. "The 'Reinventing Government' Exercise: Misinterpreting the Problem, Misjudging the Consequences." *Public Administration Review* 54, no. 2 (March/April): 111–22.

National Performance Review. 1993. *From Red Tape to Results: Creating a Government That Works Better and Costs Less.* Washington, D.C.: U.S. Government Printing Office.

Osborne, David, and Ted Gaebler. 1992. *Reinventing Government: How the Entrepreneurial Spirit Is Transforming the Public Sector.* Reading, Mass.: Addison-Wesley.

Pfiffner, James P. 1997. "The National Performance Review in Perspective." *International Journal of Public Administration* 20, no. 1: 41–70.

Rainey, Hal G. 1997. *Understanding and Managing Public Organizations.* 2d ed. San Francisco: Jossey-Bass.

Relyea, Harold C. 1993. *Reinventing Government and the 103d Congress: A Brief Overview.* CRS Report for Congress, 93-859 GOV. Washington, D.C.: Library of Congress.

Sanders, Ronald P. 1994. "Reinventing the Senior Executive Service." In *New Paradigms for Government: Issues for the Changing Public Service,* edited by Patricia W. Ingraham, Barbara S. Romzek, and Associates. San Francisco: Jossey-Bass.

Seidman, Harold. 1993. "Reinventing the Wheel, Not Government." *Government Executive* 25, no. 4 (April): 32–33.

Shoop, Tom. 1993. "The Executive Transition." *Government Executive* 25, no. 9 (September): 22–25.

———. 1994a. "Targeting Middle Managers." *Government Executive* 26, no. 1 (January): 10–15.

———. 1994b. "True Believer." *Government Executive* 26, no. 9 (September): 16–23.

Thompson, James R., and Vernon D. Jones. 1995. "Reinventing the Federal Government: The Role of Theory in Reform Implementation." *American Review of Public Administration* 25, no. 2 (June): 183–99.

10 Institutional Paradoxes
Why Welfare Workers Cannot Reform Welfare

Marcia K. Meyers and Nara Dillon

BETWEEN 1985 and 1993, California lawmakers made significant changes in the major welfare program for families, Aid to Families with Dependent Children (AFDC).[1] These changes had important consequences for poor families. They also had important implications for the local organization of welfare services. Although the California welfare reforms were generated by state-level lawmakers, they were finally delivered by implementing agents in each of fifty-eight county welfare departments. To gauge the extent to which front-line workers or "street-level bureaucrats" in the county welfare programs were actually delivering new welfare policies, we observed the delivery of welfare services between 1993 and 1994 in local welfare offices in four counties. We found that ambitious promises to transform welfare programs had not been realized on the front lines of service delivery. This case raises important questions about the role of organizational and bureaucratic factors in the implementation of policy reforms, particularly in the case of social policy reforms for which the goals of government interventions are highly contested.

Background: Policy Reform and Organizational Reform

An important consequence of a liberal federalist government is that law-makers rely on the cooperation of multiple public and private authorities to achieve policy objectives. To the extent that policy objectives are clear, desired outcomes are unambiguous, and the interests of all relevant actors converge, multiactor policy implementation can be expected to proceed smoothly toward anticipated policy outcomes (Palumbo and Calista 1990; Ingram 1990; Sabatier and Mazmanian 1983). Policy implementation under these conditions is relatively rare, however. More often, policies adopted at any level of government contain some challenge to the perspectives, interests, or priorities of other organizational entities that are key to implementation success (Ingram 1990; Ferman 1990).

The persistence of political conflicts introduces considerable uncertainty into the implementation process. Policies are adopted by lawmakers but are finally enacted by implementing agents who, as organizations and as individuals, can be expected to bring their own interests to the implementation process (Ferman 1990; Brandl 1989; Stoker 1991). Because they control critical resources for the enactment of policies and the flow of critical information about policy outcomes, implementing agents also enjoy considerable discretion in the production of policy outcomes (Kelman 1987; Wilson 1989). In social programs, where implementing agents deliver services and enforce rules directly with clients, the discretion of front-line workers is especially ubiquitous and important in determining policy outcomes (Lipsky 1980; Hasenfeld 1983). Because policies are finally delivered by multiple organizations and individuals, each with their own and often divergent interests, policy-making principals can achieve policy goals only by gaining the cooperation of what Stoker (1991) terms "reluctant partners": "implementation participants who enjoy substantial autonomy and whose cooperation is uncertain and may be difficult to achieve" (4).

The uncertainty of the implementation process is often exacerbated by conflict and ambiguity in the policy objectives themselves. Because American politics are coalition politics, elected officials often build a convergence of interests by adopting vague, broad, and even internally contradictory policies in an effort to satisfy multiple interests (Ferman 1990; Brodkin 1990). Implementing agents receive ambiguous directives and multiple, often competing demands from various interests. Conflicts of interest may be especially prominent in the case of social policies that have redistributive consequences (Ingram 1990). Brodkin (1990) argues that the most contested policy issues on which elected officials cannot forge agreements may be passed out of the political arena altogether in the form of ambiguous statements of principle, symbolic policies, and nondecisions. Elected officials "delegate to the bureaucracy the hard task of giving specific meaning to vague or contradictory statements of legislative policy intent" (111).

Locating and Defining the Outcomes of Social Policies

Because social policies frequently embrace unresolved political conflicts and because policy-making principals must depend on implementing agents who have divergent interests and substantial discretion, the content of social policy is rarely defined once and for all at any level of government. This raises particularly vexing problems in studying implementation (Ingram 1990; Ferman 1990). If policy makers do not always mean what they say (or say what they mean), and implementing agents do not always do as they are told (nor are they always told what to do), by what yardstick can we measure policy outcomes?

One option is to focus on policy as it is enacted or delivered to citizens. In his seminal study of street-level bureaucrats, Lipsky (1980) describes social policies as the product of the actions of front-line workers in social agencies because "although they are normally regarded as low-level employees, the actions of most public service workers actually constitute the services delivered by government" (3). Policy is delivered at the end of an oftentimes long chain of nested principal-agent relationships among elected officials, bureaucrats, managers, and workers (Lynn 1993).[2]

Given the complexity of implementing relationships, how can policy analysts hope to define a concrete measure of the success of policy implementation? Richard Elmore (1982) suggests that implementation researchers begin with "backward mapping" of the policy to be delivered. The analysis begins "not with a statement of intent, but with a statement of the specific behavior at the lowest level of the implementation process that generates the need for policy" (142). When the behaviors desired at the end point of service delivery have been precisely described, the analysts work backward through the chain of implementing agencies asking, at each level, what is the ability of this unit to affect the behavior that is the target of policy? And what type of transaction would be most congruent with this outcome?

Managing Policy at the Street Level: Incentives or Inspiration?

If social policies are finally "produced" by legions of front-line workers, we would expect the management, coordination, and performance monitoring systems in local organizations to have important policy consequences. The success or failure of *policy* reform will often depend on the success or failure of *organizational* reform. The tools that government bureaucracies and other complex organizations use to direct their members have been considered in two scholarly traditions as structures (rules and incentives) and leadership (inspiration). Although usually considered the province of management studies, organizational structure and leadership are also critical variables in policy outcomes.

From early work in the rational-legal bureaucratic and administrative management traditions, analysts have identified organizational structures as mechanisms for aligning the actions of members with organizational goals. One tradition in organizational analysis has focused on concrete dimensions of structure such as lines of authority, spans of control, and production and coordination mechanisms (e.g., Thompson 1967; Mintzberg 1979). Other analysts have explored the ways in which control is embedded in standard operating procedures and in the reward, training, and communication procedures that provide individuals with the specific and limited knowledge they need to make decisions that further organizational objectives (March and Simon 1958; March and Olsen 1989; Perrow 1986). Agency theorists have added another important dimension by emphasizing the role of information and incentive structures and the choice between hierarchical or marketlike relationships as mechanisms for coordinating the actions of self-interested but interdependent parties (Eisenhardt 1989; Moe 1984).

A second tradition in organizational scholarship challenges what are often described as reductionist structural theories by emphasizing the role of leadership and inspiration in aligning the work of individuals with the goals of the organization. As J. Q. Wilson (1989) notes: "It is a commonplace that people do not live by bread alone, but it is one often forgotten by scholars seeking to find the most parsimonious explanation of human action and the most elegant prescription for how to induce that action" (157). Barnard (1938), Selznick (1957), and others have argued for the critical role of leadership and organizational mission in motivating the cooperation of individuals within the organization. More recently, organizational analysts have described the unifying role of mission in terms of organizational culture (e.g., Schein 1992) and commitment (e.g., Ouchi 1981). Although many observers have pointed out ways in which leadership is constrained, particularly in public organizations, others convey a more optimistic view. Wilson (1989) reminds us that, contrary to the predictions of formal economic theories, most government managers do succeed in making things happen—delivering services, enforcing rules, and so on—even in the absence of compelling economic incentives for their employees. Several recent works provide examples of successful leadership in the execution and reform of social programs (e.g., Behn 1991; Golden 1990).

Welfare Reform as a Problem of Bureaucratic Reform

This model of implementation suggests that social policies, as enacted, can be observed in the actions of street-level bureaucrats who are the end point in a chain of nested principal-agent relationships linking policy makers to the front lines of service delivery. Although policy analysts usually confine their focus to the study of social policy inputs (e.g., legislation and administrative directives) or outputs (e.g., changes in clients' characteristics or circumstances), policies are substantially shaped by the organizations that operate *between* inputs and outputs. The structure and leadership strategies in these organizations are critical variables in policy results.

This study examines the implementation of welfare reform in California as an example of the organizational challenges that arise in the implementa-

234 | *Meyers and Dillon*

tion of new policies in complex, intergovernmental bureaucratic systems. Although the chronology of reform to welfare policies has been well documented, the implementation of these policies—and consequences for policy outcomes—are less understood. The implementation of state-level welfare reform experiments has been studied in several sites, but most of these studies have described the delivery of services under the specialized conditions that characterize demonstration projects. They have not addressed the question of how complex welfare changes are delivered in established welfare bureaucracies. Recent studies of the Family Support Act (Lurie and Hagen 1993; Hagen and Lurie 1994; Brodkin 1997) suggest that as states go to scale, welfare reforms may be substantially diluted due to a scarcity of organizational attention and resources.

If, as argued earlier, social policies are ultimately produced in transactions between clients and street-level bureaucrats, it is important to open the "black box" of local welfare bureaucracies to understand better what occurs in these transactions and the organizational variables that direct them. This study examines the implementation of welfare reform in California from the "bottom up" by considering the work of front-line workers in welfare offices. Using data from interviews and observations conducted in local welfare offices in 1993 and 1994, we analyze the extent to which transactions between welfare workers and their clients reflected the stated goals of legislative and administrative directives. We then consider how organizational factors in local welfare offices—particularly issues of organizational structure and inspiration—help explain the gap between the policies articulated by elected officials and the policies finally delivered by street-level bureaucrats.

The Case: Work Pays in California

In his 1992 state of the state address, Governor Pete Wilson articulated a new mission for the California AFDC program when he pledged to "make welfare what it should be: transitional aid to the needy, not a permanent way of life." The AFDC program was included in the 1935 Social Security Act to provide economic protection for dependent children and to keep widowed mothers out of the labor market. By the 1980s, welfare policies were shaped by a quite different set of expectations and concerns. Beginning with the creation of a state welfare-to-work training program in 1985 (the Greater Avenues to Independence or GAIN program), California was a leader in a new generation of state-level experiments designed to move recipients, including single mothers, *out of* the welfare system and into employment. Between 1991 and 1993, amid contentious public and political debate, the California legislature approved additional changes to the AFDC program as part of the "Work Pays" demonstration project.[3] Work Pays made two important changes in the objectives and rules of the AFDC program.

First, Work Pays emphasized *transitional assistance.* Although AFDC continued to be an entitlement, policy makers attempted to reduce caseloads by creating financial disincentives to long-term welfare receipt. Since 1988, eligibility for most welfare has been contingent on participation in work or employment preparation.[4] California lawmakers created additional disincentives for welfare receipt by reducing the value of AFDC through elimination of all cost-of-living adjustments and through reduction of benefits by nearly 13 percent in real terms.

Second, Work Pays policies explicitly promoted *work and economic self-sufficiency* for welfare recipients. As described by state officials in 1993, Work Pays was designed to "substantially change the focus of the AFDC program to promote work over welfare and self-sufficiency over welfare dependence." Employment disincentives were reduced by lowering the marginal tax on earnings, allowing recipients to offset benefit reductions partially through earnings ("fill the gap" policies), and lifting the ceiling on employment hours. Employment preparation was emphasized by strengthening requirements for GAIN participation and by creating financial incentives for adolescents to remain in school and for families to save for education. Program rules were also modified to ease the financial difficulty of leaving AFDC by extending child care and Medicaid benefits for a longer period after cash aid was terminated. The chronology of work-related welfare reforms in California is set out in table 1.

The state Department of Social Services (DSS) was responsible for overall management of the AFDC program and the new Work Pays demonstration. Because welfare is locally managed in California, however, the ultimate design and delivery of welfare services, and of welfare reforms, was the responsibility of each of fifty-eight county welfare departments. Between 1991 and 1993, state DSS officials issued "All County Letters" informing county welfare directors about changes in AFDC benefits and rules. In 1993, concerned that clients were not being informed of the new employment incentives and obligations, state DSS officials stepped up efforts to communicate policy changes. A public information campaign was launched with public service announcements and eye-catching "Work Pays" brochures and posters that were distributed to local welfare, public health, and social service agencies. A toll-free number was established (1-800-WRK-PAYS) to provide welfare clients with information about work incentives and access to a state DSS worker. The governor proclaimed a "Work Pays" month and joined the director of the California DSS at press conferences and other media events. The director of the

Table 1. Chronology of Work–Related Welfare Reforms in California, 1985–1994

Year	Program/Project	Changes
1985	California GAIN Program	Created county programs of education, training, and job preparation services for AFDC recipients
1988	Federal Family Support Act	Imposed work or training requirements on most AFDC recipients. Authorized matching federal funds for state welfare-to-work programs (JOBS program) and entitlement of matching federal funds for support and transitional child care and Medicaid services
1991	Assistance Payment Demonstration Project	Reduced AFDC maximum aid payment 4.4 percent ("fill the gap budgeting"); froze COLA for AFDC maximum aid payments
1992	Assistance Payment Demonstration Project	Reduced AFDC maximum aid payment additional 5.8 percent; eliminated hourly work limits for AFDC recipients; reduced AFDC maximum aid payment additional 2.7 percent
1993	Work Pays Demonstration Project (SB 35 and SB 1078)	Extended AFDC disregards that lower marginal tax on earnings; created "supplemental child care" program for employed recipients; created program of financial incentives, case management, and support services for pregnant and parenting teens (Cal-Learn)

state DSS prepared letters to county welfare workers asking them to participate in the outreach campaign by wearing "Work Pays" buttons and delivering the message to clients that "it always pays to work."

What Would It Mean to Implement Work Pays?

Between 1992 and 1994 we studied the implementation of Work Pays in local welfare offices in four California counties. We were particularly attentive to how front-line workers were communicating information about the new policies and what type of signals they were sending to clients about the new employment expectations and benefits of the program.

We focused on the content and the approach of front-line communications for several reasons. First, we assumed that providing substantial information to clients would be a necessary step in implementing the reforms. Work Pays created complicated new program interactions, opportunities, and incentives for clients who began paid employment.[5] Although complete information about the opportunities and penalties was not a *sufficient* condition for clients to comply with new work and self-sufficiency obligations, it was arguably a *necessary* condition for a successful transition to economic independence given the complexity of welfare rules and the limited economic prospects of most welfare clients.

Second, the communication of information about Work Pays was assumed to serve an important signaling function. Although the changes in welfare policies were relatively modest, state officials promoted Work Pays as an important shift in the *mission* of the program—a shift from provision of permanent assistance to keep mothers *out* of the labor market to provision of transitional assistance to move them *into* paid employment. State officials used a variety of public information techniques to get the word out about these changes. Their most effective tool in this regard, however, was the front-line worker in the local welfare office, who had face-to-face contact with all applicants and clients and who was often the only individual with whom welfare recipients ever had direct contact. As described by the director of the California DSS in a 1993 letter to local eligibility workers: "These changes are complicated, and can make your job more difficult. Fortunately, one aspect of the program has become easier to understand: *it always pays to work*. . . . It's an important message, and it's one we hope you will help us deliver. . . . You are a vital link to the AFDC population and we can't hope to reach recipients without your support."

Third, we expected the *form* of communication to serve as an indicator of the extent to which local operations reflected the emphasis on transitional aid and employment. Since the formal separation of federally funded social services and cash assistance in the 1970s, local welfare offices, in California as elsewhere, have been preoccupied with processing claims for cash welfare assistance (Goodsell 1981; Simon 1983; Bane and Ellwood 1994). Implementation of reforms such as Work Pays, which emphasized changes in clients' employment behaviors and use of welfare, would demand substantial changes in philosophy and approach. Local welfare programs would need to modify operations that had been designed for what Hasenfeld (1983) has called "people sustaining" services that increase clients' well-being without attempting to change their personal attributes in order to deliver a new type of "people changing" or transforming services that would alter clients' personal attributes, motivation, and behaviors. As the director of DSS described it, "The goal [of Work Pays was] to materially influence the work behavior of AFDC recipients" (Anderson 1995, 44).[6] Because welfare recipients differ in their individual characteristics, needs, and prospects for self-sufficiency, no single strategy was likely to work with everyone. Developing the type of personalized services that might influence work behavior of this diverse population would be a dramatic departure for local programs that had been pressed for several decades to develop standardized operations geared toward efficiency, accuracy, and consistency in the processing of welfare claims (Simon 1983; Brodkin 1987, 1990).[7]

The face-to-face transactions between line workers and clients provided a useful unit of analysis for studying each of these aspects of the Work Pays implementation: the information that was transmitted to clients about the reforms, the explicit and implicit signals about welfare and work, and the extent to which programs provided more individualized "people changing" services. To operationalize measures of these outcomes, we made use of Richard Elmore's (1982) model of "backward mapping." We reasoned backward from the desired outcome of the Work Pays reforms (to influence materially clients' work behaviors) in order to identify specific characteristics of worker-client communications that were most consistent with the production of these outcomes.[8]

Welfare workers were quite limited in their ability to produce employment outcomes: they could not force clients to go to work, control the job opportunities that clients encountered, or even change clients' employment potential.[9] Nevertheless, in the delivery of cash assistance, welfare workers were positioned to control at least three factors that might have been used to "influence materially" work behaviors. First, in their role as gatekeepers and eligibility technicians, workers could provide or withhold important *information* about complex program rules, interactions, and services that were available to support clients' efforts to leave welfare for work. Second, because they were necessarily selective in their communication and application of welfare rules that were simply too voluminous to enforce in their entirety, workers actively *constructed the meaning* of opportunities and obligations associated with welfare participation. Finally, because they delivered this information in an unpredictable and partially uncontrollable personal encounter with a highly diverse population of claimants, workers exercised considerable *discretion* in the extent to which they personalized services to apply the right mixture of teaching, assistance, and exhortation that would help different clients go to work.

"Backward mapping" the implementation of Work Pays suggested that, if the reforms were fully implemented at the street level, we would observe a new type of transaction between workers and their clients. We would expect to find that many workers were replacing or supplementing traditional *instrumental* client transactions, which emphasized collecting and verifying information for claims processing, with *transformational* transactions that used "people changing" approaches to increase clients' employment, self-sufficiency, and rapid exits from the welfare system. In transformational interactions, the explicit and implicit messages about work and self-sufficiency would be high, as workers communicated expectations about work and the transitional nature of assistance, provided information on work-related rules and benefits, and assisted clients with securing supportive services such as training, job referral, child care, and transitional benefits. Personalization and individualization would also be evident, as workers modified their transactions to match services and other types of assistance to clients' needs and helped clients understand how, in their own situation, it "paid to work."

Was Work Pays Implemented?

Between 1993 and 1994 we observed face-to-face transactions between welfare workers and their clients in several offices in four California counties.[10] These observations were supplemented in each office with semi-structured interviews with front-line workers and their supervisors.

Our observations revealed little evidence that workers had incorporated any elements of Work Pays into their communication with clients. Workers were observed to engage in any *transformational* transactions in fewer than 20 percent of interviews. In these rare cases, the worker provided at least some information about self-sufficiency or work and tailored some of the information to the needs or circumstances of the client. In the majority of interviews, however, transactions were purely *instrumental:* workers provided no information about programs, incentives, services, or expectations regarding work and self-sufficiency and took no steps to tailor their interactions to the individual needs of their clients. These interviews were dominated by an emphasis on determining eligibility and by an instrumental concern for collecting and verifying eligibility information. Instrumental transactions ignored or even discouraged clients' interests in issues of work and self-sufficiency. If information about work or self-sufficiency was referenced at all, it was done so in an instrumental fashion that emphasized program rules and regulations and discouraged clients' active engagement or involvement.

The remaining workers were observed to respond in limited ways to the Work Pays reforms. In about one-fifth of the transactions observed, the worker responded to the increased information load by *routinizing* discussions of work and self-sufficiency with clients. In these interviews, workers provided some information related to work and self-sufficiency, but their standardized recitation of incentives and rules did little or nothing to explain complex program information and did not link it in any way to clients' individual needs or circumstances. Other workers, about 10 percent of those observed, responded to the welfare reforms by *particularizing* their transactions with clients. These workers continued their instrumental concern for determining program eligibility but deviated from routinized scripts on an ad hoc basis to give advice, guidance, or individualized information. Because these deviations were idiosyncratic and driven principally by workers' conceptions of program expectations and client needs, they provided clients with partial, confusing, and sometimes incorrect information about new expectations and resources.

Interviews with workers and supervisors confirmed the accuracy of the observations. Workers placed low priority on informing clients about work incentives, encouraging them to leave welfare, or referring them to training or other support services. Nearly all indicated that they did not routinely initiate discussions about work and that they discussed the impact of work on benefits only when clients asked or reported new earnings. Only one worker indicated that it was important to communicate "the importance of work" to clients. None routinely included discussions of "fill the gap budgeting," the lifting of the one-hundred-hour work rule, or other work provisions with clients. As one described it, "If they are exempt from GAIN, we don't talk about work issues; if they are eligible we tell them about GAIN. Other than that, if they don't push it, we don't push it."

Organizational Factors: Why Did Workers Fail to Reform Welfare?

Direct observations revealed that the majority of welfare workers were failing to communicate either concrete information or a new message about welfare to their clients. To understand why workers failed to implement Work Pays fully, it is necessary to look in some detail at the organization of work in local welfare offices. Interviews with front-line workers and their supervisors suggested that the organizational mechanisms used to align individual actions with agency objectives—especially the structure of work and understanding of mission—were fundamentally incompatible with the type of activities called for by the welfare reforms.

Structural Constraints: Rules, Standard Operating Procedures, and Incentives in the Welfare Office

Rules, standard operating procedures, and incentives are used in all complex organizational systems to align the actions of members with the goals of the organizations and, in public organizations, with larger policy goals. In the local welfare offices we visited, rules and incentives were seen to direct the actions of street-level bureaucrats, including the content and quality of their transactions with clients. Rather than supporting workers in the provision of information about work and self-sufficiency or in the provision of individualized assistance in interpreting work incentives and expectations, the structure of work directed workers toward instrumental transactions that emphasized routinization, control, and extracting information.

Organizing Pressures: Rules and Clients

The job of a welfare worker in California was demanding. If the person was an AFDC intake worker, he or she was responsible for determining eligibility for the AFDC, Emergency Assistance, and Food Stamps programs. With thirty to fifty clients per month, each worker completed a long application form, collected and verified supporting documentation, and determined initial eligibility. If the individual was a continuing worker, he or she was responsible for processing monthly reports for as many as 270 active cases, calculating the allowable benefit after disregards and deductions, submitting paperwork, and authorizing payment. The worker met with clients annually to redetermine eligibility and, as often as needed, to solve problems, reconcile errors, answer questions, and ferret out fraudulent claims.

These difficult jobs were driven by two organizing pressures: extensive program rules and unpredictable, largely unobservable, program clients.

Welfare workers delivered programs that were governed by extensive, complex, and frequently changing rules. Rules were extensive because welfare was allocated on the basis of detailed categorical and means-tests. Rules were complex because they reflected policy makers' efforts to target assistance on specific groups under varying conditions; any one applicant might have qualified for several programs, resulting in complex interactions between programs. Rules were constantly revised because programs were jointly managed by federal, state, and local governments, with substantial judicial involvement.

As eligibility rules have become more elaborate over the years, so too have the monitoring systems needed to hold workers and agencies accountable and to discourage fraudulent claims. One of the most pressing accountability demands has been quality control standards, adopted in the 1970s, that hold state welfare departments strictly accountable for AFDC overpayments. California passed this accountability structure on to local officials through an extensive quality control monitoring system; county welfare systems, in turn, adopted detailed rules to prevent, detect, and reverse erroneous eligibility determinations and payments. Workers felt the pressure of these monitoring systems directly. They were expected to enforce rules as specified in extensive and frequently updated program manuals; they were explicitly directed in the execution of various eligibility tests and verifications; and the accuracy of their eligibility determinations was constantly monitored through local quality control systems.

Clients were the second organizing pressure on the street-level welfare bureaucrats. Workers responded to a large and varied client population that had, at the time of this study, both a legal entitlement and oftentimes urgent need for assistance. Clients came in person to apply for aid and on an annual basis to recertify their eligibility. They communicated monthly through reapplication forms and supporting documentation. On a daily basis, many contacted workers in person or by phone to complete paperwork, ask questions, update addresses or other information, resolve problems with missing or late payments, and register complaints.

It was one of the paradoxes of welfare workers' jobs that they were simultaneously in control of their clients' fate and dependent on their clients for the production of welfare services. To enforce program rules and produce income transfers, workers needed extensive information about their clients. Yet they had little direct access to this information because most of it—from clients' financial need to their household characteristics and their prospects for self-sufficiency—was revealed only outside the welfare office. Welfare clients, like most individuals, could be expected to vary in their honesty and reliability. Workers, however, could do little to verify the information that was provided entirely through reports and supporting documents provided by clients themselves.

Workers' Response: Standardization, Routinization

Welfare workers thus faced pressures from above, in their need to be accountable to supervisors and quality control audits, and from below, in their dependence on uncontrollable and largely unobservable clients. The information that welfare workers obtained from applicants and clients was a critical resource for managing these pressures, but workers faced formidable information asymmetries. The solution for most was adoption of routinized, instrumental procedures designed to control interactions with, and extract maximum information from, their clients.

The instrumental approach to client transactions was evident when workers described the information they considered critical to exchange with clients. When asked what was most important to communicate during client interviews, workers were nearly unanimous in identifying rights and responsibilities and especially clients' responsibility to report *everything* to the welfare office. By reading aloud the official summary of clients' legal rights and reporting responsibilities, workers tried to impress on clients their responsibility to disclose the information needed by the worker to do the job. As one supervisor described it, she expected her workers "to emphasize to clients that they must report all changes and *let the worker assess* whether it will affect benefits."

Routinized and instrumental approaches were reinforced by a structure of employment rewards that provided few if any incentives for workers to engage in extensive or individualized interactions with their clients. Workers described performance evaluation in uniform terms across the four counties: informal evaluations by supervisors on an ongoing basis, and formal, written performance reviews quarterly or annually. The criteria for good performance mentioned most frequently were organization, speed in processing claims, ability to meet deadlines, accuracy in paperwork, number of cases processed, and general "work habits" such as punctuality, attendance, and dress. The quality of interactions with clients was mentioned occasionally as an element in performance reviews. When asked how interactions were evaluated, however, both workers and supervisors agreed that client complaints were the only mechanism. None knew of performance standards for the quality of staff interactions with clients or of mechanisms, such as regular observation, through which supervisors might evaluate these interactions. None of the workers indicated that providing more information, counseling, or referrals for clients would be noticed or rewarded by supervisors; a few indicated that they had been specifically advised that such "social work" activities were not part of their job.

The criteria for performance evaluations were clear; the rewards for doing a good job were much less so. When workers were asked, "What happens when you do a good job around here?" the most frequent response was "Nothing." Good workers were recognized through certificates, "employee of the month" awards and positive written reviews, and informal praise and recognition by their superiors. Yet salaries were raised through annual step increases, and promotions were widely believed to depend on standardized civil service tests rather than on-the-job performance. If the workers were not cognizant of organizational rewards for good performance, neither did they complain about harsh or even very specific penalties for poor performance. Some thought that poor workers would be transferred to a different desk or unit; many did not know of any specific sanctions for errors or poor performance.

The Penalty for Poor Work: More Work

Workers had to correct errors or incomplete information on client applications. Documents were "bounced" from the computer back to the worker if there were errors; cases were returned from supervisors or auditors for more processing if information was incomplete or calculations were incorrect; serious errors that delayed claims generated time-consuming client complaints to the worker and the supervisor.

Given this incentive structure, there were few if any rewards for workers who made an effort to educate or counsel their clients. In fact, there were substantial disincentives for workers to engage in transactions with clients that could either delay welfare claims or lead to client complaints about fair treatment. Client satisfaction was rarely noted, but client complaints were because they created more work: more work for the supervisor, who had to resolve the dispute, and more work for the worker, who had to resolve the problem. At their most serious, complaints become requests for fair hearings to contest eligibility decisions. Supervisors rarely, if ever, heard from *satisfied* clients; as neatly summed by one worker, "The less the supervisors hear about you from clients the better."

The need to control work demands created another, even more direct incentive for workers to routinize transactions and avoid lengthy discussions of employment and self-sufficiency. Welfare clients are very heterogenous in their individual characteristics, their needs for assistance, their personal and family resources, and their management of the welfare application process. For workers, these differences, particularly special or complicated circumstances that affected benefit levels, created even more uncertainty. Special circumstances made processing claims more time-consuming up front and increased the chances for error, additional work, and, possibly, client complaints. To minimize these risks, workers strove to standardize applications and, by extension, their knowledge of client characteristics. When asked which cases were the most difficult to process, workers pointed to families with unusual circumstances, such as non-English-speaking parents, transitions in household structure, and, notably, earned income. Although workers had strong incentives to extract information from clients, they also had strong incentives to standardized that information whenever possible. For example, workers commonly voiced the opinion that clients had earnings they did not report to the welfare office. Nonetheless, workers rarely probed clients for information about work or earnings unless clients volunteered that they were employed. It was even more uncommon for workers to direct, encourage, or exhort clients to change their employment status. "When the client calls and tells you they are working," one worker described, "then you talk about it [work]."

Inspiration and Mission in the Welfare Office

The structure of the local welfare offices did little to encourage workers to provide information or individualized counseling about work and self-sufficiency to their clients. Yet, as many observers have argued, the importance of welfare "reform" may lie not in the details but in the new signal it sends—to clients and to workers—about the responsibility of individuals to pursue self-sufficiency outside the welfare system. Effectiveness on this dimension may depend less on formal rules, procedures, and directives for welfare workers and more on inspiration through leadership that engages workers and clients with a new program mission.

Leadership and inspiration are likely to be difficult, however, when the goals are conflicting or ambiguous, as is the case with many welfare programs. Both public opinion data and the vacillating history of welfare reform reveal a persistent tension between support for government programs to alleviate disadvantage and the expectation that individuals can and should achieve self-sufficiency without government assistance (Heclo 1994). These tensions have been routinely passed out of the political arena and into administrative channels of the welfare system in the form of "policies that simultaneously preach compassion and stress deterrence" (Katz 1986).

Perennial controversies about the mission of welfare, and the uncertainty of a joint production process that relies heavily on sometimes uncooperative clients, could make the job of delivering even basic welfare services nearly impossible. The Work Pays reforms exacerbated this tension by charging local welfare programs with potentially conflicting objectives: to provide equitable and equal treatment of all claims for assistance while discouraging use of assistance and modifying the behaviors of claimants. In the county welfare offices that we observed, managers and workers resolved these contradictions by constructing their understanding of the mission of welfare and of Work Pays in ways that were consistent with actual capacity: they substituted means for ends, adopted simplified and proximate goals for their work, and separated operational activities from larger, more controversial, and less certain program outcomes.

Workers in the front lines of welfare offices concerned themselves with processing applications and supporting paperwork to get welfare checks to their clients. When asked to describe what was most important about their job, they consistently described deadlines for processing claims: completing application documents, processing monthly eligibility adjustments, making address changes, responding to client appeals, and absorbing the contents of state letters that notified local offices of changes in program rules. Occasionally, workers volunteered that service to clients was an important aspect of their job. When pressed to describe service, however, these workers spoke in terms of completing paperwork and meeting deadlines to ensure timely and accurate benefits. Nearly as many stated that the aspect of their work that they would most like to *reduce* was contact with clients. This narrow conception of the role of the welfare worker was consistent with the views of immediate supervisors. As one supervisor put it, "The job [of a worker] is to serve the public, so getting people their entitlement is my highest priority."

The county welfare systems did not operate *without* articulated mission statements or goals. Shaped by incremental policy making and contested interests, however, local programs constructed an understanding of mission that largely substituted means for ends. Consider the following mission statement from a county in northern California: "To promote the social and economic well-being of individuals and families . . . through a responsive, accessible, and flexible service delivery system that recognizes the importance of the family, culture and ethnic diversity, and the increased vulnerability of populations at risk." Although the mission statement clearly articulates process values, it sidesteps fundamental controversies over *outcomes* by failing to define "well-being." Welfare programs can strive either to reduce clients' poverty or to reduce their dependency on welfare; the substantial body of research on welfare-to-work programs suggests that it is exceedingly difficult to accomplish both. The choice between these objectives was notably absent in this mission statement and in the descriptions of program goals from workers themselves. When a worker described her job, she did not speak about *outcomes,* such as reducing poverty, hardship, or inequality. Nor did she talk about the Work Pays goals of supporting self-sufficiency and work. She spoke instead about the *process* of determining and dispersing entitlement. *The larger mission and associated controversies and uncertainties were neatly shorn from the day-to-day work of street-level bureaucrats.*

Structure, Inspiration, and the Work Pays Reforms

These conditions of work and the understanding of program mission had important implications for the implementation of Work Pays. If welfare workers did not communicate information or signals about the goals of Work Pays, much less engage their clients in an active effort to increase self-sufficiency, it was not because they were opposed to the intent of these policies. On the contrary, when asked about welfare reform, workers frequently described the problems of the welfare system in terms of client dependency and barriers to self-sufficiency and expressed support for initiatives directed at increasing work and independence. Workers were generally quite clear in their personal and professional understanding of the rhetorical goals of welfare reform. As described by one, "The biggest problem is that the system doesn't expect responsibility. If there is no time limit for receiving AFDC, then there should be something to help clients get out and contribute to society. This might keep them on welfare longer, but less will be paid for by their grant, they will have more money in the home, be able to contribute to the economy, increase their self-esteem and maybe be motivated to get off welfare."

If welfare workers did not fully implement Work Pays, it was not due to their opposition to the policy changes. Welfare workers rarely engaged in transformational transactions with their clients because they *could not,* given the structure of their jobs and their understanding of the mission of the welfare system.

The strongest disincentive to engaging in transformational activities was the instrumental structure of workers' routine transactions with their clients. Workers emphasized repeatedly that processing claims was their main, and, for some, their only, legitimate role with clients. The structure of formal and informal incentives reinforced this instrumental approach. Workers were rewarded, and were best able to manage their workload, when they maximized the number of claims they processed in the least amount of time with the fewest errors. The greatest penalties workers faced were not direct sanctions, but instead extra work resulting from errors or delays: claims to reprocess, errors to be corrected, and client complaints to be resolved.

Rewards for modifying the message or the quality of their transactions with clients were uncertain. There were no mechanisms to observe or evaluate communication of the new message that welfare was transition or that "work pays." Workers were given no authority to impose work requirements or expectations about transitioning out of the welfare system; they had few mechanisms for tracking clients' progress toward self-sufficiency. They could neither reward clients for making use of work-related information and referrals nor sanction them for ignoring or even abusing this information by "gaming" the system for additional benefits. In their role as claims processors, their work actually became harder, more prone to errors and complaints if the case included earned income. Although the official message was that "it pays to work," in most respects it *did not* pay for welfare workers to engage their clients in planning for work and self-sufficiency.

The limited role that workers took advising and counseling clients was consistent also with a pervasive lack of resources for providing this type of assistance. The changes in California welfare policy were implemented without providing local welfare offices with new operational resources. Time was the most obvious limitation. Workers carried caseloads in excess of 200 or 250 clients. Processing claims, associated paperwork, and routine client inquiries left no time for individualized counseling about work and self-sufficiency. One program manager described the problem this way: "Workers do what is mandatory, and 'Work Pays' is nice, but it is at the bottom of the line in workers' priorities."

Workers also lacked information about services and resources available to help welfare recipients achieve self-sufficiency. Workers had to rely on their own "homework" or what their peers could tell them in order to make referrals. A few had compiled extensive catalogues of community resources; many simply referred clients to the county hotline for assistance. With each change in welfare programs or expansion in transitional assistance, workers noted that the rules became more difficult for them to understand and to communicate to clients.

The second important constraint at the street level was a narrow and technical understanding of the mission of the welfare system. Welfare workers and their supervisors consistently described their jobs in technical terms that severed the process of their work from its possible outcomes. The substitution of means for ends was prominent in workers' understanding of Work Pays. The "comprehensive" welfare reform promoted by the governor and state welfare officials was communicated to local welfare offices through a series of notices about changes in benefit levels, eligibility rules, and program regulations. Workers learned about the *content* of changes in routine staff meetings, through written directives about changes in eligibility rules, and through updates to their voluminous procedure manuals. Workers were rarely informed about the *purpose* of the rule changes through any of these channels.

Left to their own devices to interpret the goals and probable effects of Work Pays, workers were strikingly uninformed, misinformed, or skeptical about the goals articulated by elected and bureaucratic officials. When asked to describe the specific changes that had been made in the AFDC program, all could relate in detail the dates and procedures used to modify benefits, inform clients of benefit cuts, update forms, and so on. When asked to consider *why* these changes had been instituted, workers gave vague and contradictory responses. *Almost none described the changes as work incentives or support for client self-sufficiency.* Many saw the changes as routine modifications to already complex and frequently changing rules governing welfare programs. When pressed to consider the purpose of the changes, the majority of workers responded that the state was trying to save money. Others frankly admitted that they did not know and had not "given any thought" to why the policies had been adopted. A few connected the changes to work and self-sufficiency but were doubtful that they would have a meaningful impact. "I really have no idea about the purpose" was a typical response. "I don't see how less money is supposed to help anything."

The severing of the mechanics of welfare reform from its goals was carried over into workers' transactions with clients. Workers did not routinely communicate welfare reforms to their clients beyond required notifications of benefit reductions and rule changes. When clients asked directly, workers did their best to respond. Nonetheless, lacking a meaningful understanding of the goals of welfare reform, they were seriously limited in what they could tell their clients. Most said that the state "was running out of money" and had to reduce benefits. For some, responding to clients' concerns about benefit reductions was acutely painful. "The decreases in grants are awful," one worker commented. "I got lumps in my stomach when I heard about it." Others responded to clients' distress by disavowing the policies entirely. "It's the lawmakers' position," one told her clients. "We have no control over it."

Conclusions

This study of welfare reform in California suggests that policy makers failed to align the actions of street-level bureaucrats with their policy goals. Workers persisted in their instrumental transactions not because they disagreed with the policy intent but because the structure of their jobs and their understanding of program mission created significant disincentives for cooperating with policy reforms. Hence the institutional paradox: as presently organized, the welfare bureaucracy makes it nearly impossible for workers to cooperate with the intent of welfare reform.

This paradox can be understood as failure on the part of policy makers to understand and to manage the implementation process. Prescriptively, it would suggest that policy makers turn their attention to the structure of rules and incentives in local offices and to better communication of the goals of the reform. The source of the paradox may go deeper, however. If policy makers could not forge agreement on their welfare policy goals, their inattention to organizational constraints may be evidence of "successful" policy politics that shifted conflicts from the political to the administrative arena. If the problem is largely one of political will and coherent policy formulation, organizational reforms will do little to solve the underlying dilemma.

Structural Failure or Leadership Failure?

One interpretation of the gap between legislated and enacted welfare reform in California is that policy-making principals failed to modify the service delivery structure in order to direct bureaucratic agents toward their policy goals. In both rhetoric and legislation, the governor, state legislature, and
state welfare bureaucracy shifted the emphasis of the AFDC program. In the
local welfare offices, however, street-level bureaucrats exercised their substantial discretion and control over line operations to ignore and even undermine
these policy goals. Workers "did their jobs" as defined by formal operating procedures and performance reviews; they also structured their jobs to cope with
the informal system of incentives that penalized processing errors but rarely
rewarded provision of extra information or encouragement to clients. By just
"doing their jobs," however, they displaced their efforts from transforming clients to processing claims. This could be interpreted as widespread shirking
because workers, as agents, did not pursue policy makers' interests in changing
welfare programs.

Viewed through this lens, the lack of cooperation with policy goals on the
street level can be traced to structural factors. The job of the street-level bureaucrats in local welfare offices was constrained by pressures toward timely,
accurate, and standardized processing of claims for financial assistance. Workers
were observed to cope with the routinely difficult tasks of claims processing
by engaging in highly routinized and instrumental transactions with their clients. Welfare reforms adopted by California policy makers added new complexity and uncertainty to the already difficult job of working with a diverse
population of clients but did not provide additional resources to support implementation. Street-level bureaucrats coped with the reforms as they coped
with other aspects of their jobs: they enforced the reforms as administrative
rules, incorporated them into standardized determinations of clients' eligibility, and only selectively informed clients about related opportunities or obligations.

An alternate interpretation would suggest that the gap between stated and
enacted policy was evidence that policy makers failed to exercise leadership in
communicating the goals of welfare reform. Although elected and bureaucratic officials talked about comprehensive welfare reform, there was little evidence that workers and supervisors in local welfare offices understood the
reforms in these terms. Workers understood the mission and goals of their organizations in proximate and technical terms that focused on producing payments, controlling errors, and minimizing client complaints. They understood
welfare reform in similarly narrow and proximate terms that incorporated the

means, in the form of rule changes and benefit reductions, while ignoring the anticipated ends in clients' work and self-sufficiency behaviors.

Viewed through the lens of leadership theory, limited cooperation in the implementation of welfare reform can be seen as a failure by the governor and state DSS officials to send clear and consistent signals about policy intent to implementing bureaucrats. Although they emphasized work and self-sufficiency repeatedly in public relations and campaign materials, policy makers failed to incorporate this message in the formal transmission of policy changes to the county welfare offices. They emphasized rule changes but did not link these to anticipated client outcomes or create new performance standards for local programs. The failure to provide new resources for implementing welfare reforms reinforced the mixed signals from public officials. Workers who did not know, misunderstood, or were skeptical of officials' policy goals were poorly equipped and had little motivation to convey new expectations or new opportunities to their clients.

Successful Policy Politics?

It is also possible that the gap between stated and enacted policy reflects a different and more fundamental political failure. As Evelyn Brodkin (1990) has pointed out, in highly conflictual political environments, unresolved policy conflicts are often passed from the political to the administrative arenas. Implementing agents become an alternate channel for policy formulation, and they both resolve and obscure the political conflicts. Administrators commonly respond to political conflict by breaking down new mandates into a series of apparently unrelated, discrete operational activities. Each individual policy component is then recast as a technical, rather than political, problem.

Americans and their elected officials are exceptionally ambivalent about welfare. Given the operational difficulties of simultaneously helping the deserving poor while deterring the undeserving poor, and of solving problems of poverty and welfare use without substantial financial transfers, politicians may derive more political rewards from proposing than from implementing welfare reform (Heclo 1994). They are particularly rewarded for proposing policies that promise the impossible: for example, to save taxpayers' money while bringing about dramatic changes in chronic poverty and associated social and economic dysfunctions.

In crafting welfare reform in the 1990s, political officials in California followed the pattern that has characterized other welfare reforms. Welfare reform was debated in dramatic and highly partisan terms among the governor and liberal and conservative state legislators. The debate was made more visible by the inclusion of a welfare reform initiative on the California ballot (Proposition 165, the Government Accountability and Taxpayer Protection Act) in 1992. The governor's comprehensive welfare reforms, a good number of which were finally adopted by the state legislature, promised sweeping changes in the welfare system and dramatic changes in recipients. Yet, the policies that were finally adopted reflected political compromise and made relatively minor changes to the AFDC program. In their lack of clear direction and support for the implementation of these policies, state officials reflected the political compromise by sending mixed signals to local welfare offices about their commitment to their own reforms.

The disjuncture between the promise and the delivery of welfare reform may reflect not only a failure to implement the will of the policy makers but also a failure of will by policy makers. Political officials promised dramatic and politically popular "reforms" but finally adopted minor changes in program rules. They left the resolution of the inherent contradiction to their implementing agents, who responded by implementing the letter of the reforms. Whether they implemented the spirit of the reforms is more difficult to judge, given evidence that elected officials themselves failed to make choices among competing priorities.

Implications for Welfare and Bureaucratic Reform

This study of the implementation of welfare reform in California must be considered exploratory. Welfare systems vary widely between states, and both the sample and the data collection methods limit generalization to other regions of the country. Our measure of the gap between policy intent and achievement may also be debated. The use of backward mapping is useful to develop a counterfactual for what "would have" happened had front-line workers cooperated fully with the intent of welfare reform. Nevertheless, it may not produce the only or even the best measure of implementation success.

Despite these cautions, some lessons about the implementation of welfare reform may be usefully derived from this case. With the devolution of welfare programs to the states under the 1996 Personal Responsibility and Work Opportunities Act, these insights seem particularly important for both policy and management analysts.

A careful study of the organization of the welfare offices suggests that neither the structure nor the mission of those programs, as presently organized in California, are designed to support the work of changing the characteristics and behaviors of welfare recipients. The prevailing political consensus at the national and state levels suggests that welfare should be transitional assistance that encourages, facilitates, and, if necessary, imposes work on recipients. This implies substantial changes in policy delivery on the front lines. Changing

AFDC from a "people sustaining" program to a "people changing" or transforming program will require that the transactions between welfare workers and their clients be both more complex—in terms of information exchanged—and more personalized to engage diverse clients themselves in the achievement of these outcomes.

This case suggests that, no matter how much welfare workers in local offices support the intent of welfare reform, necessary changes in the operations and goals of local programs will not happen automatically. The structure of rules, operating procedures, and monitoring systems create too many disincentives for welfare workers to take on the additional and highly uncertain work of transforming their clients' behavior. The legacy of contradictory goals and impossible expectations has produced too strong a tendency to substitute means for ends in the understanding of program mission.

One lesson from this case may be that officials need to invest the resources necessary to undertake activities to bring about bureaucratic reforms: articulating a clear mission and measurable outcomes for the welfare system, linking goals to program operations, revising performance reviews to reward workers who help and encourage clients toward self-sufficiency, engaging workers in efforts to reengineer their transactions with clients, decreasing caseloads, increasing workers' discretion in processing individual claimants, and so on. This course of action is warranted if policy makers are serious about changing the AFDC system from an open-ended entitlement to a program of transitional assistance and work support. If the apparent gap between policy intent and enactment results from policy politics rather than failed implementation, however, efforts to secure the cooperation of implementing agents by better management of bureaucratic organizations may have unanticipated consequences. As Ferman (1990) cautions, the gap between policy intent and implementation outcomes may be the result of "policy makers and bureaucrats doing what they have to do to get things done in our political system. . . . If the true culprit is our political system, changes in one part (e.g. limiting bureaucratic discretion) will not alter that system and will probably create more difficulties in one little area" (50).

In the case of welfare reform, efforts to reform welfare bureaucracies toward unobtainable goals may create unanticipated difficulties. In the California welfare offices we observed, most workers continued in their instrumental transactions with clients. A fraction did show signs of more engaged and transformational interactions, but a larger fraction could be seen to cooperate only partially with the reform efforts. Some workers attempted to incorporate new information about work and self-sufficiency; faced with the ongoing pressure toward timely processing of claims, however, they coped by routinizing this information into their eligibility determination scripts. Others responded by particularizing their transactions: deviating from the script on an ad hoc basis and using their considerable discretion in transactions with clients to pursue their own, idiosyncratic understanding of the goals of the program and the best interests of the clients.

Efforts to reform the welfare bureaucracy without first resolving the internal contradictions of welfare policy and loosening the structural constraints on implementing agents may produce coping behaviors in place of policy reform. For example, if officials demand that workers provide more and more complex information about work and self-sufficiency to clients but fail to provide resources and or specify reasonable outcomes to be achieved through this information exchange, workers are likely to respond by even greater routinization of their transactions. If officials give workers more discretion and control over the content and quality of their transactions with clients but fail to convey a clear and consistent vision of the behavioral and motivational outcomes they hope to produce, workers may respond with more particularistic application of program rules and inequitable allocation of program resources.

Brandl (1989) reflects the prevailing debate about policy implementation when he writes, "There appear to be two broad approaches to aligning the actions of employees or agents with the missions of their organization: incentives and inspiration" (490). This analysis of welfare reform underscores the importance of both in achieving policy goals. Incentives are unlikely to work in the absence of the inspiration that comes from an understanding of organizational mission; inspiration will be equally ineffective if it is inconsistent with organizational structures and incentives. This case also suggests an important caveat: neither incentives nor inspiration are likely to work if policy makers pass unresolved political conflicts to their implementing agents through policy directives that are too contradictory or ambiguous to achieve.

Notes

Earlier versions of this chapter were presented at the 1995 Annual Meeting of the American Political Science Association, September 1995, and at the Third National Public Management Research Conference, October 5–7, 1995, University of Kansas. The help of Barbara Snow and Henry Brady in the collection and interpretation of these data is gratefully acknowledged. Thanks also to Evelyn Brodkin, Irene Lurie, Charles Goodsell, and Jodi Sandfort for comments on earlier drafts and to the welfare employees in Alameda, San Joaquin, San Bernardino, and Los Angeles counties of California for their cooperation with this research. All errors of fact and interpretation are, of course, the responsibility of the authors.

1. Since replaced by the Temporary Assistance Program for Needy Families by the 1996 Personal Responsibility and Work Opportunities Reconciliation Act.

2. The focus on the *interaction* between street-level bureaucrats and clients underscores the related point that social policies are jointly produced by the state and the recipient or citizen. Hasenfeld (1992) notes that a defining characteristic of social agencies is the use of technologies designed to process, sustain, or change people who come under their jurisdiction. Individuals in their roles as clients become one of the "raw materials" in the production of social programs or enactment of social policies. Nonetheless, street-level bureaucrats can rarely produce social policy outcomes without the active cooperation of their human "raw materials." Furthermore, individuals in their roles as clients are neither inert nor necessarily passive. They *react* to transformational process, and therefore affect their outcomes, and often actively *participate* in those processes, thereby engaging in a form of joint production with the worker.

3. Work Pays was the last in a series of AFDC program reforms initiated between 1991 and 1993 under a system of state-run and federally approved demonstration projects. Because these policies modified federal law under the Social Security Act, most were adopted under federal waivers as welfare demonstration projects. Although authorized as demonstration projects using experimental designs, however, the policy changes affected all but a small group of five thousand AFDC recipients "held harmless" as a control group.

4. With some exemptions, the 1988 Family Support Act required welfare recipients whose youngest child was at least six years of age to participate in work or work preparation activities, contingent on space in local JOBS programs.

5. In the estimation of one state DSS worker, the new "fill the gap budgeting" under Work Pays required a calculation "about as complicated as an income tax form" for each month (Johnson 1993).

6. Anderson continued: "Our rationale for incrementally reducing AFDC MAP [maximum aid payment] levels is to create a financial incentive for adults in AFDC households to work, and thus contribute to their own financial support and that of their children, and to reduce the financial incentive to enroll in AFDC in the first place. Coupling the MAP reductions with program policy changes, such as elimination of the 100-hour rule and removing the time limits for the $30 and one-third income disregards, provides California AFDC recipients with the financial incentives to seek employment and increase their earnings" (44).

7. The standardization of operations at the local level was a response to several pressures, including the official separation of federal social services and cash assistance in the 1970s, the elaboration of welfare eligibility rules through legislation and court cases, and the adoption of rigid quality control standards that penalized states for AFDC overpayments. For a good discussion of these factors see Brodkin (1987, 1990) and Simon (1983).

8. This analysis and empirical findings are described in more detail in Meyers et al. (1995) and Meyers, Glaser, and Mac Donald (1997).

9. Workers in the JOBS employment preparation program, authorized and funded under the federal JOBS program of the 1988 Family Support Act, did control access to education and training programs and some support services. Nevertheless, these were operated as separate programs in which no more than 20 percent of AFDC clients were ever enrolled.

10. Observational and interview data were collected in local welfare offices in four counties between 1993 and 1994. The four counties ranged from a very large dispersed bureaucracy to a small and highly centralized system. In order to tap variation within counties, researchers visited at least two different district offices in each county. The unit of analysis for data collection was the transaction between eligibility workers and their clients. Field researchers observed sixty-six intake or redetermination interviews between workers and clients. A structured observation form was used to record the frequency with which topics were discussed by workers with their clients, to record the content of other discussions, and to collect information about the characteristics of the AFDC case. Observational data were later coded on two dimensions of substantive interest: the *content of information* about Work Pays and other employment-related welfare reforms that was given to clients and the *exercise of positive discretion* by workers to explain, individualize, or interpret welfare policies, including the reforms. Semistructured interviews were later conducted with forty-three intake and redetermination workers and supervisors to verify and extend the conclusions from direct observations.

References

Anderson, Eloise. 1995. "Welfare by Waiver." *Public Welfare* 53: 44–49.

Bane, Mary Jo, and David Ellwood. 1994. *Welfare Realities.* Cambridge: Harvard University Press.

Barnard, Chester I. 1938. *The Functions of the Executive.* Cambridge: Harvard University Press.

Behn, Robert. 1991. *Leadership Counts.* Cambridge: Harvard University Press.

Brandl, John E. 1989. "How Organization Counts: Incentives and Inspiration." *Journal of Policy Analysis and Management* 8, no. 3: 489–94.

Brodkin, Evelyn Z. 1987. "Policy Politics: If We Can't Govern, Can We Manage?" *Political Science Quarterly* 102, no. 4: 571–87.

———. 1990. "Implementation As Policy Politics." In *Implementation and the Policy Process,* edited by Dennis J. Palumbo and Donald J. Calista. New York: Greenwood Press.

———. 1997. "Inside the Welfare Contract: Discretion and Accountability in State Welfare Administration." *Social Service Review* 71, no. 1: 1–33.

Eisenhardt, Kathleen M. 1989. "Agency Theory: An Assessment and Review." *Academy of Management Review* 14, no. 1: 57–74.

Elmore, Richard. 1982. "Backward Mapping: Implementation Research and Policy Decisions." In *Studying Implementation,* edited by Walter Williams. Chatham, N.J.: Chatham House.

Ferman, Barbara. 1990. "When Failure Is Success: Implementation and Madisonian Government." In *Implementation and the Policy Process,* edited by Dennis J. Palumbo and Donald J. Calista. New York: Greenwood Press.

Golden, Olivia. 1990. "Innovation in Public Sector Human Services Programs: The Implications of Innovation by 'Groping Along.'" *Journal of Policy Analysis and Management* 9, no. 2: 219–48.

Goodsell, Charles T. 1981. "Looking Once Again at Human Service Bureaucracy." *Journal of Politics* 43: 761–78.

Hagen, Jan L., and Irene Lurie. 1994. *Implementing JOBS: Progress and Promise.* Albany, N.Y.: Nelson A. Rockefeller Institute of Government, State University of New York.

Hasenfeld, Yeheskel. 1983. *Human Service Organizations.* Englewood Cliffs, N.J.: Prentice-Hall.

———. 1992. *Human Services As Complex Organizations.* Newbury Park, Calif.: Sage.

Heclo, Hugh. 1994. "Poverty Politics." In *Confronting Poverty,* edited by Sheldon H. Danziger, Gary D. Sandefur, and Daniel H. Weinberg. Cambridge: Harvard University Press.

Ingram, Helen. 1990. "Implementation: A Review and Suggested Framework." In *Public Administration: State of the Discipline,* edited by Naomi B. Lynn and Aaron Wildavsky. Chatham, N.J.: Chatham House.

Johnson, Mark. 1993. "Complex New Welfare Rules Work against Those Hoping to Get Off." *San Jose Mercury News,* June 24, page 18A.

Katz, Michael B. 1986. *In the Shadow of the Poorhouse: A Social History of Welfare in America.* New York: Basic Books.

Kelman, Steven. 1987. *Making Public Policy: A Hopeful View of American Government.* New York: Basic Books.

Lipsky, Michael. 1980. *Street Level Bureaucracy: Dilemmas of the Individual in Public Services.* New York: Russell Sage Foundation.

Lurie, Irene, and Jan L. Hagen. 1993. *Implementing JOBS: The Initial Design and Structure of Local Programs.* Albany, N.Y.: Rockefeller Institute of Government, State University of New York.

Lynn, Laurence E. 1993. "Policy Achievement As a Collective Good: A Strategic Perspective on Managing Social Programs." In *Public Management: The State of the Art,* edited by Barry Bozeman. San Francisco: Jossey-Bass.

March, James G., and Johan P. Olsen. 1989. *Rediscovering Institutions: The Organizational Basis of Politics.* New York: Free Press.

March, James G., and Herbert A. Simon. 1958. *Organizations.* New York: John Wiley and Sons.

Meyers, Marcia K., Bonnie Glaser, Nara Dillon, and Karin Mac Donald. 1995. *Institutional*

Paradoxes: Why Welfare Workers Can't Reform Welfare. UC-DATA Working Paper. Berkeley, Calif.: University of California.

Meyers, Marcia K., Bonnie Glaser, and Karin Mac Donald. 1997. "On the Front Lines of Welfare Delivery: Are Workers Implementing Policy Reforms?" *Journal of Policy Analysis and Management* 16, no. 4: 426-39.

Mintzberg, Henry. 1979. *The Structuring of Organizations.* Englewood Cliffs, N.J.: Prentice-Hall.

Moe, Terry M. 1984. "The New Economics of Organization." *American Journal of Political Science* 28: 739–77.

Ouchi, William G. 1981. *Theory Z: How American Business Can Meet the Japanese Challenge.* Reading, Mass.: Addison Wesley.

Palumbo, Dennis J., and Donald J. Calista, eds. 1990. *Implementation and the Policy Process: Opening Up the Black Box.* New York: Greenwood Press.

Perrow, Charles. 1986. *Complex Organizations: A Critical Essay.* New York: Random House.

Sabatier, Paul, and Daniel Mazmanian. 1983. "The Implementation of Public Policy: A Framework of Analysis." In *Effective Policy Implementation,* edited by Daniel Mazmanian and Paul Sabatier. Lexington, Mass.: D. C. Heath.

Schein, Edgar H. 1992. *Organizational Culture and Leadership.* San Francisco: Jossey-Bass.

Selznick, Philip. 1957. *Leadership in Administration.* Berkeley, Calif.: University of California Press.

Simon, William H. 1983. "Legality, Bureaucracy, and Class in the Welfare System." *Yale Law Journal* 92: 1198–1250.

Stoker, Robert P. 1991. *Reluctant Partners: Implementing Federal Policy.* Pittsburgh: University of Pittsburgh Press.

Thompson, James D. 1967. *Organizations in Action: Social Science Bases of Administrative Theory.* New York: McGraw Hill.

Wilson, James Q. 1989. *Bureaucracy.* New York: Basic Books.

11 | Contracting In
Can Government Be a Business?
Eric Welch and Stuart Bretschneider

RECENT POPULAR MANAGEMENT rhetoric and public management research have been concerned with the answers to two fundamental questions regarding what is considered to be inefficient delivery of government services: (1) How can internal government processes function with greater flexibility and efficiency? (2) To what extent are the role and scope of government activity warranted? The solutions offered by researchers and practitioners have often carried a heavy dose of the "new managerialist" assumptions that the key to a more efficient government is a greater infusion of private sector practices and thinking (Osborne and Gaebler 1992). Examples of remedies for internal efficiency problems include greater decentralization of decision making, greater entrepreneurial incentives for public managers, and the use of specific tools such as total quality management. These innovations promise to improve the way government works (Osborne and Gaebler 1992). Remedies to issues of role and scope of government have often revolved around the contracting out of government services to the private sector. "Contracting out" can be defined as the process by which government decides to have its services, goods, or both provided beyond the organizational boundary by profit or not-for-profit organizations. This activity must be motivated by the assumption that the results will decrease cost without reducing service levels (Prager 1994).

Of course, these remedies have spurred a third question regarding the broader non-efficiency-based consequences to government and society of private sector prescriptions to issues of public efficiency. Concerns with privatization include the hollowing out of government, public accountability, and customer/client orientation in a nation of citizens (Milward 1994; Kettl 1988; Deakin and Walsh 1996). In addition, giving government managers greater discretion in decision making as a way of encouraging quicker, more appropriate government responses has raised questions of internal accountability and responsiveness (Romzek and Dubnick 1994).

Regardless of the recent trends in rhetoric and research, these twin pillars of internal and external efficiency enhancement of the delivery of public services do little to describe the actual array of interaction that exists among public agencies, private businesses, and not-for-profit organizations. For example, recent work by Perlmutter and Cnaan (1995) has identified the systematized activity of fund-raising and donation seeking from private sources as one way in which public agencies are attempting to offset double constraints of lower tax base and higher demand for better services. Other examples of nontraditional government activities include the Onondaga County Morgue (central New York State) selling autopsy services to neighboring counties for profit and a nationwide trend at the county level where information services departments sell data to private businesses for profit (*Syracuse Herald Journal* 1995). It is difficult to describe this activity by government as an effort to reduce the size of government, nor is it accurate to describe this activity as enhancing the efficiency of the internal processes of government. Instead, this type of government activity is new and tends to take place outside government's traditional service and geographic boundaries. As such, there is a need to develop a fuller understanding of this activity and to explain the impetus behind it.

This chapter considers only the entrepreneurial activity by which the government sells its resources or service delivery capacity to profit, not-for-profit, or other government organizations beyond its organizational boundary. We call this *contracting in* and consider it to be the converse of contracting out. The sale of these services or resources is designed to help the purchasers carry out their organizational objectives. These do not include services directed to individuals or citizens such as parks, libraries, and so on. Similarly, it does not include public enterprises that are viewed here as quasi-governmental organizations. A key ingredient to contracting in is that the government unit expects to make a profit (e.g., a revenue enhancement.)

Such boundary-spanning activities—in which government agencies expand their traditional boundaries as a means of enhancing their funding base—are often conducted in the name of entrepreneurship. Peters and Waterman (1982) have argued previously that it is the responsibility of public administrators to assume a greater entrepreneurial role. Others have identified government sector entrepreneurial activity as a potential solution to the problem of fiscal constraint as well as a general source for managerial improvement (Osborne and Gaebler 1992). Of course the underlying assumption of entrepreneurship is that closer proximity and greater interaction with markets is efficiency enhancing and revenue producing—both of which are good things for overall social welfare. In part, it is argued in this chapter that this emphasis on entrepreneurship, combined with greater decision-making discretion on the part of administrators, an environment of fiscal constraint, and the new managerial emphasis on private market solutions has created a situation in which contracting in is more likely to occur and an environment in which a wide variety of implications for public service may be hypothesized. The degree to which contracting in is normatively a good or bad thing, although worthy of discussion, lies beyond the scope of this chapter.

This chapter will attempt to follow the research trajectories already well established for contracting out. First, we will provide some concrete examples of what contracting in is and what it is not. Second, we will establish a structural theory to explain the emergence of contracting in along with a set of hypotheses that helps identify and clarify the potential reasons why government organizations might contract in. This is followed by an empirical test of our contracting in framework using the sale of data by county information service and county program directors as an example. Finally, we will conclude with some observations regarding the potential implications of contracting in on public organizations.

Examples of What Contracting In Is and What It Is Not

Contracting in is not necessarily a newly coined term. Nevertheless, this is the first time a theoretical framework has been developed and tested empirically. There are four necessary conditions that must be satisfied before a specific government activity can be considered contracting in. First, the service must be provided by a public agency. This condition distinguishes public enterprise activity that is, for all practical purposes, financially independent from government agencies that are financed through allocation of public funds. Second, contracting in activity represents delivery of a service or product as an intermediate or final good (capital or labor) that helps another external organization carry out its own objectives. Third, contracting in activity is new in the sense that the service or product provided is outside what are considered to be organizational boundaries. As such, there is an implicit requirement that this service adds value to what otherwise may be a freely available public good, that the government provides a service in a geographical location outside its tax base of support, or some combination of the two. Fourth, contracting in is done for profit. Government activity must satisfy all four of these to be considered contracting in.

For example, national laboratories are public organizations that provide resources in the form of human capital and physical capital to companies throughout the nation. The human capital consists of skilled researchers and technicians, whereas physical capital encompasses a range of resources from basic laboratory space to expensive and rare equipment used for the purpose of research, analysis, and development. For its part, the national laboratory is able to provide existing resources as inputs to the innovation process of companies for a profit. The service provided by the federal lab is considered to be outside its organizational boundary because contracting in with a private company has altered the array of projects in which it is involved.

A second example of contracting in activity is the selling of autopsy services by a county morgue in one locality to neighboring counties for profit. In such an instance, the contracted county is extending the definition of its own boundaries by providing a service to a locale outside its own tax base. The county morgue capitalizes on economies of scale, slack, or special circumstances such as temporary lack of service in the other county by providing the service for a profit.

A third example is the sale of data by county government agencies to private companies for a profit. The data typically comprise a broad range of demographic data that are specific to a locality. Companies seek out such data either to repackage for resale or to use internally for development of marketing purposes. The government resource is thereby used as an intermediate or final product that assists companies to carry out their organizational goals. In this case as well, provision of this good is beyond what the organization would consider its range of traditional activities.

Contracting in is conducted at all levels of government—federal, state, and local. It is also conducted without regard to the buyer. That is, the buyer can be another government agency, a private company, or a nonprofit organization as long as the four necessary conditions are met. In this sense, contracting in is a pervasive activity of government.

The Theory of Contracting In

Organizations have three basic levels for analysis: the external environment, the internal environment, and interaction between the external and internal (see figure 1). With respect to contracting in, the external environment contains two fundamental forces that act on government organizations: fiscal stress and society's value structure. The internal environment can be represented by at least five broad categories of variables: the value orientation of the organization or its cultural environment, internal fiscal stress, control and authority structures, the extent of bureaucratization, and technological resources and task requirements. The degree of interaction between the agency and the environment simply describes the boundary-spanning activity of the agency. A theoretical framework that describes the propensity of a government agency to contract in must include all of these categories.

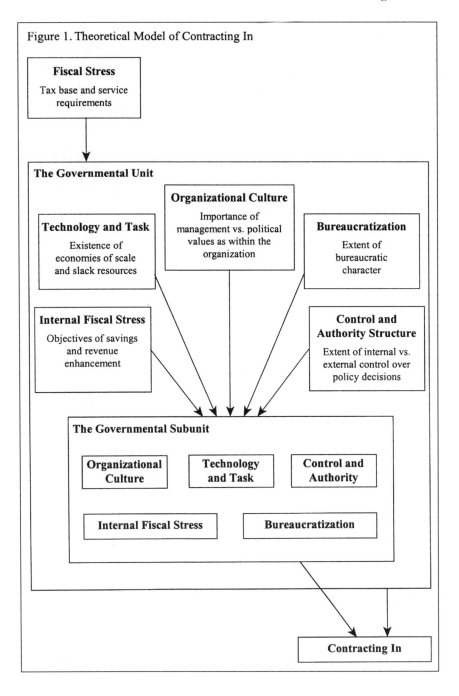

Figure 1. Theoretical Model of Contracting In

External Environment

Because the definition of contracting in has as one of its fundamental tenets the objective of profit making, fiscal stress in the environment is perhaps the most obvious factor that would motivate organizational propensity toward contracting in. Recent public and political insistence on tax reductions and spending controls have often led to restrictions in budgetary allocation for public agencies. In many cases, agency funding has been cut while demands for service have increased both in absolute terms and in terms of quality of service. Such environmental constraints can be seen to frame the decision-making environments of public managers who are then required to apply their entrepreneurial skills to the task of boosting internal efficiency, identifying alternate revenue sources, or both.

A second force in the environment that affects the propensity of a government unit to contract in is that of society's value structure. Although the degree to which society's values can be effectively measured and interpreted to impact on an agency's propensity to contract in is problematic, it undoubtedly has some influence on the internal decision-making process. Societal values will to some degree dictate a range and ranking of possible solutions to problems of administration. Therefore, the degree to which government agencies identify and adopt contracting in as a policy alternative depends in part on their receptivity to societal values that favor contracting in.

Internal Environment

Each of the five internal environment categories is discussed in turn below.

Organizational Culture (Value Orientation and Cultural Environment)

The extent to which one set of values predominates over another set within organizations is a critical factor in determining the motives for their responses to fiscal stress. In the case of contracting in, two broad sets of values exist in a state of potential conflict: managerial values and political values. Managerial values simultaneously describe the extent to which actual organizational objectives and processes are based on the tenets of managerialist thinking in which values of efficiency, economy, and entrepreneurialism are dominant. As such, managerialism often looks to the private sector for examples to increase productivity and service improvement (Pollitt 1990, Savoie 1994). The ability of the public sector to approximate the private sector's level of efficiency is often considered to be based on its proximity to and interaction with private markets. In addition, managers may be driven by dominant societal values that consider embracing markets and entrepreneurial activity to be positive, regardless of their impact on service delivery. Therefore, in the case of contracting in, profit-making ventures conducted with the private sector are considered to be appropriate sources of revenue for organizations in which managerial values dominate.

Political values (and political reality) conflict with the values of managerialism. Political values, at least in the U.S. context, hold that issues of public service, accountability to citizens, responsiveness to politicians, fairness, equity, justice, representation, and participation are primary considerations of public service. To the extent that political values override managerial values, organizations will be less likely to contract in. One possible alternative outcome for organizations faced with fiscal stress is an increased propensity to save or avoid costs or even cut service levels instead of increasing revenues through contracting in.

Internal Fiscal Stress

Internal fiscal stress can be thought of as the organizational interpretation or response to the broader fiscal stress in the environment. This can be thought of as microenvironment application of a macroenvironment state. As such, external fiscal stress is either mitigated or intensified within the organization due to specific characteristics of the organization. For example, organizational capacity as measured by the skill base and experience of the employees may affect how an organization views external fiscal constraint. Greater internal capacity organizations may be better able to develop cost-saving work flows, whereas lower capacity implies intensification of a sense of crisis and a search for other means of support. Also, overriding public interest values in the organization may cause managers to develop such organization-based cost-saving solutions as increased coordination and networking across organizational boundaries. In contrast, overriding managerial values may identify a greater array of profit-making activities such as contracting in as a means of mitigating external fiscal stress. In summary, physical endowments and value emphases or cultural environment are two factors that will influence the range of available solutions to external fiscal constraint. The actual translation of these factors into action, plans, or values is the essential nature of internal fiscal stress as it is expected to affect the propensity of governmental units to contract in.

Control and Authority Structures

This variable refers to the extent to which managers have control over decision making. This concept covers all the dimensions of decision making, including organizational goal setting and resource allocation. Structural considerations that increase the extent and scope of control include three separate issues: decentralization, deregulation, and devolution. Decentralization refers to the flattening of the organizational structure as shown through an organizational chart (i.e., removal of middle management). This gives lower-level managers a greater de facto role in decision making. Deregulation refers to the reduction in rules and regulation that guide decision making, which gives managers greater discretion in decision making. Devolution refers to instilling a greater degree of *du jour* authority in decision making in lower levels of the bureaucracy. This results in greater accountability by managers at lower levels of the hierarchy. Devolution of decision-making authority is not necessarily a result of decentralization of structure.

Placing greater capacity for discretion in the hands of public managers in charge of service delivery may also induce managers to perceive their organization's survival to be dependent on their own actions rather than on the actions of superiors. Therefore, increased internal control over policy may enable managers to search for revenue-enhancing methods that help secure the organization's future.

Bureaucratization

This term refers to the extent to which barriers exist within the organization that either prevent efficient functioning of the internal administrative or service delivery process or prevent interconnections and interactions with other organizations in the environment that may be efficiency enhancing. Barriers to efficient functioning of internal administrative processes may be associated with red tape. It is possible that higher barriers imply lower propensity to contract in. Bureaucratization is clearly related to authority and control in public organizations. It might be best then to think of bureaucratization in terms of negative impacts of control when the control is specifically oriented to reduce decision discretion and enhance accountability. Whereas the cluster of variables above focus on control and authority structure and locus of control, bureaucratization emphasizes the effect of structures on process.

Technology and Task

Technical complexity refers to the inherent characteristics of the work task such that agencies with more complex services and duties may also require unique or specialized resources. Similarly, increased technical complexity creates barriers to communication and sharing of information due to the potential gap between the highly specialized and competent agency on the one hand and less sophisticated external organizations on the other. It is also possible that a higher technical complexity of task within an organization may provide opportunities for the provision of a unique service or product that has higher potential marketability on the one hand and lower potential ease of transfer on the other.

Whereas the potential impact of technical complexity of task is relatively apparent, the effects of technological sophistication are not. New technologies are important contributors to improvements in economic productivity. New technological applications and improvements in human capital can be employed to provide an existing service at lower cost, higher quality, or both. For example, an agency in one county that provides analysis of subsidized elderly care provision is able to process more applications with greater computing power and better software than a similar agency in a different county that processes hard copies of claims by hand. Increased productivity is also linked to the size of the client base and length of time devoted to a specific task where learning and on-the-job experience improve an administrator's skill levels. All of these forces can generate potential economies of scale. For example, one organization in operation for one month will probably be a less efficient producer of completed claims than one in operation for a year. Similarly, an organization that serves one hundred recipients may be less efficient at the margin than an organization that serves one thousand recipients.

Increasing internal economies of scale can lead to several results. First, the skill level of the workers increases, and their ability to use a specific technology more effectively leads to the production of organizational slack. This slack can be allocated to increase work loads, cost reductions, or new services. Second, depending on the entrepreneurial interest and intuition of the manager, improved familiarity with the service inputs and outputs may reveal hidden or latent resources within the agency that have market value. Either of these could lead to an increased propensity to contracting in. The enhanced ability to manipulate the agency's work load, extract and package a new service or product, or perceive the existence of slack resources may provide the organizational capacity to respond to or seek out external market demand for a new service.

Interaction between External and Internal Environments

Contracting in is, by definition, one type of interaction with the environment. Therefore, the extent to which an agency is already interacting with the environment in the broad range of its activities will have an impact on whether contracting in is a viable alternative to relieve fiscal stress. The greater the a priori interaction between an organization and its environment, the more likely contracting in will be considered as an option.

Hypotheses

On the basis of the above theoretical framework for contracting in, a series of hypotheses are suggested.

H1. The greater the fiscal stress, the greater the demand for cost reduction and revenue enhancement. These forces will increase the likelihood that the governmental unit will contract in.

H2. The impact of fiscal stress is in part facilitated or mitigated by the specific organizational culture as it leads to increasing the likelihood of contracting in.

H2a. The role of values: the more managerial values dominate, the more fiscal stress is likely to lead to increased contracting in (versus public interest and political values).

H2b. The role of control: the greater the organization's control of its own policies and procedures, the more fiscal stress is likely to lead to increased contracting in.

H3. The greater the bureaucratization of the organization, the less likely it will be to contract in.

H4. The task environment.

H4a. The larger the organization, the more likely economies of scale and slack resources exist. These factors will increase the likelihood that an agency will contract in.

H4b. The more complex the task or technology, or the more specialized the information, the more likely the organizations will be to contract in.

H4c. Professional capacity and experience: the more familiar and confident employees are with the task, the more likely they will be able to contract in for the information.

Empirical Analysis

Sampling

In order to test our theory we collected data on county government practices associated with the selling of data. The original data collection effort was part of a national study of information resource management in county governments (Fletcher et al. 1992), which included mail surveys, phone surveys, and detailed case studies. Two of the groups targeted for mail surveys in this study, information service (IS) managers for the central data-processing activities of the county and selected program managers representing four major functional area in county government—solid waste, criminal justice, public works, and aging or elderly services—were asked a series of questions regarding their efforts at selling data.

All of the survey forms were pretested before they were mailed out. IS managers and program directors in selected case study counties as well as members of the National Association of Counties' (NACo) Research and Technology Focus Group commented on early drafts of all the survey forms. The sample frame for the mail surveys consisted of all counties with population in excess of 100,000, excluding New England. New England counties are not full function county governments and consequently were deemed not typical of county government in the rest of the United States. Names of IS managers and program directors were obtained from NACo mailing lists and the *1991–1992 County Executive Directory.* All names and addresses were verified by phone before mail surveys were sent out. Each individual was first sent an alert letter explaining the purpose of the study and assuring appropriate privacy protections for individual responses. One week later the surveys were mailed. A follow-up mailing of surveys to all nonrespondents was conducted three weeks after the initial survey mailing.

The survey processes yielded 176 IS manager responses, for a response rate of 43 percent, and 570 program director responses, for a response rate of 45 percent. The low response rate raises issues of selection and nonresponse bias. Various statistical tests were conducted to compare population size, growth rates, and geographic distribution of the sample cases with the sample frame. In all cases, no statistically significant differences were found. Although this does not eliminate the possibility of selection or nonresponse bias due to other factors, it suggests that the sample is at least representative of the largest counties in the United States. Certainly our reliance on counties at the outset limits generalizability of our study to other governmental units. Nevertheless, the use of these data provides an initial exploratory view of the phenomena of contracting in.

Measurement

The basic phenomenon of interest is contracting in with particular reference to selling data or information services for profit beyond the governmental unit's boundary for profit. As a practical matter it is very difficult to know the extent to which a particular governmental operation is generating net profits; consequently, we opted to identify those organizations (i.e., central county information service agencies or program agencies) as contracting in if they sold data and indicated the use of a full-cost billing system. Although this type of billing does not insure that the service was for profit, it provides the best approximation available from the survey data. We recognize that this provides us with an imperfect measurement of contracting in but given the general bias in government toward cross-subsidizing operations, the use of a full-cost basis suggests a more managed and deliberate activity. At the very least, a full-cost billing approach is a necessary precondition for contracting in. Approximately 45 percent of the central IS managers sold data using a full-cost approach to billing, whereas only 7 percent of the program units did.

Independent variables suggested by our structural theory can be organized into the following groups: external fiscal stress, culture in terms of values, internal fiscal stress, control and authority structures, bureaucratization, and technology and task.

External Fiscal Stress

The first group of variables should capture variation in access to resources (i.e., tax base) and demand for services. Three variables were used to capture this potential source of variation: the size of the county in terms of its 1990 population, the growth rate as measured by the percentage change in population for the county between 1980 and 1990, and the percentage of minority population in the county. We expect size and growth rate to be inverse measures of fiscal stress. Large counties are more likely to have access to slack resources, and growing counties will similarly have increasing demand but also increasing revenues. Larger minority populations will signal increased demand of public services, especially social services, which will be positively related to fiscal stress.

Values and Organizational Culture

In order to tap potential variation between organizational cultures, we developed two aggregate variables, one to measure the extent to which the culture emphasizes managerial values and another to tap the importance of higher-level social values. Each survey respondent was asked to indicate the importance, on a scale from 1 to 7, of a series of strategic objectives considered when investing in information technology. Although these are not direct measures of overall organizational cultural values, they do require respondents to rate values and objectives. We would expect a high correlation between these measures and overall measures of organizational culture, thus providing these measures as reasonable surrogates or instruments.

Seven items associated with managerially oriented objectives included reduced paperwork burdens on business and citizens, better information to the public, improved analysis of information associated with existing and emergent social problems, increased quality of work, increased service quality, improved strategic decision making, and efficient administrative control of resources. These seven measures were added together to create a management values variable. The Cronbach's alpha, a measure of reliability, associated with this variable was 0.79 for the IS managers' surveys and 0.84 for the program directors' surveys.

The second aggregate measure of culture summed five of the importance scales—free access to information, protection of individual privacy and confidentiality, protection of proprietary information, promotion of economic development, and protection of historically valuable records and information. For the IS managers' responses, this social value variable generated an alpha of 0.81, and the program directors' data alpha was equal to 0.83. We consider this package of society-related variables to represent the political value set described in our theoretical framework. We would expect that management values are positively associated with contracting in whereas political values are negatively associated with contracting in.

Internal Fiscal Stress

In an effort to identify different internal management responses to fiscal stress, two measures were again developed from respondents' assessments of specific objectives associated with obtaining new information technology. The survey included three financial objectives: avoid cost, save money, and enhance revenues. The two cost-related scores were summed, producing an aggregate index with a Cronbach alpha of 0.78 within the program director responses and a 0.65 for the IS manager responses. It was clear that when the inclusion of the revenue enhancement objective was attempted, overall reliability dropped significantly, thus suggesting that this should be a separate dimension. These two variables represent different responses to fiscal stress, cost cutting, and revenue enhancement, and they permit us to consider a wide array of mixed motivations or responses to fiscal stress, ranging from the extremes of exclusive focus on cost cutting and focus on revenue enhancements.

Control and Authority

A major characteristic of public organizations is the diffusion of control and authority across multiple structures. A series of questions asked respondents to indicate the extent to which various actions were controlled internally by their unit or externally by another unit, where a response of 1 indicated complete external control and a 5 indicated complete internal control. The ten activities included program policy, administrative procedures, organizational structure, client qualifications, service delivery, supplier selection, personnel, information systems, planning process, and reporting requirements. In both surveys the reliability measure was 0.78. This aggregate measure varies from a low of 11 to a high of 55. The larger the value, the more internal or local overall control of the IS function or program function, as perceived by the unit's manager.

Bureaucratization

Four questions were asked regarding the extent of perceived bureaucratization or red tape present in respondents' organizations. The questions were asked along a seven-point scale, where 1 indicated no problems or difficulty in getting work done was associated with bureaucracy and a 7 indicated extreme problems or difficulty in getting work done was associated with bureaucracy. Three of the questions related to the negative aspects of red tape, and one dealt with the extent of autonomy (discretion) provided to professionals. Reliability analysis suggested that the three negative measures—extent of bureaucracy slowing down activities, red-tape delays, and the frequency of having to do work over—could be aggregated into a single measure. This aggregate measure of red tape generated an alpha score of 0.76 in both survey groups. Because the two measures reflect different dimensions, the use of the two variables provides the ability to capture situations with mixed levels of bureaucratization and professional autonomy.

Technology and Task

The variables associated with task and technology are designed to capture several important aspects of the production process associated with generating and selling data. First we consider the issue of economies of scale. Size of the organization and the relative size of the IS component of the organization are important. In the case of the central county IS unit, the number of full-time equivalent staff (FTEs) simultaneously captures the organization's size and the technical capacity of the county to use IS technology to collect and disseminate information and data. At the program unit level we consider both the overall size of the unit in terms of total FTEs and the number of FTEs dedicated to managing the unit's IS technology. All of the size variables are transformed by using the log value in order to account for potential nonlinear effects that are commonly associated with this type of size measure.

The actual process of moving or sharing data in its various forms as an organizational task are also affected by two general factors. Barriers to the free movement of data exist at the procedural, legal, and technical levels. To account for potential variations in barriers as constraints to action, we aggregated a series of questions about barriers into a single measure. Both IS managers and program directors were ask to rate on a seven-point scale (1 indicating not a barrier and seven indicating an extreme barrier) six potential barriers to the exchange or movement of data—high cost of providing data, lack of authority to provide data, personal privacy concerns, loss of data integrity if shared, technical barriers such as media compatibility, and problems of common user definitions. The alpha reliability of the aggregate measure was 0.64 for the IS manager responses and 0.74 for the program manager responses.

The second task for which we developed a control measure was the current extent of data sharing going on by the organization. This related to the potential capacity, economies of scale, or both that might be present. For organizations that are already transmitting large amounts of data to various users, the marginal cost for providing the service to one more user should be less, thus increasing the likelihood of contracting in. Respondents were given a list of nine different target groups—legislative body, other agencies in the county, other agencies in other counties, local governments, state governments, federal government, news media, private businesses, and nonprofit corporations. Information from the unit could be shared with any of these groups. Respondents indicated on a scale from 1 (no sharing) to 5 (extensive transfers of data) the extent to which they shared data with these target groups. The Cronbach alpha for this measure in the IS manager survey was 0.64, and for the program director sample it was 0.76.

Findings

Given that the dependent variable is binary in nature, our multivariate model estimates the impact of the independent variables on the probability that a unit will engage in contracting in. We use a probit model that links increasing probability of contracting in to the inverse cumulative normal probability distribution (Judge et al. 1985).

In general, our findings only partially support our theoretical construct. This is not necessarily surprising because the survey instrument was not specifically designed to test our theory. That is, some of the variables may not adequately measure the conceptual categories of our framework. Nevertheless, the framework is not entirely without support as the following description of findings will show. The results are summarized in table 1.

With regard to external fiscal stress, the results support our general hypothesis that external fiscal stress on the information service department is an important factor in determining whether agencies contract in. Although population size, growth rate, and percent minority are all inversely related to contracting in, population size and growth rate effects are statistically significant (p values of 0.02 and 0.03 respectively). Therefore, a smaller relative tax base

Table 1. Impact of Variables on Decisions to Contract In

Variable	Information Service Managers			Program Managers		
	Sign	Estimate	p Value	Sign	Estimate	p Value
External fiscal stress						
County population size	−	1.3 E-6[a]	0.02[a]	+	5.3 E-8	0.53
Growth rate	−	0.019[a]	0.03[a]	−	3.3 E-4	0.93
Percent minority population	−	0.007	0.52	+	0.004	0.39
Value orientation						
Political value orientation	+	0.039	0.59	−	0.024	0.45
Management value orientation	+	0.147	0.20	+	0.004	0.92
Internal fiscal stress						
Saving objective	−	0.074	0.50	−	0.041	0.27
Revenue objective	+	0.166	0.14	+	0.092[a]	0.06[a]
Control and authority						
External control	+	0.069	0.36	−	0.069[a]	0.02[a]
Bureaucratization						
Autonomy of professionals	+	0.158	0.14	+	0.020	0.68
Red tape	−	0.073[a]	0.06[a]	−	0.005	0.78
Technology and task (Economies of scale						
Agency size (log fte)	+	0.474[a]	0.01[a]	+	0.022	0.61
Size of information service dept. (log fte)	NA	NA	NA	+	0.080[a]	0.02[a]
Interaction barriers	+	0.041	0.56	+	0.002	0.95
Technical image concern	−	0.023	0.83	−	0.070[a]	0.04[a]
Share with other organizations	−	0.160	0.36	+	0.067	0.19

[a] $p \leq .10$.

E, exponential notation.

and a reduction in the tax base increase the likelihood of contracting in. This finding supports our first hypothesis that increased fiscal stress will lead to a greater likelihood of contracting in.

These findings are not replicated at the program manager level, however. For example, only growth rate is inversely related to contracting in—both county population size and percent minority population are positively associated with contracting in. In addition, none of the variables are statistically significant indicators. It must be remembered, however, that the internal structural position of the programs, which usually obtain some direct appropriation, tends to insulate them from the direct effects of the external environmental. Access to a stable source of funding makes program agencies more dependent on internal funding mechanisms such as the traditional budget process.

With regard to the internal environment, results indicate no statistically significant relationships. Although these results may indicate problems at the theoretical level, it is also possible that the measurement problems have caused these results. Therefore, little support exists to confirm our second hypothesis (H2a) that the more managerial values dominate, the more fiscal stress is likely to lead to increased contracting in.

Responses to internal fiscal stress variables provide some degree of support to the hypothesis that contracting in is positively associated with objectives of revenue enhancement but negatively associated with savings and cost-avoidance objectives. Although this trend is true for both program managers and information service managers, only the objective of revenue enhancement is statistically significant for program managers. It is possible that interest in revenue enhancement for IS managers is mitigated by other issues such as the fact that many of the revenues may not be returned to the IS department but rather enter the general fund. Perhaps revenue enhancement activities at lower levels of government are more likely to return revenues to the contracting organization. In general, however, this seems to indicate additional mild support for our first hypothesis.

The extent of internal control and authority over policy decisions provided interesting and interpretable results. Although the control and authority structure is not associated with contracting in activity in the case of IS managers, greater internal control is significantly associated ($p = 0.02$) with contracting in for program managers. The findings for the program managers confirm our hypothesis that greater internal control is positively associated with increases in contracting in. Therefore, evidence indicates some support for our third hypothesis (H2b) that greater organizational control will lead to contracting in for more specialized and decentralized government agencies. The strength of this finding, however, is questioned by the unexpected results for IS managers.

Findings indicate that greater red tape at both the program and IS department level implies a decreased likelihood to contract in. Similarly, a greater degree of perceived professional autonomy is positively associated with contracting in. Even though the directional trends are consistent with our hypotheses that increased autonomy and less red tape are associated with contracting in, lower levels of red tape are statistically significant only for IS managers' decisions to contract in. This may imply that red tape is a relatively less important inhibitor to contracting in at the program level than at the department level. In addition, red tape may be associated with external political control. Also, the degree of autonomy of professionals in the organization may be a poor surrogate for bureaucratization because managers may be thinking about the constraints on others in the organization rather than on their own actions. This finding provides some degree of general support for our fourth hypothesis (H3) that greater bureaucratization leads to less contracting in.

We find that size does relate to the likelihood that a governmental unit will contract in. More specifically, the size of the relevant production function component of the organization is positively and significantly related to contracting in. These results provide some support for our hypotheses that larger agencies potentially enjoy economies of scale and greater slack resources that facilitate contracting in. These results tend to provide good support for our fifth hypothesis (H4a) that larger organizations will be more likely to contract in.

In addition, high barriers to sharing technology are positively associated with contracting in, whereas greater concern for technical image is negatively associated with contracting in. Although these general trends hold true for both IS managers and program managers, only technical image for program managers is statistically significant (p = 0.04). These findings indicate that greater technical complexity and less concern for technical image (greater familiarity with the task, greater confidence in technical ability, and greater professionalism) favorably affect the probability of contracting in.

Last, no significant relationships exist between the probability of contracting in and information sharing. Therefore, our sixth and seventh hypotheses (H4b and H4c)—that increased task complexity and professional capacity are important indicators of contracting in—seem to be mitigated by agency position and service orientation.

Conclusions

We find that limited support can be gleaned from our empirical test of the theoretical framework for contracting in. Although it is true that statistically significant results exist in five of the six categories of variables, only larger agency size was a consistently significant indicator of contracting in activity for both IS managers and program managers. Other categories were either important only for information service managers' decisions to contract in (external fiscal stress, bureaucratization), only for program managers (internal fiscal stress, control and authority), or for neither (value orientation). The limited ability to generalize these findings indicates two potential areas of concern: measurement problems and theoretical problems.

As mentioned previously, the survey instrument was not designed as a means to analyze the contracting in phenomena. Many of the measures are weak surrogates of the theoretically defined concept. For example, many of the measures attempting to identify existing economies of scale are indirect. Future research should attempt to develop a survey instrument that better reflects the theoretical framework and to achieve a better understanding of such issues as pricing, revenue beneficiaries, and internal resource reallocation.

With regard to the theoretical model, we find that the organizational environment and agency orientation are more complex than initially indicated by our theoretical framework. It is our contention that the position of the organization within the administrative system needs to be better explained. For example, the probability of contracting in for information service managers may be positively (although not significantly) correlated with greater external control and public interest values, whereas it is negatively correlated with bureaucratization. This contrasts with the governmental program unit in which bureaucratization and public interest values are negatively correlated (again, not significantly) with the probability of contracting in, whereas higher internal levels of control are significantly associated with the probability of contracting in. This may suggest greater underlying complexity than is accounted for through our initial model. Future research should work to provide a greater sense of causality and influence between the environment and the governmental unit, between the environment and the subunit, and between the governmental unit and the subunit.

Despite these shortcomings, this research provides some important results and raises some interesting questions. For example, the meaning of the result that size of the IS function is important for both IS and program managers in making decisions to sell data should not be overlooked. This finding indicates that large, specialized organizations are more likely to contract in due to possible power, autonomy, control, capacity, complexity, and economies of scale. The highly professional and specialized nature of the U.S. bureaucracy may provide a rich environment for contracting in activities.

In addition, statistically significant findings that revenue enhancement, degree of professionalism, and policy autonomy are all identified with programs having larger IS divisions may indicate a potential application for theories of the self-interested bureaucrat. Although we must be careful not to overgeneralize, there seems to be some mild indication that more highly decentralized, professional agencies that are able to build an internal capacity for the generation of marketable goods may be doing so either as a means of providing some security against arbitrary budget decisions or as a means of enhancing the size of their bureaucracies. These two opposing outcomes deserve further study.

Organizations face uncertain environments in which the traditional political nature of the budgetary process is compounded by the increasing fiscal constraints. Managers may, either as a result of structural design or value orientation, respond to budgetary uncertainty by identifying a marketable product or service and selling that service for a profit as a means of providing greater financial stability to service provision. Through the creation of alternative sources of funding, managers are making decisions in the public interest based on their own interpretations at a local level that may contradict the demands by the broader population. At the same time, they are also inadvertently increasing their ability to continue to make such decisions. That is, they are increasing their de facto autonomy at the expense of external political control.

The second alternative depicts a manager who believes that the objective of contracting in is not only to stabilize the budgetary process but also to increase their autonomy and the size of their organizations. This scenario differs from the first because here the self-interested bureaucrat acts as if private sector market activity first improves the organization's power, status, and autonomy. Stabilization of the fiscal environment is a second consideration. In this scenario, the bureaucrat may be less risk averse and more prone to contracting in decisions that extend organizational boundaries more dramatically.

The implications of both of these scenarios are similar. The end result is greater autonomy by the organization, less responsiveness to politicians and the creation of new constituencies in the private sector, and the subsidization of new and unproved business ventures that require start-up capital. New constituencies are not without power, and business ventures that are originally developed to generate profits also create new interest groups. As with all interest groups, they are likely to exert political pressure to prevent their demise. Thus, contracting in may result in government subsidization of activities that actually lose money.

Finally, potential effects on the accountability of government to citizens are mixed and would require a much clearer understanding of the long-term effects of contracting in. On the one hand, self-interested bureaucrats are making decisions that reflect their own preferences (preferences that may conflict with those of the citizenry). This results in a breakdown in accountability in the entire system. The public-interested bureaucrat intent on maintaining services deemed important at the street level in specific locations, however, is making the system more accountable to smaller sections of the citizenry in the face of broader political demands for reduction of service.

References

Deakin, Nicholas, and Kieron Walsh. 1996. "The Enabling State: The Role of Markets and Contracts." *Public Administration* 74: 33–48.

Fletcher, P., S. Bretschneider, D. Marchand, H. Rosenbaum, and J. Bertot. 1992. *Managing Information Technology: Transforming County Governments in the 1990s.* Syracuse, N.Y.: Syracuse University School of Information Studies.

Judge, George G., W. E. Griffiths, R. Carter Hill, Helmut Lutkepohl, and Tsoung-Chao Lee. 1985. *The Theory and Practice of Econometrics.* 2d ed. New York: John Wiley and Sons.

Kettl, Donald F. 1988. *Government by Proxy: (Mis?)Managing Federal Programs.* Washington, D.C.: Congressional Quarterly Press.

Milward, H. Brinton. 1994. "Implications of Contracting Out: New Roles for the Hollow State." In *New Paradigms for Government: Issues for the Changing Public Service,* edited by Patricia W. Ingraham, Barbara S. Romzek, and Associates. San Francisco: Jossey-Bass.

Osborne, David, and Ted Gaebler. 1992. *Reinventing Government: How the Entrepreneurial Spirit Is Transforming the Public Sector.* Reading, Mass.: Addison-Wesley.

Perlmutter, Felice D., and Ram A. Cnaan. 1995. "Entrepreneurship in the Public Sector: The Horns of a Dilemma." *Public Administration Review* 55, no. 1: 29–36.

Peters, Thomas J., and Robert H. Waterman. 1982. *In Search of Excellence: Lessons from America's Best-Run Companies.* New York: Harper & Row.

Pollitt, Christopher. 1990. *Managerialism and the Public Service: The Anglo-American Experience.* Cambridge: Basil Blackwell.

Prager, Jonas. 1994. "Contracting Out Government Services: Lessons from the Private Sector." *Public Administration Review* 54, no. 2: 176–84.

Romzek, Barbara S., and Melvin J. Dubnick. 1994. "Issues of Accountability in Flexible Personnel Systems." In *New Paradigms for Government: Issues for the Changing Public Service,* edited by Patricia W. Ingraham, Barbara S. Romzek, and Associates. San Francisco: Jossey-Bass.

Savoie, Donald J. 1994. *Thatcher, Reagan, Mulroney: In Search of a New Bureaucracy.* Pittsburgh: University of Pittsburgh Press.

IV | Politics, Governance, Reform, and Innovation

The PUBLIC ADMINISTRATION community has long acknowledged that the American administrative state is fundamentally shaped by politics. Despite the obstinate legacy of the politics–administration dichotomy, scholars emphasize that effective public management, and successful reform, are essentially political: "The problems are power and politics, not bureaucracy" (Frederickson 1992); "If we want better government, we better talk politics" (Rosenbloom 1993); "The key problems are failures of electoral institutions rather than failures of bureaucracy" (Meier 1997). A major political issue affecting public management is the allocation of power between the legislative and executive branches: executive branch managers execute and supplement political decisions that have been made in the legislative branch. Two of the chapters in this section (Golden and Kaboolian) examine the responsiveness of such public managers to citizens and their interest group representatives. The two chapters wrestle with the difficult and complex issues facing public managers responsible for executive agency rules and administrative processes. The final chapter (Berry, Chackerian, and Wechsler) assesses a state-level government "reinvention" with attention to the importance of coherent theory and sustained, genuine political leadership in guiding and supporting reform efforts.

Marissa Martino Golden's chapter analyzes the role of interest groups in executive rule making. Her motivation stems in part from her interest in ascertaining "the extent to which [public interest] participation requirements compensate for delegated power to an unelected branch." Golden's objective is to determine patterns of public participation in the rule-making process and the impact of such participation on executive agency decisions.

Golden's methodology consists of a careful review of written comments submitted to three federal agencies during the notice-and-comment period required under the Administrative Procedures Act. She finds that although business interest groups are much more active participants in the comment process relative to citizen groups, there is no evidence of "undue business influence" on final agency rules. Instead, she argues, "the agency tends to hear most clearly the voices that support the agency's position," particularly when there is conflict among the interest groups. Golden proposes that while her findings provide empirical support for the "issue networks" model of interest group influence in the rule-making process, they also add a new component to the model. Instead of simply playing roles of roughly equal power in the network, agencies in fact act as "arbiters," refereeing among the supporters and critics of proposed rules. She also suggests that executive agencies must work harder to reach out to citizen groups because currently most citizen groups have limited access to information that would enhance their opportunity to participate in the rule-making process.

Linda Kaboolian's chapter focuses on the "reengineering" of the disability determination process in the Social Security Administration (SSA). Kaboolian examines the barriers to effective dialogue between the SSA and disability advocacy groups. She notes that although the agency and the advocacy groups both strive to serve the same group of clients better, SSA managers could lose "their neutrality and detachment" if they identify too closely with the advocates' positions, whereas advocacy groups are often suspicious of agency motives. Managerial responsiveness is therefore a risky venture for public managers.

In the case of the SSA reengineering process, managers worked to weaken the barriers to effective advocacy participation. They invited the advocates to tour their facilities, providing them with a clearer perspective on the agency's constraints. The managers adopted other strategies, including incorporation of the advocates as "partners" in the process instead of limiting them to their traditional "advisory" role. Perhaps most important, the SSA managers breached the conflicts within the advocacy coalition, collecting information from various coalition subgroups and mediating among them to "help them resolve their differences." Unfortunately, the reengineering recommendations were opposed by those advocates who had chosen to be only marginally involved in the dialogue. Kaboolian concludes that the outcome of the SSA efforts left the managers "feeling burned" and concerned about the "dangers and costs of working with advocates." She recommends that in the future, executive agencies and advocacy groups must work harder to reduce barriers to communication. One simple solution might consist of "tours of duty" in which advocates and SSA managers familiarize themselves more thoroughly with the two sets of organizational cultures and missions.

Berry, Chackerian, and Wechsler use the case of "reinvention" in the state of Florida to inform and refine administrative reform theory. They observe that reform is steeped in politics and is "a seamless process in which interest groups and elected officials struggle to increase their power and control over resources." In the 1990 Florida gubernatorial race, administrative reform was central to the campaign waged by Lawton Chiles and Buddy MacKay (Chiles's lieutenant governor running mate). On their election, the Chiles administration solicited input from a wide range of stakeholders. Citizens, executive agencies, newly formed advisory commissions, and other groups were asked to contribute ideas for the reform design. The result, the authors suggest, is that "on their face, the proposed reforms seemed to lack a single overarching theme or approach." The excessive scope of reform meant that sustaining and monitoring the process would be very difficult.

The authors review the major components of the reforms, which included such familiar themes as "results-oriented government and performance-based budgeting" and "total quality management (TQM)." As the reforms progressed, emphases on "empowerment" of lower-level executive branch managers and related cultural changes were superseded by efforts to enhance powers at upper levels of the agencies and to increase executive control. The authors conclude that the Florida reforms were moderately successful, and they offer a set of "lessons" that can be used to refine existing reform theory. For example, the political impetus for the reforms (i.e., the Lawton/MacKay campaign) generated excessive commitments that proved to be impossible to sustain. The early stages of the reform process were characterized by symbolic gestures, but genuine political support waned as reform became more difficult. In addition, skepticism set in among public employees and other constituents, particularly when, despite pleas for financial sacrifice in the interests of better government, Governor Chiles paid his top administrators significantly higher salaries than previous governors had. Revenue shortfalls and "divided" government further complicated reform efforts. In short, reform in Florida was overly ambitious, and it fell victim to difficulties associated with inadequate sustenance from political leaders.

These chapters demonstrate that the management of reform and innovation is dominated by political struggles. Decisions concerning the extent to which resources are allocated—to specific groups of citizens, to different levels of public agencies and organizations, and to competing branches of government—are fundamental to the work of public managers engaged in implementing reform. Consequently, public management theory must clearly acknowledge that managers are not insulated from politics and that they typically work in highly charged arenas of political conflict. The authors of these chapters have provided us with insights into the political challenges that continue to frame the management of reform.

References

Frederickson, H. George. 1992. "Painting Bull's Eyes around Bullet Holes." *Governing* 6 (October): 13.

Meier, Kenneth J. 1997. "Bureaucracy and Democracy: The Case for More Bureaucracy and Less Democracy." *Public Administration Review* 57, no. 3 (May/June): 193–99.

Rosenbloom, David. 1993. "Have an Administrative Rx? Don't Forget the Politics!" *Public Administration Review* 53, no. 6 (Nov./Dec.): 503–7.

12 | Interest Groups in the Rule-Making Process
Who Participates?
Whose Voices Get Heard?

Marissa Martino Golden

I<small>N THE TEXTBOOK</small> version of American politics, Congress is responsible for lawmaking. This has led scholars to study the legislative process and to pay particular attention to the role of interest groups in that process. Particularly since the 1960s, however, Congress has delegated significant portions of its lawmaking responsibilities to federal administrative agencies. The administrative analogue to lawmaking is known as rule making—the process by which federal agencies issue regulations. We are all familiar with these regulations—Environmental Protection Agency regulations dictate the standards that our cars must meet with respect to auto emissions, Food and Drug Administration regulations govern the labels that appear on the products we buy at the supermarket, Security and Exchange Commission regulations determine the information provided to shareholders—and they are a major determinant of public policy.

There is an important distinction between congressional lawmaking and agency rule making, however: although Congress has voluntarily delegated its power, it has delegated it to an unelected branch of government. To compensate for this fact, Congress has developed an elaborate set of procedures (codified in the Administrative Procedure Act [APA]) designed to build democratic safeguards into the rule-making process. Foremost among these are requirements for "public" participation in agency rule making known as "notice and comment" provisions. The assumption underlying these safeguards is that public participation requirements will force unelected bureaucrats to consider the public interest in the formulation of federal regulations. In essence, Congress created a legally mandated avenue for interest group participation in the rule-making process.

Yet despite all of the attention paid to interest group influence in Congress, little attention has been paid to this facet of agency rule making. Most scholarly attention has focused on either the technical facets of rule making, such as the use of cost-benefit analysis, or on interest groups in the congressional context. It is important to turn our attention to interest group participation in agency rule making for a number of reasons. First, we need to determine the extent to which participation requirements compensate for delegated power to an unelected branch. Does public and interest group participation constitute a sufficient "check" on the bureaucracy? Second, it is important to study interest group involvement in the regulatory process for the same reasons that it is important to study interest group involvement in the legislative arena. The normative desire for political equality and the pluralist belief that one cure for the "mischiefs of faction" is to ensure that all groups in society are represented in the political arena dictate that we examine which groups participate in politics and the extent to which they influence policy outcomes. As E. E. Schattschneider asked more than thirty-five years ago, "What accent the heavenly chorus?" Scholars have paid insufficient attention to the heavenly choir's accent in the rule-making process despite its emergence as the major avenue for regulatory policy development.

This chapter has two objectives. The first is to identify patterns of citizen and interest group participation and influence in agency rule making. The second is to assess these patterns in the context of models of the policy-making process as well as in the contexts of public administration and democratic theory.

This chapter examines these issues using a previously overlooked approach. It uses the actual written comments submitted to federal agencies by interest groups during the APA-mandated notice-and-comment period to answer two questions: (1) Who participates in federal agency rule making? (2) To what extent do participants influence final agency decisions?

Previous Research

As discussed above, the current research asks two questions: Who participates in agency rule making, and how much influence do they have over rule-making outcomes? In this section, the literature on each of these two questions will be treated separately.

Who Participates?

There is a small cottage industry devoted to answering the question, "What accent the heavenly chorus?" and that literature provides a useful point of departure for the present study. Attention to this question stems from Schattschneider's (1960) observation that "the flaw in the pluralist heaven is that the heavenly chorus sings with a strong upper class accent" (35). Schlozman (1984) and Schlozman and Tierney (1986) led the way in attempting to answer this question empirically. The study of the seven thousand organizations listed in the directory *Washington Representatives* (Schlozman 1984) led to the conclusion that "the evidence indicates clearly that the pressure system is tilted heavily in favor of the well-off, especially business, at the expense of the representation of broad public interests and the interests of those with few political resources. . . . Thus, Schattschneider's observation (1960, 35) that 'the flaw in the pluralist heaven is that the heavenly chorus sings with an upper-class accent' continues to be accurate" (1028–29). Caldiera and Wright (1990) and Danielian and Page (1994) posed Schattschneider's question in the narrower contexts of interest group participation as amicus curiae and interest group representation in the media, respectively. Caldiera and Wright (1990) found that citizen groups submitted amicus briefs more than either corporations or trade associations, though slightly less than the two combined. They concluded that overall "our findings on the participation of amicus curiae reveal that the Supreme Court is remarkably accessible to a wide array of organized interests. . . . In this sense, the Court is very much a representative institution, and in terms of the variety of organizations from which it hears, quite representative of the general mix of organizations represented in Washington" (802–3). Danielian and Page (1993) found that public interest groups receive coverage on television news equal to that received by corporate America. In their content analysis of network news over a thirteen-year period, they found that 32 percent of the groups covered were "citizen action" groups, and groups representing business interests received 36.5 percent of the coverage. These studies provide us with useful points of comparison, but they tell us little about who participates in federal agency rule making.

Studies of rule making tend to be of two genres. Many are case studies of particular rules. These studies tend to examine high-profile rules such as the cigarette labeling rule from the Federal Trade Commission (Fritschler 1989; West 1982, 1985), cotton dust standards from the Occupational Safety and Health Administration (Bryner 1987), or ozone standards and Resource Conservation and Recovery Act (RCRA) regulations from the Environmental Protection Agency (Landy et al. 1994). Moreover, although they include some discussion of interest group participation in agency rule making, they do not make it the focus of their inquiry, and their case studies focus more on the role of the Office of Management and Budget, Congress, and internal agency procedures in the rule-making process (Bryner 1987). The second type of study zeroes in on one facet of the rule-making process. Common subjects here are the use of cost-benefit analysis in agency rule making (McGarity 1991; Smith 1984) and regulatory review (Bowers 1993; Cooper and West 1988; Duffy 1994; Furlong 1995; Portney and Berry 1995). These are important subjects for inquiry, but they do not address the one facet of the rule-making process explicitly designed to foster direct accountability.

Finally, a few recent studies have turned their attention more directly to the question of who participates in agency rule making (Furlong 1993; Kerwin 1994). These studies, however, rely on survey research for their evidence. They ask interest groups whether, and the extent to which, they participate in agency rule making and the extent to which they perceive themselves to be influential in that process. There are two problems with this approach. First, these studies base their surveys on the directory *Washington Representatives*. As shown later in table 3, however, more than half of the groups submitting comments do so from outside of Washington, D.C., and many represent types of groups (e.g., individual citizens, public housing authorities) that are not captured by this sampling procedure. Thus, surveys do not render an accurate portrait of who participates in agency rule making. A review of the actual comments submitted, the method employed in the current study, provides a more accurate measure. Second, with respect to influence, groups have an incentive to overreport their influence, and federal agencies have an incentive to underreport interest group influence. What is needed is an objective analysis of the changes sought by rule-making participants and a measure of the extent to which the agency altered its proposal to reflect group desires.

Whose Voices Get Heard? Theories of Interest Group Influence

The traditional models of interest group relations with federal agencies are of iron triangles and agency capture (Bernstein 1955; Fritschler 1989). In the model of agency capture, agencies are captive to the clientele they serve—the railroad industry, truckers, or farmers (Bernstein 1955). Iron triangles assume more complex relations whereby congressional committees, agency clientele, and agency personnel all enjoy low-visibility, cordial relations and produce policy that favors all parties involved. These triangles are characterized by consensus, a limited number of participants, and policy expansion. Classic examples include agricultural policy and water resource policy (Cater 1964; Fritschler 1989; Maass 1950). This model is more than just a straw man. It continues to have adherents and empirical evidence produced in its support, and it is the model presented in even the most current textbooks (Berry 1989a; King and Shannon 1986; Knott and Miller 1987; Miller 1985).

By contrast, the issue network model asserts that the iron triangle model no longer applies to the policy process, if it ever did (Heclo 1978; Berry 1989a; Gais et al. 1991). Whereas iron triangles are characterized by a small number of consistent participants, participation in issue networks is fluid, is based on expertise and knowledge, and involves large numbers of participants. Whereas iron triangles are characterized by consensus, the mark of issue networks is conflict and competition among groups. Thus, issue networks "are shared knowledge groups that tie together large numbers of participants with common technical expertise" (Heclo 1978, 126). Among the features that distinguish them from their predecessors are their size and accessibility and the unpredictability of their policy outcomes.

As Jeffrey Berry (1989a) observes, it is clear that these two models posit "two very distinct and contradictory views regarding what kinds of policy communities are most descriptive of modern Washington politics" (243). He adds: "No one argues that there are only issue networks or only subgovernments active in policymaking. Rather, the argument is over what is most typical and most descriptive of the policy process. Which should serve as our framework for analyzing how laws and regulations are made?" (243–44). The data presented below provides a variety of measures with which to compare the empirical support for each theory in the rule-making domain.[1]

In order to understand the research method employed here, it is first necessary to understand the rule-making process itself. Under the APA, federal agencies are required to publish proposed regulations in the *Federal Register.* These are known as Notices of Proposed Rulemaking (NOPR). In the notice announcing their proposal, agencies are also required to invite public comment on their proposal. This is known as the notice-and-comment period. Following the receipt of public comments, the agency reviews the comments it receives, adopts its final regulation, and publishes it in the *Federal Register.* The regulation then carries the weight of law. In essence, as diagrammed below, interest group participation can be thought of as an intervening variable in the sequence of events that comprise the rule-making process.

Proposed Rule→Notice-and-Comment Period→Final Rule (NOPR)

Agencies retain records of the comments they receive, and these are available to scholars (as well as to the general public) under the Freedom of Information Act. This study makes use of these comments in three ways. First, it uses them to paint a descriptive portrait of who participates in the rule-making process. Second, it uses them to examine interest group influence over policy outcomes. Here changes between the proposed and final regulations are compared with the content of interest group comments.[2] Third, the comments are used to test the theories presented above.

The study examines eleven regulations in three federal agencies. The three agencies were selected to provide variation with respect to agency type, policy area, and the nature of the groups impacted by the agency's regulations. The three agencies are the Environmental Protection Agency (EPA), the National Highway Traffic Safety Administration (NHTSA), and the Department of Housing and Urban Development (HUD). These agencies were selected primarily for three reasons. First, agencies were selected that were hypothesized to serve different "clientele" and hence to precipitate participation from different types of interest groups. For example, the two regulatory agencies (the NHTSA and the EPA) greatly impact the business community, whereas HUD's rules impact urban and rural public housing residents. Moreover, although both the EPA and the NHTSA regulate industry, EPA's rules tend to impact "industry" writ large, whereas NHTSA's regulations primarily impact one specific industry (the auto industry). Second, almost all studies of agency rule making limit the locus of their inquiry to regulatory agencies (Bryner 1987; West 1985). Rule making, however, is not limited to regulatory agencies; almost all federal agencies issue rules, and some nonregulatory agencies rely quite heavily on the rule-making process. It is therefore critical to include these nonregulatory, rule-generating agencies in order to ensure that our understanding of the rule-making process is comprehensive. Hence, HUD was included in the agencies selected for this analysis to represent the class "nonregulatory agencies that engage in rulemaking." Third, all three are agencies that acquired considerable rule-making responsibility as a result of the passage of new legislation in the 1970s.

The eleven rules were selected with equal care. Of the eleven rules examined, three were issued by HUD, three were from the EPA, and five were from the NHTSA. Here the goal was to be able to generalize beyond a single rule per agency. Any given rule could be an atypical outlier, but three seemed sufficient to be able to detect patterns.

The specific regulations were selected to be representative of the rules issued by each agency but to be drawn from a single presidential administration. Both the NOPR and the final rule had to be issued during the same presidential administration. This was necessary in order to control for the party in the White House. My concern was that changes between the NOPR and the final rule might otherwise reflect the change in presidential administration rather than the comments received during the notice-and-comment period. Accordingly, for all of the rules contained in this study, both the NOPR and the final rule were published during the Clinton administration.

Once rules that did not fall within this time period were eliminated, rules were selected at random from the *Federal Register*. The aim was to examine "typical" rules. This research seeks to determine who participates in an average, run-of-the-mill rule-making procedure. This avoids any bias that might be introduced by examining only high-profile rule makings. Background information about the eleven rules is provided in the appendix and in table 1.

Table 1. Background Information

Rule	No. of Comments	Significance[a]	Hearing	Date of NOPR	Date of FR
EPA					
Emissions standards	43	Y	N	8/12/93	9/8/94
Hazardous waste	60	N	N	8/31/93	4/4/95
Acid rain	48	Y	Y	9/24/93	4/4/95
NHTSA					
Child restraint	9	N	N	1/9/92	4/16/93
Air brakes	12	N	N	3/11/93	2/14/94
Theft prevention	4	N	N	7/21/93	4/26/94
Warning devices	16	N	N	5/10/93	9/29/94
Electric vehicles	7	N	N	1/15/93	3/9/94
HUD					
Elderly and disabled	268	Y	N	1/7/94	4/13/94
Drug elimination	6	N	N	8/9/94	1/26/95
Income eligibility	1	N	N	7/1/93	3/23/94

NOPR, Notice of Proposed Rule; *FR*, Final Rule; *EPA*, Environmental Protection Agency; *NHTSA*, National Highway Traffic Safety Administration; *HUD*, Housing and Urban Development.

[a]Significance refers to whether the agency designated the rule to be "major" or "significanct" as these terms are defined by the Office of Management and Budget. Significant rules require preclearance by the Office of Management and Budget and are judged to have significant impact on the economy.

The data for this study are the actual written comments submitted to the agency in each of the eleven rule-making proceedings. These comments were obtained directly from the public docket rooms of each agency. The written comments were supplemented by a telephone survey of a sample of commentators drawn from the comments submitted. The survey was concerned with the question of *how* the participants became informed about the NOPR for which they submitted comments—in other words, how they knew when and where to comment.

Findings

Who Participates?

To reiterate, the Administrative Procedure Act and subsequent statutes were designed to foster public participation in the federal rule-making process. Our concern is with how well the notice-and-comment provisions fulfill this goal.[3] Tables 2a–2c report the percentage of each type of interest group submitting comments on each of the rules and in each of the agencies. The strongest and most striking finding is the dominance of business commenta-

Table 2a. EPA Rule Making: Comments Submitted by Type of Group

Category	Emissions Standards		Hazardous Waste		Acid Rain	
	%	N	%	N	%	N
Business						
Corporations	67.4	29	75.0	45	18.8	9
Trade associations	16.3	7	10.0	6	29.2	14
Coalitions	2.3	1	0.0	0	2.1	1
Total	86.0	37	85.0	51	50.1	24
Unions	0.0	0	0.0	0	0.0	0
Citizens' groups						
Public interest	2.3	1	0.0	0	4.2	2
Advocacy	0.0	0	0.0	0	0.0	0
Total	2.3	1	0.0	0	4.2	2
Citizens (individuals)	0.0	0	0.0	0	0.0	0
Professional associations	0.0	0	0.0	0	0.0	0
Government						
Federal agencies	2.3	1	1.7	1	2.1	1
State/local	7.0	3	3.3	2	8.3	4
Congress	0.0	0	0.0	0	2.1	1
Public housing authorities	0.0	0	0.0	0	0.0	0
Total	9.3	4	5.0	3	12.5	6
Other						
Academics	0.0	0	1.7	1	0.0	0
Utilities	2.3	1	0.0	0	29.2	14
Total	2.3	1	1.7	1	29.2	14
Missing data	0.0	0	8.3	5	4.2	2
N		43		60		48

tors in the rule-making process at the EPA and the NHTSA. Between 66.7 percent and 100 percent of the comments received were submitted by corporations, public utilities, or trade associations.[4] For five of the eight rules, citizen groups did not submit any comments.[5] In no case did the percentage of citizen group participation exceed 11 percent. Neither the NHTSA nor the EPA received a single comment from an individual citizen on any of the eight rules examined.[6] There was modest participation by other government agencies, including the Department of Energy and the National Transportation Board, and by a few academic experts.

With respect to HUD (table 2c), the pattern of participation is different.

Table 2b. NHTSA Rule Making: Comments Submitted by Type of Group

Category	Warning Devices		Air Brakes		Child Restraint		Electric Vehicles		Theft Prevention	
	%	N	%	N	%	N	%	N	%	N
Business										
Corporations	62.5	10	83.3	10	44.4	4	100	7	100	4
Trade associations	12.5	2	16.7	2	22.2	2	0.0	0	0.0	0
Coalitions	0.0	0	0.0	0	0.0	0	0.0	0	0.0	0
Total	75.0	12	100	12	66.6	6	100	7	100	4
Unions	0.0	0	0.0	0	0.0	0	0.0	0	0.0	0
Citizens' groups										
Public interest	0.0	0	0.0	0	11.1	1	0.0	0	0.0	0
Advocacy	0.0	0	0.0	0	0.0	0	0.0	0	0.0	0
Total	0.0	0	0.0	0	11.1	1	0.0	0	0.0	0
Citizens (individuals)	0.0	0	0.0	0	0.0	0	0.0	0	0.0	0
Professional associations	0.0	0	0.0	0	0.0	0	0.0	0	0.0	0
Government										
Federal agencies	0.0	0	0.0	0	11.1	1	0.0	0	0.0	0
State/local	0.0	0	0.0	0	0.0	0	0.0	0	0.0	0
Congress	6.3	1	0.0	0	0.0	0	0.0	0	0.0	0
Public housing authorities	0.0	0	0.0	0	0.0	0	0.0	0	0.0	0
Total	6.3	1	0.0	0	11.1	1	0.0	0	0.0	0
Other										
Coalitions (business and citizen groups)	6.3	1	0.0	0	0.0	0	0.0	0	0.0	0
Academics	12.5	2	0.0	0	0.0	0	0.0	0	0.0	0
Utilities	0.0	0	0.0	0	0.0	0	0.0	0	0.0	0
Total	18.8	3	0.0	0	0.0	0	0.0	0	0.0	0
Missing data	0.0	0	0.0	0	11.1	1	0.0	0	0.0	0
N		16		12		9		7		4

Here, there is minimal business participation and considerable participation by government agencies, public interest groups, and citizen advocacy groups. In one case twenty-four individual citizens submitted comments to HUD regarding its rule on designated housing for the elderly and disabled. Here, fully 9 percent of the comments HUD received on this rule were submitted by individual citizens.

Two clear patterns emerge regarding interest group participation in agency

Table 2c. HUD Rule Making: Comments Submitted by Type of Group

Category	Elderly and Disabled		Drug Prevention		Income Eligibility	
	%	N	%	N	%	N
Business						
Corporations	0.4	1	50.0	3	0.0	0
Trade associations	0.7	2	0.0	0	0.0	0
Coalitions	0.0	0	0.0	0	0.0	0
Total	1.1	3	50.0	3	0.0	0
Unions	0.0	0	0.0	0	0.0	0
Citizens' groups						
Public interest	1.1	3	16.7	1	0.0	0
Advocacy	5.6	15	0.0	0	0.0	0
Total	6.7	18	16.7	1	0.0	0
Citizens (individuals)	9.0	24	0.0	0	0.0	0
Professional associations	2.2	6	0.0	0	0.0	0
Government						
Federal agencies	0.7	2	0.0	0	0.0	0
State/local	12.3	33	16.7	1	0.0	0
Congress	0.4	1	0.0	0	0.0	0
Public housing authorities	61.6	165	16.7	1	100.0	1
Total	75.0	201	33.4	2	100.0	1
Other						
Academics	0.0	0	0.0	0	0.0	0
Utilities	0.0	0	0.0	0	0.0	0
Total	0.0	0	0.0	0	0.0	0
Missing data	6.0	16	0.0	0	0.0	0
N		268		6		1

rule making. The first pertains to interagency comparisons. The two regulatory agencies—EPA and NHTSA—have extremely limited participation by public interest or citizen advocacy groups. On the other hand, HUD commentators include citizen advocacy groups, individual citizens, and a wide range of government agencies—especially state agencies and public housing authorities. The second pertains to the accent of the heavenly chorus. Here, at least in the regulatory arena, there is a striking absence of citizen representation. In addition, even at HUD, although there were many advocates on behalf of the elderly and the disabled, the "poor" had few advocates in any of the three rules examined.

Table 3. Geographical Location of Commentators

Rule	Washington %	N	Other Locations %	N	Not Identified %	N	N
EPA							
Acid rain	29.2	14	66.6	32	4.2	2	48
Emissions standards	16.3	7	83.7	36	0.0	0	43
Hazardous waste	0.0	0	0.0	0	100.0	69	69
NHTSA							
Air brakes	8.3	1	91.7	11	0.0	0	12
Child restraint	55.6	5	44.4	4	0.0	0	9
Warning devices	18.7	3	68.7	11	12.6	2	16
Theft prevention	0.0	0	100.0	4	0.0	0	4
Windshields	42.9	3	57.1	4	0.0	0	7
HUD							
Designated housing for elderly and disabled	4.5	12	94.8	254	0.7	2	268
Income eligibility	0.0	0	100.0	1	0.0	0	1
Drug prevention programs	16.7	1	83.3	5	0.0	0	6

EPA, Environmental Protection Agency; *NHTSA,* National Highway Traffic Safety Administration; *HUD,* Housing and Urban Development.

With respect to geography, it turns out that, contrary to public perception, rule making is not the sole province of "Washington insiders." As shown in table 3, with the exception of two NHTSA rules, all three agencies received more comments from "outside the beltway" than from inside it. Commentators were not "hired guns" but rather were technical staff, in the case of corporations, or directors, in the case of government agencies and not-for-profit groups. One of the purposes of the notice-and-comment provisions of the APA is to enhance the legitimacy of resulting regulations. The fact that voices are heard from areas as different as South Dakota and New Hampshire adds to the diversity of rule-making participants. This finding also has implications for scholars. Research on interest groups, including the highly acclaimed work by Heinz et al. (1993), focuses its attention entirely on Washington actors. Yet "lobbying" is being conducted from a much greater distance, and these participants must also be taken into account.

Finally, it is important to examine the extent to which the same groups participate in the process regularly or whether different groups submit comments for different rules. In other words, to what extent are rule-making participants "repeat players"? Table 4 shows the extent to which the same group

Table 4. Frequency of Interest Group Participation in Agency Rule Making

Agency	Number of Rules					N
	1	2	3	4	5	
NHTSA	42	5	0	1	0	48
EPA	152	8	0	NA	NA	160
HUD	274	1	0	NA	NA	275

NHTSA, National Highway Traffic Safety Administration; *EPA*, Environmental Protection Agency; *HUD*, Housing and Urban Development.

commented on more than one rule. At the NHTSA only six of the forty-eight commentators commented on two or more rules, and only one (Ford) commented on four out of the five rules examined. Eight commentators out of 160 submitted comments to the EPA on two of the three rules for which data was collected. At HUD only 1 of the 275 commentators commented on more than one rule. The evidence here is conclusive that each NOPR, even those issued by the same agency, catalyzes different groups to comment. Each NOPR results in a strikingly different set of participants.

We have created a portrait of rule-making participants—spokespeople representing business interests at the regulatory agencies, citizen advocates and state and local governmental organizations at HUD. Yet how do these groups know to comment on agency proposals? How do they become aware of the proposals that will affect their groups? How do they monitor federal agency rule-making activity? The answers to these questions shed light on understanding the documented patterns of interest group participation and assessing the presence of iron triangles and issue networks.

The findings here focus our attention not so much on interagency differences as on differences among interest groups. As table 5 highlights, business groups—be they corporations or trade associations—utilize much more sophisticated monitoring techniques than the smaller advocacy groups. Governmental organizations (public housing authorities, state agencies, and so on) fall somewhere in between. In addition, the few large advocacy groups (the American Association of Retired Persons and the National Resources Defense Council) resemble the corporate commentators.

Almost all business commentators receive and read the *Federal Register* and receive information about pending regulations from such trade associations as the Chemical Manufacturers Association and the Steel Institute. A few even subscribe to on-line services that provide them with continuously updated information regarding agency business. On the other hand, advocacy groups rely almost exclusively on informal networks of similar groups, whereby larger groups keep smaller groups informed of HUD matters. Only three of the

Table 5. Methods for Monitoring Agency Rule Making[a]

| | Type of Group | | | |
| | Business | | | |
Source of Information	Corporation[b]	Trade Association	Citizens	Government
Trade association	10	1	0	0
Professional association	0	0	1	9
Informal network	1	1	7	0
Trade journal	3	0	0	1
Federal Register	15	4	3	8
On-line sources	2	0	0	1
Subscribe to service	0	0	0	2
Issuing agency	0	0	1	7
Total number of groups surveyed[c]	16	4	10	11

[a]The numbers provided are frequencies.

[b]For purposes of this analysis, utilities were included with corporations.

[c]The sum of the numbers exceed the total because organizations use multiple methods to monitor agency rule making.

citizen groups surveyed receive the *Federal Register*. Governmental organizations such as state agencies and public housing authorities, like corporations and trade associations, tend to receive the *Federal Register* and frequently receive information from professional associations (e.g., the Public Housing Authorities Directors Association). In addition, unlike the other types of commentators, these organizations are frequently notified about NOPRs directly by federal agencies. Finally, the few large advocacy and public interest groups, such as the American Association of Retired Persons and the National Resources Defense Council, are more like their corporate and governmental counterparts. The American Association of Retired Persons, for example, has a full-time staff member whose sole job is to monitor the *Federal Register*.

The result is that the groups who submit comments to federal agencies obtain their information about pending regulations via very different means, depending on the type of group. Groups representing business interests have more sophisticated methods of staying informed, and citizens' groups rely on less sophisticated informal networks for their information.

Whose Voices Get Heard? Interest Group Influence in the Rule-Making Process

Influence poses one of political science's thorniest problems. How does one measure influence? Scholars of Congress have, for the most part, concluded that it is not possible to measure interest group influence in the congressional arena, and they have settled on the notion that "money buys access" (Conway 1991). The research design and data set developed for this study, however, facilitates the study of influence because the change between the agency's NOPR and its final rule can be measured and because it can be assumed with some confidence that the interest group comments submitted during the notice-and-comment period were the catalyst for these changes.

The Administrative Procedure Act is silent with respect to instructing agencies regarding what to do with the comments they receive. As Kerwin (1994) notes, "The agencies were not instructed anywhere in the act to take heed of what they learned from the public in written comments" (106; see also West 1985). So, the first question becomes, does the final rule differ from the proposed rule as a result of the comments received? In other words, do federal agencies take public comments into account, or are they ignored?

As table 6 depicts, eight of the ten final rules were changed, at least a minimal amount, from the proposed rules in response to interest group comments.[7] Still, in only one case did the agency change a rule "a great deal." In that case (NHTSA's electric vehicle rule), in response to objections from all seven commentators, the NHTSA abandoned altogether its proposal to require electric-powered vehicles to contain a gauge and symbol to warn drivers when the batteries were in need of recharging. In the other cases, although commentators requested more substantial changes, alterations were limited to definitional changes, changes in deadlines, and modifications to procedural issues such as record-keeping requirements. In short, in the majority of cases, the agency made some of the changes requested by commentators but rarely altered the heart of the proposal. In only two of the ten cases did the agency refuse to make any modifications to its NOPR; moreover, in one of those two rule makings, only one comment was submitted regarding the rule.

The agency is most likely to modify its NOPR in those cases where there is consensus among the commentators. In the two instances where commentators were united in their opposition to the NOPR (NHTSA's electric vehicle and theft prevention rules), the agency made significant modifications to its NOPR. The agencies were also likely to alter their rules at least "some" when there was a very large volume of objections (HUD's designated housing rule, which received 268 comments) or when there was a large contingent of objectors with a common objection and only a few commentators dissenting from the majority (EPA's emissions standards and acid rain rules where virtually everyone [except the public interest groups and other government agencies] objected to the reporting requirements).

Moreover, for each rule examined in this study, the agency included a detailed discussion of its response to all of the comments it received in the final

Table 6. Amount of Change Resulting from Comments

Rule	A Great Deal	Some	Minimal	None
EPA				
Emissions standards		X		
Acid rain		X		
NHTSA				
Child restraint			X	
Air brakes			X	
Theft prevention		X		
Warning devices			X	
Electric vehicles	X			
HUD				
Designated housing for elderly and disabled		X		
Drug prevention programs				X
Income eligibility				X

EPA, Environmental Protection Agency; *NHTSA,* National Highway Traffic Safety Administration; *HUD,* Housing and Urban Development.

rule published in the *Federal Register.* In one case, EPA's hazardous waste rule, in addition to providing the discussion contained in the *Federal Register,* the agency wrote a 145-page document that treated each of the issues raised by the sixty commentators and included it as part of the public docket for that rule. So here, although the agency did not always alter its regulation, it did provide a detailed discussion of the comments it received.

To return to our theoretical concerns: there is little evidence of agency capture in these data. With the exception of the electric vehicle regulation, all three agencies ignored the often irate pleas of their "clientele" and stuck with their initial proposals, albeit with some modifications.

The question of whose voices get heard remains. Here, the weight given to the comments received may compensate for the imbalance in the rates of participation documented above. In other words, it may not matter if there is only one lone public interest group commenting on a given rule if its voice gets heard above the din of the larger number of industry commentators. It turns out, however, that the answer to the question of whose voices get heard has less to do with agencies favoring business over public interest groups or with the number of commentators (the squeakiest wheel gets the grease) than it has to do with the degree of conflict among commentators, the sides in the conflict, and the paucity of repeat players.

With respect to the specific issue of agency responsiveness to citizen groups, the best sources of evidence are the three regulatory rules for which public interest groups submitted comments. In two cases (one at the EPA and one at the NHTSA), the lone public interest group was virtually ignored. In one case, the Natural Resources Defense Council wanted a stronger rule than that proposed by the EPA; in the second case, the Center for Auto Safety raised the sole objection to a rule supported by manufacturers. In the third case (EPA's acid rain rule), however, the National Resources Defense Council and the Environmental Defense Fund supported the EPA's definition of thermal energy with which commentators from industry, utilities, and municipal governments all found fault. In that case, the agency's final rule granted what the public interest groups sought.

The conclusion to be drawn from these findings is not that agency responsiveness to public interest groups varies. It is that when there is conflict rather than consensus among the commentators (as there was in six of the ten rules examined), the agency tends to hear most clearly the voices that support the agency's position.[8] In the acid rain case, the public interest commentators were supportive of the NOPR. In the other two cases, the public interest groups sought change. The voices of critics tend to be heard less clearly than the voices of rule supporters, even when there are more critics than supporters. This finding applies not just to those rules where there is conflict between citizen groups and business but also where the conflict is among business commentators. For example, in NHTSA's proposal to issue a rule regarding safety standards for air brakes, the voice of the lone air brake manufacturer who supported the rule was heard over the voices of the six spring brake manufacturers and trade associations who objected to the standards set by the rule.

Second, I did not find undue business influence in the rules examined. This is due, in part, to the fact that in a number of cases, "business" did not present a united front. There were frequently divisions within the business community. To use the example mentioned above, the air brake rule pitted air brake manufacturers against spring brake manufacturers. Accordingly, not all business interests could be accommodated. In other cases, particularly at the EPA, business influence was limited by the fact that industry opposed the agency's proposals and that the agency made only minor concessions to the commentators. Finally, influence was limited by the absence of repeat players. Because different groups commented on each rule, few groups, corporations, or industries were in a position to influence more than one rule, even within the same agency. The rule's beneficiaries were different in each case, making "capture" unlikely.

Thus, the primary bias that was detected in my examination of ten federal rule-making procedures was the agencies' tendency to favor supporters of its rules over critics. It did not matter if the critics were the big three automakers or the Center for Auto Safety; those submitting comments in support of a rule were more likely to get the final rule they desired, and those with objections were most likely to get only minor concessions.[9]

In sum, there seem to be two consistent findings regarding interest group influence via notice and comment. First, significant influence is limited. Only one of the ten rules examined was changed significantly from the NOPR. Second, with respect to whose voices are heard, no clear pattern emerges. Citizens' influence was obviously limited to those rules where there was citizen group participation. Where there was public interest participation, voices on all sides seemed to be taken into account. Of equal interest, in those rules without citizen participation, business influence was nonetheless variable due to conflict within the business sector and the tendency on the part of federal agencies to favor supportive commentators over critics. I will argue below that these "nonpatterns" make sense if viewed in an issue network framework.

Issue Networks and Influence in Agency Rule Making

When viewed in the aggregate, the data presented above paint a clear portrait of interest groups in the rule-making process. Moreover, that portrait clearly resembles an issue network.

First, the rule-making process is characterized by a large number of participants, not the small numbers in iron triangles. For example, HUD received 268 comments on one of its rules.

Second, the absence of repeat players is evidence of the fluidity and porous nature of the process. For example, as discussed above and presented in table 4, of the 160 organizations who submitted comments to the EPA, only 8 submitted comments for more than one NOPR, and none submitted comments for all three of the rules examined. At the NHTSA, where five rules were included in the study, only five out of forty-eight commentators commented on more than one rule, and only one commented on four of the five rules. At HUD, only 1 out of 275 commentators commented on more than one rule. These figures mask part of the story. The lists of commentators for each rule reveal strikingly different sets of participants. For example, utilities commented extensively on the acid rain opt-in rule, but the hazardous waste rule elicited comments from chemical, gas, and waste management companies but not utilities. Even at the NHTSA, where the agency's rules target a single industry, and where one would expect to see the big three automakers and the leading consumer advocacy groups as regular participants, most commentators are not regular participants in the rule-making process. Instead, the groups who comment on agency NOPRs vary widely. They are different each time. These findings support the notion of issue networks. As Gertrude Stein would say, "There is no there there."

Third, the means by which rule-making participants keep abreast of agency rule-making activity also paints a picture of loose networks bound not by iron but by issues and information. Here, there is a great deal of information exchanged across and among groups. Government organizations and business organizations rely heavily on their membership in trade and professional associations to stay informed. These associations regularly alert their members about federal agency activity. In addition, citizen groups rely equally heavily on informal networks to keep informed. The picture that emerges from the telephone survey of these citizen groups is of organizations in constant contact with each other and heavily reliant on each other for information. By this measure, there are teams, or networks, of groups circulating information and assisting each other in their battle against the common enemy that is the federal agency issuing the rules.

Fourth, this study found a high degree of conflict among commentators. The elderly did not want to share their housing with the disabled. The spring brake manufacturers did not want the air brake manufacturers to have different safety standards. The public interest groups wanted more stringent regulation than that sought by industry. This provides an additional measure for, and is further evidence of, the prevalence of issue networks in the rule-making arena.

Finally, our examination of the rule-making process draws attention to a feature absent in the current issue network model. Missing from the theory but present in the current study is the role of the agencies themselves. In the issue network model, agencies are treated as coequal players in a complex web or network. In fact, at least in the rule-making process, federal agencies serve as arbiters. They arbitrate among opponents and supporters of federal regulations. Ultimately, agency officials, not interest groups, make the final judgment on the content of the rule. The federal agency can accommodate or ignore the comments it receives, thus highlighting a hierarchy of relations within the issue network. Thus, this study of interest groups in the rule-making process not only demonstrates the utility of the issue network model in the rule-making arena but also adds to that model by positing a more accurate role for federal agencies in models that attempt to explain the policy process.

How does this model speak to the question of influence? The model enhances our understanding of interest group influence in agency rule making in at least two ways. First, by according agencies their rightful place as arbiters rather than coequal participants, it explains the limits of interest group influence over final rules. Of equal importance, by emphasizing the unpredictability of policy outcomes, it explains the absence of consistent patterns of influence. "Whose voices were heard" varied in the rules examined as they are theorized to vary by the issue network model (and as contrasted with capture and iron triangle theories). Where issue networks are operative, it is difficult to predict who will influence policy outcomes. This is in keeping with the study's findings regarding patterns (or nonpatterns) of influence in agency rule making. In short, the issue network model helps us to understand interest group influence in the rule-making process and seems to describe more accurately that process than the iron triangle model.

Implications for Public Administration

It is important to discuss this study's implications for public administration and public administrators. The findings presented in this chapter regarding participation rates for groups representing the public interest suggest the need for federal agencies to play a more active role in ensuring that affected groups are informed about NOPRs and invited to comment. Agencies need to do a better job of outreach to affected parties.

This research has also drawn attention to the fact that rule making is embedded in issue networks. This has two consequences for public administrators. First, it highlights the role of federal agencies not just as regulation writers but as arbiters among groups demanding vastly different types of regulations. Federal agencies are faced with the daunting task of mediating among competing claims, and it is not possible to please all of the rule-making participants. Second, the large number of participants, the conflict among them, and the technical nature of the issues involved all make rule making, indeed policy making in general, difficult. As students of public administration we need to be aware of the difficulties this presents for public administrators and to give these difficulties further study.

Conclusions

What are we to conclude from this examination of interest groups in the federal rule-making process? First, the findings presented in this chapter should give both scholars and practitioners pause. This is due to the chapter's findings regarding the skew in interest group participation and the dominance of business in federal agency rule making. Although, as Schlozman (1984) notes, it is difficult to specify "what an unbiased pressure system would look like," it is clear "that an unbiased pressure system would be quite different from what presently obtains" (1021). Federal agencies do not seem to be doing a very good job providing adequate notice of their proposed actions. The bias in participation rates of business and citizen groups and the virtual absence of actual citizen participation demonstrate conclusively that the accent of the heavenly choir in the rule-making process is off-key.

Second, the patterns of participation documented in this chapter have all the hallmarks of issue networks. Groups moved in and out of the policy process depending on the issue. There were different participants in each rule making, even within the same agency. Most of the rules pitted groups against each other and featured identifiable winners and losers. Yet there was a fair amount of communication among groups; indeed, information was the currency of the networks. Examining interest group participation in agency rule making provides concrete and tangible evidence of issue networks—a heretofore fuzzy and amorphous concept. Moreover, our focus on agency rule making adds to the issue network model by developing the concept of agency rule makers as arbiters. In the rule-making process, agency personnel give shape to the heretofore formless issue networks.

Finally, this chapter draws attention to the many facets of interest group involvement in agency rule making that require further research. Questions remain regarding the extent to which the study's findings regarding patterns of participation and issue networks are generalizable to other agencies, rules, and policy domains, and much work remains to be done with respect to refining our understanding of interest group influence in the rule-making process.

Appendix
List and Description of Rules Examined

EPA Rules

1. National Emission Standards for Hazardous Air Pollutants for Industrial Process Cooling Towers *(Emissions Standards)*

    This rule sets final standards that limit the discharge of chromium compound air emissions from industrial process cooling towers (ICPTs). Because chromium compounds are considered to be hazardous air pollutants (chromium is a known human carcinogen that can cause lung cancer), the rule seeks to limit their emission by prohibiting the use of chromium-based water treatment chemicals in new and existing ICPTs.

2. Hazardous Waste Management System: Testing and Monitoring Activities *(Hazardous Waste)*

    This rule proposes a revision in the testing and monitoring methods that are used by organizations that are seeking to comply with the requirements of Subtitle C of the Resource Conservation and Recovery Act. The proposed rule specifies the physical and chemical test methods to be used for evaluating solid waste.

3. Opting into the Acid Rain Program *(Acid Rain)*

This rule complements EPA's acid rain program, which was set up to reduce sulfur dioxide and nitrogen oxide emissions, the primary components of acid rain. The acid rain program has set up a sulfur dioxide allowance trading system in which utility units are allocated allowances based on their historic emissions and can trade allowances with each other (at prices determined in the marketplace), provided that at the end of each year, each unit holds enough allowances to cover its annual sulfur dioxide emissions. The opt-in rule implements the Clean Air Act Amendments of 1990 and allows sources that are not required to participate in the acid rain program the opportunity to participate on a voluntary basis. The rule targets industrial boilers and other combustion units ("all stationary combustion units burning fossil fuels") and specifies the procedures that they must follow if they wish to opt into the sulfur dioxide allowance program.

NHTSA Rules

1. Federal Motor Vehicle Safety Standard; Warning Devices *(Warning Devices)*

This rule sets standards for warning devices carried in cars and other vehicles. Warning devices are placed on the highway to inform approaching traffic that there is a stalled vehicle on the road. Prior to this rule, NHTSA standards specified the design of warning devices. This rule states that these design standards are mandatory only in buses and trucks that weigh more than ten thousand pounds. These vehicles must adhere to the standards. The rule provides warning device manufacturers with greater design flexibility for devices carried in automobiles, however.

2. Federal Motor Vehicle Safety Standard; Air Brake Systems; Air-Applied, Mechanically Held Brake Systems *(Air Brakes)*

This rule amends an existing rule that specified the requirements for parking brakes in vehicles (cars, for example) equipped with air brake systems. Manufacturers have traditionally equipped air-braked vehicles with spring brake systems in order to comply with these brake requirements. The old rule thus discouraged the manufacture and use of other forms of nonspring air brake systems, such as mechanically held air brake systems. The NHTSA decided to amend its "design restrictive" attitude toward air brake systems to encourage nonspring brake manufacturers in response to a petition for rule making from ITI, a manufacturer of mechanically held air brake systems.

3. Federal Motor Vehicle Safety Standard; Child Restraint Systems *(Child Restraint)*

This rule amends NHTSA's previous safety standard on child restraint systems. It seeks to expand the definition of child restraint systems so that (1) systems installed in vehicles other than passenger cars are included (such as minivans); (2) both restraints built into the cars and added on later are included. The expanded definition will ensure that the requirements apply to a larger number of child restraints. The rule also simplifies the existing labeling requirements for child restraint systems so that information about the child restraint (date of manufacture, name of manufacture, and so on) does *not* have to be included in the owner's manual for the motor vehicle or on the label that accompanies the child restraint.

4. Federal Motor Vehicle Safety Standard; Electric Vehicle Control and Displays; Windshield Defrosting and Defogging Systems *(Electric Vehicles)*

There are two parts to this rule: one applies to the display of battery-level information in electric vehicles; the other applies to the windshield defrosting and defogging systems in such vehicles. Part (a) considers whether controls and displays for electric-powered vehicles should be standardized, and part (b) amends existing standards on windshield defrosting and defogging systems in order to make them more appropriate for electric-powered vehicles. For (a), the regulatory issue was whether a standardized gauge and symbol should be required to indicate battery energy level. These indicators would inform drivers of electric vehicles about the vehicle's remaining range capability before recharging is necessary. The NHTSA proposed the use of an illuminated telltale, with the word "recharge" and an ISO battery symbol. For (b), NHTSA proposed that the reference to "engine warm-up" in Standard No. 103 (the standard requires that the defrosting and defogging system of a vehicle be capable of melting a specific amount of windshield ice within a specified time period after allowing time for engine warm-up) should be revised for electric-powered vehicles so as to specify that "the warm-up procedures should be the one that the manufacturer recommends for cold-weather starting."

5. Motor Vehicle Theft Prevention; Procedures for Selecting Lines Subject to Theft Prevention Standard *(Theft Prevention)*

This rule sets up a time frame for automobile manufacturers to notify the NHTSA about new lines of cars (along with information about the theft rate for each line) and requires that the manufacturers should notify the NHTSA no less than eighteen months before the introduction of the planned line. The NHTSA requires this notification about new lines of cars in order to decide which lines are subject to the theft prevention standard—i.e., this particular final rule lays the groundwork for the NHTSA to engage in "procedures for selecting lines subject to theft prevention standard" (59 FR 21638).

HUD Rules

1. Designated Housing; Public Housing Designed for Occupancy by Disabled, Elderly, or Disabled and Elderly Families *(Elderly and Disabled)*

    This rule was developed to implement section 622(a) of the Housing and Community Development Act of 1992. Section 622(a) was written so as to allow public housing authorities to designate certain portions of their buildings as "elderly only" and others as "disabled only" so that elderly and disabled residents would not have to live together. Section 622(a) is basically a set of procedures that public housing authorities must follow if they want to designate portions of their properties as "elderly only" or "disabled only."

2. Income Eligibility for Tenancy in New Construction Units *(Income Eligibility)*

    This rule amends existing section 8 (Housing Assistance Payments) regulations in order to comply with the National Affordable Housing Act of 1990. The Affordable Housing Act requires that any housing that is constructed with funds from the section 8 program should be reserved for low- and very low–income families. The rule makes one major change: it applies to all housing units that are assisted by section 8 funds, regardless of *when* they actually entered into the section 8 assistance contract (known as a Housing Assistance Payment contract or HAP contract). Prior to this rule, existing regulations exempted units that had entered into HAP contracts before October 1, 1981. This exception is no longer valid; thus *all* public housing that is constructed by funds from the section 8 program must be reserved for low- and very low-income families.

3. Federally Assisted Low-Income Housing Drug Elimination Program *(Drug Elimination)*

    This rule implements a program (the Assisted Housing Drug Elimination Program of the National Affordable Housing and the Housing and Community Development Acts of 1992) that authorizes HUD to make drug elimination grants to federally assisted low-income housing with private, for profit, or not-for-profit owners, whereas previously these grants were only available for public housing authorities and Indian housing authorities. Drug elimination grants are designated for use in eliminating drug-related crime and the problems associated with it.

Notes

An earlier version of this chapter was presented at the Third National Public Management Research Conference, Lawrence, Kansas, October 5–7, 1995. Thanks to Deborah Chasan and Srirupa Roy for their research assistance and to Caren Addis, Mina Silberberg, and Phil Cooper for their helpful comments. Data collection for this project was funded by a grant from the University of Pennsylvania Research Foundation.

1. In addition to these two theories, "hollow cores" and an "advocacy coalition framework" (ACF) are also posited as alternatives to iron triangles (Heinz et al. 1993; Jenkins-Smith and Sabatier 1994). Although both are germane to our discussion, space constraints do not allow for their treatment here.

2. I want to be explicit about the limits of this study. The analysis is limited to interest group influence in the official, APA-mandated, rule-making process. The data cannot address the question of how issues get on the agenda, nor can it address issues that never make it to the agenda in the first place (see, for example, Bachrach and Baratz 1962; Crenson 1971). Moreover, the findings reported here are limited to the traditional rule-making process and do not address negotiated rule making or dispute resolution. These are, however, important areas for future research because the current literature on negotiated rule making and dispute resolution does not currently provide an adequate answer to the questions posed in this chapter (but see Bingham and Wise 1996; Fiorina 1988; Funk 1987).

3. It is important to note here that Congress took a number of steps in the 1970s that added participation requirements beyond those included in the Administrative Procedure Act. (See, for example, Gormley 1989; Kerwin 1994; Schlozman and Tierney 1986 for a discussion of these additional participation requirements.) As Schlozman and Tierney note, one of the aims of these changes was to correct "imbalances in representation by facilitating the participation of representatives of broad publics" (346). More recently, Congress has passed the Negotiated Rulemaking Act of 1990 and the Administrative Dispute Resolution Act of 1990 whereby federal agencies can invite interested parties to the negotiating table prior to the issuance of an NOPR.

4. For purposes of this analysis we will consider public utilities to be businesses. Nevertheless, they are listed separately in the table to acknowledge their distinct characteristics.

5. This figure does not include the comment submitted by the Advocates for Highway and Auto Safety regarding NHTSA's warning devices rule. Because this coalition of the insurance industry and consumer advocates is funded by the insurance industry, it is not coded as a citizen's group. It is included in table 2b under the heading "Other." Nonetheless, its comment did provide consumers with some representation in that rule making where they were otherwise unrepresented.

6. The NHTSA did receive comments from two individual inventors, but because their comments were economic in nature and pertained to the finances of their businesses, they were classified as corporations.

7. EPA's hazardous waste rule was not included in our analysis of influence because of the length and technical nature of the comments received. It is included in the discussion of participation because a list of commentators was provided in the public docket. As a result, this section of the chapter presents the results of an examination of ten rather than eleven rules.

8. In the remaining rules the conflict was between the commentators and the agency. In these cases, commentators objected to some or all of the agency's NOPR.

9. I want to reiterate here a point made earlier in the chapter. The research reported in this chapter is limited to interest group influence in the official, APA-mandated, rule-making process. This research cannot address biases that go into the type of rules that are developed in the first place or rules that never get written due to influence, capture, or bias at other stages of the rule-making process. Nor can it take into account the types of participants and the degree of influence of those participants in those cases where negotiated rule making is undertaken.

References

Bachrach, Peter, and Morton Baratz. 1962. "The Two Faces of Power." *American Political Science Review* 56 (December): 947–52.

Bernstein, Marver. 1955. *Regulating Business by Independent Commission.* Princeton, N.J.: Princeton University Press.

Berry, Jeffrey. 1989a. *The Interest Group Society.* New York: Harper Collins.

———. 1989b. "Subgovernments, Issue Networks, and Political Conflict." In *Remaking American Politics,* edited by Richard Harris and Sidney Milkis. Boulder, Colo.: Westview Press.

Berry, Jeffrey, Kent Portney, and Ken Thomson. 1993. *The Rebirth of Urban Democracy.* Washington, D.C.: Brookings Institution.

Bingham, Lisa, and Charles Wise. 1996. "The Administrative Dispute Resolution Act of 1990: How Do We Evaluate Its Success?" *Journal of Public Administration Research and Theory* 6 (July): 383–414.

Bowers, James. 1993. "Looking at OMB's Regulatory Review through a Shared Powers Perspective." *Presidential Studies Quarterly* 23 (spring): 331–45.

Bryner, Gary. 1987. *Bureaucratic Discretion: Law and Policy in Federal Regulatory Agencies.* New York: Pergamon Press.

Caldiera, Gregory, and John Wright. 1990. "Amici Curiae before the Supreme Court: Who Participates, When, and How Much?" *Journal of Politics* 52, no. 3: 782–806.

Cater, Douglas. 1964. *Power in Washington.* New York: Vintage.

Conway, Margaret. 1991. "PACs in the Political Process." In *Interest Group Politics,* edited by Allan J. Cigler and Burdett A. Loomis. Washington, D.C.: Congressional Quarterly.

Cooper, Philip, and William West. 1988. "Presidential Power and Republican Government:

The Theory and Practice of OMB Review of Agency Rules." *Journal of Politics* 50: 864–95.

Crenson, Matthew. 1971. *The Un-Politics of Air Pollution: A Study of Non-Decisionmaking in the Cities.* Baltimore: Johns Hopkins University Press.

Danielian, Lucig, and Benjamin Page. 1994. "The Heavenly Chorus: Interest Group Voices on TV News." *American Journal of Politics* 38, no. 4 (November): 1056–78.

Duffy, Robert. 1994. "Regulatory Oversight in the Clinton Administration." Paper presented at the Annual Meeting of the American Political Science Association, New York.

Fiorina, Daniel. 1988. "Regulatory Negotiation as a Policy Process." *Public Administration Review* 48 (July/August): 764–72.

Fritschler, A. Lee. 1989. *Smoking and Politics.* 4th ed. Englewood Cliffs, N.J.: Prentice Hall.

Funk, William. 1987. "When Smoke Gets in Your Eyes: Regulatory Negotiation and the Public Interest—EPA's Woodstove Standards." *Environmental Law* 18: 55–98.

Furlong, Scott. 1993. "Interest Group Influence on Regulatory Policy." Ph.D. diss., American University.

———. 1995. "The 1992 Regulatory Moratorium: Did It Make a Difference?" *Public Administration Review* 55: 254–61.

Gais, Thomas, et al. 1991. "Interest Groups, Iron Triangles, and Representative Institutions." In *Mobilizing Interest Groups in America,* edited by Jack Walker. Ann Arbor, Mich.: University of Michigan Press.

Gormley, William. 1989. *Taming the Bureaucracy: Muscles, Prayers and Other Strategies.* Princeton, N.J.: Princeton University Press.

Heclo, Hugh. 1978. "Issue Networks and the Executive Establishment." In *The New American Political System,* edited by Anthony King. Washington, D.C.: AEI.

Heinz, John, et al. 1993. *The Hollow Core.* Cambridge: Harvard University Press.

Jenkins-Smith, Hank, and Paul Sabatier. 1994. "Evaluating the Advocacy Coalition Framework." *Journal of Public Policy* 14 (April/June): 175–203.

Kerwin, Cornelius. 1994. *Rulemaking: How Government Agencies Write Law and Make Policy.* Washington, D.C.: Congressional Quarterly Press.

King, Lauriston, and W. Wayne Shannon. 1986. "Political Networks in the Policy Process: The Case of the National Sea Grant College Program." *Polity* 19: 213–31.

Knott, Jack, and Gary Miller. 1987. *Reforming Bureaucracy.* Englewood Cliffs, N.J.: Prentice-Hall.

Landy, Marc, Marc C. Roberts, and Steven R. Thomas. 1994. *The Environmental Protection Agency: Asking the Wrong Questions.* New York: Oxford University Press.

Maass, Arthur. 1950. "Congress and Water Resources." *American Political Science Review* 44 (September): 576–93.

McGarity, Thomas. 1991. *Reinventing Rationality: The Role of Regulatory Analysis in the Federal Bureaucracy.* New York: Cambridge University Press.

Miller, Tim. 1985. "Recent Trends in Federal Water Resource Management: Are the 'Iron Triangles' in Retreat?" *Policy Studies Review* 5 (November): 395–412.

Portney, Kent, and Jeffrey Berry. 1995. "Centralizing Regulatory Control and Interest Group Access: The Quayle Council on Competitiveness." In *Interest Group Politics,* edited by Allan J. Cigler and Burdett A. Loomis. 4th ed. Washington, D.C.: CQ Press.

Schattschneider, E. E. 1960. *The Semi-Sovereign People.* New York: Holt, Rinehart and Winston.

Schlozman, Kay. 1984. "What Accent the Heavenly Chorus? Political Equality and the American Pressure System." *Journal of Politics* 46: 1006–32.

Schlozman, Kay, and John Tierney. 1986. *Organized Interests and American Democracy.* New York: Harper and Row.

Smith, Kerry. 1984. *Environmental Policy under Reagan's Executive Order.* Chapel Hill: University of North Carolina Press.

West, William. 1982. "The Politics of Administrative Rulemaking." *Public Administration Review* (September/October): 420–26.

———. 1985. *Administrative Rulemaking: Politics and Processes.* Westport, Conn.: Greenwood Press.

13 Dialogue between Advocates and Executive Agencies
New Roles for Public Management
Linda Kaboolian

ONE IMPORTANT SET of actors in formulation and implementation of public policy is the advocacy community. Several disciplines, however, treat advocates separately, which has led to a narrow and incomplete view of advocates and their capabilities and their effectiveness. Political scientists have examined this community as the special interests that form a corner of the "iron triangle." Heclo (1978) characterizes advocates in a variety of guises as elements of "issue networks" whose members define, comment on, and lobby on policy initiatives. Peterson and Chubb (1989) and Berry (1984) describe advocates' interactions with the legislative branch. In this literature, the role of advocates is to lobby to affect the nature and direction of public policy. An evaluation of this behavior is offered by several schools of political scientists. Some, such as the pluralists, see the engagement of advocates as a healthy aspect of democracy. Others, such as Lowi (1979), Olson (1971), and, more recently, Rauch (1994), argue that the activities of these groups are causing the political system to seize, leaving many social issues unresolved. A recent review of empirical evidence suggests that although the monopoly characterization of these organizations may be an overstatement, the organizations are still effective in their issue areas.

On the other hand, sociologists, at first interested in advocates in the context of political mass movements, now treat modern advocates as organizations with agendas and resources. Advocates are characterized as elements of an "industry" (Zald and McCarthy 1979) or as "social movement actors" whose task is to mobilize resources and pursue strategies to accomplish their goals (Gamson, Fireman, and Rytina 1982). Recent work on social movements and advocacy organizations has focused on how role identity (rather than economic or status interests) plays in the formation of advocacy organizations (Phelan 1989).

Both sets of literature have gaps that make it difficult to construe a positive role for advocacy groups as parties to a dialogue with public managers. Political scientists have largely ignored the organizational characteristics of advocacy communities (an exception is Rothenberg 1992). Little has been written about the relationship between these interest groups and the executive branch, particularly about the role of advocates in the design and delivery of services by executive agencies. Where this literature exists, it mainly focuses on local community-level grassroots organizations, which act both as policy advocates and as service delivery providers. Sociologists do little better: they focus on the contentious relationship between advocates and the legitimated bureaucracy, and as a result they have many more insights about conflict than about collaboration.

Nevertheless, scholars and practitioners have been examining cases of public deliberation, dialogue, and collaboration and have reported the value of the processes and presented models for us to consider. This chapter attempts to combine the questions asked by political scientists about the role of advocates in the political process with the concerns of sociologists interested in the organizational aspects of social movements so as to reconsider the role of advocates in the design and delivery of services in the public sector and the job of public managers relative to that role.

The issue of advocacy involvement cannot be ignored because, despite the arguments against it, it is a well-established part of the political process. Advocacy involvement typically takes two forms that advocates pursue with vigor: lobbying and litigating. The definition and shape of public services is greatly affected by these actions. Public managers can triangulate with these actions to augment their own efforts, even while they are the targets of criticism from legislators or of litigation for service provision failures. Lacking the resources, influence, or mandate to do otherwise, public managers often rely on advocates to argue for budget augmentation, or they wait to receive that mandate from the courts, courtesy of the advocacy community. However tacit the understanding may be about this strategy, it has many limitations: it is after the fact, it is indirect, it results in remedial rather than innovative actions, it produces rework for the agency, and, in an era when service delivery attempts to assess and address the needs of clients, it loses the value that consultation could provide.

There are several additional compelling, though more theoretical, reasons to consider crafting a constructive dialogue between advocates and public managers. There is a growing sense that, despite many improvements in the management of public bureaucracies, governmental institutions are neither solving society's problems nor providing good service delivery (Chrislip and Larson 1994; Osborne and Gaebler 1992). Serious questions have been raised about some of the fundamental arrangements of the public sector. As a consequence of the Progressive "good government" reforms, which attempted to separate administration from partisan politics, a classic problem emerged that organizational theorists have addressed. Because the reforms fortified public bureaucracies against partisanship by strengthening their external boundaries, they made it virtually impossible for the organizations to respond to external environmental changes, even those that would have resulted in organizational performance that was more satisfying to the citizenry.

Another reason to rethink these issues is the persuasive argument that wide participation and shared problem solving not only may increase the capacity of government to address society's problems competently (Reich 1995) but also may enhance democratic institutions and civic life. Putnam (1993) states his concern that the demands of life in the late twentieth century have taken Americans away from the type of engagement that knitted together communities and created the "social capital" that allowed citizens to be engaged with political institutions and processes. Ostrom, Schroeder, and Wynne (1993) argue that for too long, analysis of citizenship activities have focused on voting and the "consumption of public services" when in fact citizens have been "co-producers" of public goods. Recognition of this fact—and enhancements of opportunities for participation—gives citizens a greater stake in the processes as well as the outcomes of public operations.

Last, both public and private organizations have been challenged to question the Weberian notion that bureaucracy is the best form of organizational design and that hierarchy is inherently effective. Flatter organizational structures and wider job descriptions with greater discretion have accompanied the shift from the manufacturing-based paradigm of scientific management to the more service provision–based production modes. The importance of knowledge about processes known only to frontline employees has been recognized, and joint problem solving and other forms of employee participation programs have been designed to solicit that information. Concurrent with this shift within organizations is the notion that adequate expertise about problem solving does not necessarily exist solely within organizations. Organizations are motivated to monitor external environmental changes and to adapt as needed. In order to respond adequately to external stakeholders, they are required to "learn" more about stakeholder needs and desires by becoming "closer to customers" (Osborne and Gaebler 1992). For these reasons, it is time to consider the efficacy of a more direct relationship between executive agencies and the advocacy community in the design and delivery of services. However bountiful the potential gains, it has been difficult to craft these working relationships. Although advocates and public managers recognize overlaps in their interests (they often have, after all, the welfare of the same "customers" at the center of their activity), the two parties seem to have a difficult time working collaboratively. There are several reasons for this. First, it is difficult to accomplish constructive engagement in a highly charged political arena (Reich 1995). Advocates are not always a unitary force; they may represent a fractured community, one that is not well prepared to engage with a monolithic bureaucracy. Perhaps worse than lack of consensus within the advocate community is the lack of an infrastructure that helps the various members of the community articulate their objectives or visualize (or recognize) a satisfactory solution to a problem.

In addition, the relationship between public managers and advocates is role bound, with each actor in possession of a self-defined role and script. The advocates are saviors of the exploited clients and adversaries of the impersonal bureaucracy, embodied by the public manager, against which the fight for improved service to their constituents must be waged. The public manager is the underappreciated, technically expert, politically savvy, service-providing servant who balances the multiple and conflicting demands of legislators, unions, political appointees, the courts, and advocates. The strategies pursued by each emanate from these roles: advocates sue, and public managers guard against the involvement of advocates by limiting the advocates' access to the organization, information, and organizational resources. These strategies, forged in conflict, are not well suited to a more collaborative problem-solving process.

Dialogue and collaborative activities put the various parties together and require sustained interaction. Where this has happened, for example in labor-management relationships, the result has been concern about "capture" and "co-option." Capture, a problem often discussed in the context of the relationship between regulators and the regulated (Kagan 1982), is more generally a problem of agency (Perrow 1986). Public managers run a risk of losing their neutrality and detachment if they start to identify with the claims of advocates (Kettl and DiIulio 1995); advocates can become sympathetic to public managers' responses to criticism if they try to incorporate bureaucratic imperatives into their world view.

An additional difficulty stems from the fact that not all public service operations are "service" operations; many are compliance functions. Not all people and organizations in direct contact with public operations are customers; some are simply "inputs" to the production process or "targets of a service encounter." A more complete depiction of the complexity of these relations is illustrated in table 1.

This table differentiates "service" from "service encounters." The former is the type of product produced; the latter is the production process itself. The table also shows that public operations that are "compliance functions" can have a "service encounter" component, but the "target of that encounter" is not the "customer" of that encounter. The importance of these differentiations

Table 1. Relationships in the Production Process

Production Function	Customer (for whom the work is done)	Other (to whom the work is done)
Service	May not be present at service encounter	Is an "input" or target of service encounter
Compliance	May be willing coproducer	May not be willing coproducer

is not simply to create a new vocabulary, or to overemphasize the usefulness of the term "customer" to the public sector (Barzelay 1992) but to make clear the implicit authority relationships between the "providers" (read public agencies) and the "targets of the encounters" (read clients).

In a service production function there is little exercise of authority between the providers and the targets of the service. In addition, the customers may also be targets of the service encounter and therefore have not only a stake in the outcomes but also an interest in the operation of the production process. As a result, an organization might want to allow "customers" and "targets" to design the service delivery process. In a compliance function, there is an authority or regulatory relationship between the provider and the target so that even when the targets are also "customers" and have a stake in both the outcomes and operation of the production process, it distorts the authority relationship to allow targets to design the compliance process. This complex set of relationships begs the question: What is the proper role for advocates in a collaborative dialogue about operations that are largely a compliance function?

Last, the choices facing public managers and advocates are not always good ones. Instead of conversation about how best to use increases in operation budgets, many conversations are about downsizing, overwhelming workloads, and unmet needs of clients. In such environments, it is difficult for public managers to understand their mandate fully, and it is particularly difficult for advocates to participate in the redesign of reduced services. Here is a good example of how a potential benefit of collaboration can also be a deterrent. Whereas participation in a decision-making process may strengthen the legitimacy of the decisions, when the nature of the decisions is negative, as they are in service reductions, participation may signal tacit approval and therefore may not occur.

It is my contention that in order to design an optimal relationship between advocates and mangers, we need to understand better the self-constructed identities, world views, and environments of advocates for clients of a social welfare program and of the managers who design programs, implement them, and are accountable for their outcomes. Inherent in that relationship are many contextual factors, including the political complexities of constituent politics, accountability, technical expertise, organizational imperatives, and the nature of symbolic politics.

Reengineering the Disability-Determining Process at the Social Security Administration

In 1993, under the umbrella of the National Performance Review[1] and in reaction to growing criticism of its disability determination process,[2] the Social Security Administration (SSA) charged a team of experienced managers and consultants with the task of "re-engineering the process."[3] The only constraints on the team were the statutory definition of disability and the right of claimants to an appeal before an administrative law judge. The agency committed significant resources to an in-depth examination of the process's poor performance, to the causes of the poor performance, and to a radical redesign.[4]

Using the methodology outlined by Hammer and Champy (1994), the SSA team began with an enumeration of the concerns about the process's performance, mapped out the "as is" process, and conducted a thorough analysis of the systemic causes of performance problems. The team employed a variety of methods, including traditional analyses of workflows; focus groups with claimants; an internal scan involving three thousand interviews with executives, former executives, managers, and frontline employees at the state and federal levels; computer modeling of new processes; and monthly meetings with representatives of the advocacy community to discuss options for the new process.

Disability

The Social Security Administration administers two disability programs, Disability Insurance (DI) and Supplemental Security Income (SSI).[5] Together they represent the fourth largest entitlement, costing an estimated $52 billion in fiscal year 1994. Disability is statutorily defined as the "inability to engage in any substantial gainful activity by reason of any medically determinable physical or mental impairment which can be expected to result in death or can be expected to last for a continuous period of not less than 12 months." To meet this definition an individual must be severely physically or mentally impaired, and that impairment must prevent his or her performance of past work.

In addition, considering age, education, and work experience, the individual must be incapable of performing any other kind of work that exists in the national economy.

The Disability Determination Process

Although the SSA oversees the disability programs and conducts the quality assurance operations, the initial decision is made and the first level of appeal is conducted at one of the fifty-three state Disability Determination Services (DDS).[6] This arrangement, an enormous and complex production system encompassing federal, state, and nongovernmental entities, is a vestige of the consolidation of the federal disability program from existing state programs. The initial determination is made in four administrative steps, which are as follows.

1. *Initial decision.* Claimants who meet the eligibility criteria (DI and SSI), that is, they are not performing substantial gainful activity, present their medical evidence to the DDS. At this level in the determination process a team of medical professionals and a disability examiner determine whether, on the basis of the medical evidence provided,[7] the claimant's condition meets the "listing of impairments." If it does not, the team must determine whether the claimant has enough residual functional capacity to work. Claimants are notified when their claims have been approved or denied. The allowance rate at this level for fiscal year 1992 was 43 percent.
2. *Reconsideration.* Claimants have the right to appeal the initial decision by requesting that their files be reconsidered by a different DDS review team. This is a paper review of the evidence examined at the initial level. The allowance rate at this level for fiscal year 1992 was 17 percent.
3. *Appeals to an administrative law judge.* Claimants who have been denied at the reconsideration level can appeal within sixty days of the date of the denial. At this level the appeal is conducted under the guidelines of the Administrative Procedures Act of 1946. Hearing officers, known as administrative law judges, are technically employees of the agency and are bound by its policies, but the Administrative Procedures Act grants them judicial independence, which allows greater latitude in their decisions than was allowed at earlier levels. The review of claims at this level differs from that of earlier levels. Claimants often appear at the hearing and are allowed representation. The agency is not represented. Of importance, the review is de novo, that is, additional evidence can be considered at this time. The allowance rate at this level for fiscal year 1992 was 68 percent.
4. *Appeals to the Appeals Council.* Claimants who have been denied by an administrative law judge may appeal to the Appeals Council, the final level of

administrative procedure. The Appeals Council represents the secretary of the Department of Health and Human Services. The allowance rate at this level for fiscal year 1992 was 8 percent.

Appeals beyond the Appeals Council level are heard in federal district court.[8] For fiscal year 1992, .005 percent of cases were appealed to the federal courts, and, of those, one in five was allowed.

Program Challenges

From 1985 to 1993, disability programs grew enormously and at a rate greater than expected. In the past decade, the disability-prone age cohort of the population increased by 17 percent, and the number of persons who received disability benefits grew from 4.9 million to 7.3 million, an increase of 49 percent. Program and administrative costs increased 108 percent, from $25 billion in 1985 (55 percent in constant dollars).

The increase was the result of several factors over which the SSA had no control. The recession of 1990–1991 saw a rise in claims both from insured workers who had lost jobs and unemployment benefits and from others whose household income had decreased. Independently and concurrently, the lack of health insurance coverage for poor working families also stimulated claims for DI and SSI.

Court decisions and congressional action also generated increases in both the volume of SSA claims and the complexity of eligibility rules. In 1990 the Supreme Court required the SSA to revise its criteria for assessing childhood disabilities. The Zebley decision[9] led both to a reconsideration of more than 400,000 claims, some a decade old, and to 150,000 back payments. The new regulations stimulated new claims.[10] Class action suits with narrow applicability and circuit court decisions with which the SSA disagreed helped fragment the national program. In addition to Court actions, congressional pressure led to changes both in the regulations covering the assessment of claims based on mental disorders and in the reassessment of recipients' conditions to determine continuing eligibility.

At the same time these increases occurred, the SSA was the target of a substantial downsizing effort, one that neutralized the significant gains the agency made in increased productivity and investments in new technology. Financial relief for the agency was not provided. The SSA shifted a significant portion of its budget allocation to support such disability programs as retirement, thereby mortgaging its future. Despite these problems, the agency received only a modest waiver of government-wide constraints on personnel levels.

Increases in the number of claims filed and the number of recipients, program complexities, and budgetary constraints are not in and of themselves a problem, but they reflect other important economic and social changes. They do raise questions about the performance of the disability programs and the process by which they are delivered. Collectively, these increases had a great impact on the programs' viability. The DI trust fund was projected to be insolvent by 1995.[11] Congressional support for the SSI benefit to drug- and alcohol-dependent recipients waned because television news programs filmed recipients using their SSI checks for the purchase of alcohol and illegal drugs. Aged alien recipients were the target of increasing criticism of benefits to noncitizens.

Symptoms of the Breakdown of the Disability Determination Process

Those who are unfortunate enough to become disabled find their problems compounded by inefficiencies at SSA.

—Representative Dan Rostenkowski, May 1991

Evidence of the breakdown of the disability determination process was, unfortunately, easy to observe. The following is a shortened list of the concerns raised by oversight authorities and SSA itself.

Decisions took a long time. Increased volume and backlogs caused claimants to wait 155 days from the date of filing for initial decisions about their claims—a task that required thirteen hours of staff time.[12] If they appealed a rejected claim they could expect to wait up to 550 days. The entire process up until this point required thirty-two hours of staff time. This meant that persons who, in order to qualify for benefits, earned virtually no income for five months prior to their applications had to wait at least five more months to learn whether they would receive benefits they may have been entitled to on the day they applied. The wait for an initial decision was projected to increase 50 percent by fiscal year 1995.

The backlog of work grew at each level of the process. Backlogs are the natural consequence of a system that handles sharp increases in volume and differential processing times at each level. The backlog of claims awaiting hearings by administrative law judges increased from 142,000 at the end of fiscal year 1989 to 205,000 at the end of fiscal year 1992. As a result of the pending work load, important work with consequences for program costs went undone. Continuing Disability Reviews for DI recipients are required every three years (except where disability is assumed to be permanent). Each year between four hundred thousand and five hundred thousand recipients should be reviewed. In fiscal year 1994, 1.2 million cases needed reexamination. The actual cessation rate due to improvements in the beneficiary's condition was estimated to be quite low—less than 10 percent.[13] Continuing Disability Reviews, however, are still cost-effective and important to both program integrity and the knowledge base about probabilities of rehabilitation on which to base future decisions.[14]

The percentage of denials being appealed was growing, as was the percentage of appeals ultimately awarded benefits. Over time the rate of appeals and the rate of awards by administrative law judges both rose despite extremely high accuracy rates for the initial decision (96.4 percent for approvals and 93.4 percent for denials). Nearly half of all rejected claims were appealed, and two out of three appeals were approved by administrative law judges.[15] Appeals have costs associated with them, even when they do not lead to awards. Each appeal to an administrative law judge cost $894 to process in fiscal year 1992. When claimants are represented by an attorney, up to 25 percent of initial payment may be used for attorney fees. This is money that the claimant does not receive.

Patching up the process creates more work. Even agency attempts to improve service delivery exacerbated the problem. SSA regulations provide for a percentage fee from back awards to attorneys who have represented rejected claimants in administrative appeals. The fees are deducted from the claimant's benefit check and sent to the representative. The agency provides this service in order to ensure and regulate representation for rejected claimants. These representatives have learned, however, that the longer an appeal takes, the larger the award and the larger the fee. Therefore, these representatives have little incentive to facilitate the resolution of a case.

Ironically, the breakdown of the service delivery system created more work for the system. The appeals process generated rework, i.e., the reprocessing of claims. The increasing probability of awards at higher ends of the production chain meant that those familiar with the system would advocate appeals by clients and create more rework. Clients increasingly used representatives to advocate for them within the system, requiring the SSA to process more payments to advocates.

Almost needless to say, the effects of these systematic problems were keenly felt by SSA clients. As a result, the advocacy community was a frequent and vocal critic of the agency and its operations and a powerful lobbying force on behalf of the disabled.

The Advocate Community

The SSA identified 252 stakeholders in its reengineering plan. The vast majority were organizations in the advocacy community for the disabled. This community was relatively new, though several of its members, notably those associated with childhood diseases and veterans causes, are considerably older than average. Within the community are multiple overlapping coalitions such as "Save Our Security" and "Concerned Citizens for the Disabled Coalition," which consisted of member organizations. These coalitions are loose confederations without formal structure, but they are tied together through interlocking directorates, a revolving pool of staff, and, in some cases, shared offices and support staff. Many of the professional staff of these organizations are lawyers and have a history of legal advocacy for children or the poor. Although some have had policy jobs at the legislative or executive branches, almost without exception they had very little experience either as service providers or as managers of service delivery operations.

The structure of this community is worth noting. Although the constituents of the community are numerous—an estimated thirty-five to forty-three million people have disabilities—and are thereby a potential force to be reckoned with, the community "spans a splintered universe." There are many types of disabilities: physical, mental, sensory impairments, cognitive processing impairments. There are many sources of disabilities: genetic, congenital, accidental, disease related. Disabilities can occur at any time over the life course, and, as a result, the interests of the members of the coalition are often at odds.

In 1991 the advocacy community won a stunning victory with the passage of the Americans with Disabilities Act (ADA), a comprehensive bill guaranteeing the right to participation in public and economic life through "reasonable accommodations." The ADA has had enormous implications for the business and the public sector, which has been required to make public buildings and infrastructure accessible to people with physical disabilities. The passage of this bill was the result of a savvy political strategy. The advocate community made it an issue before the 1992 campaign by empirically demonstrating their voting strength to incumbent president Bush. Advocates also staged dramatic street theater in Washington, D.C., crawling up the steps of the Capitol to demonstrate the consequences of insensitivity to the users of wheelchairs.

The Agency

At approximately the same time that the ADA passed, children's advocates won the *Zebley* decision. This was not only a blow to the Social Security Administration but also a source of great frustration to the career public managers of the SSA who had disagreed with the Reagan administration's switch from "presumptive" disability for children (that is, the granting of benefits until the child is proved to not be eligible) to the more adversarial "presumptive non-disability." As a result of the Reagan policy, many families had to wait for the adjudication process to grind on, often missing developmental opportunities for their children. The Court's order that the SSA readjudicate four hundred thousand cases per the *Zebley* decision, further burdening the already broken disability process, was a bitter pill for the career managers who had disagreed with the policy. It also placed the public managers in an awkward position relative to the advocacy community, which remained skeptical of the managers' sentiments about the policy.

SSA managers had little experience with advocates except in adversarial situations. No SSA manager at the strategic or operations level had worked for an advocate group. (This is not the case at the level of political appointees.) The SSA itself is located outside of Washington, D.C., in Woodlawn, Maryland—in part to keep it apart from Congress and its lobbyists. The practical implications were that any face-to-face interactions required enormous logistical planning. The public managers often found themselves vilified by advocates, even though they agreed with advocate positions. If anything, the managers believed that they worked on behalf of the disabled. They perceived their jobs as stewarding the resources of the trust fund; maintaining the legitimacy of the adjudication process by careful, methodical (albeit slow) measurement; and providing excellent service in the form of legal representation against itself and other resources.

In fact, the SSA, as an organization, had a difficult relationship with the disability program. Increasingly, the applicants were not simply the sick and elderly working insured and their families but also the uninsured poor applying for SSI benefits. The history of the SSA's struggle to incorporate the SSI program into its culture is well known (Derthick 1990). In addition, disability—both the DI and SSI programs—differs from old age and retirement insurance in that it operationally requires adjudication rather than accounting and benefit issuance. As a result, disability has come to represent a compliance function largely for poor clients in an agency that sees itself as a service delivery operation for the entitled beneficiary.

The Dialogue

From December 1993 through May 1994, the reengineering team for the disability determination process met monthly with members of the Concerned Citizens for the Disabled Coalition. The purposes of the dialogue were to brief the coalition on the progress SSA was making on its design for a new determination process and to solicit input on design features. Very quickly, the advocates expressed their suspicions that SSA was not sincere about this dialogue and that the best course of action was to not participate. An invitation to visit Woodlawn and the SSA headquarters for a tour of operations, however, kept the relationship alive through the second month. The tour of the facilities and the backroom operations made it clear that the advocates had no idea of the complexity or scale of the adjudication operation. Issues that they dealt with on a microlevel and suggestions they made for marginal improvements in idiosyncratic cases had enormous consequences for the operation simply because of its scale. As a result of this tour, the advocates left expressing admiration for the amount of work that did get done at the agency and interest in future tours, particularly in meetings with the developers of the agency's software systems.

As the analysis of the disability process progressed and ideas for new designs were solicited and considered by the team, the managers of the SSA began to share the reform options under consideration. This was a difficult act for the managers. They were used to seeing advocates in the "advisor" role, sitting on policy commissions, listening to their testimony—not acting as partners. Ultimately they were convinced that they must present their ideas for service delivery options to the advocates and ask them for their preferences. Accustomed to presenting a single option, the managers were not prepared to create alternatives, some of which maximized interests other than those held by the organization.

The fractured interests within the advocate group emerged as soon as the options were outlined. The inability of the advocates to resolve their disagreements concerning alternative proposals became clear. As a result, the SSA managers wanted to halt the dialogue, but they became convinced that they could help to create the capacity within the group to do this work. It quickly became apparent that the advocates were not knowledgeable enough about SSA's operations to make concrete counterproposals. As a result, the managers began to solicit information from subcoalitions about their interests and preferences and to mediate between the subcoalitions to help them resolve their differences. For the managers, this activity required a new set of tasks and skills, and it repositioned them relative to the advocates. They had been battling for so long that it was difficult to imagine themselves as coaches and mediators.

Toward the end of the six-month dialogue period, it seemed that the advocate community believed it had been "heard" by the SSA and that it had made a significant contribution to the design process. One last meeting was held to review the recommendations of the reengineering team. It was at this meeting that the limitations of the process became apparent. After the reengineering team made a presentation of its proposal, the advocates made it clear that they had every intention of lobbying against it in Congress. This seeming reversal of position was the result of several factors. First, the coalition had worked hard to get every member to attend this last meeting, even though many members had expressed little interest during the previous six months. The lack of a decision-making process within the coalition allowed the members who had sat outside the process to veto the work of those who had worked with the SSA. In addition, the smallest disagreement between the SSA and the advocates became the focus of the advocates' criticism and a justification for withdrawing support from the proposal. The advocates could do this because there was no system that held them accountable to the process. Instead, they saw that they would only close off their appeal path to Congress if they signed on to anything that was less than 100 percent of what they wanted. In fact, over the course of the dialogue, they had moved the SSA closer toward their own goals, silently reserving the right to withdraw support from that position.

The outcome of the process left the SSA managers feeling burned. They had invested in the relationship, opened themselves up to new tasks and skills, worked with the advocates to design acceptable choices, and helped the advocates choose among them. Yet, in the end, the SSA managers had little to show for their work. Unfortunately, although the programmatic consequences of this failed dialogue were not great, the personal experiences reinforced the managers' sentiments about the dangers and costs of working with advocates.

Conclusions and Recommendations

Analysis of this experience has been enhanced by the use of a sociological framework to consider the dilemma of dialogue and participatory processes between public managers and advocacy organizations. Future efforts, both theoretical and practical, should expand on this analytic framework and consider the potential for partnership.

An additional frame of reference might be provided by reviewing negotiations in public sector disputes. Understanding the organizational capacity of the partners to collaborate, the issue cultures around which they are collaborating, and the incentives to seek viable solutions to problems would be of enormous consequence.

One practical recommendation for an agency and advocate community that might help break down the barriers between the organizations and maintain appropriate boundaries is short-term tours of duty at each other's organizations. Such terms could provide two benefits. Advocates might become better versed in the operational and organizational (as well as political) issues facing an agency, and public managers might lower the barriers of professional isolation that keep them apart from the advocates with whom they share many concerns.

Notes

1. The National Performance Review, in addressing the Department of Health and Human Services and the Social Security Administration, recognized increases in productivity in the disability program and noted the need for dramatic improvements in the administration of the program in order to meet the increasing workload.

2. The General Accounting Office had issued several critical reports on the administration of disability programs. See, for example, Social Security Disability: Growing Funding and Administrative Problems (GAO/T-HRD-92-28); Social Security: SSA Needs to Improve Continuing Disability Review Program (GAO/HRD-93-109; Social Security: Increasing Number of Disability Claims and Deteriorating Service (GAO/HRD-94-11).

3. Reengineering is defined by its leading proponents, Hammer and Champy (1994), as "the fundamental rethinking and radical redesign of business processes to achieve dramatic improvements in critical contemporary measures of performance, such as cost, quality, service and speed" (32).

4. The initial proposal of the team was issued in spring 1994, six months after the reengineering project began. Public comment on the proposed design was solicited and analyzed before pilot projects began.

5. Title II of the Social Security Act established the Disability Insurance program for eligible workers, their disabled children, and widow(er)s. Benefits are disbursed from the Social Security Trust Fund. Title XVI of the act provides for Supplemental Security Income, a needs-based benefit for the aged, blind, and disabled that is funded from general revenues.

6. In addition, there is one federally run determination service.

7. Medical evidence of record is obtained either directly from the treating sources used by the claimant's provider or from an independent source and is referred to as a "consultative examination."

8. Judicial review of disability claims at the district and circuit courts levels has less to do with the fragmentation of the program by judicial district. For more on this topic, see the *Status of the Disability Programs of the Social Security Administration* (1994), a Congressional Research Service Report, June 1994.

9. *Sullivan v. Zebley* (493 U.S. 521 [1990]).

10. The Court required the SSA to consider as a disabling impairment behavior that is not "age appropriate."

11. It was not insolvent by 1995. The SSA is pursuing legislation to reallocate payroll taxes from the Old Age and Survivors Insurance (OASI) program to the DI program.

12. This is an aggregate number. In actuality, Title II claims (DI) generate a shorter wait than do Title XVI claims (SSI).

13. Reviews of DI beneficiaries typically result in conversion to retirement benefits.

14. No formal procedures for review have been established for the majority of beneficiaries of the SSI program. Even where they exist, however, they are not performed. The treatment plans required of the drug- and alcohol-dependent recipients are not adequately monitored, further eroding support for this program.

15. In 1993, the accuracy rate for rejected claims was 93.4 percent; however 47 percent of rejected claims were appealed.

References

Barzelay, Michael. 1992. *Breaking through Bureaucracy: A New Vision for Managing in Government*. Berkeley: University of California Press.

Berry, Jeffrey M. 1984. *The Interest Group Society*. Boston: Little, Brown.

Chrislip, David D., and Carl E. Larson. 1994. *Collaborative Leadership: How Citizens and Civic Leaders Can Make a Difference*. San Francisco: Jossey-Bass.

Derthick, Martha. 1990. *Agency under Stress: The Social Security Administration in American Government*. Washington, D.C.: Brookings Institution.

Gamson, William A., Bruce Fireman, and Steven Rytina. 1982. *Encounters with Unjust Authority*. Homewood, Ill.: Dorsey Press.

Hammer, Michael, and James Champy. 1994. *Reengineering the Corporation: A Manifesto for Business Revolution*. New York: Harper.

Heclo, Hugh. 1978. "Issue Networks and the Executive Establishment." In *The New Political System,* edited by Anthony King. Washington, D.C.: American Enterprise Institute.

Kagan, Robert A. 1982. *Going by the Book: The Problem of Regulatory Unreasonableness*. Philadelphia: Temple University Press.

Kettl, Donald F., and John J. DiIulio, Jr., eds. 1995. *Inside the Reinvention Machine: Appraising the National Performance Review.* Washington, D.C.: Brookings Institute.

Lowi, Theodore. 1979. *The End of Liberalism: The Second Republic of the United States.* 2d ed. New York: Norton Press.

Olson, Mancur. 1971. *The Logic of Collective Action: Public Goods and the Theory of Groups.* Cambridge, Mass.: Harvard University Press.

Osborne, David, and Ted Gaebler. 1992. *Reinventing Government: How the Entrepreneurial Spirit Is Transforming the Public Sector.* Reading, Mass.: Addison-Wesley Publishing.

Ostrom, Elinor, Larry Schroeder, and Susan Wynne. 1993. *Institutional Incentives and Sustainable Development: Infrastructure Policies in Perspective.* Boulder, Colo.: Westview Press.

Perrow, Charles. 1986. *Complex Organizations: A Critical Essay.* 3d ed. New York: Random House.

Peterson, Paul, and John E. Chubb, eds. 1989. *Can the Government Govern?* Washington, D.C.: Brookings Institution.

Phelan, Shane. 1989. *Identity Politics: Lesbian Feminism and the Limits of Community.* Philadelphia: Temple University Press.

Putnam, Robert D. 1993. *Making Democracy Work: Civic Traditions in Modern Italy.* Princeton, N.J.: Princeton University Press.

Rauch, Jonathan. 1994. *Demosclerosis: The Silent Killer of American Government.* New York: Times Books.

Reich, Charles A. 1995. *Opposing the System.* New York: Crown Publishers.

Rothenberg, Lawrence S. 1992. *Linking Citizens to Government: Interest Group Politics at Common Cause.* New York: Cambridge University Press.

Zald, Mayer N., and John D. McCarthy, eds. 1979. *The Dynamics of Social Movements: Resource Mobilization, Social Control and Tactics.* Cambridge, Mass.: Winthrop Publishers.

14 Reinventing Government
Lessons from a State Capital
Frances S. Berry, Richard Chackerian, and Barton Wechsler

ADMINISTRATIVE REFORM IS once again on the public agenda as a new generation of strategies for reinventing the way government is managed has achieved
surprising attention and interest. Driven by citizen dissatisfaction with government performance, serious and persistent fiscal problems, and the example
of seemingly successful restructuring in the private sector, political leaders at
every level of government and a growing number of reinvention advocates
have argued forcefully for fundamental changes in government operations
(Osborne 1988; Osborne and Gaebler 1992; National Performance Review
1993; National Commission on the State and Local Public Service 1993;
Thompson 1993; Barzelay 1992; DiIulio 1994).

As with previous generations of administrative reform, many of the current reform prescriptions call for managing government more like a business and recommend strategies generated by the private sector (Osborne and
Gaebler 1992). Some of these efforts, however, reflect a more complex understanding of government reform than earlier efforts. For example, Florida's
blueprint for reform (Governor's Commission for Government by the People
1991) goes well beyond the Grace Commission, which focused on federal staff
cutbacks, productivity improvement programs, and privatization as the solutions for an inefficient federal administration. Similarly, the state and federal
reform efforts in the 1990s build on the extensive experience of states in the
1980s as "laboratories" for new administrative and policy reforms (Osborne
1988).

The dominant view of administrative reform in the academic literature is
that it is the consequence of short-term struggles for political access and symbolic rewards (Radin and Hawley 1988). From this perspective, administrative
reform is part of a seamless process in which interest groups and elected officials struggle to increase their power and control over resources. Power struggles, however, can be played out in any number of ways not restricted to administrative reform. Administrative reform is episodic, surging during some
periods while ebbing during others. Some have argued that the surges of
administrative reform are related to long-wave changes in the economy

(Chackerian 1996). Long-term economic decline and related decline in government revenues create a series of programmatic crises that suggest to the public and to political leaders that comprehensive changes are required in the way the government does business. In the short run, the administrative reforms that are chosen by political leaders to address problems of decline are those that are available in the institutional environment (Meyer 1979; Meyer and Rowan 1983).

Administrative reform is inevitably influenced by the process of developing support for change among relevant authorities. Obviously, it is easier to develop support for reforms that have widespread institutional legitimacy. The reforms may be embedded in the wider political culture, expressed in exemplar organizations and given rhetorical support by experts, think tanks, editorial writers, and, eventually, political leaders. As a consequence, reforms tend to be taken from a set of solutions that are fashionable in the relevant institutional environments.[1] From this perspective, it is not surprising that the track record of administrative reform does not inspire confidence. It is also not surprising that reformers themselves may be frustrated by the consequences of their actions.

Although some writers argue that administrative reform has not been particularly successful, a more careful analysis suggests that the empirical evidence about the consequences of administrative reform is largely nonexistent (Chackerian 1996). There is little debate, however, over the fact that there have been major changes in administrative arrangements in state governments since the turn of the century. State governors have garnered much more control over budgets, personnel, and organization. Interestingly, no one suggests that these changes be reversed.

Florida, led by Governor Chiles and Lieutenant Governor Buddy MacKay, has undertaken one of the most comprehensive reform efforts in the current period (U.S. General Accounting Office 1994). From the start of the 1990 gubernatorial campaign, it was clear that Chiles and MacKay intended to put administrative reform at the top of their policy agenda. They argued in their campaign that a large part of the problem of poor governmental performance in Florida could be traced to rigid bureaucratic structures, to overly constraining administrative rules and procedures, and to outmoded management systems. In order to fix Florida's government, to make it more efficient and effective, Chiles and MacKay prescribed a comprehensive program of administrative reform.

"Reinvention" has been the popular rhetoric used by Chiles and MacKay to describe their reform efforts. The press picked up the term as well and used it to label anything that was designed to improve the administration of state government. Since the idea of reform was introduced in the midst of the gubernatorial campaign, a large number of initiatives were introduced using the legitimating language of "reinvention." Included in this package were many of the most popular contemporary management innovations, such as total quality management (TQM), strategic planning, deregulation, downsizing, and civil service reform. Yet it also included old standbys, such as organizational restructuring, decentralization, performance measurement, and performance-based budgeting.

This chapter describes the efforts of the Chiles-MacKay administration to reinvent and restructure government in Florida, focusing on the key initiatives and the lessons to be drawn from them. After discussing the context in which Florida's administrative reforms took place, we describe some of the key reform initiatives.[2] Then, we seek to draw out lessons from Florida's experience.

The Context of Reform

After decades of rapid growth and change, Florida has become the nation's fourth largest state, with a population of more than thirteen million. Accompanying this tremendous growth in population have been even larger increases in state government. Fueled by needs for new schools, roads, and sewers; increased demand for law enforcement and corrections; rising health care costs; increased demands for child protection and adult day care; and virtually every other government service, state government expenditures grew rapidly during the 1980s. Florida's problems have been compounded by an outdated tax system that limits its fiscal capacity and a relatively conservative political culture that blocks innovation and change (Chackerian 1994a). Perhaps as much as any other state, Florida entered the 1990s facing an environment in which it was forced to "do more with less."

By their political biographies, Lawton Chiles and Buddy MacKay were well suited to address the challenges of a growing but troubled Florida. Both had achieved political prominence in the 1970s and 1980s, first in the Florida legislature and then in the U.S. House and Senate. Chiles had retired after three terms in the Senate, disenchanted by his experience and disheartened about the prospects for improving government from Washington. MacKay, after losing a bruising campaign to succeed Chiles in the Senate, also returned to private life in the late 1980s. Less than two years later, reportedly influenced by writings suggesting that the states would be the proving ground of reform, the "laboratories of democracy" (Osborne 1988), they ran together in the 1990 gubernatorial race. Chiles and MacKay made administrative reform a central element in their 1990 campaign and the themes they developed in that campaign would be carried forward throughout their administration.

Florida's Reform Initiatives

The structures and methods of operating developed during the 1990 gubernatorial campaign provided both principles and processes that were replicated during the administrative reform efforts that followed. Large working groups of twenty to thirty-five high-profile people were put to work on a variety of issues, including transportation, social services, and growth and the environment.[3] These working groups became the prototype for transition task forces that mobilized large numbers of people inside and outside the government to investigate the workings of each agency and to review their current and past performance. Chiles and MacKay also asked for in-house reviews from the agencies; this redundancy was intended to give them multiple perspectives and a basis for their own independent judgment about agency performance.

In addition, the Governor's Commission for Government by the People, popularly referred to as the Frederick Commission, was established in early 1991, with David Osborne and Doug Ross as primary consultants. This group, borrowing heavily from what became *Reinventing Government* (Osborne and Gaebler 1992), helped to articulate the Chiles-MacKay philosophy of administrative reform. According to the report of the Governor's Commission for Government by the People (1991), government should be:

1. Catalytic: it steers more than it rows.
2. Community-oriented: it empowers more than it serves.
3. Customer-driven: it meets the customer's choice rather than the bureaucracy's.
4. Value-oriented: it stresses prevention rather than cure.
5. Results-focused: it funds outcomes rather than inputs.
6. Market-oriented: it uses competition rather than monopoly (10–11).

The report also proposed a series of initiatives that operationalized the principles of a "reinvented" government and that came to define the administration's approach to reform (23). During the Chiles-MacKay administration, the personnel system would be revamped by reducing the number of classifications, increasing pay flexibility, and making it easier to hire and fire civil service employees. Organizational processes would be transformed through the use of modern management techniques, especially total quality management. Agency management structures would be streamlined, layers of middle management would be eliminated, and agencies would be decentralized. A new Department of Management Services would be created to oversee personnel, planning, budgeting, procurement, and other administrative services. Moreover, a new budget policy and format would shift the focus of the state budgeting system from inputs to outcomes.

The reforms articulated by the Frederick Commission report touched in some way virtually every aspect of government in Florida. Some, like civil service reform and total quality management, were proposed with the intent of government-wide adoption (Wechsler 1994). Others were begun as experiments in one or two agencies, such as the budget and pay flexibility granted to the Department of Revenue. Still other strategies were more narrowly focused to address specific problems, such as restructuring the now defunct Department of Health and Rehabilitative Services (HRS) and the merger of the Departments of Administration and General Services.

On their face, the proposed reforms seemed to lack a single overarching theme or approach. This may have been the result of the large number of groups and individuals who were invited to contribute their ideas during the campaign and the early part of the administration. Inclusion is a very effective campaign technique, but it inevitably leads to an eclectic approach to reform. The administration's public rhetoric was that reforms would benefit all of the affected stakeholders—citizens, state government managers, and public employees. Soon after the election divisions developed among the relatively small circle of trusted allies that surrounded Chiles and MacKay. Part of the struggle was for personal advantage, but significant differences emerged over the relative importance of discretion for high-level managers and true decentralization. For some, administrative reform was a process of giving those who could be trusted to steer greater flexibility to make policy as well as freedom from bureaucratic and legal constraints. For others, the priority was to make agencies smaller, more driven by those at the operational and community level. Over time, it became clear that empowerment of lower-level managers was not as high a priority as giving more power to upper-level managers and increasing executive control.

This struggle within the administration can also be seen in another set of conceptual tensions. Some of the reform proposals, particularly TQM, were designed to change the culture of government whereas others were more focused on the structure of incentives. Pay for performance, performance budgeting, budget flexibility, and strategic planning are essentially methods to insure rationality from the perspective of policy makers. For a variety of reasons to be developed below, the effort to transform the culture has been abandoned in favor of a focus on the structure of incentives. One is tempted to conclude that this change took place as it was gradually decided that executive control was the more important and that it was easier to achieve than cultural transformation and decentralization.

Civil Service Reform

Civil service reform received the greatest attention in the early years of the administration. Extensive criticisms of the existing system were reported to the Chiles-MacKay transition teams, and the Frederick Commission concluded that reform of the personnel system was necessary for the development of a quality work force. Architects of civil service reform claimed that it would "reduce waste, increase productivity, and enhance human resources" (Frederick Commission 1991, 2). As a result of reform, they promised, agencies would be empowered; managers, supervisors, and employees would receive needed training; performance evaluation would be improved and linked to the reward system; and employees would be involved in improving the quality of services. Civil service reform proposals called for changes in employee selection and retention, classification and pay systems, training and human resource development, and performance appraisal (Wechsler 1994).

Although legislation authorizing changes to the personnel system was passed in December of 1991, implementation of the new civil service system was slow and piecemeal. According to a group of personnel officers interviewed in 1995, only a part of the changes promised by the administration had occurred, principally in the area of pay and hiring flexibility. Linking pay to performance, a key feature of reform, was authorized in limited situations by the legislature, but this has not been widely used due to the lack of merit money as well as the difficulty of measuring performance. Civil service reform, they said, produced some benefits but on the whole had not done much to improve the system. The role and capacity of personnel management, however, has been greatly diminished in the restructured Department of Management Services (formed by the merger of the old Departments of Administration and General Services). At the same time, the interest of political leaders in civil service reform has waned, with the result that there is weak administrative and political support for continued improvements in personnel management or in full implementation of civil service reform.

Restructuring

A second element of Florida's reforms focused on restructuring the executive branch of state government. From the perspective of the administration, the structural arrangements that they had inherited were messy and unwieldy,

Table 1. Agency Restructuring in the Chiles Administration: Splits, Consolidations, and Privatization

Date	New Agency	Source
Splits		
1990	Veterans Affairs	Governor's Office
1990	Elder Affairs	Health and Rehabilitative Services
1992	Health Care Administration	Governor's Office
1994	Juvenile Justice	Health and Rehabilitative Services
1996	Health	Health and Rehabilitative Services
1997	Children and Family Services	Health and Rehabilitative Services
Consolidations		
1992	Managment Services	General Services and Administration
1993	Environmental Protection	Environmental Regulation and Natural Resources
1993	Business and Professional Regulation	Business Regulation and Professional Regulation
Privatization		
1996	Enterprise Florida	Commerce

improperly aggregated in some places and disaggregated in others. No coherent theory, however, provided a rationale for the rash of structural changes that followed. In some cases agencies were merged, in others they were divided, and in yet other cases efforts were made to decentralize policy making to citizen boards. In addition, in the most current round of restructuring, one agency was privatized (see table 1).

Chiles and MacKay inherited a structure of departments and agencies that was the product of a massive reorganization in 1969, the first major change in Florida government organization since 1885 (Chackerian 1994b). Consolidation, a major feature of the 1969 reorganization, was not central in the period thereafter nor in the Chiles reorganization proposals, with some important exceptions (e.g., Management Services, Environmental Protection, and Business and Professional Regulation). Constituency-driven reorganizations, however, were quite important as the Chiles administration began its reform efforts.

Two constituency organizations were created by constitutional amendment in 1990, Veterans Affairs and Elder Affairs. Veterans, unhappy with the arm's-length treatment the Office of Veterans Affairs was receiving in the Executive Office of the Governor, put an issue on the state ballot that provided constitutional status for a new Department of Veterans Affairs. The logic for the creation of Elder Affairs was similar: seniors desired more attention and prominence for their issues and concerns than was given by placement within HRS.

In 1992, the Agency for Health Care Administration was created by splitting functions away from HRS, but it could as easily be seen as a new agency. This new organizational structure was seen as a way to give emphasis to a policy area particularly important to the governor. As a division in the huge HRS, Health was not thought to be flexible enough nor sufficiently committed to health care reform to drive policy changes through the legislature or to manage the implementation of any changes that might be adopted. In 1996, in part as a quid pro quo for making permanent the Agency for Health Care Administration,[4] the governor bowed to demands from physicians and other medical health care professionals to dismember HRS further by creating a separate Department of Health.

The Department of Management Services, the Department of Business and Professional Regulation, and the Department of Environmental Protection were distinctive structural reforms. Unlike the other post-1969 reorganizations, these were not splits from existing agencies, but resulted from combining existing departments. In addition, they were unique in that they involved cabinet as well as gubernatorial agencies. Management Services combined a cabinet agency, the Department of General Services, and the Department of Administration, which was under the control of the governor; the new Department of Environmental Protection, established in 1993, combined the functions of the governor's Department of Environmental Regulation with the cabinet's Department of Natural Resources; and, finally, the Department of Business and Professional Regulation was created to combine the functions of the Department of Business Regulation and the Department of Professional Regulation. The espoused logic of these latter mergers was that regulations could be reduced and made more consistent if administered by a single consolidated agency. Although not tied directly to the merger, the regulatory and oversight functions of Management Services were reduced; in this case, consolidation supported the administration's desire to decentralize responsibility for personnel management to the operating departments. What better way to expedite this process than to weaken the organizational position of the central regulatory agency?

The centerpiece of the Chiles-MacKay effort to decentralize government operations was their attempt to reorganize Florida's human services system. HRS was the largest comprehensive human services agency in the country— its creation as a consolidated agency was driven equally by federal initiatives and by urban reformers in the Florida legislature who emerged as leaders after reapportionment in the late 1960s. Many in the legislature concluded that the agency, after twenty years in existence, was too large to be managed effectively. The consequence of this was a slow decline in the scope of the agency and the spinning off of functions to several new agencies. A major element in the 1990 Chiles-MacKay campaign was their pledge to increase community control and citizen involvement in health and human service decision making. The administration attempted to achieve decentralization of agency operations and community control through the establishment of Health and Human Services Boards (HHSBs). In 1992, the Florida legislature passed the HRS Reorganization Act, which created four new administrative districts and new community boards in each of the now fifteen districts that covered the state. The HHSBs have joint responsibility with the HRS district administrators to:

1. Establish district goals and objectives.
2. Conduct needs assessments.
3. Develop and approve a district service delivery plan.
4. Provide policy oversight, including development and approval of district policies and procedures.
5. Act as a focal point of community participation in department activities.
6. Participate with the secretary of HRS in the selection of the district administrator.

The governor appoints roughly one-fifth of the members of HHSBs, and the boards of county commissioners appoint the remainder. The community boards operate through annual agreements negotiated with the secretary of HRS. The agreements include expected service outcomes, core service elements, and a dispute resolution procedure.

The role of the HHSBs and the powers given them by the legislature are evolving. The essential issue is the extent to which the boards should move from having joint planning and oversight responsibilities with the district administrator to having complete responsibility. The governor has been strongly supportive of such a move to "managing partners," but key legislators are resistant. Among their concerns are the possibility of uneven services and service levels in different parts of the state, the difficulty of meeting federal requirements, and the loss of control over contract funds. The governor, in spite of these concerns, remains committed to further decentralization, arguing that community ownership is the only way to increase the efficiency and effectiveness of social services and to increase the willingness of communities to support additional funding. The 1996 Florida legislature has further complicated the outcome by removing health-related programs from HRS and by creating a new and separate Department of Health to be administered by a physician. The final demise of HRS was accomplished in 1997 when its name was changed to Children and Family Services to describe more accurately its remaining functions.

Finally, restructuring also has included the elimination of the Department of Commerce. Its main function of business development was transferred to an existing nonprofit organization, Enterprise Florida. The state contracted with Enterprise Florida to provide business development services. Other functions of the eliminated Department of Commerce were transferred to other state agencies. The intention was that after an initial period of state fiscal support, Enterprise Florida would become self-supporting through subscriptions from various benefited state enterprises. It is, of course, too soon to say how well this will actually work, but the early results have been mixed. Enterprise Florida continues to be very heavily dependent on state financial support. As a consequence, the state legislature has begun to tighten oversight. In the 1997 legislative session, the director of Enterprise Florida was "called on the carpet" for failing to keep the legislature informed of agency activities. Legislative oversight has reached the point that some now regard Enterprise Florida functionally, that is, as a regular state agency that retains the facade of a public nonprofit organization.

The structural changes over the past seven years have been massive, responding initially to no clearly articulated theory but, in retrospect, reflecting a theory in use (Argyris and Schon 1978) based on three assumptions: (1) smaller agencies are better, (2) citizen/community input is good in health and human services programs, and (3) more gubernatorial control is better. The first and third assumptions have been the subject of debate since the turn of the century in administrative theory; the second assumption comes from Osborne and Gaebler (1992) and the political realities of different community tastes for diverse service packages. The Chiles-MacKay administration seems to have used the seemingly contradictory principles of increasing top policy makers' discretion while at the same time increasing policy input from grassroots citizens, presumably to circumvent middle managers and professional staff who were seen as unresponsive to their wide-ranging administrative and policy reforms. How well these principles work in Florida will take some further time to assess.

Results-Oriented Government and Performance-Based Budgeting

The Frederick Commission set a primary goal of changing to a results-oriented state government and recommended that performance measures be established for all government agencies. A number of follow-up reforms were initiated, spearheaded by the governor's Office of Planning and Budgeting, to give life to the commission's recommendation. Partners in Productivity—a group established in 1987 with membership from Florida Tax Watch, the Florida Council of 100, and the state of Florida—formed a task force to develop comprehensive performance and productivity measures for state government (Florida Department of Management Services 1995, 3–4).

Partners in Productivity was especially visible in overseeing the pilot productivity enhancement programs from 1991 to 1994, which included flexibility in merit pay, budget flexibility whereby partial savings were retained by agencies for other investments, and personnel flexibility experiments.[5] The Partners in Productivity task force realized, however, that it could not develop the detailed performance measures that were needed for all programs the state operated, and this work was carried forward in two major initiatives: The Florida Commission on Government Accountability to the People (GAP Commission) and the Government Performance and Accountability Act of 1994. The GAP Commission was composed largely of business executives who were charged with developing quality-of-life measures for the state of Florida. From the commission's work, seven areas were identified for improving government performance and accountability, and benchmarks were developed in each area to measure the state's progress in improving the well-being of Florida's citizens. The GAP Commission's state benchmarks are now being fully integrated into the budget process after four years of development, public hearings, and extensive agency participation in a Technical Task Force that pulled together the overall framework and indicators for the state's quality of life.

The Government Performance and Accountability Act, containing numerous reforms, was enacted in 1994. The most visible was performance-based budgeting, with a phased-in implementation of five to seven agencies a year until 2002, when all state agencies and their major programs will be functioning under the new budget format. For the major programs, agencies develop input, output, and outcome measures and establish "standards" for each of these measures as well as for actual performance based on prior years' performance level. Once performance-based budgets are approved, managers are given lump-sum funding for the program and flexibility in how the funds can be spent without following rigid line-item budget constraints. The Departments of Revenue and Management Services undertook the first pilot programs in performance-based budget in 1994. Progress has been limited, but it has been generally viewed by the legislative committees, the governor's office, and the involved agencies as positive. The governor's recommended budget for fiscal year 1995–1996 contained lump-sum appropriations and performance measures for general tax administration and property tax administration in the Department of Revenue and for the facilities program in the Department of Management Services.

Strategic Planning

In 1992, after a task force reviewed the state's established agency functional planning process and found it lacking, the governor's Office of Planning and Budgeting initiated an agency strategic planning process that was designed to link the planning process with budget development and submission. The agency strategic planning process included a model format for agencies to follow, including the development of an agency mission and vision, goals, trends and conditions (that documented the problems in society and the obstacles facing each problem's solution), issues, and objectives focused on achieving the agency's goals.

An evaluation of strategic planning in the Department of Corrections (Huang and Berry 1995) found a high proportion of senior managers (94 percent) committed to the strategic planning process, with positive assessments of many of its outcomes, including less-centralized control of department decision making and a view that planning and budgeting were finally becoming linked, which was widely supported as necessary to fulfill strategic planning's promise. Managers also believed that the plan's emphasis on quality management had enabled the department to enhance the quality of its services. Still, a number of negative findings emerged that focused on the lack of integration of the strategic plan into daily management activities and a lack of accountability. Managers did not think they had the resources to involve lower-level staff in the planning process and did not have enough feedback on how their programs and actions were related to the achievement of the plan's goals and objectives.

In the then-existent HRS, the strategic planning process was integrated into the department's two-year effort to decentralize decision making. Service groupings were developed by top staff to show how outcomes cross traditional program lines; the fifteen regional human services boards have used these service outcomes in their needs assessment to find gaps in service requirements. Each of the district strategic plans uses the same framework to prioritize and rank each of the outcomes. The district HHSBs then construct their budget request by these priority outcomes. As the departmental strategic plan is finalized, the HRS secretary and the district boards contract for services for the upcoming year, with the most important outcome indicators and standards spelled out in the contract. According to a senior staffer, the strategic planning process and the outcome orientation allowed service integration at the same time that HRS moved toward greater decentralization of decision making through the district boards. This process is said to have forced integration of programs with similar services and service goals as program resources are cut and workload continues to grow. Nevertheless, others in the advocacy groups and the district offices were more skeptical about whether integration was really occurring. After the failure of the agency's three-year fight with the legislature and the governor's office to stay intact, the reorganization resulted in deep budget cuts for program services and in plummeting morale.

Total Quality Management

When Governor Chiles appointed John Pieno as the new director of the Department of Administration (DOA), he announced that the department would undertake a major initiative to bring TQM to state government. From the beginning, the TQM effort was linked to civil service reform and the deregulation promised through the process of applying sunset provisions to the state's civil service law and starting anew with a substantially different personnel management system. In fact, this linkage was merely a marriage of convenience because the two reforms were linked only in that they were together under the leadership of the DOA. The task forces established to review and rewrite the civil service regulations were not given extensive training in TQM and were not expected to become TQM experts. A few people within the DOA did work full-time on developing training on TQM basics. Just as the training was ready for implementation, however, the DOA training unit was eliminated in a round of budget cuts; as a result, only a few agencies received the basic TQM training. After this, agencies were on their own with regard to developing quality management programs; most never went beyond basic training and fragmented implementation.

In interviews with top agency staff on the results of TQM programs four years after initial efforts began, two themes emerged. First, innovation requires resources, and most of Florida's reinvention efforts not only had no new resources but also coincided with across-the-board budget cuts in 1991–1993. A top agency appointed official said bluntly, "Florida is not committed to TQM because they have not put up the money to pay for it." Another offered, "Our biggest obstacle is the lack of funds to train people properly."

When state agency directors were asked whether the governor should continue major efforts in quality management initiatives, responses reflected their mixed feelings about the four-year TQM experiment. The manager in the agency reporting the most success with quality management stated flatly, "It's our only hope for state government, our only hope to manage more efficiently with fewer resources." Most agency heads wanted to see the governor's office give support for TQM while allowing agencies total flexibility in deciding how to implement it. No agencies wanted the governor's office to start a highly centralized program. Several acknowledged that they needed technical assistance and training resources if they were to make headway. A number of directors said TQM should be folded into other efforts, especially the rule-reduction initiative. "Don't call it TQM," said one agency head, "because of the negative baggage associated with it. Focus on deregulation, but keep it decentralized."

Deregulation and Innovation

In his 1995 state-of-the-state address, Governor Chiles challenged state agencies to cut rules by one-half and asked Lieutenant Governor MacKay to head a task force to achieve that goal. Each agency was asked to review its rules and redline those that were outdated, unnecessary, or redundant. A senior staff member of the Office of Planning and Budgeting recently claimed that they had identified about a one-third reduction in rules through agency efforts and were working on the rest of the promised reduction. Still, this staff person noted the different perceptions that agencies and legislators have about rules: legislators tend to believe that agencies wildly promulgate unnecessary rules without regard to legislative intent, whereas agencies see rules as a way to keep exceptions filed by interest groups from overwhelming their work. Other agency-specific efforts at deregulation, such as the Department of Transportation's proposal to suspend rules for three years, are being developed and implemented. The 1996 legislature passed a law that takes a legislative perspective on this issue by making it easier for the legislature to block the implementation of new rules rather than trying to reduce the number of rules already on the books.

The Chiles administration has tried with some success to address the disincentives that managers face in trying to innovate under tight fiscal constraints. A productivity enhancement program returned about 25 percent of the cuts that agencies sustained in the period of 1991–1992. This was a one-time effort, however, and did not lead to long-lasting changes. In the 1994 budget reform law, a new Innovations Investment Program was established to solicit and fund proposals from agencies, but this, too, has met with little long-term success. Similarly, the administration has been effective in using pilot projects to promote innovation and to initiate systemic reforms under conditions most conducive to success before seeking legislative support for full-scale reform implementation.

A final reform geared to increasing competition and reducing costs was embodied in the Florida Council on Competitive Government, established by the 1994 Government Performance and Accountability Act. The process is "designed to open up state services to competition among the private and public sector in an effort to improve performance and reduce costs" (Florida Council on Competitive Government 1995). The council, composed of the Florida cabinet, other state agency representatives, and a smaller number of private sector representatives, will soon vote on a cost model with specified criteria and procedures for determining whether a project or government services should be advertised for competition. It is still too early to tell how far-reaching this initiative might be, but preliminary discussions include advertising a broad range of agency administrative services for competitive bids. The Department of Commerce was privatized, but the experience has been mixed because after an initial legislative hands-off period, the new public non-profit agency, Enterprise Florida, has been increasingly subjected to legislative controls.

Where Does Reform Stand?

The Chiles administration began its reform effort by using the language of "reinventing government" developed by Osborne and Gaebler (1992). How does its progress to this point measure up against those principles? Any fair observer would certainly conclude that there have been real successes. With agency strategic planning now nearly fully implemented, and with performance-based program budgeting now extended to designated programs for about seven agencies, state government is clearly more results focused; benchmarks from the private and public sectors are used as standards of excellence. Competition in government is considered by the legislature when agency budgets and programs are under review. The governor's office has taken the lead in establishing the Florida Council on Competitive Government, which may bring far-ranging changes based on competition and privatization to government service delivery. The Department of Commerce, a small agency focused on economic development, has been privatized. Nevertheless, most of state government has yet to be brought under the control of these principles (though we would not argue that all of government should be subject to external market competition). Performance-based program budgeting is now in its fourth year of gradual implementation across Florida's state agencies. Twelve agencies submitted program-based performance budgets (for a partial group of each agencies' programs) for fiscal year 1997–1998. Concerns exist (see, for example, Florida Taxwatch 1997), but the budgeting process has survived despite early concerns that it would not be implemented.

State government also is modestly more community oriented and relies more on citizen input. Many agencies now conduct citizen (or "customer") surveys to determine service quality and to solicit input on needed changes. The decentralization of the human services agency and the greater functional homogeneity of state agency structures may draw them closer to their "customers." In another instance, Governor Chiles has made Healthy Start, a prenatal care program for all women designed to prevent low birth weight babies and reduce infant mortality, a priority in his legislative agenda. Healthy Start combines his three-pronged interest in prevention programs, improved conditions for children and families, and public-private community partnerships.

Unlike the experience with the National Performance Review, civil servants have not controlled the reform process. Indeed, public employees in many agencies seem to feel less empowered than before the reform efforts began, and civil service reform, decentralization, privatization, and budget cuts have made employees feel less supported and more under attack.

Is the government more "catalytic"? Does it "steer more and row less"? Perhaps it is modestly more catalytic, but perhaps not. If by "the government" one means the administrative agencies, there is little evidence to support the proposition. The events noted above that have disempowered the civil service are not conditions that encourage risk taking and innovation. If, on the other hand, one is referring to executive and legislative initiatives that support private and nonprofit service delivery, the answer might be "modestly more catalytic."

In sum, modest but real progress has been made toward the general objectives the Chiles–MacKay administration set for itself in 1990. Furthermore, for those interested in learning from Florida's experience, there are important lessons to be grasped.

Lessons from Administrative Reform in Florida

Lesson 1: Reformers tend to use popular writings without determining their application to the local situation. Administrative reform has been fueled by a set of ideas in good currency, popular prescriptions that have attracted the attention and support of local reformers. In the case of Florida's administrative reforms, many of the most popular reform prescriptions were adopted with great fanfare but with little understanding of their application to the local situation.

This has meant that few real models of how the reform rhetoric should function in practice were available, and the process of implementation truly meant creating new processes and new incentives in each agency. Thus, while "a thousand flowers bloomed," many wilted long before real, sustained changes could be made. TQM and civil service reform provides the clearest examples of these failures. Better understood and more tractable reforms—strategic planning and performance-based budgeting—are slowly being implemented and have generally depended on using one or two agencies as models that other agencies can then emulate. Pilot projects (in performance measurement and deregulation) have been used to test reform principles, and these experiments have laid the groundwork for future implementation.

Lesson 2: When administrative reform proposals develop in the context of a political campaign, advocates tend to overpromise results to develop political support. In order to build support for administrative reform among skeptical constituencies, advocates of reform tend to make large claims about the impact reforms will have on government performance. According to its advocates, Florida's administrative reforms were to produce large costs savings, eliminate large numbers of bureaucrats and cut bureaucratic red tape, reduce waste and inefficiency, provide higher quality public services at lower cost, and restore government by the people. The claim of savings to be achieved through civil service reform illustrates the problem of overpromising.

Most studies (e.g., Stepina, Hennessey, and Wechsler 1987) concluded that Florida put too few resources into every aspect of its personnel system. Both the state's personnel agency and the governor's Commission on Civil Service Reform called for increased funding for employee training and development as well as for a market-based pay system. In 1992, estimates of the costs of closing the pay gap were more than $1 billion. Nonetheless, the administration repeatedly promised that civil service reform would result in significant savings, more than $200,000,000 in the first four years. Although the promise of big savings was probably necessary to gain political support, these savings were never realized.

TQM was also started with the promise of significant cost savings, but the reality has been different for most agencies. Only three agencies could supply examples of cost savings when asked by the governor's office, and only two claimed that they had saved large amounts. The Department of Labor and Employment Security has documented more than $1 million in savings in the Division of Unemployment Compensation, and the Department of Revenue has cut nineteen supervisory positions and increased revenue collection fivefold. Most agency directors believe that TQM training and various components of the quality management process (such as problem-solving teams and citizen surveys) have contributed to improved service delivery and helped the agency keep up with increased workloads while absorbing budget cuts. Still, large cost savings across the agencies have not been documented.

Lesson 3: Under fiscal constraints, reforms with low implementation costs and uncertain benefits tend to be favored over reforms with high implementation costs and high benefits. Reformers are under intense pressure from the public, the media, and the political calendar to produce immediate results. Their credibility and political futures depend on being able to demonstrate that positive improvements have occurred as a result of their efforts. As a result of these pressures, there is a tendency to take actions that look good in the media or that appeal to the public but that are easy to do because they involve low implementation costs.

Because Chiles and MacKay had made administrative reform a leading theme of their administration and tied improved administrative performance to future funding requests, the need to gain credibility by achieving immediate results was extremely important. This led them to make a number of largely symbolic gestures, including Buddy MacKay's brief service as secretary of HRS. MacKay spent a short time at HRS, and, in addition to trying to get a handle on a major scandal inherited from the previous administration, he moved a modest number of headquarters staff out into the field, restructured some administrative and support operations and eliminated some jobs, proclaimed a successful reform of an intractable bureaucracy, and moved on to other issues.

Another factor influencing reformers' preference for low-cost efforts is the length of time required to achieve really significant results. Because political attention spans tend to be short, reforms that take any length of time to implement or to achieve results tend to lose support or slip off the agenda. Civil service reform began with the passage of legislation with sunset provisions for the existing career service system and was followed by legislation authorizing the development of a new system as sketched out in the report of the governor's Commission on Civil Service Reform. Once legislation was passed, however, other issues came to the forefront, and the administration seemed to lose interest. Actions taken on other reform projects (i.e., administrative restructuring) further decreased the attention given to civil service reform. After several years, there were few resources and little activity devoted to this effort.

Total quality management provides a different kind of example. TQM began as a fairly decentralized process that agency directors could tailor to meet their own program needs. Central support from the governor's Department of Management Services consisted primarily of limited train-the-trainer courses on TQM basics without more extensive technical assistance. Most agencies highlighted some TQM processes in their 1991–1993 strategic plans, in keeping with Governor Chiles's inclusion of TQM in his reinvention efforts. Although TQM was seen as a way to change the organizational culture and front-line employees' approach to their job, a comprehensive survey of state agency directors by the governor's office in 1995 found a low level of TQM activity in most agencies. Even such agencies as the Department of Corrections, which had engaged in extensive TQM training for staff, reported only sporadic organizational changes, primarily linked to using crosscutting ad hoc task forces. Only one agency, the Department of Revenue, has fully embraced quality management practices and changed its overall culture. Sustained leadership (more than six to seven years), access to new resources, and persistence in implementing quality management even through dead-end efforts have clearly paid off for the agency and prove how extraordinary its success is among state agencies.

On the other hand, the administration was much more successful in reorganizing agencies. These reforms were relatively easy to carry out because the principles of reorganization are understood relatively well, and, no matter how you reorganize, there is a widely known theory that provides justification for your approach. There also are established legal procedures and formal and informal routines for carrying out reorganizations. From this perspective, reorganization carries relatively low implementation costs. Little follow-up has been conducted to show whether the cost savings and other efficiencies attributed to reorganization have actually occurred as a result of the reform, however.

Lesson 4: When reforms accomplish less than was promised, they are perceived as failures and tend to lose support. Because advocates tend to overpromise results and because at best there is substantial skepticism about claims, the actual accomplishments of reform are often perceived as disappointing. When reforms produce only minimal improvements in service delivery or reduce costs only a little, they are regarded as failures. In the early days of the administration, reengineering experiments in the Department of Revenue and the Department of Labor and Employment Security were promoted as providing evidence that government could be made to work substantially better. These projects involved the most routine work activities in two of the state's smaller agencies. It was soon clear that these efforts were very limited in their impact and in their generalizability to other government functions. Eventually, after an auditor general's report found little evidence of any lasting effect on agency operations, the legislature withdrew special legislation allowing the experiments. The disappointment extended to the public. Chiles's popularity sank in the polls, and he narrowly escaped defeat when he ran for a second term in 1994, although he came into office via a landslide in 1990.

Lesson 5: Because political support for administrative reform tends to erode and because reform takes longer than expected, sustained leadership from within the agencies is critical for success. Although nearly everyone supports improving the efficiency and effectiveness of government operations, relatively few stakeholders understand the complex issues involved in reforming administrative systems or are prepared to engage in or support the extended effort and many compromises required to improve public management. Elected officials offer rhetorical support for administrative reform and, in the case of the Chiles-MacKay administration, have made considerable efforts to change the policy framework. Nevertheless, it is also true that quick political gains rather than long-term improvements in service delivery or financial management are important. Citizens are often cynical or naive about reform. The cynics distrust the motives of the reformers and have low expectations about the prospects for reform. Naive citizens see reform in terms of catchy phrases—"Run government more like a business"—and have little patience for those who suggest administrative reform is long and hard work. Because of past experiences, those most immediately and directly affected by administrative reform, public managers and employees, tend to be fearful of costs and skeptical about the benefits of strategies that have political legitimacy but no systematic testing. Furthermore, although many believe that administrative reform is necessary, they see much of the reform agenda as driven by antigovernment rhetoric, cost cutting, and downsizing rather than by a genuine desire for improved government performance.

Government reinvention efforts in Florida coincided with major budget cuts resulting from revenue shortfalls. Thus, many in the agencies suspected the reinvention rhetoric was just a cover for the deep personnel and program cuts that were going to come. For example, passage of the Florida Education Accountability Act in 1991 shifted planning and outcome responsibilities to individual schools and required a transformation of the Department of Education from a mission of regulation to one emphasizing technical assistance. In attempting to make this transformation, the Division of Public Schools used strategic planning, crosscutting task forces, and organizational development processes to redesign the division's mission and new ways of carrying out its work. Although the plans were fully developed, very little implementation occurred, leading one bureau chief to remark, "That was the fastest failure of organizational change I've ever seen." Administrative staff joked openly with black humor in their planning meetings that they were laying the groundwork to cut positions to make up needed budget savings and mostly did not see these efforts as ways really to improve their ability to work. As further ammunition for skeptical attitudes, some Republican policy makers (including 1994 Republican gubernatorial candidate Jeb Bush) openly called for the abolition of the department.

Among agency directors who assessed why TQM faced difficulties in implementation in their agencies, a frequent response was that midlevel managers opposed it. One respondent said, "Supervisors and midlevel managers opposed employee empowerment efforts." Explanations included the shift of power away from managers and the unwillingness to take risks. One agency director who had not participated in early pilot projects to return agency savings back to the agencies said that "risk taking is forbidden or prohibited. If our agency achieves efficiencies and cost savings due to TQM, then the governor or legislature cuts our budget and takes the savings." This was not just abstract speculation. Sales commissions in the Department of Lottery were canceled by the legislature when word leaked out about their size. Similarly, savings from work restructuring in the Department of Labor and Employment Security were taken back by the legislature and not shared with employees as promised. The attempt to implement a frontline change in management and decision making seems destined to fail without the support of frontline supervisors and their bosses. In addition, without added resources or incentives to be efficient, many managers see no positive value in radically restructuring how they work.

Sustained leadership also permits the continuity needed to implement complex reforms. As the Chiles-MacKay administration moves further into its second term, sustained efforts within certain agencies is clearly paying off both in terms of the success of certain reinvention efforts and in the increased potential of others to be successful. For example, performance-based budgeting is being implemented only now, although the success of the Department of Revenue in moving to an outcome-oriented budget for its programs has shown that this format can be developed. It also took more than a full year to develop a working agreement between the governor's office and the house and senate appropriations committees about how the budgeting process would actually unfold. It also took the first year to get agency staff conversant with the intent and format of the new process, despite extensive training opportunities and communication between the Office of Planning and Budgeting and agency budget offices. Reform efforts may depend on the easy initial wins to look successful, but once these have been achieved, sustained leadership, flexibility in implementation methods, and access to additional resources for innovative experiments as well as training are going to be needed.

Lesson 6: Unintended consequences, both positive as well as negative, are endemic to administrative reform. The reform initiatives were not developed as a comprehensive package, but rather in response to particular pressures and ideas. As a consequence, the interactions between initiatives were not considered fully and in some cases had unintended effects. The clearest example of this was the destructive effects of the agency reorganizations on TQM initiatives. Incipient TQM efforts in a number of agencies were derailed by the relatively low-cost and high-visibility reorganization efforts. Another example is related to public support for administrative reform, which was based largely on the claim that it would lead to greater economy and efficiency in government. This was a credible appeal for a variety of reasons, not the least of which was that Florida had experienced significant revenue shortfalls and budget cuts. This appeal was undercut, however, when Governor Chiles decided to pay his top-level appointees substantially more than their predecessors had earned. The move not only lent credibility to Republican charges that Chiles was not serious about cutting back government, but, perhaps more important, also was a source of profound disappointment to the administration's rank-and-file supporters. When Chiles spoke to state employees, he urged sacrifice to improve the lives of Floridians. After he raised the salaries of his top appointees (and purchased a highly publicized ice maker for his poolside drinks), there was a palpable loss of enthusiasm for sacrifice and administrative reform.

Although the reinvention efforts cover a broad range of organizational culture and structural reforms, significant learning can occur and has occurred from one reform effort that can be applied to enrich the implementation of the next effort. A brief discussion of how the Department of Revenue has integrated these reform efforts into an overall reinvention strategy illustrates how crosscutting reforms become more than the sum of their parts when the organizational culture shifts toward a "learning organization" approach (Argyris and Schon 1978). The Department of Revenue began strategic planning in the late 1980s under the leadership of Tom Herndon, who was widely perceived as one of the state's best managers. In addition to its strategic planning process, the agency was designated in the period of 1990–1993 as one of two agencies given authority to develop pilot projects to implement quality management, flexibility on personnel rules and bonuses, and program budgeting.[6] The agency persisted in its attempt to implement team-based decision making, beginning again after the first year's effort did not produce the desired results. Its use of monies from productivity enhancement programs and vacant positions to provide bonuses to data entry staff based on meeting higher performance goals became well-known throughout state government and contributed to a real sense in the agency that difficult organizational change could be positive for both individual employees and the organization as a whole.

Even when Tom Herndon left the Department of Revenue to become Governor Chiles's chief of staff, the new executive director, Larry Fuchs, made a commitment to continue the reinvention efforts and kept Jim Zingale, deputy executive director, in place to ensure continuity. Team-based and decentralized decision making has been widely adopted, with enough success that early resistance has been overcome. The agency discusses its operations and budgets against the goal of enhancing quality services. A senior manager in the department summarized their philosophy about reinventing government: "Fewer rules won't change the way government works, quality will. Rules are necessary when the culture has deteriorated. By cutting rules, we are attacking the symptoms and not the disease. The disease is that we have got very efficient at doing the wrong things."

At the Department of Revenue, the 1993–1994 performance-based program budgeting was tied closely to the department's quality management initiatives. As the departmental leadership developed critical outcome measures for its general tax administration program, they asked themselves, "Are these the critical outcomes we should be achieving? Do we need to be doing all the activities we currently fund? Should we be shifting funds to higher-priority areas? What are our core processes that cut across current division structures? And how can we best organize so that divisions work more effectively together?" As a result of performance-based budgeting and the department's core process mapping, the agency reorganized to place more emphasis on its key processes. The insights gained from performance-based program budgeting into the agency's priorities, now reflected in some 200 to 250 performance measures, have been used as feedback to advance continuous improvement in the operations and management of that program.

Conclusions

The lessons of Florida's administrative reform effort are complex, reflecting the real challenges and opportunities encountered in reinventing government. Lawton Chiles and Buddy MacKay promised that they would fundamentally change government and government operations. Their promises raised expectations to unrealistic levels, and, as a consequence, the perception of failure set in early. Still, Chiles and MacKay were not politically naive, and they attempted to build support for their efforts by involving a diverse set of groups on the assumption that these reforms would benefit all of the affected stakeholders—citizens, state government managers, and public employees. In spite of their efforts at coalition building, the scope of change was so vast that the conflict and uncertainties generated defied any disciplined monitoring of the implementation process. Over the six-year reform process, as the perception of failure began to develop, there was a tendency to move from the hard and costly reforms, such as TQM, to a greater emphasis on technical and less-expensive reforms, such as reorganization, performance appraisal bonuses, and performance-based budgeting.

The reform process was greatly affected by unpredicted events, the most important of which were serious budget shortfalls and the election of a Republican majority in the state senate. The senate proved to be far more interested in reducing the size of government than in reforming it. Budget shortfalls virtually assured that expensive reforms would be abandoned or undertaken by persistent agency leaders without much fiscal support from the governor's office. What little progress was made in changing the culture of government was largely lost in those agencies that were reorganized by the governor's office, which over the period of 1993–1996 placed more emphasis on reorganization and other structural reforms than on quality management initiatives. A survey conducted by the governor's office in 1995 suggests that TQM efforts usually foundered or were abandoned when an agency was reorganized. As a consequence, Florida's reforms have gone slowly and have had an uneven impact. The reformers themselves were not without blame for these results. The administration overpromised what would come from its efforts, too often resorted to symbolic over substantive change, lost interest at critical moments, and showed too little confidence in the rank-and-file administrators critical to the implementation of reform.

Nonetheless, some important changes have occurred, and current efforts to deregulate government and to link budgeting to measurable outcomes show considerable promise. Several state agencies with strong continuous leadership have been successful in implementing comprehensive quality programs and have re-created their workplace. Whether the promise will be more broadly fulfilled will probably depend on the strength of leadership from professional administrators and their ability to sustain interest and support among their staff people as well as elected officials. Florida does not have a strong tradition of professional civil servants. The "every man for himself" culture that was described many years ago by V. O. Key (1949) has institutionalized a professional culture that emphasizes loyalty to persons rather than to standards of practice. That said, there are also major changes in the institutionalized environment that may lend energy to the incipient reform efforts, including good-government groups such as Florida Taxwatch and award programs that promote innovation, quality improvements, and productivity reforms. Pilot projects and a few exemplar agencies provide models and technical advisors to agencies lower on the learning curve. A core of professional staff in the governor's Office of Planning and Budgeting has also supported quality management initiatives and state agency innovations in a range of areas. The small successes in strategic planning, performance-based budgeting, reengineering and core process mapping, and even TQM will make it easier to institute reforms in other parts of the state government if there is the "local leadership" and desire to do so.

Some have suggested that the slow progress of Florida's reform represents a failure of theory. Although it is true that there was no clear articulation of a theory of administrative reform, there were clearly articulated objectives, primarily coming from the "reinvention" literature. On balance, the pockets of reform are consistent with these objectives of anticipatory government, the emphasis on competition and market orientation, more community and citizen orientation, and the focus on outcomes rather than inputs.

Notes

1. The reasons for the ebb and flow of reform fashion is beyond the scope of this chapter, but it seems to be influenced by private sector management rhetoric (Chackerian 1996). For a particularly interesting discussion of the ebb and flow of private sector management rhetoric, see Barley and Kunda (1992).

2. The methods of data collection for this study included a review of the primary government reports on administrative reform and a series of structured interviews with Chiles administration officials on programs and agency efforts. We also had access to the transcripts from the governor's office of interviews with agency directors discussing quality management programs in their agencies and assessing impacts from these programs. Quotations appearing in the chapter are drawn from these sources. The three authors have each written on aspects of the Florida reforms and have consulted with the administration in the reform process: Wechsler and Chackerian served as consultants to the Chiles administration on civil service reform; Berry served as consultant to the governor's office on performance-based budgeting; both Wechsler and Berry consulted with numerous state agencies on strategic planning and quality management initiatives; and Chackerian consulted on agency restructuring.

3. James Krog, interview with Richard Chackerian and Frank Sherwood, Tallahassee, Florida, December 23, 1990.

4. And to garner needed votes to prevent a veto override of 1995 legislation that allowed the state government to bring suit against tobacco companies to recover Medicaid costs incurred in treating smoking-related health problems.

5. These pilot programs are detailed in a series of reports, including Productivity Ad-

visory Group, *Interim Report;* Productivity Advisory Group, *Final Report;* and the Florida Office of the Auditor General, *Special Review of the Personnel and Budgeting Pilot Projects Administered by the Department of Labor and Employment Services and the Department of Revenue.*

6. A top-level staff person for one of the appropriations committees noted that the Department of Revenue was selected as a pilot for performance measurement because legislators trusted its leadership and believed it was well managed.

References

Argyris, Chris, and Donald Schon. 1978. *Organizational Learning: A Theory of Action Perspective.* Reading, Mass.: Addison-Wesley.

Barley, Stephen R., and Gideon Kunda. 1992. "Design and Devotion: Surges of Rational and Normative Ideologies of Control in Managerial Discourse." *Administrative Science Quarterly* 37: 363–99.

Barzelay, Michael. 1992. *Breaking through Bureaucracy: A New Vision for Managing in Government.* Berkeley, Calif.: University of California Press.

Chackerian, Richard. 1994a. "The Bureaucracy: Historical Development and Reform." In *The Florida Public Policy Management System,* edited by Richard Chackerian. Tallahassee, Fla.: Florida Center for Public Management.

———. 1994b. "Agency Splits, Creations and Consolidations in Florida: Why Is It Done and What Are the Consequences?" Paper delivered at a special conference on governmental reform, University of South Florida, Tampa, Florida.

———. 1996. "State Government Reorganization: 1900–1985." *Journal of Public Administration Research and Theory* 6, no.1: 25–48.

DiIulio, John, Jr., ed. 1994. *Deregulating the Public Service: Can Government Be Improved?* Washington, D.C.: Brookings Institute.

Florida Council on Competitive Government. 1995. *Orientation Package: Procedures and Guidelines.* Tallahassee, Fla.: Florida Council on Competitive Government.

Florida Department of Management Services. 1995. *Building a Better Government.* Tallahassee, Fla.: Florida Department of Management Services.

Florida Office of the Auditor General. 1993. *Special Review of the Personnel and Budgeting Pilot Projects Administered by the Department of Labor and Employment Services and the Department of Revenue.* Tallahassee, Fla.: Florida Office of the Auditor General.

Florida Taxwatch. 1997. *Putting Taxpayers First: Steps to Improve Florida's Performance-Based Budgeting.* Tallahassee, Fla.: Florida Taxwatch.

Frederick Commission. 1991. *Report.* Tallahassee, Fla.: Florida Department of Administration.

Governor's Commission for Government by the People. 1991. *Final Report.* Tallahassee, Fla.: State of Florida.

Huang, James, and Frances Stokes Berry. 1995. *Strategic Planning in the Florida Department of Corrections.* Tallahassee, Fla.: Florida Department of Corrections.

Key, V. O. 1949. *Southern Politics in State and Nation.* New York: Knopf.

Meyer, J. W., and B. Rowan. 1983. "Institutionalized Organizations: Formal Structure as Myth and Ceremony." In *Organizational Environments: Ritual and Rationality,* edited by J. W. Meyer and W. Richard Scott. Newbury Park, Calif.: Sage.

Meyer, Marshall W., ed. 1979. *Change in Public Bureaucracies.* London: Cambridge University Press.

National Commission on the State and Local Public Service. 1993. *Hard Truths/Tough Choices: An Agenda for State and Local Reform.* Albany, N.Y.: Nelson Rockefeller Institute of Government.

National Performance Review. 1993. *From Red Tape to Results: Creating a Government That Works Better and Costs Less.* Washington, D.C.: U.S. Government Printing Office.

Osborne, David. 1988. *Laboratories of Democracy.* Boston: Harvard Business School Press.

Osborne, David, and Ted Gaebler. 1992. *Reinventing Government: How the Entrepreneurial Spirit Is Transforming the Public Sector.* Reading, Mass.: Addison-Wesley.

Productivity Advisory Group. 1993. *Interim Report.* Tallahassee, Fla.: State of Florida.

———. 1994. *Final Report.* Tallahassee, Fla.: State of Florida.

Radin, Beryl A., and Willis D. Hawley. 1988. *The Politics of Federal Reorganization.* New York: Pergamon Press.

Stepina, Lee, Harry W. Hennessey, and Barton Wechsler, eds. 1987. *Florida's Compensation System: A Comprehensive Study of Career Service Pay and Benefit.* Tallahassee, Fla: Florida State University.

Thompson, Frank. 1993. *Revitalizing State and Local Public Service.* San Francisco: Jossey-Bass.

U.S. General Accounting Office. 1994. *Managing for Results.* Washington, D.C.: U.S. Government Printing Office.

Wechsler, Barton. 1994. "Reinventing Florida's Civil Service System: The Failure of Reform?" *Review of Public Personnel Administration* 14: 64–76.

Conclusion

Jocelyn M. Johnston

THIS BOOK REPRESENTS the work of leading scholars in the field of public management—scholars who belong to a community interested in acquiring a better understanding of how reform and innovation occur and how managers can facilitate the success of efforts to improve government and governance. The scholars who have contributed to this volume span a wide spectrum of the disciplines that comprise the field of public management. They include specialists in interest group representation in the policy process, social science theorists, experts on the administrative state and democracy, management and leadership theorists, implementation scholars, policy analysts, and organization theorists. The diversity of their scholarly interest is indicative of the scope of challenges that face public managers. The charge for public management scholars is, consequently, one that requires an interdisciplinary perspective and demands a broad view of the work of public managers.

The chapters in this book clearly demonstrate that public management scholars have embraced that charge. Researchers in the field continue to enlighten our understanding of the processes and structures that affect government management. They formulate new theories and refine and test existing theories in order to understand better the determinants of effective public management and organizations. Despite the substantial contributions of scholars—and practitioners—to the field, many important gaps remain. Yet we know that sometimes government performance can and does improve and that innovation and reform are successfully adopted and implemented. We recognize successful public management reform when we see it, and we can sometimes articulate how and why it happened.

The need for government management reform often goes unquestioned, however. Too often, we tend to assume that reform can and will improve government. Clearly, citizens find many government services lacking, and their disenchantment is often greatest with those services provided by the federal government (Advisory Commission on Intergovernmental Relations 1994)— the level of government on which many of the chapters in this book focus. Yet this should hardly surprise us. Services and programs properly carried out at the federal level are often characterized by attributes that inhibit individual "customer" satisfaction. Many goods and services provided by the federal government have "public" features that render them less amenable to private provision. The work of federal managers is further complicated by the nature of federal government services, which often keep federal-level managers distant from citizens or "customers" with infrequent, if any, direct contact (Kettl 1995). In addition, managers in all levels of government, plagued during the last two decades by serious resource constraints, hear voices that constantly clamor for a government that does more with less. Unfortunately, the clamor is often reinforced by unenlightened—and sometimes counterproductive—demands for further reforms and improvements.

Elected officials and citizens want public managers who can deliver a government that is more efficient and more responsive. Nevertheless, the extent to which managers can "deliver" may often be determined in part by the function of the agency and by the level of government in which the agency is located. Frameworks for reform are therefore shaped by the missions of government units and organizations, and those vary greatly—across different governmental agencies and certainly across levels of government (Kettl 1995). Consequently, sweeping generalizations about effective public management are difficult. Some common conditions prevail, however. All public managers work in organizations molded by political environments. This fact complicates their efforts to maximize managerial efficiency (Behn, chapter 3), and it affects the incentives that determine the inclination of managers to embrace, promote, and implement reform (Larkey and Devereux, chapter 7; Meyers and Dillon, chapter 10; Ingraham and Jones, chapter 9; Berry, Chackerian, and Wechsler, chapter 14). In addition, public managers often confront problems that defy easy solutions—problems with which social science theory and research continue to wrestle (Mohr, chapter 1; Weiss, chapter 2).

The Challenges of Public Management

Government reform is inherently political. How can bureaucrats manage the dual objectives of managerial effectiveness and efficiency, and accountability to the people, their representatives, and the laws of the land? Herein lies one of the greatest challenges for public management. Complex accountability systems seriously confound the work of public managers (Romzek and Dubnick 1994; Romzek and Ingraham 1994), and they frequently preclude strict comparisons between public and private management tasks (Moe 1994).

Kettl (1995) emphasizes that "the problem of reinventing government really revolves around these issues: Just what *do* citizens expect government to do? How can the bureaucratic power required to do the job well be held accountable to elected officials and, in the end, to the people?" (75). The first question is one that must be answered primarily through our political process. Assuming it can be answered satisfactorily, we can turn to the second question, which has been addressed by several chapters in this book.

Simply put, the political framework within which public managers function limits their ability to offer the "efficient" government sought by reformers. For example, Larkey and Devereux (chapter 7) suggest that reforms designed to make public budgetary processes more "democratic" have seriously altered the incentives for budgetary decision makers and that they work against effective, or "efficient," budgeting. These authors argue that the "openness movement . . . greatly increases the stakes of taking a position against specific interests in favor of broader interests." Similarly, Berry, Chackerian, and Wechsler (chapter 14) point out that the success of Florida's government reinvention process was compromised to some extent by efforts to incorporate the views of multiple citizen groups. On the other hand, real program gains can often be realized from administrative processes that are more open and that strive for responsiveness. Golden (chapter 12) and Kaboolian (chapter 13) provide insights into how public managers respond to citizen input and how managers' responses to that input shape their efforts to serve elected officials and citizens. Balancing these dual objectives—responsiveness and efficiency—is a fundamental component of public management, yet it is one that is frequently overlooked by reformers. As Moe (1994) notes, reform is too often driven by the emphasis on "customer satisfaction" at the expense of political accountability (or, in more explicit terms, by the ascendancy of economic considerations over law).

Public management scholars know that efforts to view public management as isolated from politics are misguided; there are dangers in assuming a strict distinction between "rowing" and "steering." Yet current federal reform rhetoric minimizes the importance of the political environment within which public organizations function. For example, the influence of the law (determined by political processes) on public managers (Moe 1994; Rosenbloom 1993; Frederickson 1996; Rosenbloom and Ross 1994; Cooper 1994; O'Leary and Wise 1991) receives little attention by reinvention proponents. In addition, federal reinvention reforms have virtually ignored the "people's" branch of government—i.e., Congress. Public management analysts are well versed in the importance of all three branches of government—executive, legislative, judicial—to public managers in all government levels. The political and legal structures that constrain public managers have a powerful impact on managers and their ability to implement or influence reform (Evans and Wamsley, chapter 5; Wise and Stengård, chapter 6; Roberts, chapter 4). Nonetheless, reinvention advocates continue to stress values—such as efficiency and economy—that are often antithetical to democratic responsiveness.

In addition to the effects of political institutions and structures on public management and reform, the tendency to combine reforms with "downsizing"—or the reduction of resources—also challenges public management (Berry, Chackerian, and Wechsler, chapter 14). Ingraham and Jones (chapter 9) document the difficulties faced by public managers who have to deal with uncertainty, a loss of resources, and the need to manage change, downsizing, and substantial changes in their work roles. Middle managers, in particular, who are often targets of the downsizing rhetoric, are forced to manage competing objectives while doing "more with less." Their skepticism about the true objectives of reform can hardly be criticized, given their position relative to the politics of resource allocation. For frontline workers implementing welfare reform in California, the incentives to adopt the reforms fully are weak and mixed. The predilection of workers to reform their interactions with clients is further hampered by inadequate resources. Similarly, the need to replace diminishing resources, discussed by Welch and Bretschneider (chapter 11), provides yet another illustration of the impact of resource constraints on the adaptation of public managers to a "reinvention" environment. At the very least, such resource constraints limit the range of financial incentives with which public managers—and their staffs—can be motivated. Although other incentives—such as strong motivational leadership—are certainly available (Behn, chapter 3; Meyers and Dillon, chapter 10), the absence of financial resources adds to the management challenges faced in the public sector.

Management in the public sector can and should use lessons from private sector management practices whenever possible, as suggested by Thompson and Johansen (chapter 8). The applicability of private sector and market mechanisms, however, must be tempered by the unique political and institutional features in which public management must function. Public managers are challenged by myriad, competing interests, accountabilities to multiple parties, and wary scrutiny from citizens whose dissatisfaction is sometimes unavoidable. As a result, it is inappropriate to expect public managers to "produce" with exclusively private managerial tools. In addition to political challenges, public managers are also charged with providing services that can often be categorized as public goods and that further compromise their ability to "borrow" strategies from the private sector.

Finally, public managers are at the helm of the "implementation" phase of the policy process. All too often, however, they are responsible for implementing policies that are theoretically unsound and invalid (Pressman and

Wildavsky 1979). Thus, the successful management of reform requires a foundation of valid public policy.

What We *Do* Know about Effective Reform and Innovation

The state of public management theory is still maturing. Yet even if public management is only a "distinctive approach to knowledge, rather than a distinctive body of theory" (Bozeman 1993, 17), it does offer some coherence to the varied problems faced by managers in the public sector. Public management theorists are like most other social scientists; they frequently draw from related social science disciplines to inform their conceptualizations of public management. For example, elements of rational choice theory, which provide insights into the motivations that guide individual public manager actions, are used to understand better how and why public managers do what they do. Public management scholars have clarified the need for award systems that are based on a sound understanding of the motives of managers and of how those managers calculate the costs and benefits associated with their decisions. As a result of this knowledge, the incentives for public managers to engage in reform effectively can be carefully analyzed in an effort to understand better the dynamics of management reform (Larkey and Devereux, chapter 7; Ingraham and Jones, chapter 9; Meyers and Dillon, chapter 10; Welch and Bretschneider, chapter 11). In addition, specific management strategies (Behn, chapter 3; Roberts, chapter 4) can be used to enhance the success of reform management, particularly when those strategies are tailored to individual organizational missions and contexts (Kettl 1995; Peters 1994).

Thus, despite its youthful state, public management theory *does* enhance our understanding of the intricacies of managing the work of government and of managing public sector reforms. The complex challenges that face public managers, however, are further complicated by the inescapable fact that we are still very limited in our capacity to "produce" reform and innovation. As Paul Light (1994) notes, "Governments can *increase the probability* that innovation will both occur and endure" (65). The work of the authors in this book represents efforts to identify factors that increase that probability.

What We *Don't* Know

Despite significant contributions from public management scholars, many of the field's theoretical propositions remain underdeveloped (Lynn 1996). Mohr (chapter 1) offers a persuasive explanation for this problem. He reminds us that for the social sciences in general, and for public management in particular, it is likely that theories are permanently limited to probabilistic explanations. Because we study human behavior, which is intensely complex, our ability to construct invariably valid theories is severely constrained. Current reformers seem to ignore this principle. For example, the National Performance Review clearly articulates the problem that drives reform (government can do better) and the ultimate objective of the reform (government will do better), but because of its "atheoretic" approach (Ingraham and Jones, chapter 9), it fails to wrestle with the thorny problems associated with limited social science theory: which interventions will work (Weiss, chapter 2)? When will they work? Most important, *why* will they work? Will X *cause* Y?

Many of the chapters in this volume wrestle with these questions. For example, Larkey and Devereux (chapter 7) remind us that one reason for the failure of past efforts to reform budgetary processes is that "there has always been too much pretense that we can know the effects of adopting policy A versus policy B. The reality is that the effects of A or B depend on poorly understood causal mechanisms and conditions that are not easily forecast. The difficulty is compounded because the research that would improve our understanding of the causal mechanisms or improve our forecasts of base conditions is usually infeasible intellectually, politically, or both." Similarly, Meyers and Dillon (chapter 10) note that the implementation of welfare reforms has been hampered by the "black box" that intervenes between policy inputs and outputs (see also Mohr, chapter 1, and Weiss, chapter 2).

These questions remain elusive, and they will continue to challenge public management scholars for the foreseeable future. This is certainly not the last wave of government reform. Nonetheless, the efforts of public management scholars to understand and explain the management of current reforms better will, we hope, enhance the success of future reforms. Furthermore, we are confident that the scholarship contained in this volume will contribute substantially to existing theory and to the application of those theories in the interest of managerial effectiveness in a democratic society.

References

Advisory Commission on Intergovernmental Relations. 1994. *Changing Public Attitudes on Governments and Taxes.* Washington, D.C.: Advisory Commission on Intergovernmental Relations.

Bozeman, Barry. 1993. "Searching for the Core of Public Management." In *Public Management: The State of the Art,* edited by Barry Bozeman. San Francisco: Jossey-Bass.

Cooper, Phillip J. 1994. "Reinvention and Employee Rights: The Role of the Courts." In *New Paradigms for Government,* edited by Patricia W. Ingraham, Barbara S. Romzek, and Associates. San Francisco: Jossey-Bass.

Frederickson, H. George. 1996. "Comparing the Reinventing Government Movement with the New Public Administration." *Public Administration Review* 54, no. 3: 263–70.

Kettl, Donald F. 1995. "Building Lasting Reforms: Enduring Questions, Missing Answers." In *Inside the Reinvention Machine: Appraising Governmental Reform,* edited by Donald F. Kettl and John J. DiIulio, Jr. Washington, D.C.: Brookings Institution.

Light, Paul. 1994. "Creating Government That Encourages Innovation." In *New Paradigms for Government,* edited by Patricia W. Ingraham, Barbara S. Romzek, and Associates. San Francisco: Jossey-Bass.

Lynn, Laurence E., Jr. 1996. *Public Management as Art, Science, and Profession.* Chatham, N.J.: Chatham House.

Moe, Ronald. 1994. "The 'Reinventing Government' Exercise: Misinterpreting the Problem, Misjudging the Consequences." *Public Administration Review* 54, no. 2: 111–22.

O'Leary, Rosemary, and Charles Wise. 1991. "Public Managers, Judges and Legislators: Redefining the 'New Partnership.'" *Public Administration Review* 52, no. 4: 316–17.

Peters, B. Guy. 1994. "New Visions of Government and the Public Service." In *New Paradigms for Government,* edited by Patricia W. Ingraham, Barbara S. Romzek, and Associates. San Francisco: Jossey-Bass.

Pressman, Jeffrey, and Aaron Wildavsky. 1979. *Implementation.* Berkeley, Calif.: University of California Press.

Romzek, Barbara S., and Melvin J. Dubnick. 1994. "Issues of Accountability in Flexible Personnel Systems." In *New Paradigms for Government,* edited by Patricia W. Ingraham, Barbara S. Romzek, and Associates. San Francisco: Jossey-Bass.

Romzek, Barbara S., and Patricia W. Ingraham. 1994. "The Challenges Facing American Public Service." In *New Paradigms for Government,* edited by Patricia W. Ingraham, Barbara S. Romzek, and Associates. San Francisco: Jossey-Bass.

Rosenbloom, David H. 1993. "Have an Administrative Rx? Don't Forget the Politics!" *Public Administration Review* 53, no. 6: 503–7.

Rosenbloom, David H., and Bernard H. Ross. 1994. "Administrative Theory, Political Power, and Government Reform." In *New Paradigms for Government,* edited by Patricia W. Ingraham, Barbara S. Romzek, and Associates. San Francisco: Jossey-Bass.

Contributors

Robert D. Behn is professor of public policy at Duke University and director of its Governors Center. His recent articles include "The Big Questions of Public Management" in *Public Administration Review* and "Public Management: Should It Strive to be Art, Science, or Engineering?" in the *Journal of Public Administration Research and Theory*. He wonders why the eighty-year goal of winning a World Series has not helped the Boston Red Sox become an innovative organization.

Frances S. Berry is an associate professor in the Reubin O'D. Askew School of Public Administration and Policy at Florida State University. She has held senior management and consulting positions at the Council of State Governments and the Florida Center for Public Management at Florida State University. Her research interests include strategic management, policy and management innovation, and state public policy. She has published articles in numerous journals, including the *Public Administration Review,* the *American Political Science Review,* the *American Journal of Political Science,* the *Public Productivity and Management Review,* and the *Policy Studies Journal.*

Stuart Bretschneider is a professor of public administration at Syracuse University's Maxwell School of Citizenship and Public Affairs. He received his Ph.D. in public administration from the Ohio State University in 1980. His primary fields of research include public organizations' use of information technology and the effects of those technologies on public organizations; how public organizations employ forecasting activities; and how sector differences affect administrative processes. He has also worked on numerous funded projects associated with the evaluation of public policy in both the energy and environmental areas. A past president of the International Institute of Forecasters (IIF), Dr. Bretschneider is a director of the IIF and an associate editor the *International Journal of Forecasting.* He is also the managing editor of the *Journal of Public Administration Research and Theory.* An avid *Star Trek* fan, Dr. Bretschneider is also the director of the Center for Technology and Information Policy at the Maxwell School, where he also coordinates the Ph.D. program in public administration.

Richard Chackerian is professor of public administration and policy at Florida State University and director of the Ph.D. program. His main research interest is organization structure and change.

Erik A. Devereux is senior lecturer in politics at Carnegie Mellon University, where he also serves as director of the Master of Science in Public Policy and Management Program. He was trained in the political economy of the United States at the Massachusetts Institute of Technology (B.S. 1985) and at the University of Texas at Austin (Ph.D. 1993), and his research mainly focuses on the politics of mass media. Devereux is the author of several articles on media politics during the 1960s and of the textbook *Political Analysis: Interests, Institutions, and Possibilities in the Policy Process.* In collaboration with Patrick Larkey, Devereux is conducting a multiyear project on political incentives in democratic policy processes.

Nara Dillon is a Ph.D. candidate in the Department of Political Science, University of California, Berkeley. She is a scholar of comparative politics with a particular interest in welfare programs in the United States and the Republic of China.

Karen G. Evans is a doctoral candidate at the Center for Public Policy at Virginia Polytechnic Institute and State University. Her research interests center on pragmatism in administrative structure and reform and on the new sciences. Her work has been published in the *Public Administration Review* and *Administrative Theory and Praxis,* and she has coauthored entries in *The International Encyclopedia of Public Policy and Administration.*

H. George Frederickson is the Edwin O. Stene Distinguished Professor of Public Administration at the University of Kansas. He is the editor-in-chief of the *Journal of Public Administration Research and Theory* and the author of *The Spirit of Public Administration.* He is a past president of the American Society for Public Administration and a fellow of the National Academy of Public Administration.

Marissa Martino Golden is assistant professor of political science at Bryn Mawr College. She is a past recipient of the Leonard D. White Award and the author of the forthcoming book *Bureaucratic Behavior in a Political Setting: Exit,*

Voice, and Loyalty during the Reagan Years. She received her Ph.D. from the University of California, Berkeley.

Patricia W. Ingraham is a professor of public administration at the Maxwell School of Citizenship and Public Affairs, Syracuse University, where she also serves as the director of the Alan K. Campbell Public Affairs Institute. She is currently directing the Government Performance Project, a four-year study funded by the Pew Charitable Trusts. She is the author of *The Foundation of Merit: Public Service in American Democracy.* Ingraham's awards include the National Academy of Public Administration's Brownlow Book Award, the American Society for Public Administration/National Association of Schools of Public Affairs and Administration Distinguished Research Award, the Levine Award, and the American Society for Public Administration's Mosher Award. She is a past president of the National Association of Schools of Public Affairs and Administration.

Carol K. Johansen is currently associate professor of management and organizational studies, University of Southern Maine, where she is chair of the academic senate and interim chair of International Academic Programs. Previously she taught and directed the Legislative Internship Program at the School of Planning Public Policy and Management, University of Oregon, and at the Graduate School of Management, University of Maryland. She also directed the Presidential Management Intern Program, Office of Personnel Management, and coordinated all long-term development programs for civil service personnel and directed the Joint Military Intelligence Masters Program at the U.S. State Department. Her Ph.D. and A.B. are from the University of Oregon.

Jocelyn M. Johnston is an assistant professor in the Department of Public Administration at the University of Kansas. Her current research focuses on intergovernmental policies and programs, the privatization of social services, and property tax administration. In addition, she is participating in a study of the implementation of welfare reform through the Rockefeller Institute's State Capacity Project and in a national analysis of county fiscal conditions. She received a Ph.D. from Syracuse University in 1994.

Vernon Dale Jones is a lieutenant colonel in the United States Air Force. He is an associate professor and chief of the American and Policy Studies Division in the Department of Political Science at the U.S. Air Force Academy in Colorado Springs. He is a 1997–98 fellow in the Council for Excellence in

Government Fellows Program. His professional interests and research are focused on public leadership and management, public administration, organizational change in government agencies, and state and local intergovernmental relations. He is the author of *Downsizing the Federal Government: The Management of Public Sector Workforce Reductions.*

Linda Kaboolian is an assistant professor of public policy at the Kennedy School of Government, Harvard University. She received her Ph.D. from the University of Michigan. Her research interests include evaluating federal efforts to reform labor unions and innovation in traditional labor-management relations in the public sector. Kaboolian has conducted extensive analysis of management issues in the Social Security Administration.

Patrick D. Larkey is professor of decision making and public policy at Carnegie Mellon University, where he has also been head of the Department of Social and Decision Sciences, associate dean for academic affairs at the H. J. Heinz School of Public Policy and Management, and chair of the faculty senate. He is the author of numerous books and articles, including *The Search for Government Efficiency: From Hubris to Helplessness* (with G. W. Downs) and *Evaluating Public Programs: The Impact of General Revenue Sharing on Municipalities.* His work has been recognized with the 1976 Outstanding Doctoral Dissertation in Public Finance Award of the National Tax Association/Tax Institute of America and the 1988 Louis Brownlow Book Award from the National Academy of Public Administration for "the outstanding original contribution to the public administration literature." He is presently editor-in-chief of *Policy Sciences.*

Marcia K. Meyers is currently assistant professor of social work and public affairs at Columbia University and associate director of the New York City Social Indicators Survey Center. She also works closely with the Survey Research Center (and UC-DATA Data Archive) at the University of California, Berkeley, on state-level welfare data collection projects. Dr. Meyers's research focuses on public policies and programs for vulnerable populations, including public welfare services, child welfare programs, and child care services. In collaboration with the State Capacity Project of the Rockefeller Institute of Government, Dr. Meyers is beginning a new multistate study of the implementation of welfare reforms at the "front lines" of service delivery.

Lawrence B. Mohr received his A.B. from the University of Chicago in 1951 and his M.P.A. and Ph.D. degrees from the University of Michigan in 1963 and 1966, respectively. He has spent his career at the University of Michigan, where he teaches organization theory, program evaluation, and research methods. He is currently professor of political science and public policy. His books include *Expanding Organizational Behavior, Impact Analysis for Program Evaluation,* and *The Causes of Human Behavior.*

Nancy C. Roberts is a professor of strategic management in the Department of Systems Management at the Naval Postgraduate School in Monterey, California, and a codirector of the Institute for Whole Social Science in Carmel Valley, California. She has been a visiting associate professor at the Graduate School of Business at Stanford University and an assistant professor of behavior at the Carlson School of Management at the University of Minnesota. Roberts received a Diploma Annual (1966) from the Sorbonne in Paris, France, and a B.A. (1967) in French and an M.A. (1968) in Latin American and South Asian history from the University of Illinois. She received a Ph.D. from Stanford University with a specialization in organization change and development.

Per Stengård has deep and diversified experience in public management from a career working within the Ministry of Public Administration, in government task forces, and in a handful of central agencies. Mr. Stengård holds the master of public administration and is responsible for coordinating and heading different research programs at the Swedish Agency for Government Employers. He served as secretary of the Board of Government Employers and policy adviser to the former director general. In his work for the Swedish Council for Developing Government Administration he heads the development and implementation of a master's program for civil servants. In 1993 Mr. Stengård wrote a master's thesis titled "Perspectives on Change—The Policy Process behind the Abolishment of the National Board for Juvenile Education," which gave echo in the Swedish discourse about organizational change in government administration.

Fred Thompson is Grace and Elmer Goudy Professor of Public Management at the Atkinson Graduate School of Management, Willamette University. He is a recipient of the Willamette Trustees' Teaching Award, the Gold Medal of the American Society of Military Controllers, the *Public Administration Review*'s William E. Mosher and Frederick C. Mosher Award, and the Academy of Management's Outstanding Public Management Paper Award. He is a member of the Oregon Government Standards and Practices Commission and chairs the Association for Budgeting and Financial Management. His Ph.D. is from the

Center for Politics and Economics, Claremont Graduate University, and his B.A. is from Pomona College.

Gary L. Wamsley is the founding director of the Center for Public Administration and Policy at Virginia Polytechnic Institute and State University. He is best known for his work as editor and contributing author of *Refounding Democratic Public Administration* and for his work with Mayer Zald, *The Political Economy of Public Organizations.* He has been editor of *Administration and Society* since 1979. His expertise covers selective service, national security, emergency management, and budgeting.

Barton Wechsler (Ph.D., Ohio State University) is dean of the Edmund S. Muskie School of Public Service and professor of public policy and management and community planning and development at the University of Southern Maine. He has also been a faculty member at the University of Illinois and at Florida State University. His recent research has been concerned with public sector reform, human resource management, and strategic planning.

Janet A. Weiss is the Mary C. Bromage Collegiate Professor of Organizational Behavior and Public Policy in the Business School and the School of Public Policy at the University of Michigan.

Eric Welch is an assistant professor at the University of Illinois at Chicago. He conducts research in the areas of public management, comparative management, technology policy, and environmental policy. He is currently working on several projects related to the environmental behavior of organizations. Professor Welch has published in such journals as *Public Administration Review,* the *International Journal of Forecasting,* and the *International Journal of Environmental Studies.*

Lois R. Wise is professor of policy and administration in the School of Public and Environmental Affairs, Indiana University. She is a recipient of a Fulbright Senior Research Fellowship and the Swedish Institute Jubilee Prize for International Scholarship. She is the author of numerous articles and book chapters on public management reform and pay policy. She has served as a visiting scholar and research consultant to organizations in the United States and abroad. Between 1995 and 1997 she collaborated on different research projects on behalf of the Swedish Agency of Government Employers.

Index

Adams, Henry Carter, 186
Administrative Procedures Act, 281, 285, 286,
  289, 291, 295, 298, 308, 309, 318
administrative responsibility, 127
Advisory Committee on Intergovernmental Re-
  lations, 356, 361
advocacy community, 312, 313, 314, 315, 321,
  322, 323, 324, 325, 326
AFDC. *See* Aid to Families with Dependent
  Children
agency capture, 288, 299, 300, 303, 315
Aid to Families with Dependent Children, 230,
  231, 235, 238, 241, 242, 247, 248, 250, 252,
  253, 255, 256
Allison, Graham, 37, 67, 68
American Association of Retired Persons, 296,
  297
Americans with Disabilities Act, 322
Anderson, Eloise, 238, 255, 256
Angle, Harold L., 93, 109
Anthony, Robert N., 191, 200, 201, 203
antigovernment movement, 4, 6
antitax movement, 4
APA. *See* Administrative Procedures Act
Arendt, Hannah, 141
Argyris, Chris, 338, 350, 354
Aristotle, 122
Arnold, Doug, 183, 187
Atkins, Charles, 73, 83
Atkinson, John W., 26, 34
authority, governmental, 52, 53, 54, 55, 56, 59;
  as mechanism of intervention, 54, 56, 62; as
  policy instrument, 52, 55; weakness of as pol-
  icy mechanism, 58
auto safety legislation, 94, 100

Bachrach, Peter, 308, 309
balanced budget amendment proposals, 178
Ban, C., 151, 164
Bane, Mary Jo, 237, 256

Baratz, Morton, 308, 309
Barber, Benjamin, 128, 130, 137, 141
Bardach, Eugene, 104, 107
Barley, Stephen R., 353, 354
Barry, Maureen, 154, 165
Barzelay, Michael, 200, 204, 209, 211, 228, 316,
  327, 329, 354
Base Realignment and Closure Commission,
  217
Baum, L. Frank, 117, 131, 139, 141
Beard, Dan, 218
Becker, S., 91, 107
Behn, Robert D., 5, 13, 14, 70, 71, 73, 74, 79,
  83, 86, 87, 88, 89, 94, 98, 102, 107, 123, 133,
  140, 141, 233, 256, 357, 359, 360
Bernstein, Marver, 288, 309
Berry, Frances S., 4, 8, 281, 282, 340, 353, 355,
  357, 358, 359
Berry, Jeffrey M., 287, 289, 309, 311, 312, 327
Bertot, J., 279
"best practices," 2, 4
Bingham, Lisa, 308, 309
Bolles, Albert S., 187
BOR. *See* Bureau of Reclamation
Borins, Sanford, 189, 204
Bower, Joseph L., 192, 204
Bowers, James, 287, 309
Bozeman, Barry, 2, 9, 12, 123, 124, 141, 360, 361
Brandl, John E., 231, 254, 256
Bretschneider, Stuart, 5, 7, 8, 209, 279, 359, 360
Brodkin, Evelyn Z., 231, 234, 238, 251, 255, 257
Brown, Donaldson, 191
Brown v. Board of Education, 97
Brunsson, Nils, 145, 164
Bryan, William Jennings, 117
Bryner, Gary, 287, 290, 309
Budget Act of 1921, 114, 202, 203
budgetary process: effects of increased openness
  on, 173, 176, 177, 183; differences and simi-
  larities between government and business,

Redman, Eric, 104, 108
red tape, 40, 136, 266, 272, 275, 276, 345
Reich, Charles A., 314, 315, 328
Reid, T. R., 104, 108
reinventing government, 4, 8, 111, 136, 137,
    138, 207, 208, 211, 213, 216, 217, 282, 329–
    53; elements of, 212; role of middle managers
    in, 213; theoretical faults with, 212, 213. *See
    also* National Performance Review
Resource Conservation and Recovery Act, 287
responsibility budgeting, 193, 194, 201, 202
results-oriented government, 283
revenue enhancement, 260
Ribicoff, Abraham, 94, 95, 106
Rivlin, Alice, 176
Roberts, Kenneth, 95
Roberts, Marc C., 287, 310
Roberts, Nancy C., 6, 7, 14, 89, 90, 91, 92, 93,
    108, 359, 360
Roche, James M., 96
Rochefort, David A., 43, 68
Roethlisberger, E. J., 23, 36
Roe v. Wade, 98
Rogers, E., 25, 27, 30, 35, 36, 91, 108
Rogers, Will, 168
Romzek, Barbara S., 211, 228, 259, 357, 362
Rosenbloom, David H., 281, 284, 358, 362
Ross, Doug, 332
Rossi, Peter, 66, 68
Rothenberg, Lawrence, 312, 328
Roth v. United States, 98
routine change theory, 32, 33, 34
Rowan, B., 330, 355
Rubin, Irene, 195, 204
Rytina, Steven, 312, 327

Sabatier, Paul, 230, 258, 308, 310
Salamon, Lester, 52, 67, 69
Sallee, N., 198, 204
Sanders, Ronald P., 213, 229
Sanger, J. B., 89, 93, 102, 104, 109
Sanger, Mary Byrna, 102, 108
Savoie, D., 160, 162, 164, 264, 279
Schattschneider, E. E., 286, 287, 311
Schein, Edgar H., 233, 258
Schlozman, Kay, 286, 287, 303, 308, 311
Schmidt, Mary R., 124, 143
Schneider, Anne, 49, 69
Schon, Donald, 338, 350, 354
Schroeder, Larry, 111, 115, 314, 327
Schroeder, R. G., 92, 109
Schultze, Charles, 67, 69

"science of muddling through," 133
Scott, G., 198, 204
Scott, W. Richard, 99, 109
Scriven, Michael, 21, 22, 23, 36
Scudder, G. D., 92, 109
Securities and Exchange Commission, 285
Seidman, Harold, 212, 229
Selznick, Philip, 127, 143
Senge, Peter M., 126, 142
Senior Executive Service, 213, 215
separation of powers, 8
Shannon, W. Wayne, 288, 310
Shaw, Jerry G., 216, 228
Shelly v. Kraemer, 97
Sherwood, Frank, 353
Shoemaker, F., 25, 27, 36
Shoop, Tom, 214, 216, 229
Simon, Herbert A., 140, 143, 186, 188, 233, 257
Simon, William H., 237, 238, 255, 258
Singer, Jerome E., 211, 228
Sjöland, M., 154, 163, 165
Slemrod, Joel, 190, 204
Smircich, Linda, 132, 143
Smith, Kerry, 287, 311
Social Democrats, Sweden, 151, 152, 162
social science: aesthetic dimension of, 23; histori-
    cal perspective in, 21, 22; prevailing theories
    in, 11; research in, 17
Social Security Act, 234, 255, 326
Social Security Administration, 163, 282, 317,
    318, 319, 320, 321, 322, 323, 326, 327
Sorensen, Richard E., 29, 36
SSA. *See* Social Security Administration
Statistics Sweden, 158, 159, 164, 165
Steisel, Norman, 74
Stengård, Per, 5, 111, 112, 359
Stepina, Lee, 345, 355
Stivers, Camilla M., 126, 127, 143
Stockman, David, 175, 180
Stoker, Robert P., 231, 258
Stokes, Donald E., 121, 143
Stone, Deborah, 52, 59, 69
strategy of unobtrusive leadership, 83, 84
street-level bureaucrats, 230, 232, 234, 241, 242,
    246, 249, 250, 255. *See also* front-line workers
Sullivan, William M., 128, 136, 138, 139, 144
Sullivan v. Zebley, 319, 322, 323, 326
Sundelson, J. Wilner, 170, 187, 188
Supplemental Security Income, 317, 318, 319,
    320, 323, 326, 327
supply side economics, 175
Sweden, 198; deployment and staffing practices

in, 160; government reform efforts in, 113; labor unions in, 147, 151, 152; reform implementation in, 112, 146, 147, 148, 151–52, 153, 154, 155, 161, 162; strategy to reduce central government staff in, 157–59; theories of labor markets in, 5

Sweden, government agencies of: Agency for Government Employers, 155; Job Security Foundation, 159; Labor Market Authority, 159; Ministry of Defense, 157, 158; Ministry of Public Administration, 151, 157, 158; National Board of Social Welfare, 159; National Education Authorities, 159; National Employment Training Authority, 159; National Forest Enterprise, 159; National Insurance Board, 159; National Power Board, 159; National Railway Board, 159; State Agreement on Job Security, 158; State Institute for Personnel Development, 159

Sweden Post, 159

TAC. *See* Tactical Air Command
Tactical Air Command, 73, 76, 80, 81, 85
Tang, Shui-Yan, 111, 115
Taylor, Charles, 130, 144
Taylor, Frederick W., 140, 144
Technical Task Force, 339
Teich, Alfred H., 93, 108
theoretical process description, 27
theory of the problem, 38, 39, 40, 41, 42, 43, 44, 45, 63
Thomas, Steven, R., 287, 310
Thompson, D., 130, 142
Thompson, Frank, 329, 355
Thompson, Fred, 5, 8, 111, 114, 115, 168, 169, 172, 188, 189, 201 204, 205, 359
Thompson, James D., 232, 258
Thompson, James R., 212, 229
Thompson, Robert, 60, 68
Tierney, John, 286, 308, 311
Tocqueville, Alexis de, 59, 67, 69, 128, 140, 144
total quality management, 283, 331, 332, 333, 341, 342, 345, 346, 347, 349, 350, 352
TQM. *See* total quality management
Trade Promotion Coordinating Committee, 42
Trebilcock, Michael J., 189, 205
Turner, James, 21
tutelary power, 59
two-step flow theory, 25, 27, 28, 30, 34

United States: civil service system, 146, 148, 152, 154, 161; deployment and staffing practices in, 160; federal work force, strategy to reduce, 155–57; governance in, 123; management of reform in, 112; public management reform implementation in, 146, 147, 148, 151, 152–53, 154, 155, 161, 162; theories of labor markets in, 5

United States Air Force, 85
United States Bureau of Labor Statistics, 49
United States Commission on the Organization of the Executive Branch, 168
United States Congress, 85, 96, 105, 114, 152, 153, 154, 163, 175, 176, 180, 183, 184, 187, 195, 197, 200, 201, 212, 216, 285, 287, 297, 308, 323, 325, 358; Armed Services Committee, 85
United States Constitution, 105, 186
United States Department of Commerce, 95, 96, 100
United States Department of Defense, 156, 157, 163, 168, 169, 195, 200, 215, 220
United States Department of Energy, 292
United States Department of Health and Human Services, 215, 319, 326
United States Department of Health, Education, and Welfare, 94
United States Department of Housing and Urban Development, 163, 290, 292, 293, 294, 296, 298, 301, 307; designated housing rule, 293, 298, 307
United States Department of Labor, 95, 163
United States Department of the Interior, 215
United States Food and Drug Administration, 215, 218–19, 220, 221, 285; mission of, 218
United States Forest Service, 59
United States General Accounting Office, 160, 163, 326, 330
United States House of Representatives, 97, 173, 186, 187, 331
United States Postal Service, 157
United States Senate, 97, 187, 331; Commerce Committee, 96; Operations Committee, 94
United States Supreme Court, 97, 98, 100, 101, 287, 319, 323, 326
Unsafe at Any Speed, 95. *See also* Nader, Ralph
Urwick, Lyndall, 140, 142

Vaill, Peter B., 86, 88
value-neutral management, 111
Van Cott, Harold, 211, 228
Van de Ven, Andrew, 92, 93, 109
variance theories, 25, 29, 30
verstehen school, 21, 22